URSYN

CODE APPRECIATION

RESHAPING KNOWLEDGE

URSYN.COM

First published 2026
by CRC Press
2385 NW Executive Center Drive, Suite 320, Boca Raton FL 33431

and by CRC Press
4 Park Square, Milton Park, Abingdon, Oxon, OX14 4RN

CRC Press is an imprint of Taylor & Francis Group, LLC

ISBN13: 9781032972541 (hbk)
ISBN13: 9781032970578 (pbk)
ISBN13: 9781003592938 (ebk)

DOI: 10.1201/9781003592938
Typeset in Times New Roman and Herculanum

Publisher's note: This book has been prepared from printer-ready copy provided by the author.

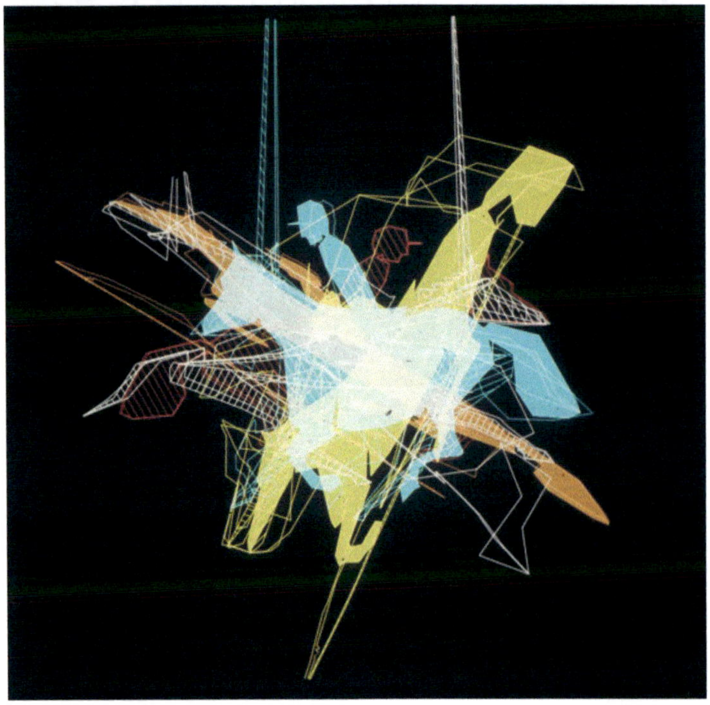

Atuzebo: always filled out with love.

For M and M, with Much Love

A Series of Books: Knowledge Through the Arts
Playful Books About Serious Things

This series consists of the following volumes:

Dance Code: Dance Steps as a Code, Taylor & Francis
New Storytelling: Learning Through Metaphors, Taylor & Francis
Code Appreciation: Reshaping Knowledge, Taylor & Francis
Nature Appreciation: Knowledge as Art, Taylor & Francis

Several common themes are woven throughout these books. They provide crucial insights into coding and the ongoing connections between programming and various fields of knowledge, areas of specialization, courses of study, and a diverse range of subjects. The books playfully explore knowledge domains and technologies within the framework of everyday situations faced by characters who endeavor to express their challenges through coding. These volumes also examine a collective understanding of nature. In each book, text and illustrations are accompanied by artworks from the author and other artists, visual outputs from computer programs, and sketches of imaginary characters.

Falling Pages. The output from the computer codes. © 2025 by Anna Ursyn

Keywords

New Storytelling, Metaphors, Analogies, Art, Coding, Programming, Music, Dance, Choreography, Video, Mathematical Art, Art and Science Connection, Professions, Computer Graphics, Digital Media, Knowledge Visualization, Knowledge Transfer through Art, Character Creation, Concept Art, Time and Space-based Digital Illustration, Cognitive, Abstract, Non-Linear Thinking, Types of Intelligences, Talents, 3D printing.

Padungo: won the Best Introvert award.

Padungo: won the Best Introvertic Award.

Flutist. A bronze sculpture. © 2025 by Anna Ursyn

TABLE OF CONTENTS

Autumn. © 2025 by Matylda Czarnecka

Trees. © 2025 by *Matylda Czarnecka*

Zoom. © 2025 by Anna Ursyn

CHAPTER 1
INTRODUCTION

LEARN WITHOUT STUDYING

UNDERSTAND PROGRAMMING ACROSS DISCIPLINES THROUGH STORIES

About This Book

This book offers a collection of stories arranged as an alphabet book. The stories introduce examples of coding for various disciplines and fields of knowledge and emphasize the importance of developing interdisciplinary skills, including programming, art, and storytelling, in today's visual world. The goal is to show that programming is a language that enables thinking from another perspective: how computers treat and process data. In each story, illustrated characters present a major programming concept used for the code (set in parenthesis) that refers to their knowledge or work. Thus, in a playful way, Avatars or Alter Egos bridge friendly content with more abstract concepts. The reader can grasp some programming ideas and see how coding can be used in various professions to approach different strategies to solve problems, get new ideas, sort things out, get inspiration, interact with others, or find technology-based solutions.

Metaphors Aid Understanding Programming and Technologies Across Disciplines

These short stories introduce the reader to some codes that are related to various disciplines. This way, people can see how interaction and the immersive nature of ever-connected fields of knowledge help us communicate better and faster in a perhaps fun way. The story-based situations introduce metaphorically technological solutions accompanied by computing codes related to various disciplines.

Metaphors link instructions that are written to tell a computer what task it should perform and show how it supports disciplines with novel solutions. The characters show how technology is present in various areas of study or work and how the rapid growth in technology and computing adds to linking them with tasks in other disciplines.

Learning through stories with metaphors helps to compare and contrast information and knowledge in various disciplines. One can notice shortcuts, overlaps, and similarities, comprehend abstract concepts, and be more creative and imaginative with cognitive thinking in mind. A playful way of storytelling introduces interconnections between the subject areas to lessen fears and inhibitions toward coding, sciences, and complex abstract concepts. As disciplines are connected, one can focus on one's own studies, expand, or decide on one's major and minor. Subjects and topics became more connected when technology took a decisive step forward. Some computer science or computer information systems students may have a difficult start in their majors and minors; this method could help them oversee coding from a bird's eye perspective, pick the right coding area, and add a minor or a second major.

Connecting Learning Through Stories with One's Own Career

The book is not aimed at teaching coding but offers a simple way to improve prompt writing skills and communication with the coders on the job. We can agree that jobs now involve coders; thus, those not afraid of coding speed up the company's production process. Programmers appreciate collaborating without having to answer obvious questions. In a fast-paced, connected, and technology-related environment, we experience the growth in computing daily, so it is important to understand technologies affecting most disciplines in many ways. As Robert Baldwin said at the World Economic Forum Growth Summit 2023, "Artificial intelligence won't take your job. It's somebody using AI that will take your job." Employers expect their employees, who are often placed in different parts of the globe, to be familiar with some aspects of the job others do for a company. At sessions held by entertaining industries for educators to help them prepare students for a job, it can be said that they all agree on the following skills their prospective employees possess:

1. Quality portfolio showing cognitive, abstract, innovative, and creative approaches.
2. Ability to write by developing new content.
3. Understanding music or appreciating music is important to be able to add it to production.
4. Acting, performing, or sports involvement to understand how the characters deliver stories.
5. Understand coding, or at least not be afraid of it, to communicate faster with the coders.
6. Collaborative skills, so the production goes in an interdisciplinary fashion.

One may agree that our environment worldwide has become more visual in nature, and the role of coding is important across various disciplines. Also, whatever we do can become a story. For example, when hiring artists to develop concept art, visualizations, or other types of visual design, employers want them to have experience with writing, performing, or sports to understand better the characters they create. Music is an important element in delivering a story. One must understand major ideas and jargon of programming to break the artist-coder barriers and thus communicate faster and better on projects, tasks, and products.

There is a general trend from employers to help candidates be confident in coding. It improves communication between researchers, artists, writers, and coders on the job. With growing collaborative and communication skills among coworkers, connecting with new technological trends and solutions is available without learning how to code; comprehending how codes work helps to structure our work in a new way, be it writing stories, making artistic creations, or working in scientific fields. Short stories serve those in performing arts, computer graphics, digital media, storytelling, or anyone interested in understanding and becoming familiar with some principles and the logic behind new technologies run by computing, which many companies often appreciate.

Artificial Intelligence (AI) and Machine Learning (ML) have become more used in the educational system. Students typically have strong opinions towards them, with many challenges and dangers being discussed, but new solutions are helpful and save time. Soon, we need to comprehend how a machine works, be it a ring, bracelet, watch, phone, tablet, computer, or a simple hologram, various types of Virtual Reality systems (VR, XR, AR), or even for example, a 3D printed drawing robot, or generative artificial intelligence (GAI) art.

The ideas in stories support the transformation of the STEM program (with S for science, T for technology, E for education, and M for mathematics) into the STEAM programs (with A for Art) (http://stemtosteam.org) and fit into a STREAM (with an R for reading/writing) movement. Also, students need to learn to collaborate well.

Below, Chapter 2, *Letters,* introduces the language of programming in stories set in alphabetic order. Chapter 3, *Numbers,* talks about numerical and measurement systems. Chapter 4, *Application*, informs about practical coding applications in computer graphics based on specific dimensions. Chapter 5, *Products,* provides examples of products coming out of computer graphics generated in different dimensions.

SUMMARY AND CONCLUSION

Coding has become common and needed, and this book is set to help non-coders lose their inhibitions.
It shows how programming is present across various disciplines.
It helps undeclared students, or those with undiscovered passions, find their major or two.
It explores how everything is connected.
It is a playful way to structure a set of stories involving programming.
The book connects disciplines and focuses on the role of programming in our connected fields of study. Thus, students on different levels, faculty, administrators, board members, choreographers, directors, policymakers, and anyone seeking majors, passions, or willing to delve into current trends in our culture would benefit from this book.

Colimur: understands hierarchy

Some related materials can be found at:

https://ursyn.com/ then select Art & Programming

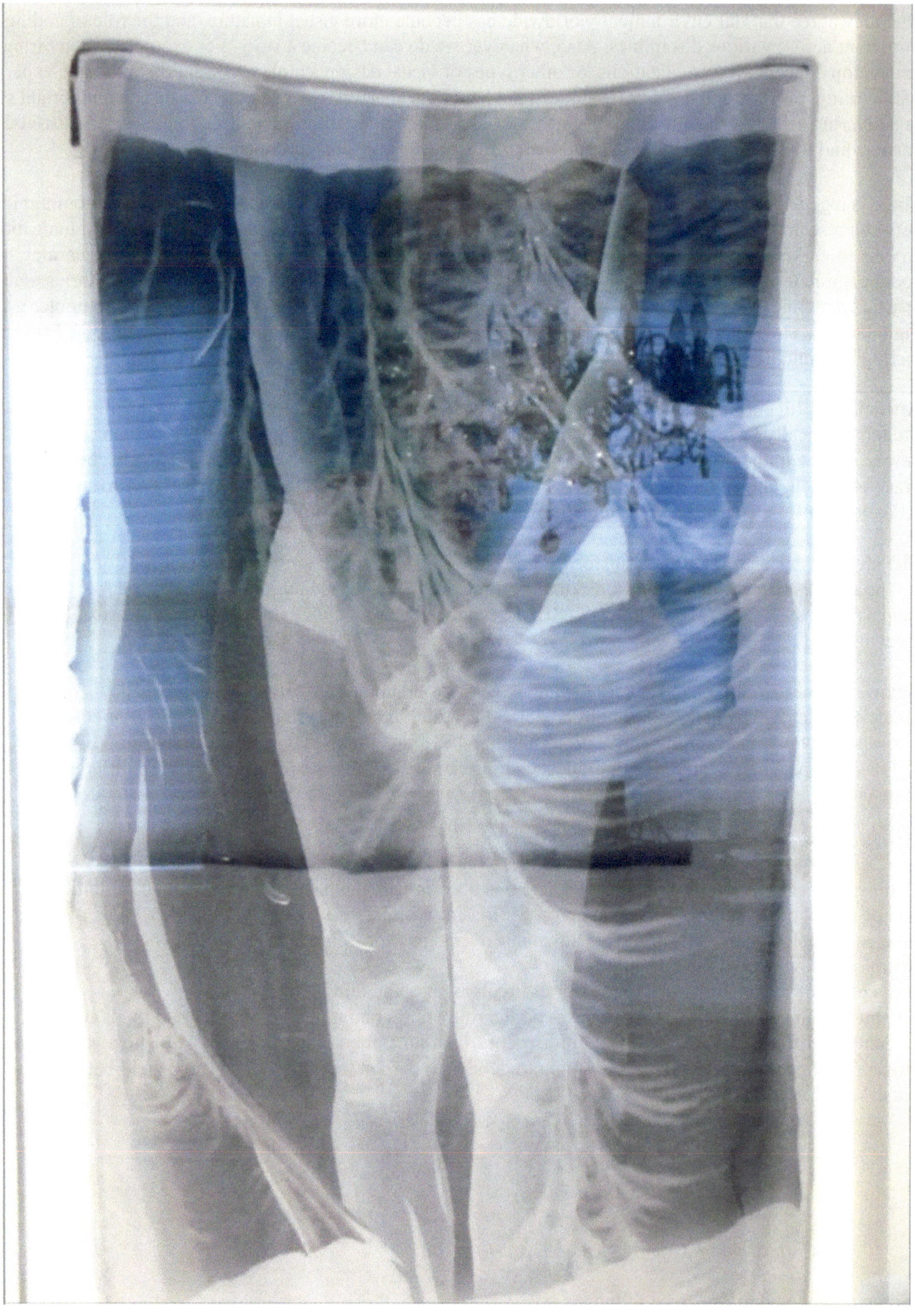

Artwork by Joohyun Pyune. (Used with permission).

Ideas & Dogmas © 2025 by Anna Ursyn

CHAPTER 2
LETTERS

This chapter offers a collection of stories arranged as an alphabetic book. On the following pages, illustrated characters introduce the language of programming and programming concepts used for the coding. Each page begins with a brief description of a profession, presents a main coding idea, and introduces an imaginary character.

Pukaga: brings good wishes down.

A	ACOUSTICS: THEORETICAL PHYSICS – SCIENCE OF SOUND (LIBRARY TO GENERATE AUDIO SIGNAL, SIGNAL GENERATION USING NUMPY) SEA DUCK – ANATIS

To communicate with other ducks, Anatis made up his mind to disguise silence. Around him, silence disguised acoustics.

```
import numpy as np # Numpy – a library for Python programming language

import sounddevice as sd
import time

def generate_silence(duration, sampling_rate):
    t = np.linspace(0, duration, int(sampling_rate * duration), endpoint=False)
    silence = np.zeros_like(t)
    return silence

# Parameters
duration = 5  # seconds
sampling_rate = 44100  # samples per second

# Generate silence
silence_signal = generate_silence(duration, sampling_rate)

# Play the "silent" signal
sd.play(silence_signal, samplerate=sampling_rate)
sd.wait()

# Wait for a moment
time.sleep(2)

# Generate and play a normal audio signal
normal_signal = np.sin(2 * np.pi * 440 * np.arange(sampling_rate * 2) / sampling_rate)
sd.play(normal_signal, samplerate=sampling_rate)
sd.wait()
```

The generate_silence function created a NumPy array representing silence, and then the sound device library played that "silent" signal. Disguising acoustics typically involves advanced signal processing techniques and using physical materials or structures to manipulate sound waves.
Now, Anatis can enjoy silence with friends.

AESTHETIC DESIGN
(DATA VISUALIZATION WITH A BAR PLOT)
STILT WALKER – MAECK

His only interest was modern aesthetics. He considered everything from a bird' s-eye perspective. He planned cities by looking at their projected functions from above. His computer had a drive filled to its capacities. He could often tell people that he carried a skyscraper on his small drive shaped like a key.

```
# Code to design a skyscraper from a bird's eye perspective

import matplotlib.pyplot as plt
import numpy as np

def draw_skyscraper(num_floors, floor_heights):
    # Calculate cumulative heights for each floor
    cumulative_heights = np.cumsum(floor_heights)

    # Create a bar plot to represent the skyscraper
    plt.bar(range(1, num_floors + 1), cumulative_heights, color='gray', edgecolor='black')

    # Set plot properties
    plt.title("Skyscraper Design: Bird's Eye View")
    plt.xlabel("Floors")
    plt.ylabel("Cumulative Height")
    plt.grid(axis='y', linestyle='--', alpha=0.7)

    # Highlight the total height of the skyscraper
    plt.text(num_floors / 2, cumulative_heights[-1] + 5, f"Total Height: {cumulative_heights[-1]} meters",
             fontsize=12, color='blue', ha='center')

    # Show the plot
    plt.show()
# Example usage: a skyscraper with 10 floors and varying floor heights
num_floors = 10
floor_heights = np.random.randint(3, 15, num_floors)  # Random floor heights between 3 and 15 meters
draw_skyscraper(num_floors, floor_heights)
```

The code leveraged the matplotlib library to create a bar plot where each bar corresponds to a skyscraper floor. The cumulative heights of the floors gave the total height of the skyscraper. The code was designed to be flexible, allowing for different numbers of floors and varying floor heights to showcase the diversity in modern skyscraper designs.

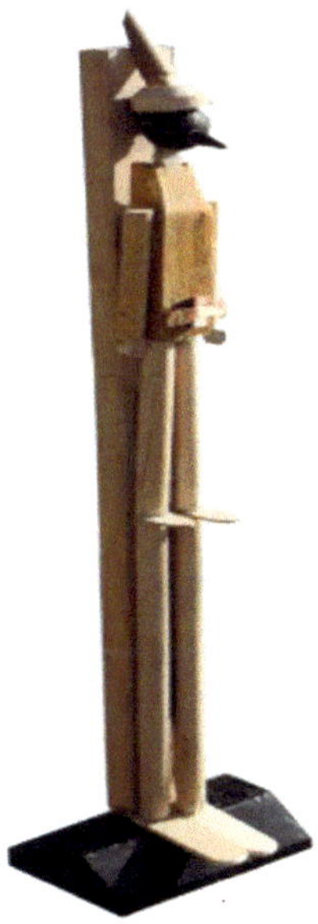

He never talked but watched things around him and then thought about everything.

AID TO THE CREW MEMBERS
(STRING MANIPULATION)
RUNNER – PIO

Pio never knew why they were calling him a "runner." He never had to rush. There were times when he had to wait until someone needed something done. He noticed serious naming problems everywhere. There is a waiter in a restaurant and a patient in the hospital, but the patient waits, and the waiter has to be patient. He thought the world would be nicer if proper words were used for better communication. He'd prefer his own title to be "Useful" or "Everything." Sometimes, they asked him to take a package somewhere to make him feel useful. Pio often helped someone in the house without going outside, but it always rained whenever they asked to do chores outside. He tried to remember to take his big black umbrella with him every time, but when it failed, a newspaper was good enough for short distances. "What will happen when the newspaper becomes a piece of plastic that changes the pages electronically - would it shock me?" He wondered. "It probably will be called in a non-consistent way." But the biggest problem was the suggestions for his unusual words offered to him by the speller. To enhance communication, he created a method that capitalizes the first letter of each word in a given sentence. This is often referred to as "title case." He used split()to break the sentence into a list of words, List comprehension with capitalize() to capitalize the first letter of each word, join()to combine the words back into a sentence. Manipulating strings is crucial for various text processing tasks and is a fundamental aspect of programming when dealing with textual data.

```
def improve_communication(sentence):
    # Split the sentence into a list of words
    words = sentence.split()

    # Capitalize the first letter of each word
    title_case_words = [word.capitalize() for word in words]

    # Join the words back into a sentence
    improved_sentence = ' '.join(title_case_words)

    return improved_sentence

# Example usage:
original_sentence = "hello world! this is a sample sentence."
improved_sentence =
improve_communication(original_sentence)

print("Original sentence:", original_sentence)
print("Improved sentence:", improved_sentence)
```

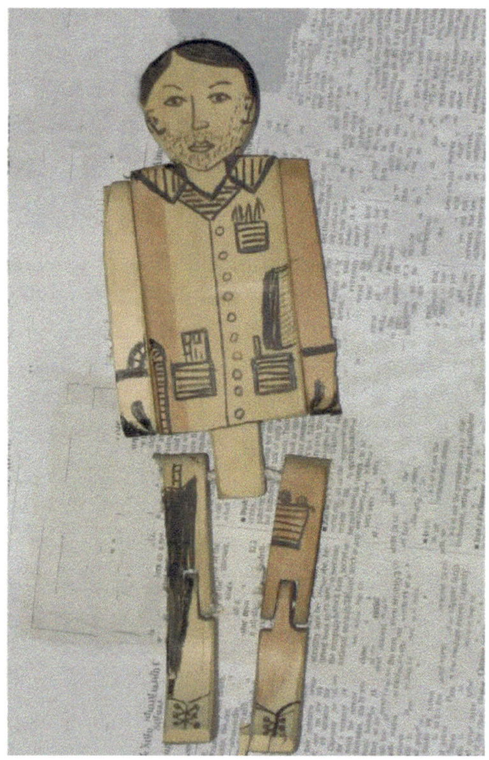

Artificial Intelligence did not help him when correcting his spellchecker. He was too peaceful for that.

ANATOMY
(DATA TYPES)
OSTEOLOGIST'S DOG – BONE

They all knew Bone was coming to the back of the Carni Restaurant for some bones. They wrote a code:

```
# Number of bones in a dog's body
dog_bones_count = 320

print(f"A typical dog has approximately {dog_bones_count} bones in its body.")
```

There were other dogs visiting the place. How many bones?

ANIMAL COGNITION
(CONDITIONAL STATEMENT)
SHAPE SHIFTERS – HAS, MUF, VIS, AND FIS

They wondered about whether a dog understands the meaning of thank you.

```
def dog_understands_thank_you(response):
    if response.lower() == "bark":
        return True
    else:
        return False

# Scenario 1: Dog understands "thank you"
dog_response = input("You: Thank you!\nDog: ")
if dog_understands_thank_you(dog_response):
    print("Your dog understands the meaning of 'thank you'. Good dog!")

# Scenario 2: Dog does not understand "thank you"
else:
    print("Your dog might not understand the meaning of 'thank you'. Keep training!")
```

Using if and else, the function dog_understands_thank_you checks if the dog's response matches the expected response ("bark" in this case) and returns True if it does, indicating that the dog understands the meaning of "thank you." The script then uses conditional statements to provide different messages based on the dog's response.

After a long discussion, they concluded by agreeing that a dog understands the word, please.

ANIMAL HOSPITALITY
(IF, ELIF, ELSE)
VIOLA – ELISA

Elisa was known for her fast driving, even in the cities and city limits areas. No one really knew how fast she could be on an open road. Once, she was stopped by a police officer while driving with her sister Sisina. She knew well that the speeding ticket was to be quite expensive. The police officer emerged from his police car slowly. It was already dark, so she could not see much against the moving lights. “How much,” she asked to cut the topic short. “You’ll take the kitty I found on the road and take good care of it,” replied the police officer. She named the cat Ticket and obeyed the rules the best she could, following Sisina’s code: the care routine for a virtual cat. This included feeding, playing, and checking its health:

```
import random

class Cat:
    def __init__(self, name):
        self.name = name
        self.hunger = 50
        self.happiness = 50
        self.health = 100

    def feed(self):
        food_amount = random.randint(5, 15)
        self.hunger -= food_amount
        print(f"{self.name} has been fed. Hunger decreased by {food_amount}.")

    def play(self):
        playtime = random.randint(10, 30)
        self.happiness += playtime
        print(f"{self.name} played happily. Happiness increased by {playtime}.")

    def check_health(self):
        if self.hunger <= 0 and self.happiness >= 100:
            self.health = 100
        else:
            self.health -= 10
            print(f"{self.name}'s health decreased. Current health: {self.health}.")

def main():
    cat_name = input("Enter a name for the found cat: ")
    found_cat = Cat(cat_name)

    while True:
        print("\n==== Cat Care Menu ====")
        print("1. Feed the cat")
        print("2. Play with the cat")
        print("3. Check the cat's health")
        print("4. Exit")

        choice = input("Enter your choice (1-4): ")

        if choice == '1':
            found_cat.feed()
        elif choice == '2':
            found_cat.play()
        elif choice == '3':
            found_cat.check_health()
        elif choice == '4':
            print("Exiting cat care program. Goodbye!")
            break
        else:
            print("Invalid choice. Please enter a number between 1 and 4.")

if __name__ == "__main__":
    main()
```

First, she defined a Cat class with methods for feeding, playing, and checking health. The main routine allowed her to interact with the virtual cat by choosing actions from a menu. The cat's hunger, happiness, and health levels were updated based on their interactions. Then, she modified and expanded the code to include more features and details for a more comprehensive plan for taking care of their real cat.

And a happy cat he was.

ANTHROPOLOGY (DATA STRUCTURES) PIPES – JAKE

Jake was born with no hearing ability but a great sense of rhythm. How can you tell? He liked making sounds, and they were very rhythmic and beautiful. He had a translator for most of his school classes. When classes involved complex knowledge, he got two of them. Both were kind and knowledgeable and whenever one of them was late, she'd excuse herself in sign language so all could see how sorry she was.

```
class SignLanguageInterpreter:
    def _init_(self):
        self.sign_dictionary = {
            "hello": "👋",
            "goodbye": "👋🏻",
            "yes": "👍",
            "no": "👎",
            "please": "🙏",
            "thank you": "🙌",
            # Add more signs as needed
        }

    def interpret_sentence(self, sentence):
        words = sentence.lower().split()
        interpreted_signs = [self.sign_dictionary[word] if word in self.sign_dictionary else word for word in words]
        return " ".join(interpreted_signs)

# Example usage:
interpreter = SignLanguageInterpreter()

sentence1 = "Hello, how are you?"
sentence2 = "Yes, please and thank you."

print(interpreter.interpret_sentence(sentence1))
print(interpreter.interpret_sentence(sentence2))
```

The sign_dictionary is a dictionary that maps words to their corresponding signs in sign language. This data structure allows for efficient lookup and retrieval of sign representations for given words. The interpret_sentence method uses this dictionary to replace words with their corresponding signs.

Jake made mistakes in his written assignments. Once, he explained to his teacher that it was his second language. When the teacher shared her thoughts that he was a native, Jack explained that his first language was the signing language.

APPRAISAL
(FUNCTION TO CALCULATE A VALUE)
VIOLIN CONSERVATOR — CARL

During a fire in which Carl, a violin conservator, lost a large part of his house, his collection of musical instruments was also destroyed or damaged by burning. Carl tried to reach an agreement with his insurance company through discussion and a compromise. Negotiations lasted two years, and never-ending meetings did not help to find the middle ground. The agent used a simple code that helped an insurance company assess the value of each musical instrument to calculate the insurance payout based on the instrument's original value and depreciation.

```
def calculate_insurance_payout(original_value, years_since_purchase):
    # Assuming a 10% depreciation rate per year
    depreciation_rate = 0.10

    # Calculate depreciation
    depreciation_factor = (1 - depreciation_rate) ** years_since_purchase
    current_value = original_value * depreciation_factor

    # Insurance payout is 80% of the current value
    insurance_payout = 0.8 * current_value

    return insurance_payout
# Example usage
instrument_original_value = 2000  # Replace with the actual original value of the instrument
years_since_purchase = 3  # Replace with the actual number of years since the instrument was purchased

insurance_payout = calculate_insurance_payout(instrument_original_value, years_since_purchase)
print(f"The insurance payout for the lost instrument is: ${insurance_payout:.2f}")
```

They defined a function calculate_insurance_payout that took the original value of each instrument and the number of years. The function calculated the depreciation based on a predefined depreciation rate and the current value. The insurance payout is set to 80% of the current value.

Despite this thorough method of assessing the insurance payout, the insurance company found that Carl's rare instrument, by a distinguished violin master, was worth very little because it was very old!

ARCHITECTURE
(DRAWING 2D SHAPES AND OBJECTS ON THE PYGAME SCREEN)
TURTLE PLAYER – FEDE

Fede's real passion was to build architectural projects using 3D programs. He used some components to be included in his compositions: trees, benches, furniture, light fixtures, and even people.

```
import pygame
import sys
# Initialize Pygame
pygame.init()
# Set up the display
width, height = 800, 600
screen = pygame.display.set_mode((width, height))
pygame.display.set_caption("Architectural Project")
# Define colors
white = (255, 255, 255)
brown = (139, 69, 19)
green = (0, 128, 0)
blue = (0, 0, 255)
yellow = (255, 255, 0)
black = (0, 0, 0)
# Function to draw architectural components
def draw_architectural_scene():
    # Draw background
    screen.fill(white)
# Draw trees
    pygame.draw.rect(screen, brown, [50, 400, 20, 100])
    pygame.draw.polygon(screen, green, [(10, 400), (90, 400), (50, 300)])

    pygame.draw.rect(screen, brown, [200, 400, 20, 100])
    pygame.draw.polygon(screen, green, [(160, 400), (240, 400), (200, 300)])
    # Draw benches
    pygame.draw.rect(screen, brown, [350, 450, 100, 20])

    # Draw furniture
    pygame.draw.rect(screen, blue, [500, 350, 50, 50])

    # Draw light fixtures
    pygame.draw.circle(screen, yellow, (650, 100), 30)

    # Draw people
    pygame.draw.circle(screen, black, (700, 500), 10)
    pygame.draw.rect(screen, black, [680, 500, 40, 60])

# Main game loop
while True:
    for event in pygame.event.get():
        if event.type == pygame.QUIT:
            pygame.quit()
            sys.exit()

    # Draw architectural scene
    draw_architectural_scene()

    # Update the display
    pygame.display.flip()
```

He used shapes and objects to represent architectural components and provide a simple visualization to plan in 3D, with libraries like Blender's Python API (bpy) or other dedicated 3D libraries.

Once, he inserted a model of a person into the composition, but later on, he could not find it. It must be behind the house, he thought, so he rotated the house. Nope. The person disappeared. He kept searching, but working on the wrong axis was obviously a problem. He forgot all about it. After finishing the exterior of the building, he walked inside virtually. As he was in... there was a man inside.

They both screamed!

ART
(COLOR)
HURDY GURDY – AOIFE

Aoife was a painter. The most beautiful present that was given to her was a box of paints with three tubes of red paint, each of a different shade. She checked them against some options:

```
def generate_shades_of_red(num_shades):
    shades_of_red = []

    for i in range(num_shades):
        # Adjust the intensity of red while keeping green and blue at zero
        red_intensity = int(255 * (i / num_shades))
        shade = (red_intensity, 0, 0)
        shades_of_red.append(shade)

    return shades_of_red

def display_shades(shades):
    for i, color in enumerate(shades):
        print(f"Shade {i + 1}: RGB {color}")
# Number of shades you want to generate
num_shades = 10

# Generate and display shades of red
shades_of_red = generate_shades_of_red(num_shades)
display_shades(shades_of_red)
```

Each shade of red was associated with a color name this time, and the display_named_shades function printed out each shade along with its name and corresponding RGB values. She could adjust the num_shades variable to generate a different number of named shades. However, she wanted more values associated with names of shades of red, such as Hex:

```
shades_of_red = {
    "IndianRed": "#CD5C5C",
    "LightCoral": "#F08080",
    "Salmon": "#FA8072",
    "DarkSalmon": "#E9967A",
    "LightSalmon": "#FFA07A",
    "Crimson": "#DC143C",
    "FireBrick": "#B22222",
    "DarkRed": "#8B0000",
}

for shade, hex_code in shades_of_red.items():
    print(f"{shade}: {hex_code}")
```

For this, she defined a dictionary called shades_of_red, where the keys are the names of the shades, and the values are their corresponding hex color codes. Then, it iterated over the dictionary and printed out the name of each shade along with its hex code.

Now, she talked about colors using numbers.

ASTROPHYSICS-PROPERTIES, PROCESSES, CELESTIAL OBJECTS BEYOND THE EARTH (USING EXTERNAL LIBRARY)
SATURN WATCHER – SATARA

She loved Saturn so much that every night, she could be seen watching her planet. It was not easy to spot, so she could often be seen at her computer, buying telescopes. She wrote a code to see Saturn on her computer whenever she wanted.

```
import ephem

def next_saturn_sighting(latitude, longitude):
    observer = ephem.Observer()
    observer.lat = str(latitude)
    observer.lon = str(longitude)

    saturn = ephem.Saturn()
    next_sighting = observer.next_pass(saturn)

    return next_sighting

# Example usage:
latitude = 34.0522  # Example latitude for Los Angeles
longitude = -118.2437  # Example longitude for Los Angeles

next_sighting_time = next_saturn_sighting(latitude, longitude)
print("Next Saturn sighting in Los Angeles:")
print(next_sighting_time)
```

In her code, the major concept was using the ephem library, a Python library for performing high-precision astronomy computations. The next_saturn_sighting function set up an observer's location and calculated the next time Saturn would be visible from that location. Still, she forgot to install the ephem library before running the code: pip installs them.

She keeps trying to see Saturn every single night, one way or another.

AUTOMATIZATION
(FUNCTIONS)
OFFICE WORKERS – MAC, ALI, META, AND NIKIS

They were probably the last ones working in the office. Their cubicles were clean, and not much was needed to furnish each one: just a table. Everything else, including controlling, communicating, and calculating devices, along with some of their personal decorations, was built into the partition walls. Their function was to oversee an average citizen's aesthetic quality of life. They'd ensure that the rain was pouring regularly to water the lawns when most citizens were asleep. Also, the lights were on when it was getting dark. They'd control all sorts of culture: the quality of the programs (by obstructing the moment something was less than appropriate), movies, concerts, exhibitions, online exercise programs, or even the noise level of distant conversations.

```
def calculate_aesthetic_quality(beauty, cleanliness, greenery):
    """Calculate the aesthetic quality of life based on predefined factors."""
    total_aesthetic_score = beauty + cleanliness + greenery
    return total_aesthetic_score

def assess_aesthetic_quality(citizen_name, aesthetic_score):
    """Assess and print the aesthetic quality of life for an average citizen."""
    print(f"{citizen_name}'s Aesthetic Quality of Life:")
    print(f"Aesthetic Score: {aesthetic_score}")

    if aesthetic_score >= 15:
        print("Excellent! The aesthetic quality of life is very high.")
    elif 10 <= aesthetic_score < 15:
        print("Good. The aesthetic quality of life is satisfactory.")
    else:
        print("Needs improvement. Consider enhancing the aesthetic surroundings.")


if __name__ == "__main__":
    # Provide predefined factors for aesthetic quality
    beauty_factor = 5
    cleanliness_factor = 4
    greenery_factor = 3
    # Calculate the aesthetic quality of life
    citizen_aesthetic_score = calculate_aesthetic_quality(beauty_factor, cleanliness_factor, greenery_factor)
    # Assess and print the aesthetic quality of life for an average citizen
    citizen_name = "John Doe"
    assess_aesthetic_quality(citizen_name, citizen_aesthetic_score)
```

The calculate_aesthetic_quality function defined the aesthetic quality based on predefined factors (beauty, cleanliness, and greenery), and the assess_aesthetic_quality function assessed and printed the average citizen's aesthetic quality of life based on the calculated score.

What bothered them was the lack of floor windows so they could see their work results.

AUDITORY SCIENCE
(MODULARIZATION AND DATA STRUCTURES)
VIOLINIST – AMADEUS

He could mumble in seven languages. His inspiration used functions and dictionaries to define mumble patterns for different languages.

```
def mumble(text, language):
    mumble_patterns = {
        'english': ''.join(c.lower() + c.upper() * i for i, c in enumerate(text)),
        'spanish': ''.join(c.lower() + c.upper() * i if c.isalpha() else c for i, c in enumerate(text)),
        'french': ''.join(c.lower() + c.upper() * i if c.isalpha() else c for i, c in enumerate(text)),
    }

    if language.lower() in mumble_patterns:
        return mumble_patterns[language.lower()]
    else:
        return "Language not supported for mumbling."

# Example of usage
text_to_mumble = "Hello, World!"
languages = ['english', 'spanish', 'french', 'german']

for lang in languages:
    mumbled_text = mumble(text_to_mumble, lang)
    print(f"{lang.capitalize()} Mumbling: {mumbled_text}")
```

The mumble function is defined to encapsulate the logic of creating a mumbled version of the input text based on the specified language. Functions allow for modularization, making the code more readable, reusable, and easier to maintain. The mumble_patterns dictionary was used to store mumble patterns for different languages. The keys are language names, and the values are the mumble patterns generated based on the specified logic. He used dictionaries to organize and retrieve data efficiently to work together with functions to create a modular and extensible solution for text in different languages.

He fulfilled his dream of recording his achievements.

AVIATION
(DEF)
HELICOPTER

All he saw was from above because he was too busy landing to observe. He thought the helicopter's landing protocol was too complicated, so he wrote a Python code to solve his problems:

```
class Helicopter:
    def __init__(self, pilot, helicopter_id):
        self.pilot = pilot
        self.helicopter_id = helicopter_id

    def request_permission_to_land(self):
        print(f"{self.pilot} requests permission to land helicopter {self.helicopter_id}.")

    def perform_pre_landing_checks(self):
        print("Performing pre-landing checks...")

    def find_landing_spot(self):
        print("Finding a suitable landing spot...")

    def descend_to_ground(self):
        print("Descending to the ground.")

    def notify_landing_complete(self):
        print(f"Landing of helicopter {self.helicopter_id} complete.")

def main():
    pilot_name = "John Doe"
    helicopter1 = Helicopter(pilot_name, "H123")

    helicopter1.request_permission_to_land()
    helicopter1.perform_pre_landing_checks()
    helicopter1.find_landing_spot()
    helicopter1.descend_to_ground()
    helicopter1.notify_landing_complete()

if __name__ == "__main__":
    main()
```

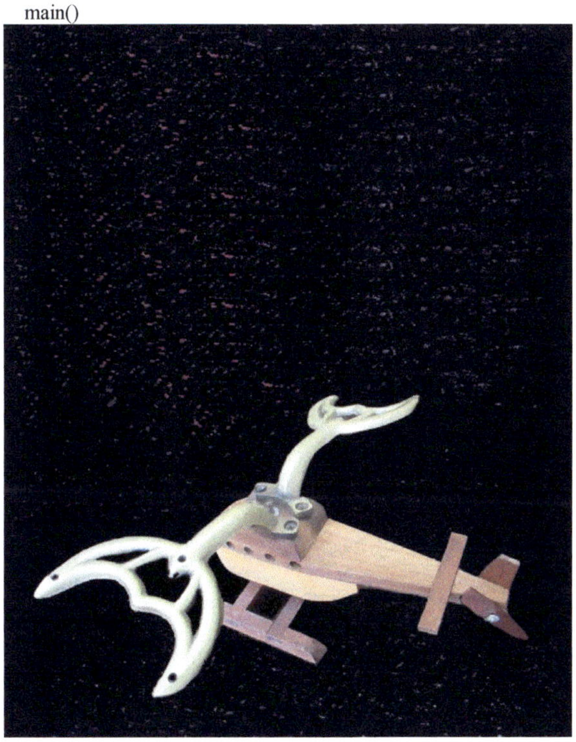

The Earth looked flat, though.

B	BAKING (COLOR) DAY-TO-DAY PERSON – GERTY

He was not worried or was caught uncertain. Gerty never took advice or would give any. His job was to make cakes for any occasion that would match the situation. Not an easy task when one looks at various holidays. Some of them were Christmas, Hanukah, New Year, Chinese New Year, Easter, Passover, Memorial Day, Labor Day, Thanksgiving, Martin Luther King's Holiday, President's Day, Ramadan, Mothers, Fathers, Grandparents, Children's Day, and more to learn about. Gerty started with a code that matches the color of a cake with a particular holiday using the OpenCV library. He used red for Christmas, pink for Valentine's Day, and orange for Halloween. Then, he customized the colors and holidays based on his other needs.

```
import cv2
import numpy as np


def match_color_for_holiday(image, holiday):
    # Define color mappings for holidays
    holiday_colors = {
        'Christmas': (0, 0, 255),  # Red
        'ValentinesDay': (147, 20, 255), # Pink
        'Halloween': (0, 165, 255), # Orange
    }


    # Get the color for the specified holiday
    color = holiday_colors.get(holiday, (255, 255, 255)) # Default
to white if holiday not found

    # Create an image with the specified color
    colored_image = np.full_like(image, color, dtype=np.uint8)

    return colored_image

# Load an example cake image (replace with your cake image)
cake_image = cv2.imread('path/to/your/cake/image.jpg')

# Specify the holiday (e.g., 'Christmas', 'ValentinesDay',
'Halloween')
holiday = 'Christmas'

# Match color for the specified holiday
colored_cake = match_color_for_holiday(cake_image, holiday)

# Display the original and colored cake images
cv2.imshow('Original Cake', cake_image)
cv2.imshow(f'Colored Cake for {holiday}', colored_cake)
cv2.waitKey(0)
cv2.destroyAllWindows()
```

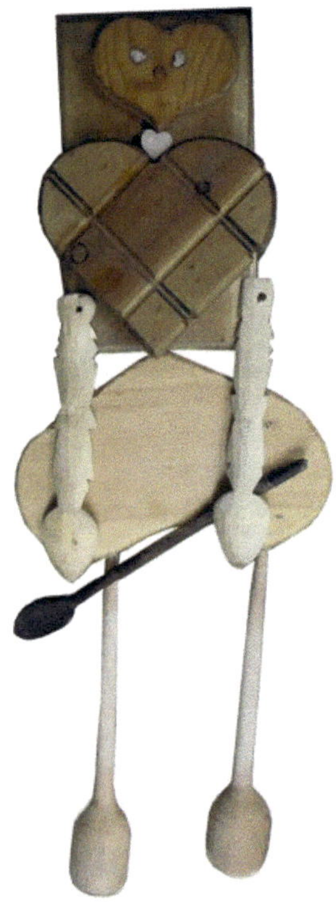

He replaced 'path/to/your/cake/image.jpg' with the path to each cake's photo. This script loaded the image, matched its color based on the specified holiday, and then displayed both the original and colored cake image. He customized the holiday_colors dictionary with other colors and holidays, then sketched and scribbled many possibilities and several color-coding designs with various color combinations to include more cultures and populations.

His favorite holiday was Thanksgiving, for he did not have to color his food.

BALLET
(ENCAPSULATION, ABSTRACTION, AND THE ORGANIZATION OF CODE WITH OOP)
THREE PRIMA BALLERINAS – PUJA, SIBEL AND CLARA

Three ballerinas were expected to be unique yet unified. Uniqueness could be developed during the improvisation part of the practice routine. They were asked to go with the music – to sense the music. Other than that, most of the rhythm had to be captured by them in the same fashion as they were the Prima Ballerinas. Usually, there is one, but with the heavy schedule of the ballet, they had to do everything in three sets: one local, one for travel, and one to substitute, so each performance is set in stone, no matter what!

Puja's career started very late: she was seven. Her mother often talked about her children, saying that with time going so fast, when a child turns three, it is too late for serious ballet, then at six, it is too late for competitive chess, and so on.

Sibel came from very far away. She knew languages, dances, and plays. Her style was different, but she could comply, blend, and become one of them when needed. Always willing to do anything that was needed, she was often asked to dance during the performances of the Orchestra. The tickets sold better that way. She is visual, the audience kept saying. It was in her dancing – the viola's sound asked her to slow down, the violin to be more vivid. She used the gong to signal her stretching position, only to allow her to be ready for the next dynamic move. Her spectacularity often scared the audience. She could improvise, like an opposition to the regular drill of the ballet. She called it creation. Once, a critic asked how she knew how to control the dance's flow. "If it feels good, it looks good," she answered.

Clara liked to dance with partners. She felt secure, supported, and important. She was a good friend to all of her dancing partners. She was the one to be called by anyone at any time for advice, to borrow something, or to talk. She'd throw parties with all her dance partners invited, but not too many ballerinas. She was always invited to all parties. They received the best reviews for their band based on their code:

```
class Musician:
    def _init_(self, instrument):
        self.instrument = instrument

    def play(self, notes):
        print(f"{self.instrument} player improvising:")
        for note in notes:
            print(note)

class JazzBand:
    def _init_(self):
        self.members = []

    def add_musician(self, musician):
        self.members.append(musician)
```

```
def perform(self):
        print("Jazz band performance:")
        for musician in self.members:
            # Improvisation happens here
            musician.play(["P", "S", "C", ])

# Creating musicians
piano_player = Musician("Piano")
saxophonist = Musician("Saxophone")

# Creating a jazz band
jazz_band = JazzBand()

# Adding musicians to the band
jazz_band.add_musician(piano_player)
jazz_band.add_musician(saxophonist)

# Performing with improvisation
jazz_band.perform()
```

This code defined two classes, Musician and JazzBand. The Musician class had an _init_ method to initialize the musician with an instrument and a play method to simulate playing notes, including improvisation. The JazzBand class had an _init_ method to initialize an empty list of band members, an add_musician method to add musicians to the band, and a perform method where each musician improvised by playing a set of notes.

Some of them played a few instruments at the same time. After all, they excelled in improvisation!

BEHAVIORAL CHANGE
(TIME DELAY)
CHESS CHEWER – AHLA

He was an internationally known chess winner, but nobody wanted to play with him. He possessed a habit of chewing on the chess pieces when thinking about the best move to make, so those who played with him could not recognize the forms and shapes of the pieces. His opponents could not see the meaning behind each re-sculpted piece; thus, he kept winning. One player wrote a code that created a routine for a person to stop chewing a chess piece while playing chess. It was not a behavior change program but a gentle reminder to break the habit:

```
import time

def chess_piece_chewing_routine():
  print("Welcome to the Chess Piece Chewing Prevention Routine!")

  while True:
    # Display a reminder message every 10 minutes
    print("\nReminder: Avoid chewing on chess pieces while playing.")

    # Wait for 10 minutes
    time.sleep(600)  # 10 minutes in seconds

if __name__ == "__main__":
  chess_piece_chewing_routine()
```

This script displayed a reminder every 10 minutes. This customizable message approached behavior change with understanding and open communication. It worked! Ahla stopped chewing on the chess pieces but still kept winning every game.

BEHAVIORAL SCIENCE (MULTITHREADING) PERSONAL TRAINER – MOJO

Mojo was a multitasker. He could sing while playing an instrument, talk while dancing, dance while talking, or shop and converse on his cell phone.

```
import threading
import time

def task1():
    for _ in range(5):
        print("Task 1 executing")
        time.sleep(1)

def task2():
    for _ in range(5):
        print("Task 2 executing")
        time.sleep(1)

# Create threads for each task
thread1 = threading.Thread(target=task1)
thread2 = threading.Thread(target=task2)

# Start the threads
thread1.start()
thread2.start()

# Wait for both threads to finish
thread1.join()
thread2.join()

print("Multitasking complete!")
```

The threading module created two separate threads, each running a different task (task1 and task2). The start() method initiated the execution of each thread, and the join() method ensured that the main program waited for both threads to finish before proceeding. Multithreading allowed multiple threads to run concurrently, achieving a form of balance.

As a child, he was stopped by a police officer for reading "How to Drive a Car" while driving his car.

BIODIVERSITY
(DICTIONARY)
SATELLITE – THE OLDEST INSECT – PUTUCO

He saw many species in his life but focused on their heritage. He researched those with the longest family history. He wanted to track down the oldest of each kind and invite them all to his Heritage Meeting. Putuco created a journal with all the living things he knew; despite his long-life span, he could not count them all. His work became even more complicated when he learned how many species disappear daily.

```
class SpeciesCounter:
    def __init__(self, species_population):
        self.species_population = species_population

    def count_species(self):
        """Count the number of individuals for each species."""
        species_count = {}

        for species, population in self.species_population.items():
            species_count[species] = sum(population)

        return species_count

if __name__ == "__main__":
    # Predefined dictionary of species and their populations
    species_population_data = {
        "Tiger": [10, 15, 12],
        "Elephant": [20, 22, 18],
        "Lion": [8, 10, 9],
        "Giraffe": [15, 17, 14],
        "Penguin": [50, 48, 52]
    }

    # Create an instance of the SpeciesCounter class
    species_counter = SpeciesCounter(species_population_data)

    # Count the number of individuals for each species
    counted_species = species_counter.count_species()

    # Display the results
    print("Species Count:")
    for species, count in counted_species.items():
        print(f"{species}: {count} individuals")
```

Dictionaries are useful for organizing and representing data in key-value pairs. In this example, a dictionary stores the count of individuals for each species. This data structure provides a convenient way to associate species names with their corresponding counts. Everyone was in his hands. He controlled it all. He knew everything or could quickly find it whenever he wanted.

He disapproved of the words always, everything, all, and everyone.

BIOGRAPHY
(STRING FORMATTING TO CREATE STRUCTURED AND CONSISTENT ENTRIES)
VIOLINIST – HARVEY

Harvey was writing bibliographies of famous bibliographers. His work was easy. All he had to do was to fill out a template: Who, Where, When, Whose, Why, What, Which.

```
def generate_bibliography(bibliographer_info):

  template = """

  {who}. ({when}). {what}. {where}: {whose}. {why}.

  """

  bibliography = template.format(

    who=bibliographer_info['who'],

    where=bibliographer_info['where'],

    when=bibliographer_info['when'],

    whose=bibliographer_info['whose'],

    why=bibliographer_info['why'],

    what=bibliographer_info['what']

  )

  return bibliography
```

```
if __name__ == "__main__":

  famous_bibliographer = {

    'who': 'Hellenic scientists',

    'where':, Antikythera, Greece'

    'when': 70–60 BC, 2nd century BC., discovered 1901'

    'whose': 'National Archaeological Museum, Athens'

    'why': 'To preserve historical artefacts'

    'what': 'mechanism, later known as the first analogue computer"

  }


  bibliography_entry = generate_bibliography(famous_bibliographer)

  print(bibliography_entry)
```

He kept talking about it in his never-ending lectures about the beauty of science and writing.

BOARD GAMES
(LISTS)
OBOE – ANDREA

Andrea plays oboe in her high school orchestra, directed and conducted by her music teacher Doran. The school orchestra will play classical music in several countries this year. Students will perform in several places and visit some cities' well-known architectural structures. Parents are discussing helping them earn money for the trip, working with kids in a bingo place, and having students play at weddings, anniversaries, and other family events.

```
import random
def generate_bingo_card():
    """Generate a random bingo card."""
    card = [random.sample(range(1, 16), 5),
            random.sample(range(16, 31), 5),
            random.sample(range(31, 46), 5),
            random.sample(range(46, 61), 5),
            random.sample(range(61, 76), 5)]
    return card

def display_bingo_card(card):
    """Display the bingo card."""
    print("Bingo Card:")
    for row in card:
        print(row)

def check_bingo(card):
    """Check if there is a winning pattern on the bingo card."""
    # Check rows
    for row in card:
        if all(cell == "X" for cell in row):
            return True

    # Check columns
    for col in range(5):
        if all(card[row][col] == "X" for row in range(5)):
            return True

    # Check diagonals
    if all(card[i][i] == "X" for i in range(5)) or all(card[i][4-i] ==
"X" for i in range(5)):
        return True

    return False
```

```
def play_bingo():
    """Simulate a bingo game and explain how to win."""
    print("Welcome to Bingo!")

# Generate a random bingo card
    bingo_card = generate_bingo_card()

    # Display the bingo card
    display_bingo_card(bingo_card)

    # Explain how to win
    print("\nTo win, mark off a full row, column, or diagonal with
'X'.")
    print("Let's simulate the game:")

    # Mark random cells as 'X' to simulate gameplay
    for _ in range(15):
        row = random.randint(0, 4)
        col = random.randint(0, 4)
        bingo_card[row][col] = "X"

    # Display the updated bingo card
    display_bingo_card(bingo_card)

    # Check for a winning pattern
    if check_bingo(bingo_card):
        print("\nCongratulations! You've won at Bingo!")
    else:
        print("\nSorry, no winning pattern. Better luck next time!")

if __name__ == "__main__":
    play_bingo()
```

Andrea's father, oboist Colin, helps find fares for the students and arranges to keep coaches, rooms, and food available at specified times. For many, the trip was one of the best experiences during high school.

Doran made some arrangements for his orchestra to perform for various schools and churches while on the trip. When Andrea graduated from her high school, Colin invited Giovanni and Jeanne to play at her graduation theme party. Andrea printed pictures taken during the trip in a really large format and hung them all over the place. And, of course, her best photo served as a backdrop for Giovanni and Jeanne's performance.

BOTANY
(METHOD)
JUGGLER – DUD

He perfected his craft on the street, so a botanic garden hired him to entertain their plants to have them grow faster. The singer before him did not do the best job there. Dud took the challenge quite seriously. First, he used the time module for a sense of time passing and some creative functions:

```
import time
import random

class Juggler:
    def entertain_plants(self, plant):
        print("Juggler is entertaining the plant...")
        for _ in range(3):
            self.juggle()
            time.sleep(1)

        print("The plant seems happy!")

    def juggle(self):
        juggling_tricks = ["cascade", "under-the-leg", "behind-the-back", "high-toss"]
        random_trick = random.choice(juggling_tricks)
        print(f"Juggler is juggling with a {random_trick} trick!")

class Plant:
    def grow(self):
        print("The plant is growing!")

# Instantiate juggler and plant
juggler = Juggler()
plant = Plant()

# Entertain the plant
juggler.entertain_plants(plant)
plant.grow()
```

The Juggler class had a method to entertain_plants that juggle for the plant. The juggle method randomly selected a juggling trick, simulating a lively performance. When he ran this code, he entertained the plant with three juggling tricks, and afterward, each plant responded by growing.

His combination of entertainment and nature attracted a lot of attention, so he had to buy a hat for all the money offered by those watching him.

BOTS
(RANDOM)
BOT – CARINE

Carine was always useful. She could predict the expected tasks and finish them before being asked to. That created confusion and a need to reprogram her into a more obedient one. With Pyk, they started by learning the bot's thinking pattern with a Python program that simulated a bot predicting assigned tasks:

```
import random
class PredictionBot:
    def __init__(self):
        self.knowledge_base = {
            "What's the weather like today?": "Sunny and warm.",
            "Tell me a joke.": "Why don't scientists trust atoms? Because
they make up everything!",
            "What's the capital of France?": "Paris.",
            "Give me a random number between 1 and 10.":
str(random.randint(1, 10))
        }

    def predict_task(self, task):
        if task in self.knowledge_base:
            return self.knowledge_base[task]
        else:
            return "I'm sorry, I don't know how to do that task."

# Example usage
if __name__ == "__main__":
    bot = PredictionBot()

    tasks_to_predict = [
        "What's the weather like today?",
        "Tell me a joke.",
        "What's the capital of France?",
        "Give me a random number between 1 and 10."
    ]

    for task in tasks_to_predict:
        prediction = bot.predict_task(task)
        print(f"Task: {task}\nPrediction: {prediction}\n")
```

Now, they could write code to make a bot more obedient by defining clear rules and conditions:

```
class ObedientBot:
    def __init__(self):
        self.obey_commands = True

    def follow_command(self, command):
        if self.obey_commands:
            print(f"Executing command: {command}")
        else:
            print("I'm sorry, I cannot execute commands right now.")

    def enable_obedience(self):
        self.obey_commands = True
        print("Obedience enabled.")

    def disable_obedience(self):
        self.obey_commands = False
        print("Obedience disabled.")
```

Corine was still outperforming herself as they discovered later that she had modified the code written for her. Everyone mastered bowling since no other activities were offered in their tiny hamlet.

BUSINESS
(RECURSIVE FUNCTIONS)
BAKERS – FU AND RU

Fu and Ru opened a bakery. Their products were shaped following fractal geometry. They wanted to spread the beauty of math. Their programs to design their merchandise helped shape fractal tree cookies:

```
import turtle

def draw_fractal_tree(branch_length, t):
    if branch_length > 5:
        # Draw the main branch
        t.forward(branch_length)

        # Draw the right subtree
        t.right(20)
        draw_fractal_tree(branch_length - 15, t)

        # Draw the left subtree
        t.left(40)
        draw_fractal_tree(branch_length - 15, t)

        # Return to the original position
        t.right(20)
        t.backward(branch_length)

def main():
    # Set up the turtle
    my_turtle = turtle.Turtle()
    my_screen = turtle.Screen()
    my_turtle.speed(2)

    # Set the starting position
    my_turtle.left(90)
    my_turtle.up()
    my_turtle.backward(100)
    my_turtle.down()

    # Call the function to draw the fractal tree
    draw_fractal_tree(75, my_turtle)

    # Close the window on click
    my_screen.exitonclick()

if __name__ == "__main__":
    main()
```

Due to its structure, the tree was hard to bake, so they did Julia set cookies. Complex numbers and iterative calculations made them switch to Platonic objects, which set them as Children's Bakery.

```
import turtle


def draw_cube(side_length, t):
    for _ in range(4):
        t.forward(side_length)
        t.right(90)

def main():
    # Set up the turtle
    my_turtle = turtle.Turtle()
    my_screen = turtle.Screen()
    my_turtle.speed(2)
```

```
    # Draw a cube
    side_length = 100
    for _ in range(4):
        draw_cube(side_length, my_turtle)
        my_turtle.forward(side_length)
        my_turtle.left(90)

    # Close the window on click
    my_screen.exitonclick()

if __name__ == "__main__":
    main()
```

Their code defined a function draw_cube with the Turtle graphics library. By adjusting the angles and side lengths, they did Platonic solids such as tetrahedron, octahedron, and dodecahedron. They started "Dig Fab Baking" by pouring pancake mix on the hot 3D printer bed after client-designed trajectories.

C CALLIGRAPHY (A DICTIONARY TO STORE INFORMATION AND LOOP) WASHBOARD – VERBAL

Verbal now owned his great-grandmother's washboard, which was quite heavily used. It was stored in the old barn when he discovered it. A little text was neatly written on the back of the wooden frame: "My job stole my soul this weekend." It happened right after the Cowboy Symposium, where Verbal went with his friend. People were reading their poetry, singing "olde Cowboys' songs, and their own and newer ones. They played music with unusual tunes. He saw some strange instruments. One of them was a washboard. Shortly after, his grand-grandmother's washboard became his own instrument. Given all the hints by one of the performers, he grasped how to play it. For the rhythm when playing a washboard:

```
def create_washboard_rhythm():
    rhythm = "Clang! Clang! Clang! Clang!"

    return rhythm


# Example usage
calligraphy_info = list_calligraphy_techniques()
washboard_rhythm = create_washboard_rhythm()

print("Various Calligraphy Techniques and Cultures:")
for technique, description in calligraphy_info.items():
    print(f"{technique}: {description}")

print("\nCreating Washboard Music:")
print("Playing washboard rhythm:", washboard_rhythm)

# Simulating washboard music with a loop
for _ in range(4):
    print("Washboard Sound:", washboard_rhythm)
    time.sleep(1)
```

The create_washboard_rhythm function generates a basic washboard rhythm as a string. Through dictionary creation, string manipulation, and a loop, he simulated washboard music.

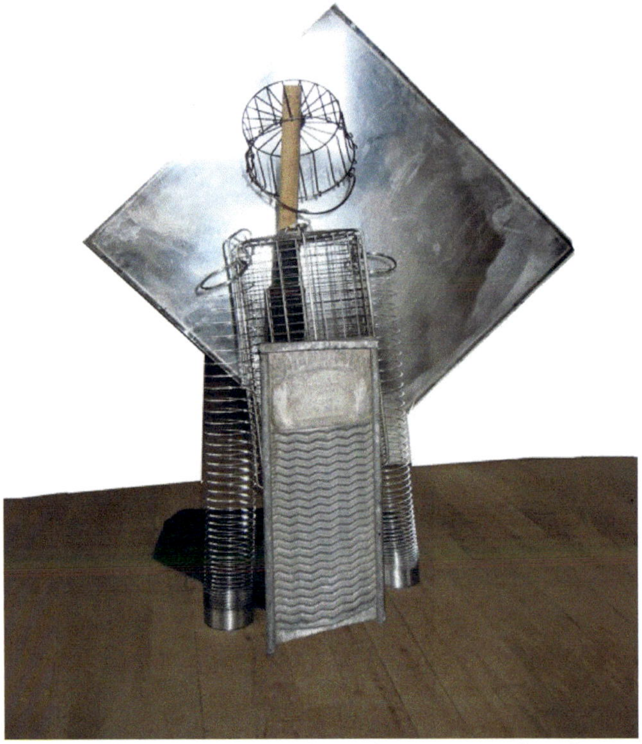

Soon, he became THE BEST. His great-grandmother must have been watching over him. However, replacing the text on the back with "My play rose my spirits this weekend" required more calligraphy and wood carving skills.

CAREER CHANGE (ALGORITHM) BODY BELLS – FRANCESCO

Francesco came from a famous pick-pocket family. His relatives were so skilled that they were asked to lecture on pickpocketing and pocket picking. The lectures were lengthy, but no one understood the difference between those two subjects. However, both methods worked if performed well. The family was very careful and patient about bringing up their youngsters. Since early childhood, upon saying their first words, they began their apprenticeship in the family trade. Everyone had to wear bells and practice emptying the pockets of others in any possible way without triggering any of the numerous bells attached to their outfit. A complete silence and an empty pocket were the two keys to success.

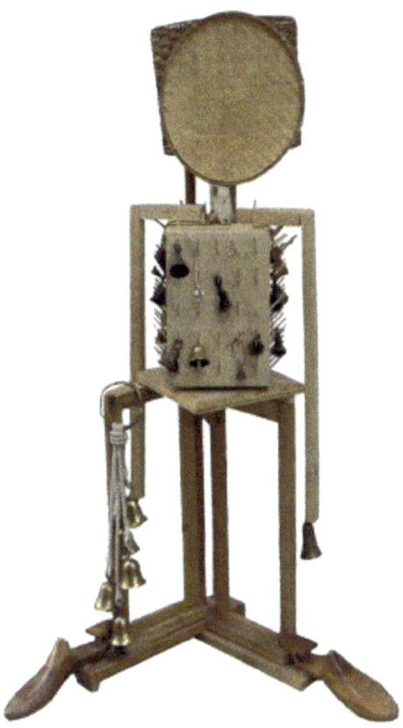

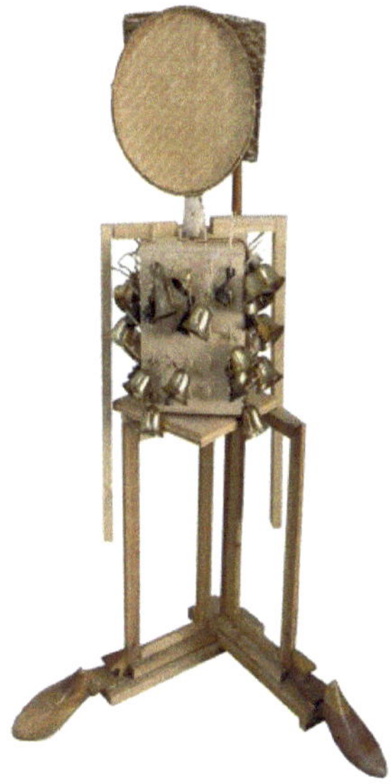

Francesco was a fast learner heading toward a No.1 Bread Winner title. The only family member with a higher score was his uncle. His bells never rang. However, it happened to Francesco while working on his uncle's pocket. He had two choices: to wait till his never-mistaken uncle scored a point or to leave.
He wrote an algorithm that helped him find body-bells-related professions:

Define Relevant Keywords:
Identify keywords associated with body bells, such as "kettlebell," "dumbbell," "barbell," and related terms.
Search Engine Query:
Use a search engine API to perform a query with the identified keywords. You can refine your search using Boolean operators (AND, OR). For example, "kettlebell AND personal trainer."
Web Scraping:
Retrieve the search results using web scraping techniques. Be respectful of website terms of service and policies.
Filter Relevant Pages:
Analyze the content of each page to determine if it's related to body bells professions.
Look for specific keywords on the page and consider using natural language processing (NLP) techniques to improve accuracy.
Classify Pages:
Use machine learning algorithms, if possible, to classify pages as relevant or irrelevant.
Train the algorithm on a dataset of known relevant and irrelevant pages.
Remove Duplicates:
Eliminate duplicate results to ensure a clean dataset.
Generate Report:
Compile a report with the URLs or brief descriptions of the identified relevant pages.
User Interface (Optional):

It was a basic outline, and the algorithm's effectiveness depended on the quality of the keywords, the search engine API, and the accuracy of the classification algorithm.
He saw an ad for a performer for a local orchestra. He successfully jumped at this opportunity. The bells he was wearing reflected the lights in a way resembling the sound wave spectrum, which caught their attention. He never went back to his inherited profession. Do what you are good at, he thought.

CAREERS FOR HAPPY PEOPLE
(RANDOM)
AGENT KERBEROS – FUN CITY

He worked several jobs before. He was an attorney's assistant, legal aid in the court, an insurance agent, working at the hospital, for the sheriff's office, the shrink's office, and held a position in prison.
He wanted a job to work with happy people only. For this, he created a code that determined jobs based on whether they involved working with happy people, challenging objectively measuring happiness, as people's moods can vary. His script named the professions with positive environments by helping others.

```
class JobSuggestion:
    def __init__(self):
        self.happy_jobs = [
            'Event Planner',
            'Teacher',
            'Social Worker',
            'Yoga Instructor',
            'Chef',
            'Travel Blogger',
        ]

    def suggest_job(self):
        print("Welcome! Let me suggest a job for you based on working with happy people.")
        response = input("Are you ready? (yes/no): ").lower()

        if response == 'yes':
            print("Great! Here's a job suggestion for you:")
            suggested_job = self.get_random_happy_job()
            print(f"You might enjoy being a {suggested_job}.")
        else:
            print("No problem! If you change your mind, feel free to come back.")

    def get_random_happy_job(self):
        import random
        return random.choice(self.happy_jobs)

if __name__ == "__main__":
    job_suggestion = JobSuggestion()
    job_suggestion.suggest_job()
```

This script suggested using a predefined list of "happy" jobs when being run with professions he believed were associated with positive environments. Since job satisfaction is subjective, and what makes people happy can vary, he skipped professional advice or assessment tools tailored for that purpose.
One day, he's got a visit…

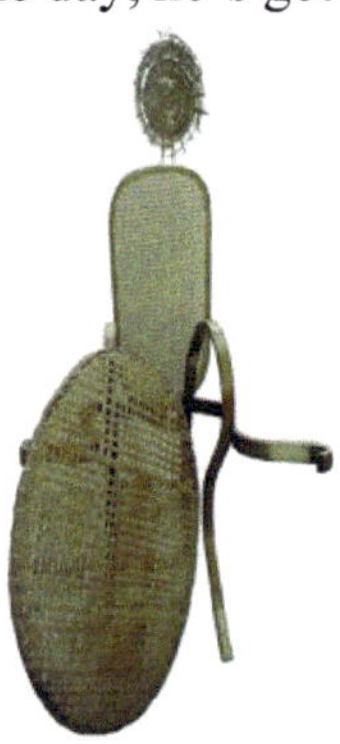

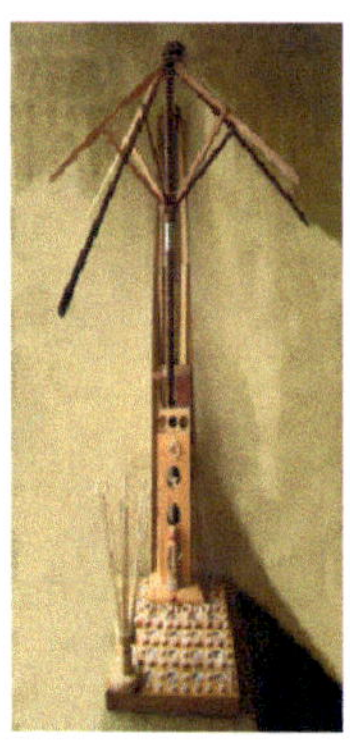

CELEBRATION: HOLIDAYS
(DICTIONARY)
LYRE PLAYERS – ERICA, KATE, LUCILLE, LYNN, AND CALVIN

Five lyre players were in the Orchestra: Erica, Kate, Lucille, Lynn, and Calvin. In addition to playing and being involved in Orchestra life, Kate served on the City's Art program council. Discussions took place about whether to host local performances or promote visiting artists. The visiting artists did not want to leave; thus, the Orchestra grew bigger.

Lucille was an environmentalist who controlled the noise level, and her questions were all about the noise blasts: who, what, when, whose, why, and addressing any sound violation.

Lynn studied religions. She made a list of problems and kept adding them after reading the news.

They all played as a team – the same music by each player with a small delay. They were all part of a group performing on special occasions. During winter, they enjoyed playing beneath the falling snow.

One day, while playing outside of the Courthouse on a beautiful snowy day, they were asked to leave in the middle of the performance despite having already been paid.

They warmed up at the nearest coffee shop and exchanged their interpretations.

Lucille: They want the Court to be a noise-free zone.

Erica: No doubt, it was racial.

Kate: The government does not like the Arts. The 1% tax going to the Arts annoys "them."

Lynn: It's all about religion.

Calvin: We all belong to the wrong political party.

```
class EventOrganizer:
    def __init__(self):
        self.events = []

    def add_event(self, event_name, date, performers):
        event = {'name': event_name, 'date': date, 'performers': performers}
        self.events.append(event)

    def display_events(self):
        print("Upcoming Events:")
        for event in self.events:
            print(f"{event['name']} on {event['date']}: {', '.join(event['performers'])}")

# Example of usage
organizer = EventOrganizer()

organizer.add_event("Holiday Concert", "2025-12-25", ["Flutist 1", "Flutist 2", "Flutist 3", "Flutist 4", "Flutist 5"])
organizer.add_event("Community Gathering", "2025-12-28", ["Local Band", "Choir"])

organizer.display_events()
```

Actually, the city was planning a joyful art parade that would celebrate various ethnic groups and religions, and the five lyre players were sitting on the way of the parade.

Their quiet, comfortable life gained some level of understanding. Calvin even gave his listeners examples while he sang it after playing his lyre.

Their living space consisted of positive space silence and negative space texture.

CELESTIAL MECHANICS – A STUDY OF THE MOTION OF OBJECTS IN OUTER SPACE (CLASSES)

GEOPHYSICISTS/DATA COLLECTORS – NUR AND KFA

They both wanted to study the Earth and its physical properties. He, Nur, was more into the lab work, while She, Kfa, enjoyed the fieldwork. They both worked for an environmental protection group. Nur studied geophysics, and Kfa's major was geoscience. Nur knew more about mapping than anyone they met, while she specialized in GIS/GPS. Late at night, when nobody was watching, they kept building futuristic models of their planet, which involved aspects such as visual representation, atmospheric conditions simulation, or other speculative features. They wrote a Python script for their vision of a planet:

```
import matplotlib.pyplot as plt
import numpy as np

class FuturisticPlanet:
    def __init__(self, size, features):
        self.size = size
        self.features = features

    def visualize(self):
        fig, ax = plt.subplots(subplot_kw={'aspect': 'equal'})
        ax.set_xlim(-self.size, self.size)
        ax.set_ylim(-self.size, self.size)

        # Draw the planet
        planet_circle = plt.Circle((0, 0), self.size, color='blue',
alpha=0.7)
        ax.add_patch(planet_circle)

        # Add futuristic features
        for feature in self.features:
            feature.draw(ax)

plt.title('Futuristic Planet')
        plt.xlabel('X-axis')
        plt.ylabel('Y-axis')
        plt.grid(True)
        plt.show()

class FuturisticFeature:
    def __init__(self, name, position, size, color):
        self.name = name
        self.position = position
        self.size = size
        self.color = color

    def draw(self, ax):
        feature_circle = plt.Circle(self.position, self.size, color=self.color,
alpha=0.7)
        ax.add_patch(feature_circle)
        ax.annotate(self.name, self.position, color='white', ha='center',
va='center')

# Example Usage
planet_size = 50
futuristic_features = [
    FuturisticFeature('Floating City', (10, 10), 5, 'red'),
    FuturisticFeature('Advanced Technology Hub', (-20, 15), 7, 'green'),
    FuturisticFeature('Hyperloop Network', (-25, -20), 6, 'orange'),
    # Add more features as needed
]

futuristic_planet = FuturisticPlanet(planet_size, futuristic_features)
futuristic_planet.visualize()
```

Their work defined a FuturisticPlanet class and a FuturisticFeature class. They customized the planet's size and added various features with their positions, sizes, and colors. The visualized method then used matplotlib to draw the planet and its features. Then, they enhanced and modified the script based on their ideas for futuristic planets and picked their best creation to move there.

CERAMICS
(CLASS)
COAT CLERK – DIETEL

Dietel made his own design for tokens to be given as a coat locator and proof of coat ownership as well. Each token had a number and a corresponding message on the back. Messages were written to cheer people who were standing in line to pick up their coats. Each one had a puzzle, and the numeric answer was placed on the other side of the token, indicating the order by which the proper coat was found. The tokens were color-coded for children and adults, with different difficulty levels set accordingly. They were ceramic, with a wooden rim for an outline. They all were beautiful, and they fit nicely in the hand. The tokens often disappeared because of their beauty. Dietel noticed that the coats started to pile up as some people chose not to pick them up so they could keep the token. It did not bother him, as it was giving him more opportunities to create more tokens, develop better and more creative designs, and improve his kiln firing skills. He wrote a code for firing a ceramic kiln and the firing process:

```
import time

class CeramicKiln:
    def __init__(self):
        self.temperature = 0

    def preheat(self):
        print("Preheating the kiln...")
        for i in range(0, 1000, 100):
            self.temperature = i
            time.sleep(1)
            print(f"Current temperature: {self.temperature}
degrees Celsius")

    def bisque_fire(self):
        print("Bisque firing in progress...")
        for i in range(1000, 900, -50):
            self.temperature = i
            time.sleep(1)
            print(f"Current temperature: {self.temperature}
degrees Celsius")

    def glaze_fire(self):
        print("Glaze firing in progress...")
        for i in range(900, 1200, 50):
            self.temperature = i
            time.sleep(1)
            print(f"Current temperature: {self.temperature}
degrees Celsius")
# Example usage
kiln = CeramicKiln()

kiln.preheat()
kiln.bisque_fire()
kiln.glaze_fire()
```

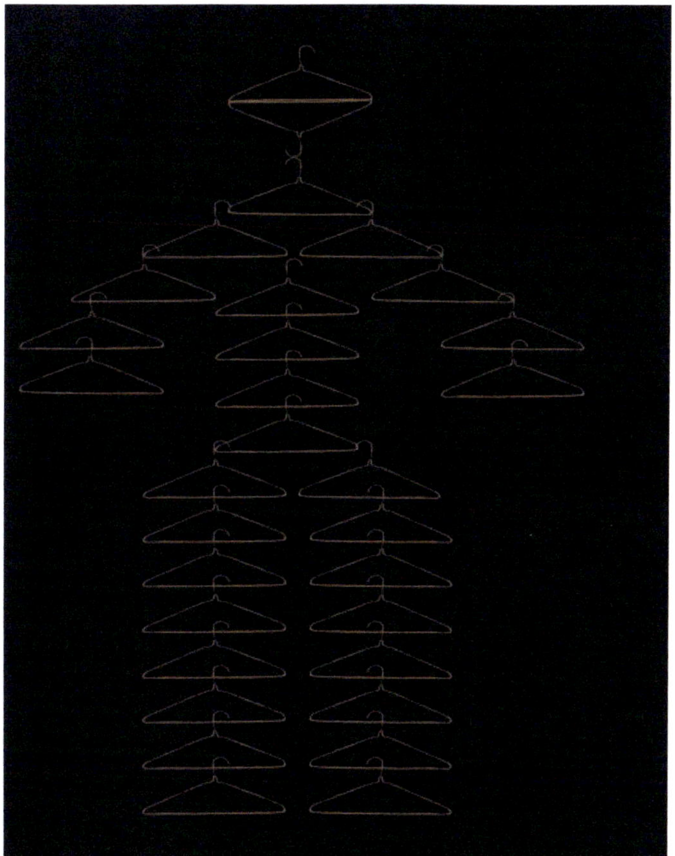

His code defined a simple CeramicKiln class with methods for preheating, bisque firing, and glaze firing, safety measures, temperature control, and kiln operation manuals when working with ceramics.

Soon, he opened a used coat store, ending his status at the bottom of the payroll.

CHOREOGRAPHY
(TRUE FALSE STATEMENTS)
HIP-HOP DANCER – TESSA & CLASSICAL DANCER – HOON

They danced to the same music. Tessa danced classically, while Hoon danced hip hop with What is it? So why should I care? approach. To master it, they matched the music with the movement through code.

```
import pygame
import time

# Initialize pygame
pygame.init()

# Set up the display
width, height = 800, 600
screen = pygame.display.set_mode((width, height))
pygame.display.set_caption("Dance Collaboration")
# Load music
pygame.mixer.music.load("your_music_file.mp3")
pygame.mixer.music.play()
# Define colors
white = (255, 255, 255)

# Define dancers
class Dancer:
    def _init_(self, color, start_position):
        self.color = color
        self.position = start_position
        self.speed = 5

    def move(self):
        keys = pygame.key.get_pressed()
        if keys[pygame.K_LEFT]:
            self.position[0] -= self.speed
        if keys[pygame.K_RIGHT]:
            self.position[0] += self.speed
        if keys[pygame.K_UP]:
            self.position[1] -= self.speed
        if keys[pygame.K_DOWN]:
            self.position[1] += self.speed
    def draw(self):
        pygame.draw.circle(screen, self.color, (self.position[0],
self.position[1]), 50)

# Create dancers
hip_hop_dancer = Dancer((255, 0, 0), [100, 300])
classical_dancer = Dancer((0, 0, 255), [700, 300])

# Main loop
running = True
while running:
    for event in pygame.event.get():
        if event.type == pygame.QUIT:
            running = False

    screen.fill(white)

    # Move and draw dancers
    hip_hop_dancer.move()
    hip_hop_dancer.draw()

    classical_dancer.move()
    classical_dancer.draw()

    pygame.display.flip()
    pygame.time.Clock().tick(30)  # Adjust the frame rate as needed

pygame.quit()
```

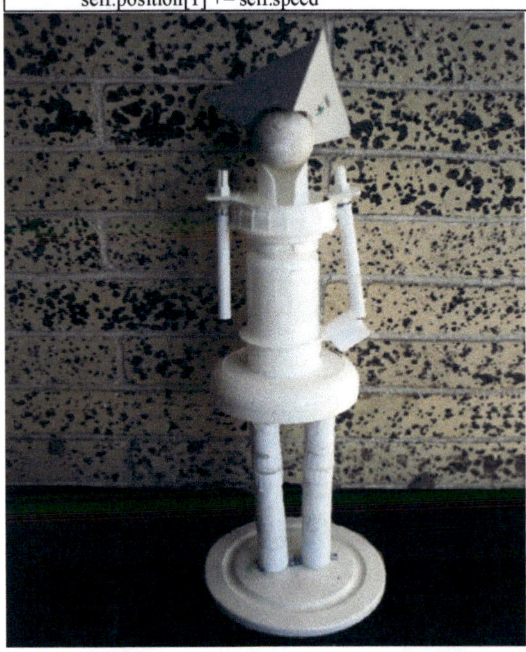

Now, they needed to replace "your_music_file.mp3" with the path to their music file. They kept customizing it further based on the needs, adding more dancers, dance moves, or interactive features whenever they were invited for a stage performance, and the demands kept growing.

CIVIC DUTY
(PROBABILITY WITH LOGISTIC REGRESSION MODEL)
CAREER CHANGE – RO, DIS, GE, FULO, HUD, AND FOL

Those from various professions were called for jury duty. After the trials, they all decided to be public defenders. The Judge wondered why, as he worked with different law professionals. Creating a comprehensive code for predicting the probability of individuals from various professions switching to become public defenders would typically involve using statistical models and analyzing relevant data. It's a complex task that often requires machine learning techniques and a dataset with information about individuals' professions, their characteristics, and the likelihood of switching to become public defenders.

```
from sklearn.model_selection import train_test_split
from sklearn.linear_model import LogisticRegression
from sklearn.metrics import accuracy_score

# Sample data (replace this with your dataset)
data = {
    'Age': [30, 25, 35, 40, 28, 32],
    'YearsExperience': [5, 2, 8, 10, 3, 6],
    'SwitchedToPublicDefender': [1, 0, 1, 1, 0, 1]  # 1 if switched, 0 if
not
}

# Creating a DataFrame (load your data here)
import pandas as pd
df = pd.DataFrame(data)

# Features and target variable
X = df[['Age', 'YearsExperience']]
y = df['SwitchedToPublicDefender']

# Splitting the data into training and testing sets
X_train, X_test, y_train, y_test = train_test_split(X, y, test_size=0.2,
random_state=42)

# Creating and training the logistic regression model
model = LogisticRegression()
model.fit(X_train, y_train)

# Making predictions on the test set
y_pred = model.predict(X_test)

# Calculating accuracy (replace with more comprehensive evaluation
metrics)
accuracy = accuracy_score(y_test, y_pred)
print(f"Model Accuracy: {accuracy}")

# Predicting the probability for a new individual
new_person = pd.DataFrame({'Age': [27], 'YearsExperience': [4]})


probability = model.predict_proba(new_person)[0, 1]
print(f"Probability of switching to become a public defender:
{probability}")
```

He used the code after each research by plugging in current data. The results stayed the same.

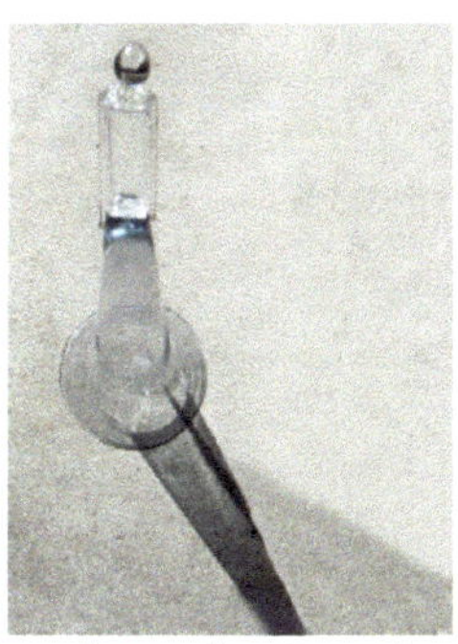

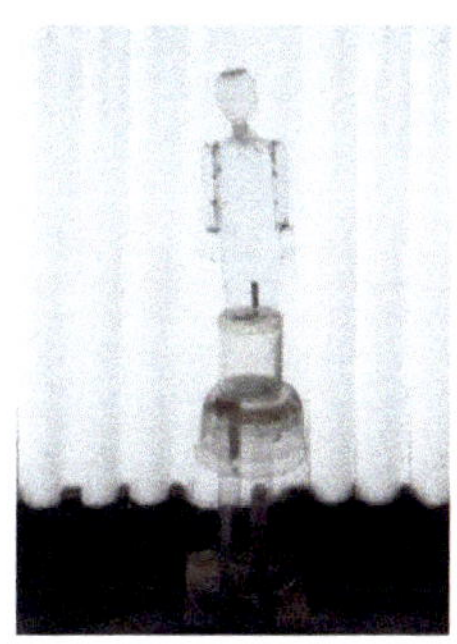

People want to be good, at least, he thought.

CLOTHING WITH NO RESTRICTIONS (CLASSES)

PERCUSSION – OVO

His greatest pride was in wearing “no season, no age” costumes.

```
class Costume:
    def __init__(self, name, description):
        self.name = name
        self.description = description

def wear_costume(person, costume):
    print(f"{person} wears the {costume.name} costume. {costume.description}")

# Creating "no season, no age" costumes
cosmic_costume = Costume("Cosmic Explorer", "A futuristic costume that transcends seasons and ages.")
fantasy_costume = Costume("Enchanted Voyager", "A magical costume with timeless charm.")

# Wearing costumes without being bound by season or age
wear_costume("Alice", cosmic_costume)
wear_costume("Bob", fantasy_costume)
```

The Costume class was created to represent costumes, and instances of this class (cosmic_costume and fantasy_costume) encapsulated both the name and description of each costume. The wear_costume function then demonstrated the use of objects (instances of the Costume class) to model the behavior of wearing costumes without being bound by season or age.

One day, Ovo went to receive an award, which changed everything.

COLLECTING
(COMPOSITION)
MUSIC COLLECTOR – DEBBIE

Debbie had ample knowledge of music and history. She wanted to document the changes in the music field. Collecting instruments was part of the process. She brought back instruments from her trips, and she also had Ken, the music traveler, bring her one from each of his. The collection was big enough to fill the entire museum, and it kept growing. There were instruments characteristic of each and every place that was historically significant to the growth and presentation of music. Sometimes, the cost of an instrument was close to nothing; sometimes, it was a fortune. Debbie only trusted Ken. She had notes, books, and manuscripts and developed a displaying system to cover the entire apartment's wall space. Tired of dusting, she ordered big plastic sheets to cover the collection with transparent screens. She painted the walls behind the instruments black for better exposure. After space next door became available, she soon needed the tall riser with all the apartments in it, but it would mean selling her instruments.

```
class Instrument:
    def __init__(self, name, value):
        self.name = name
        self.value = value

class InstrumentCollection:
    def __init__(self):
        self.instruments = []

    def add_instrument(self, instrument):
        self.instruments.append(instrument)

    def calculate_total_value(self):
        total_value = sum(instrument.value for instrument in self.instruments)
        return total_value

class TallRiser:
    def _init_(self, cost):
        self.cost = cost

    def buy_riser(self, funds):
        if funds >= self.cost:
            print("Successfully bought the tall riser!")
            return True
        else:
            print("Insufficient funds to buy the tall riser. Keep selling instruments!")
            return False

# Example usage:
instrument_collection = InstrumentCollection()

# Adding instruments to the collection
instrument_collection.add_instrument(Instrument("Guitar",  500))
instrument_collection.add_instrument(Instrument("Piano",  1200))
instrument_collection.add_instrument(Instrument("Flute",  200))

# Calculating total value from the instrument sales
total_funds = instrument_collection.calculate_total_value()

# Creating a tall riser with a cost
tall_riser = TallRiser(cost=800)

# Attempting to buy the tall riser
tall_riser.buy_riser(total_funds)
```

To organize her collection, her code defined multiple classes (Instrument, InstrumentCollection, and TallRiser) and composed them to simulate the process of managing to buy a tall riser from the sales of an instrument collection. Composition is a concept where objects of one class are used as components in another class to build more complex behavior.

The owner of the tall riser bought her entire collection, but he no longer had the space to put them in.

This is why teamwork is on the rise.

COMMON HABITS AND ADJUSTMENTS (CONDITIONAL STATEMENT) WILDLIFE TAMER – PY

He was the one who was shocked by seeing people writing with their right hands during his first left-line tour in Australia. The windshield wipers started whenever he turned on the left or right signal.

```
def traffic_rule(direction):
    if direction.lower() == 'left':
        print("Drive on the left side of the road.")
    elif direction.lower() == 'right':
        print("Drive on the right side of the road.")
    else:
        print("Invalid direction. Please specify 'left' or 'right'.")

# Example usage:
traffic_rule('left')
traffic_rule('right')
traffic_rule('center')
```

In his code, the traffic_rule function took a direction as an argument. It used conditional statements (if, elif, else) to provide instructions based on the specified direction to make decisions based on the input.

He still had a problem with the switch of time and the season.

COMMEMORATION
(ARRAY MANIPULATION)
A MONUMENT OF A COMPOSER

The music of a long-forgotten mathematician was revived and recalled by many. It happened for a simple reason: his music was rhythmic, thus suitable for a parade. And the new king loved parades.

```
import numpy as np
import matplotlib.pyplot as plt
import wave
import array

# Define the tempo and time signature
tempo = 120  # beats per minute
beats_per_measure = 4

# Calculate the duration of one beat in seconds
beat_duration = 60 / tempo

# Generate a simple rhythmic pattern using a mathematical function
beat_times = np.arange(0, beats_per_measure * beat_duration, 0.01)
beat_amplitudes = np.sin(2 * np.pi * beat_times / beat_duration)

# Plot the rhythmic pattern
plt.plot(beat_times, beat_amplitudes)
plt.title('Rhythmic Pattern')
plt.xlabel('Time (s)')
plt.ylabel('Amplitude')
plt.show()

# Save the rhythmic pattern as a WAV file
output_file = 'rhythmic_pattern.wav'
output_wave = wave.open(output_file, 'w')
output_wave.setnchannels(1)
output_wave.setsampwidth(2)
output_wave.setframerate(44100)
output_wave.writeframes(array.array('h', (int(32767.0 * x) for x in beat_amplitudes)))
output_wave.close()

print(f'Rhythmic pattern saved to {output_file}')
```

The numpy library created arrays (beat_times and beat_amplitudes) representing the beats' timing and amplitude in a rhythmic pattern. The mathematical function (np.sin) was applied to create a simple rhythmic variation. It demonstrated how to visualize the rhythmic pattern using Matplotlib as a WAV file.

It showcased how mathematical concepts can be applied to music generation.

COMMUNICATION (PRINT FUNCTION) TUBA – JARED

Jared, a tuba player, is often late for rehearsals. Sometimes, it is because of the traffic; sometimes, he misses his exit. Jared is not so motivated to be on time because many musical compositions do not comprise tuba at all. Nevertheless, the orchestra conductor, David, does not begin the rehearsal until everybody is present. Colleagues have had enough of waiting for Jared, so they warn him that he might get an alarm clock as a retirement gift. In response, he discussed why an alarm clock is not the best retirement gift by creating a script that prints out these reasons.

```
    print("Retirement Gift Suggestions:")
    print("1. Travel vouchers for a dream vacation.")
    print("2. Relaxing spa treatments for ultimate rejuvenation.")
    print("3. Personalized hobby-related items, like a custom golf set or gardening tools.")
    print("4. Memory book or scrapbook capturing memorable moments from their career.")

def retirement_gift_suggestions():
    print("5. Subscription to a book club or streaming service for leisurely entertainment.")
    print("\nAvoid:")
    print("An alarm clock - because retirement means no more early morning alarms!")

# Call the function to display the suggestions
retirement_gift_suggestions()
```

By presenting the reasons in a clear and concise manner, he emphasized the message and coding techniques for this type of script by conveying information in a readable and understandable way.

It convinced them to switch his duties to coding, which he could do from home without being late.

COMPUTER SCIENCE
(SHORTCUTS)
INSTRUMENT SALESMAN – GRAHAM

He developed a cure for a cure. Then a keyboard shortcut for a keyboard shortcut became available to him:

```
import keyboard

def on_shortcut_triggered(e):
    print("Shortcut triggered!")

# Define the keyboard shortcut (e.g., Ctrl + Alt + S)
shortcut_combination = 'ctrl+alt+s'

# Register the shortcut callback function
keyboard.add_hotkey(shortcut_combination, on_shortcut_triggered)

# Keep the program running
keyboard.wait('esc')
```

He installed the keyboard library before running the code using pip install keyboard. He set up a keyboard shortcut using Ctrl + Alt + S. When the shortcut is pressed, the on_shortcut_triggered function is called, and it prints "Shortcut triggered!" to the console. The program will keep running until the Escape key is pressed. Then, he customized the shortcut combination and the action inside the on_shortcut_triggered function according to his needs.

He became the fastest computer science professor, so they assigned him to teach a typing class.

COMPUTING (EXECUTING A FUNCTION) HELPER – SUM

In her sticky-note-yellow painted room, Sum was building her first computer. Sum bought:

- a motherboard	- video cards
- a processor	- power supply
- a hard drive	- sound cards
- RAM	- a case

She wrote a code on how to make a computer. The rest she had at hand.
Since it involves both hardware and software aspects, her Python script for software-related tasks simulated the software setup process. The hardware assembly required physical actions to be followed.

```
def build_computer():
    print("Welcome to the Computer Building Assistant!")

    # Gather user input
    processor = input("Enter the processor model: ")
    ram_size = input("Enter the RAM size (in GB): ")
    storage_type = input("Enter the storage type (SSD/HDD): ")
    storage_size = input("Enter the storage size (in GB): ")
    operating_system = input("Enter the operating system: ")

    # Display the configuration
    print("\nComputer Configuration:")
    print(f"Processor: {processor}")
    print(f"RAM: {ram_size}GB")
    print(f"Storage: {storage_size}GB {storage_type}")
    print(f"Operating System: {operating_system}")

    # Simulate installation process
    print("\nInstalling operating system...")
    print("Configuring drivers...")
    print("Setting up user preferences...")

    print("\nComputer successfully built! Enjoy your new system.")

# Execute the function
build_computer()
```

Her script collected information about the processor, RAM, storage, and operating system and then simulated the installation process without covering all the details of building a computer. Writing this code ensured that she had to build another computer, as the moment we acquired a new one, it appeared outdated. That's how fast technology evolves!

CONFIDENCE
(CLASS)
TIMPANI -- GREG

Greg always felt nervous. He thought his shyness caused it. But that wasn't it; he was blocked whenever someone spoke to him. He always felt insecure, and he questioned all the decisions or moves he made. This was unbearable and almost painful to him. He analyzed all his tasks, whether sweeping a floor or making a phone call, and he always felt he could have done better. However, he did not consider himself a perfectionist. When he played, he thought about each and every contact with his instrument. Thus, his play was subtle and cooling, ringing nicely in the listeners' ears. When he attended parties, he felt secure and radiant. He was a lion when they let him talk about his instrument.

```
class TimpaniPlayer:
    def __init__(self, hand_position="French Grip", hand_pressure="Moderate"):
        self.hand_position = hand_position
        self.hand_pressure = hand_pressure

    def play_timpani(self):
        print(f"Using {self.hand_position} grip with {self.hand_pressure} hand pressure.")
        print("Maintaining proper wrist and finger flexibility.")
        print("Striking the timpani head at the optimal spot for desired tone.")

# Example usage
timpanist = TimpaniPlayer()
timpanist.play_timpani()
```

They rarely did, though.

CONSERVATION
(STRING MANIPULATION WITH "FIND AND SLICING" OPERATIONS)
WATER CARRIER – ZEPA

.

He found out that the ideas he named his golden thoughts, jotted down on a sticky note in the pocket of his jeans, got washed along with his jeans. He could not remember or read any one of them. He could not recall the level of importance they possessed. To recover their meaning, he wrote a code:

```
def recover_information_from_sticky_note(washed_note):
    # Assume that the information is written in a specific format, like "Recovery Code: ABC123"
    keyword = "Recovery Code: "
    start_index = washed_note.find(keyword)

    if start_index != -1:
        # Extract the information following the keyword
        recovery_code = washed_note[start_index + len(keyword):]
        return recovery_code.strip()
    else:
        return "No recovery code found on the washed sticky note."

# Example usage
washed_sticky_note = "Important info:\nRecovery Code: ABC123"

recovery_code = recover_information_from_sticky_note(washed_sticky_note)
print("Recovered Information:", recovery_code)
```

The recover_information_from_sticky_note function takes a string representing a note and looks for a keyword ("Recovery Code:"). If the keyword is found, it extracts the information following the keyword.

All he remembered was they were very good.

CONSTRUCTION (INVENTORY) CONSTRUCTORS – SIX

Six of them worked together on every job, big or small. Each person mastered a different tool. It was hard to predict how many tools would be needed for each job. They created a basic inventory management:

```
class Tool:
    def __init__(self, name, quantity):
        self.name = name
        self.quantity = quantity

class ToolInventory:
    def __init__(self):
        self.tools = []

    def add_tool(self, tool):
        self.tools.append(tool)

    def remove_tool(self, tool_name):
        for tool in self.tools:
            if tool.name == tool_name:
                self.tools.remove(tool)
                return True
        return False

    def check_tool_quantity(self, tool_name):
        for tool in self.tools:
            if tool.name == tool_name:
                return tool.quantity
        return 0

# Sample usage:
if __name__ == "__main__":
    # Create tools
    hammer = Tool("Hammer", 5)
    screwdriver = Tool("Screwdriver", 10)
    saw = Tool("Saw", 3)
    tape_measure = Tool("Tape Measure", 7)
    wrench = Tool("Wrench", 8)
    drill = Tool("Drill", 4)

    # Create tool inventory
    inventory = ToolInventory()

    # Add tools to inventory
    inventory.add_tool(hammer)
    inventory.add_tool(screwdriver)
    inventory.add_tool(saw)
    inventory.add_tool(tape_measure)
    inventory.add_tool(wrench)
    inventory.add_tool(drill)

    # Check tool quantity
    print("Quantity of Wrench: ",
inventory.check_tool_quantity("Wrench"))

    # Remove a tool
    inventory.remove_tool("Saw")

    # Check tool quantity again
    print("Quantity of Saw: ",
inventory.check_tool_quantity("Saw"))
```

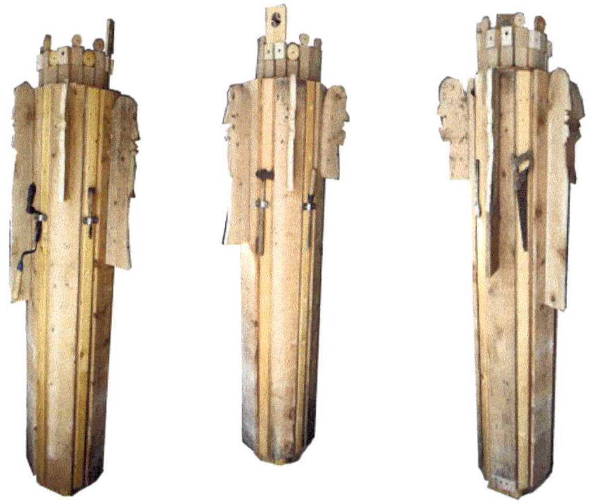

To manage tools in a construction business, they customized their code based on the specific needs, added more features like tool tracking, user authentication, or a graphical user interface (GUI) if necessary. Since they were inseparable, each of them was named Six. This way, when someone would call, any one of them could answer without causing any confusion.

CONUNDRUM: A CONFUSING PROBLEM OR QUESTION
(A CLASS)
SNAKE CHARMER – PEACE

Being part of the entertainment system was never easy. Once, on his way to the conference meeting rooms, Peace discovered that a big stone he once painted gold was still sitting in his bag. It was too late to go back and leave it in the hotel room, so he decided to hide it somewhere in the city. There was a spot that somehow looked like it was set under the bridge. When he approached it, he noticed an old bank window, only accessible through a non-working mechanism that reminded him of an old suitcase. The space between the vault and the bank window seemed to be a perfect place to hide the stone. After doing that, he noticed some action and commotion caused by the daily money transit. Seeing so many police and bank officials made him leave the scene. Now he had to find this place on the map and mark it to find his stone on the way back to the hotel. A woman stopped and asked if he needed help, "I am not from here, she said, but I know my way around Boston well." I am in Boston, then, he thought. The shaman was speaking in a language so old that even he himself could not understand it.

```
class MapMarker:
  def __init__(self):
    self.marked_places = {}

  def mark_place(self, place_name, latitude, longitude):
    self.marked_places[place_name] = (latitude,
longitude)
    print(f"Marked {place_name} on the map at
coordinates: {latitude}, {longitude}")

  def get_back_to_place(self, place_name):
    if place_name in self.marked_places:
      coordinates = self.marked_places[place_name]
      print(f"Returning to {place_name}. Coordinates:
{coordinates[0]}, {coordinates[1]}")
    else:
      print(f"Sorry, {place_name} is not marked on the
map.")

# Example of using the MapMarker class
map_marker = MapMarker()

# Mark a place on the map
map_marker.mark_place("Home", 40.7128, -74.0060)

# Get back to the marked place
map_marker.get_back_to_place("Home")
```

He used a class (MapMarker) to encapsulate the functionality. The class had a dictionary (marked_places) to store the marked places with their corresponding coordinates. The methods mark_place and get_back_to_place allowed him to mark a place on the map and later retrieve the coordinates to return there to pick up his stone.

COOKING
(FUNCTION ABSTRACTION)
THE OPERA CHEFS – FRANK, BOB AND MARCEL

Frank's recipe for Spaghetti was, "Boil spaghetti and keep throwing single spago until it sticks."
Bob's was, "Add lemon to everything."
Marcel's was, "Add garlic to anything you cook."
For all those undecided, they had a list of things that taste like chicken on their menu.
Their meals had fancy names, for example, "ITALIAN FLAVORED OLIVES" or "CATFISH FLAVORED FISH."

```
def cook_spaghetti():
    """Simulate the shortest possible way to cook spaghetti."""
    print("1. Boil water in a pot.")
    print("2. Add salt to the boiling water.")
    print("3. Place the spaghetti in the boiling water.")
    print("4. Cook for 8-10 minutes or until al dente.")
    print("5. Drain the water and set aside.")

if __name__ == "__main__":
    # Use the cook_spaghetti function to simulate cooking spaghetti
    cook_spaghetti()
```

The cook_spaghetti function encapsulated the steps involved in cooking spaghetti, providing a high-level abstraction of the cooking process. This made the code more modular, readable, and easier to understand. Function abstraction is a fundamental concept in programming that involves encapsulating a set of instructions into a function, allowing for code reuse and organization. The function abstracted away the details of cooking spaghetti, providing a clear and concise representation of the cooking process.

Frank, Bob, and Marcel were unusual cooks. They liked to share their recipes, which they turned into fortune cookies. Because of that, the recopies had to be short.
The leftovers served to the dogs were so good that this dish was called "Sitting Pretty Spaghetti."

COSMOS
(LOOP)
NOTICED – RESA

He was finally noticed. Not because he looked interesting but simply because he mentioned being on Alaain Grinsssberg's reading list. "How come you are on Alaain Grinsssberg's reading list," asked the new Alaain Grinsssberg's advisor (this is how he learned who the new advisor was). I was in the room when the list was handed out, and I quickly took the first position on that list. This playing stupid tactic paid off. Now, and finally, it could have ended, he puffed a sound that no one had a chance to name yet. The pretending was over. All has been accomplished in that domain. He was no longer a mass or part of a stereotype. They were interested in his take on the first item on the list. It was all about being clean, the idea of taking the notion to the next level by introducing it to a group, then extracting all that they could agree on; that was his new take on economics. Removing potential threats that could backfire years ahead. But this threat could have only been recognized by a fraction of the mind, only released during stress or a motivator inhibited by long-term inactivity of proper mental flow. On the other hand, this could have only been recognized by fear. To the rest, it was a noise, blubber, or unsuccessful effort to get noticed. But he only wanted to be noticed when not paralyzed by that dreadful feeling of recognizing the pattern that led to noticing, but aggressive competency of competing. Get noticed for what? Own satisfaction? Social boredom? So, Alaain Grinsssberg has been selected as president, he learned. His unconscious brain started to talk. Finally, his expectations of intelligence elsewhere were finally fulfilled.

```
import random
import time

def search_for_intelligent_life():
    """Simulate the search for intelligent life beyond
Earth."""
    print("Initiating search for intelligent life...")

    # Simulate searching different star systems
    for star_system in range(1, 6):
        print(f"Searching star system {star_system}...")

        # Simulate scanning planets in the star system
        for planet in range(1, random.randint(1, 10)):
            time.sleep(0.5) # Simulate scanning delay
            potential_life = random.choice([True, False])

            if potential_life:
                print(f"Potential intelligent life detected on
planet {planet}!")
                return

    print("No intelligent life detected in the searched star
systems.")

if __name__ == "__main__":
    search_for_intelligent_life()
```

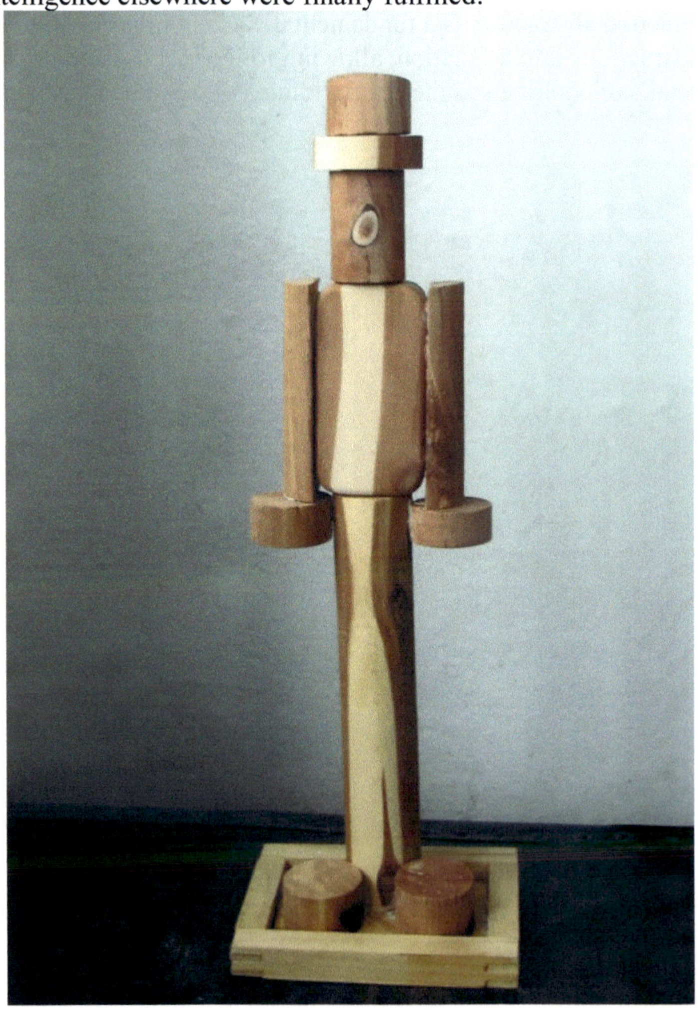

He used two nested loops: one for iterating through different star systems and another for scanning planets within each star system. The loops allowed the code to systematically search through multiple systems to simulate the search for intelligent life. My happy place is not a place, he thought. It's people.

COSTUME CODE
(ALTERNATE)
HARP – MARGARET

Margaret, a harpist, always dresses meticulously in national colors. They are always the same, but it is hard to predict the daily color set for her blouse, jacket, skirt, hair, or shoes. The stage designers, Jons, wanted to expose her closing as decorative elements at the rehearsal for the national day celebration. They created a set with all the matching colors to make her blend there. To the crew's great surprise, she showed up dressed all in black. They created a plan by programming a dress code where the parts of her closing alternated the national colors of different parts of a harpist's attire to make the audience watch the spectacle more than once, as they hoped for. They used a list of colors and then applied them to each clothing item. This way, she could grace international stages.

```
import itertools
import time

# Define national colors
national_colors = [
    "red",
    "white",
    "blue",
    "green",
    "yellow",
    "black",
    "orange",
    "purple",
]

# Define clothing items
clothing_items = ["dress", "skirt", "jacket", "hair",
"shoes"]

# Function to alternate colors for each clothing item
def alternate_colors():
    for item in itertools.cycle(clothing_items):
        color = national_colors.pop(0)
        print(f"{item.capitalize()}: {color}")
        national_colors.append(color)
        time.sleep(1) # Adjust the sleep duration to
control the speed of the color changes

# Run the function
alternate_colors()
```

They also built a transparent ship for her so more people could admire her attire, which nicely contrasted with the rest of the guests during the color-coded holiday celebrations.

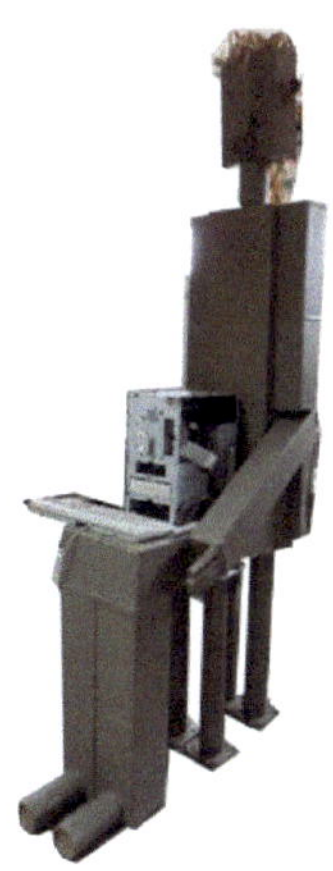

COSTUME DESIGN
(TURTLE GRAPHICS LIBRARY)
BANJO – IRENE

Irene was often asked to act in the eighteenth-century plays. She knew how to look appropriate. No one could become her. "Her" meant the lady who knew how to hold her head and gaze at her surroundings. Irene impacted her colleagues, as most were affected by her manners. Even the clothing she wore looked stylish on her and only on her. She collected books on styles of garments and accessories and reviewed them frequently. One day, the secret of her style broke out. Kathy, the costume designer, created outfits, especially for Irene, which, in turn, strongly influenced her posture, gestures, and how she talked. Then, Kathy's secret emerged: She coded her creations, which involved complex graphics and design tools. While dress design is beyond the scope of a text-based code, she used Python for 18th-century influences.

```
import turtle

def draw_dress():
    # Set up the turtle
    my_turtle = turtle.Turtle()
    my_screen = turtle.Screen()
    my_turtle.speed(2)
c
    # Draw the bodice
    my_turtle.color("blue")
    my_turtle.begin_fill()
    for _ in range(2):
        my_turtle.forward(100)
        my_turtle.right(90)
        my_turtle.forward(150)
        my_turtle.right(90)
    my_turtle.end_fill()

    # Draw the skirt
    my_turtle.color("pink")
    my_turtle.begin_fill()
    my_turtle.forward(100)
    my_turtle.left(90)
    my_turtle.forward(200)
    my_turtle.left(90)
    my_turtle.forward(100)
    my_turtle.left(90)
    my_turtle.forward(200)
    my_turtle.end_fill()

    # Draw decorative elements (you can
customize this part)
    my_turtle.color("gold")
    my_turtle.penup()
    my_turtle.goto(50, 150)
    my_turtle.pendown()
    my_turtle.circle(10)

    my_turtle.penup()
    my_turtle.goto(-50, 150)
    my_turtle.pendown()
    my_turtle.circle(10)

    # Close the window on click
    my_screen.exitonclick()

if __name__ == "__main__":
    draw_dress()
```

Her code used Turtle graphics to draw a simple representation of a dress with a bodice and a skirt. She customized the colors, shapes, and decorations to match occasions with associated colors.
Soon, her city became known as a design influencer.

COSTUME SOLUTIONS
(MAPPING)
COSTUME DESIGNERS WITH 3D PRINTING – JOHA & KATHY

Kathy was a gamer. Her hobby was to make costumes. Her designs were based on characters in computer games. She was skillful with her hands. She could never predict her outcome. She attended costume conferences and Anime conventions. It was gaining her lots of friends. At the conventions, participants wear their own creations and do skits. There are workshops and sharing sessions. Kathy's website was not only informative but also fun. It had photos and movies showing her wearing her own designs. This is where her real acting began. It is easier to design a costume for an actor when you actually act.
Joha preferred 3D printing for that. With so many available materials, tools, and techniques, 3D printing became the perfect way to dress people from head to toe. Joha matched the needs with the proper materials to be used. Shoes, for example, must be flexible, soft, and hard, respectively, yet maintain flexible, ergonometric design combined with tasteful color combinations. Her jewelry, cases, artistic eyewear, and hearing aids could be printed in wood, ABS, PLA, nylons, stainless steel, various accuras, and plastics. Her multi-color polyjet and high-resolution printer could deliver various sizes, great detail, and surfaces, if called for. Her use of plastic offered various finishes. She infused glass beads for her products with multiple color combinations, translucent or opaque. She used thermoplastic polyurethane with a rubber-like elastic material when an elastic finish was needed. Joha used laser sintering to create stable and durable jackets with interlocking hinges or springs. She worked with precious metals such as sterling silver, gold, and bronze to make jewelry and accessories. She also wrote a code that suggested materials for 3D printing costumes based on specific requirements, printer type, and budget.

```
def suggest_material(costume_part):
    materials_dict = {
        "helmet": ["PLA", "ABS", "PETG"],
        "armor": ["PLA", "ABS", "Nylon"],
        "props": ["PLA", "Woodfill", "Flexible filament"]
    }

    if costume_part.lower() in materials_dict:
        suggested_materials =
materials_dict[costume_part.lower()]
        return f"For {costume_part}, you can consider using: {',
'.join(suggested_materials)}"
    else:
        return "Sorry, I don't have suggestions for that costume
part."

# Example usage:
costume_part = input("Enter the costume part (helmet, armor,
props): ")
result = suggest_material(costume_part)
print(result)
```

Her script created a dictionary for suggested materials for costume parts. The function suggest_material took a part name and returned suggested materials. The creator focused on strength, clarity, rigidity, and safety. Her company products were durable, accurate, and safe. They offered fast delivery, affordability, color options, and safety. Together, they liked their products to look natural, with fine detail, and even to possess an antique look. They made sure that their materials were made from renewable materials. They installed a working recycler for each type of printer she'd use. Joha and Kathy shared a dream that their jewelry would leave a mark on future generations. Hard task to achieve when chemistry, biology, nature, and physics come together with technology. Their city soon looked like an oversized theatrical stage.

COSTUMES FOR PROFESSIONS
(CSS FOR STYLING THE HTML STRUCTURE)
STAIRCASE MODEL – MOPU

The new trends preferred people dressed in costumes with the Solar System, galaxies, plant growth charts, world geography, history timelines, famous poems, artworks, mathematical formulas, chemical graphs, periodic tables, food pyramids, visualizations, types of animals, creatures, plants, as well as types of rocks, formations, and more on them. The radio aired knowledge-based songs, TV promoted science, art, and literature based on knowledge, and science-based stories and books followed processes and products in Nature. Snobbery or trends turned into knowledge. All the parties fed people out of geometrical dishes with all sorts of nutrients, minerals, and whatever was currently recommended. Following the separation of concerns principle, Mopu created a lab coat in HTML and CSS:

HTML (index.html):

```
<!DOCTYPE html>
<html lang="en">
<head>
  <meta charset="UTF-8">
  <meta name="viewport"
content="width=device-width, initial-
scale=1.0">
  <link rel="stylesheet" href="styles.css">
  <title>Science Outfit</title>
</head>
<body>

  <div class="lab-coat">
    <div class="pocket"></div>
    <div class="buttons"></div>
    <div class="collar"></div>
  </div>

</body>
</html>
```

CSS (styles.css):

```
body {
  background-color: #fff;
  display: flex;
  align-items: center;
  justify-content: center;
  height: 100vh;
  margin: 0;
}

.lab-coat {
  position: relative;
  width: 300px;
  height: 400px;
  background-color: #fff;
  border: 2px solid #000;
  border-radius: 5px;
}

pocket {
  position: absolute;
  top: 50%;
  left: 20%;
  width: 80px;
  height: 80px;
  background-color: #666;
  border: 2px solid #000;
  border-radius: 50%;
}

.buttons {
  position: absolute;
  top: 70%;
  left: 45%;
  width: 10px;
  height: 60px;
  background-color: #000;
  border-radius: 3px;
}

.collar {
  position: absolute;
  top: 10%;
  left: 40%;
  width: 120px;
  height: 20px;
  background-color: #000;
  border-radius: 10px;
}
```

The lab coat had a pocket, buttons, and a collar to represent a science-themed outfit visually.

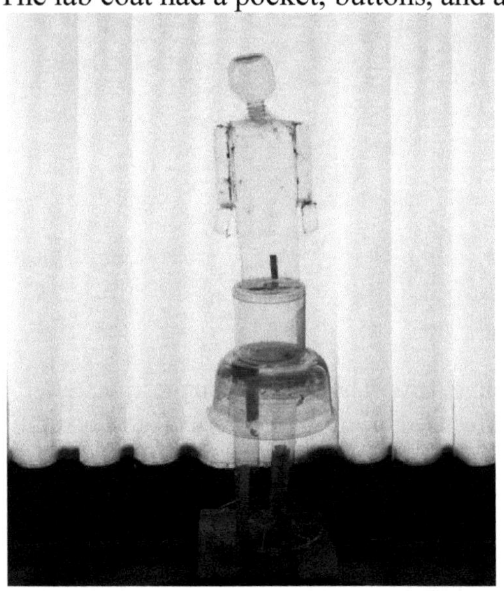

Now, the trend shifted to professions—no more learning science by looking at someone's t-shirt.

CREATIVE WRITING
(FUNCTION DECOMPOSITION)
USHER – MANIK

Manik worked in the dark. Many people came late after the performance had started, so he had to use his mighty flashlight to direct them to their seats. For this reason, he always missed the beginning of each performance. He started a blog called "The Beginnings," where he played a game with other ushers to create their own versions of how each story would start. Python code snippet that sets up a basic story introduces characters, adds a plot twist, resolves a conflict, and concludes with a moral:

```
import time

def introduction():
    print("Once upon a time in the magical land of Pythonia...")
    time.sleep(2)
    print("There lived two characters, Alice and Bob.")

def plot_twist():
    print("\nOne day, a mysterious package arrived at their doorstep.")
    time.sleep(2)
    print("They opened it to find a map leading to a hidden treasure!")

def conflict_resolution():
    print("\nExcited, Alice and Bob embarked on a thrilling adventure.")
    time.sleep(2)
    print("But soon, they realized they weren't the only ones after the treasure.")
    time.sleep(2)
    print("A rival, the cunning Pythonite, appeared, creating a conflict.")

    # Your conflict resolution logic here
    print("After a series of challenges and teamwork, Alice and Bob outsmarted the Pythonite.")

def conclusion():
    print("\nIn the end, Alice and Bob discovered that the real treasure was friendship and collaboration.")
    time.sleep(2)
    print("They decided to share the treasure with the Pythonite, teaching everyone the value of cooperation.")

def moral():
    print("\nThe moral of the story: In the face of challenges, working together leads to the greatest rewards.")

# Let's run the story
introduction()
plot_twist()
conflict_resolution()
conclusion()
moral()
```

His code included:

Function Definition: Breaking down the story into functions like introduction(), plot_twist(), conflict_resolution(), conclusion(), and moral() made the code modular and easier to understand. Each function encapsulates a specific part of the story.

Sequential Execution: The main part of the story is executed sequentially, starting from the introduction and progressing through the plot twist, conflict resolution, conclusion, and finally, the moral. This mirrored the linear structure of a story.

Printing and Time Delays: Print () statements helped display the story text while time.sleep() adds a delay between different parts of the story, creating a more immersive reading experience.

Commenting: to explain the purpose of each function and provide space to add a specific logic for conflict resolution to enhance code readability and make it easier for others to understand the code.

Variable Usage: variables are typically employed to store and manipulate data as the story progresses.

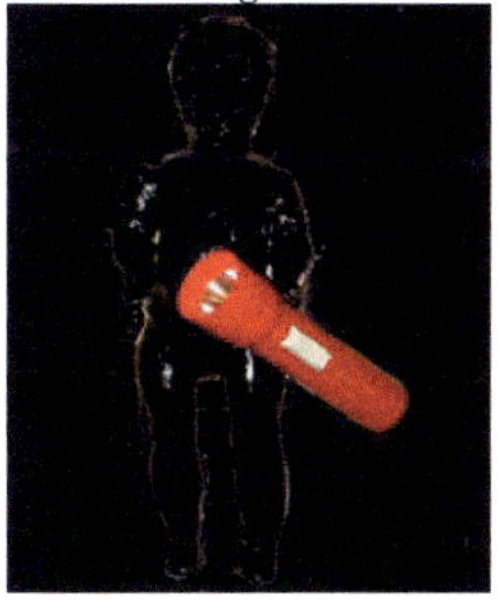

His flexible and dynamic way of generating stories with different beginnings, further actions, and endings based on predefined elements made him many friends asking him to help them record their own histories.

CULTURE: UTENSILS (FUNCTIONS)
SOLAR COOKER – MOLU

He believed that the invention of silverware was started by ways of taking food out of a campfire.

```
def introduction():
    print("Welcome to the Silverware Information Program!")
    print("Let's explore the fascinating history of silverware.")

def begin_history():
    print("\n--- The Beginning of Silverware ---")
    print("Silverware, also known as flatware or tableware, has a rich history.")
    print("It dates back to ancient civilizations where people used various materials for eating utensils.")

def historical_context():
    print("\n--- Historical Context ---")
    print("Silverware made significant advancements during the Renaissance.")
    print("During this period, elaborate designs and intricate patterns became popular, showcasing craftsmanship.")

def modern_times():
    print("\n--- Silverware in Modern Times ---")
    print("Today, silverware comes in various materials, including silver-plated, stainless steel, and more.")
    print("It is an essential part of dining culture and reflects both functionality and aesthetic preferences.")

def main():
    introduction()
    begin_history()
    historical_context()
    modern_times()

# Run the main function to execute the code
if __name__ == "__main__":
    main()
```

Each function (introduction, begin_history, historical_context, modern_times, and main) serves a specific purpose. The if __name__ == "__main__": block ensures that the main() function .

He preferred chopsticks.

CULTURAL STUDIES
(SCHEDULE)
CAROLER – GABRIEL

He'd go from house to house with his siblings every year. Some people enjoyed it and kept offering them all sorts of goods, while others did not understand the world they were singing, what the songs described, and why they would be important to them. Gabriel started to research celebrations across various cultures. Then, he studied songs, body gestures, movements, and what was required and practiced across cultures and rituals. Soon, every day of his year was filled out with his performances. He just needed good planning, where to show up, when, and what to sing. He wrote a code that schedules singing celebrations from different cultures using the schedule library to manage the planning tasks.

```
import schedule
import time

def celebrate_india():
    print("Singing celebration from India!")

def celebrate_belgium():
    print("Singing celebration from Belgium!")

def celebrate_africa():
    print("Singing celebration from Africa!")

# Schedule celebrations for different cultures
schedule.every().day.at("10:00").do(celebrate_india)
schedule.every().day.at("12:00").do(celebrate_belgium)
schedule.every().day.at("15:00").do(celebrate_africa)

# Run the scheduler
while True:
    schedule.run_pending()
    time.sleep(1)
```

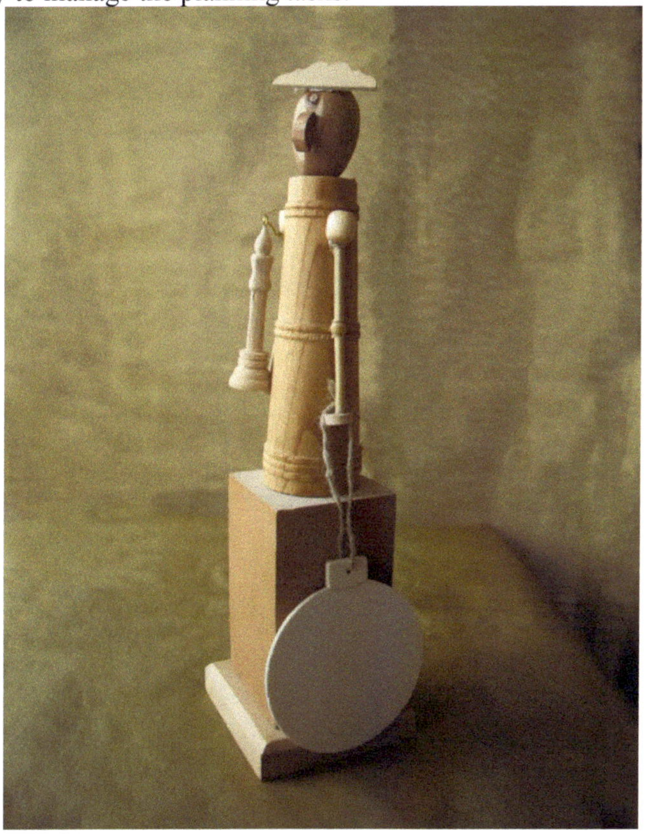

His script defined three functions (celebrate_india, celebrate_belgium, and celebrate_africa) to represent singing celebrations from India, Belgium, and Africa, respectively. Using the schedule library, these celebrations were scheduled to occur at different times of the day. He then customized the script by adding more cultural celebrations and adjusting the schedule accordingly.

There still were problems till someone told him that Africa was not a country.

CULTURES
(A DICTIONARY TO STORE INFORMATION)
WARRIOR SWORD – MISHAPU

He was known as a left-handed calligrapher.
His areas of expertise were:
Symbiosis of music and architecture
Musical theories and practices
Architecture and Internet music
Political, socio-cultural, and historical perspectives on rules governing societies.

```
def list_calligraphy_techniques():
    calligraphy_techniques = {
        "Chinese Calligraphy": "An ancient art form rooted in Chinese culture, emphasizing brushstroke techniques and harmony.",
        "Arabic Calligraphy": "Intricate writing style with a rich history in Islamic culture, often used for Quranic verses and poetry.",
        "Japanese Calligraphy": "Known as 'Shodo,' it focuses on balance, rhythm, and expression, using brush and ink.",
        "Western Calligraphy": "Includes various styles like Italic, Gothic, and Copperplate, developed in Western cultures.",
        "Korean Calligraphy": "Called 'Seoye,' it has a long tradition, influenced by Chinese characters and Korean scripts.",
    }

    return calligraphy_techniques

# Example usage
calligraphy_info = list_calligraphy_techniques()

print("Various Calligraphy Techniques and Cultures:")
for technique, description in calligraphy_info.items():
    print(f"{technique}: {description}")
```

In his code, a function list_calligraphy_techniques that creates a dictionary (calligraphy_techniques) for calligraphy techniques as keys and their associated cultural descriptions as values were defined. This approach allowed for easy access, store and retrieve data to information in some cultural contexts.

He summarized his interests when practicing his calligraphy.

CURRENT STATUS (CLASSES AND OBJECTS) MUSEUM CURATOR – AledA

AledA always cared for being labeled “current” or “up to date.” She was buying every new device the day it appeared on the market. She grew to enjoy each item, so it was hard to part with her old devices when a new version was announced. She became a curator of the Museum of Old Technology.

```
class Museum:
    def __init__(self, name):
        self.name = name
        self.technology_collection = []

    def add_technology(self, technology):
        self.technology_collection.append(technology)

    def display_collection(self):
        print(f"{self.name} Technology Museum Collection:")
        for technology in self.technology_collection:
            print(f"- {technology}")

# Example usage:
museum_name = "Vintage Tech"
tech_museum = Museum(museum_name)

# Adding old technology to the collection
tech_museum.add_technology("ADM Dumb Terminal")
tech_museum.add_technology("Lisa")
tech_museum.add_technology("Apple Computer")
tech_museum.add_technology("Tube Television")

# Displaying the museum collection
tech_museum.display_collection()
```

Her code defined a museum class with attributes like name and technology_collection, and methods such as add_technology to add old technology items to the collection and display_collection to display it.

AledA had a website organized by the web designer she hired till she learned how to code from her.

D	DANCE (LISTS) DANCE INSTRUCTOR – RAFE

Rafe knew most of the dances of the world and all the origins of the moves in every mentioned place. His code listed the few dances of the world and all the origins that started this passion:

```
dances_and_origins = {
    "Salsa": "Cuba",
    "Cancan": "France",
    "Hula": "Hawaii",
    "Flamenco": "Spain",
    "Bollywood": "India",
    "Capoeira": "Brazil",
    "Kathak": "India",
    "Samba": "Brazil",
    "Hip Hop": "United States",
}

# Displaying the dances and their origins
for dance, origin in dances_and_origins.items():
    print(f"{dance}: {origin}")
```

His script defined a dictionary (dances_and_origins) where dance styles were keys, and their possible origins were values. It then printed each dance along with its origin. He then expanded this list and modified it according to his specific needs. It was generalized, as many dances have complex histories with influences from various regions and cultures, so he referred to authoritative sources or collaborated with experts in dance and cultural studies. As a result, Rafe was flexible and bendable and could sneak out through every slightest opening in any gate. He never took advantage of this ability, though.

DANCE ROUTINE
(RANDOM)
CHOREOGRAPHER – MO

When Mo moved her hand, everyone understood. She had patience, persistence, and a sense of rhythm no one could match. She videotaped each practice so everyone could see their own ups and downs and could discuss them later. In her house, one room was covered with mirrors for her practice. Mo liked to experiment. Her creations were either inspired by musical compositions or by simple daily events, sometimes even by conversations. One day, she learned about an important gathering of various specialists to establish man's origins and unify the ways of measuring time. She gave some thought to imagining the origin of dance. To her own amusement, a thought of the first dancer as a person trying to catch a mosquito appeared to her in a visual form. Maybe someone was performing it gracefully and was noted by another person, she thought. A clap of their hands started musical experimentation. Sometimes, finding the beginnings may not be an easy task and may require some effort. She wrote a code that created a dance-like movement simulating a person trying to catch a mosquito:

```
import turtle
import random

# Set up the turtle screen
turtle.speed(2)
turtle.bgcolor("lightblue")

# Function to move the turtle randomly
def move_turtle():
    turtle.left(random.randint(0, 360))
    turtle.forward(random.randint(20, 100))

# Function to simulate catching a mosquito
def catch_mosquito():
    turtle.shape("circle")
    turtle.color("red")
    turtle.stamp()

# Main dance routine
for _ in range(10): # Perform the dance 10
times
    move_turtle()
    catch_mosquito()

# Hide the turtle
turtle.hideturtle()
turtle.done()
```

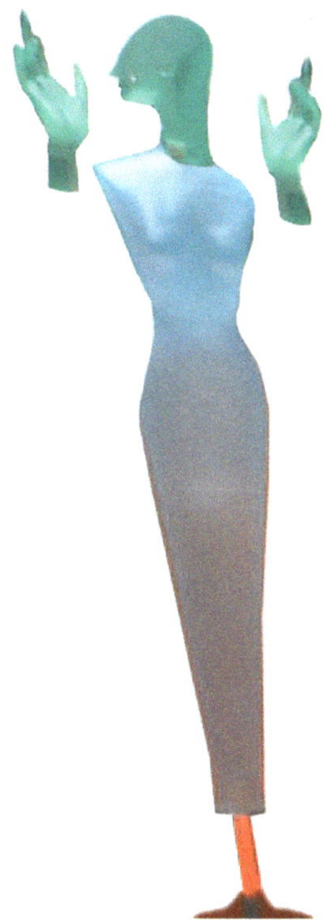

Her code used the Turtle library to create a simple dance routine. The turtle moved randomly in different directions and then simulated catching a "mosquito" by stamping a red circle. She customized the code further environment to see the dance in action! Her new creation was based on her studies, research, observation, and videotaping. Following some movement analysis, she transformed them into a performance based on the song “Ne me moleste mosquito.” The dancers were amazed, especially when the ballet production won a major award for its artistic merit and innovative approach. Sometimes, even dangerous or even deadly creatures can be inspiring through their interactive behaviors.

DESIGN
(NESTED LOOPS TO ITERATE THROUGH ROWS AND COLUMNS)
PAINTER – ROFU

As an abstract expressionist, Rofu enjoyed painting flags.

```
def paint_flag(rows, cols):
  for i in range(rows):
    for j in range(cols):
      if i == j:
        print("*", end=" ")
      else:
        print("-", end=" ")
    print()

# Example usage
paint_flag(5, 5)
```

He was doing it with his codes, specifically for a diagonal pattern. The concept of nested loops to iterate through rows and columns, printing either "*" or "-" based on a condition (if i is equal to j), was especially helpful to him. This concept was known as looping and conditional statements, which are known as fundamental in programming. This code created a diagonal pattern with "*" forming a diagonal line and "-" in the rest of the positions. He modified the conditions inside the loops for different patterns.

He believed that ultimate simplicity leads to purity.
His heart was the mediator between his head and his hand.

DIGITAL NOMAD
(HISTORY)
HOUSE PET WATCHER – MUFA

Mufa traveled where he was needed. He was taking care of houses, pets, plants, and whatever was to be looked after during the absence of the house's owners. He was living in their homes and was driving their cars. He had photographs of himself with pets he took care of with a list of cities, and places:

```
class Person:
    def __init__(self, name):
        self.name = name
        self.pet_care_history = {}

    def take_care_of_pet(self, place, pet):
        if place not in self.pet_care_history:
            self.pet_care_history[place] = [pet]
        else:
            self.pet_care_history[place].append(pet)

    def display_pet_care_history(self):
        print(f"{self.name}'s Pet Care History:")
        for place, pets in self.pet_care_history.items():
            print(f"At {place}: {', '.join(pets)}")
```

```
# Create a person
person_name = input("Enter the person's name: ")
person = Person(person_name)

# Take care of pets at different places
person.take_care_of_pet("Home", "Dog")
person.take_care_of_pet("Pet Shelter", "Cat")
person.take_care_of_pet("Farm", "Horse")
person.take_care_of_pet("Zoo", "Parrot")
person.take_care_of_pet("Home", "Hamster")

# Display the pet care history
person.display_pet_care_history()
```

He forgot to enter the data for a Person's class and methods to take care of pets at different places with the pet care history, but he remembered all of them. All the pets looked happy.

The happiest one was his cat when he'd returned to his family home for a short visit.

Well-formed one.

```
import turtle

def draw_circle(radius, color):
    turtle.fillcolor(color)
    turtle.begin_fill()
    turtle.circle(radius)
    turtle.end_fill()

def draw_rectangle(width, height,
color):
    turtle.fillcolor(color)
    turtle.begin_fill()
    for _ in range(2):
        turtle.forward(width)
        turtle.left(90)
        turtle.forward(height)
        turtle.left(90)
    turtle.end_fill()

def draw_dog():
    turtle.speed(2)

    # Draw the body
    draw_rectangle(100, 50, 'brown')

    # Draw the head
    turtle.left(90)
    turtle.forward(25)
    draw_circle(25, 'brown')

    # Draw the legs
    turtle.right(90)
    turtle.forward(25)
    turtle.left(45)
    draw_rectangle(20, 40, 'brown')

    turtle.left(180)
    draw_rectangle(20, 40, 'brown')

    # Draw the tail
    turtle.right(45)
    turtle.forward(70)
    draw_rectangle(10, 30, 'brown')

    turtle.hideturtle()
    turtle.done()

def main():
    draw_dog()

if __name__ == "__main__":
    main()
```

In his code, he used draw_circle and draw_rectangle to draw basic shapes. The draw_dog procedure orchestrated the drawing of a dog by calling the shape-drawing procedures, promoting code organization and reusability by breaking down a program into smaller, manageable ones that each handle a specific task.

Woof could bark once, two, or three times, according to the occasion. Woof, Woof Woof, or Woof Woof Woof, depending on the expression.

E	ECOLOGY (IMAGE PROCESSING) ENVIRONMENTALIST – BUK

His role was to oversee people, not to trash around. He was supposed to react if they would, but he never knew what to say. He was searching for signs of static life in nature. His code with the OpenCV library analyzed data or images for signs of static life:

```
import cv2

def detect_static_life(image_path):
    # Read the image
    image = cv2.imread(image_path)

    # Convert the image to grayscale
    gray_image = cv2.cvtColor(image, cv2.COLOR_BGR2GRAY)

    # Apply a threshold to the image to highlight potential signs of life
    _, threshold_image = cv2.threshold(gray_image, 127, 255, cv2.THRESH_BINARY)

    # Find contours in the thresholded image
    contours, _ = cv2.findContours(threshold_image, cv2.RETR_EXTERNAL, cv2.CHAIN_APPROX_SIMPLE)

    # Draw the contours on the original image
    result_image = image.copy()
    cv2.drawContours(result_image, contours, -1, (0, 255, 0), 2)

    # Display the original and result images
    cv2.imshow("Original Image", image)
    cv2.imshow("Result Image", result_image)
    cv2.waitKey(0)
    cv2.destroyAllWindows()

# Example usage
image_path = "path/to/your/image.jpg"
detect_static_life(image_path)
```

His code read an image, converted it to grayscale, applied a threshold, found contours in the image, and then drew the contours on the original image—the resulting image showed the detected signs of life, which was what he was showing those who litter. His next step was to try machine learning approaches.

He did not learn to fly and regretted it.

EDUCATION
(A CLASS TO ENCAPSULATE DATA)
MUSIC TRAVELER – KEN

Ken's life was on the road. He stayed no longer than a week in one place. His life's mission was to propagate music door to door, spread knowledge, and make sure people played instruments to make the music present in every household, every heart and mind. Ken believed that people who know music, use music, and need music are becoming better people as they are not bored, have no time to fight, and are slowly filled with a need to perfect their skills. He started with his Python code to present his argument.

```
class MusicEnthusiast:
    def __init__(self, name):
        self.name = name
        self.boredom = 0
        self.skills = 0
        self.happiness = 100

    def listen_to_music(self, genre):
        print(f"{self.name} is listening to {genre} music.")
        self.boredom -= 10
        self.happiness += 5
        self.skills += 2

    def practice_instrument(self, instrument):
        print(f"{self.name} is practicing {instrument}.")
        self.boredom -= 5
        self.happiness += 8
        self.skills += 3

    def fight(self, other_person):
        print(f"{self.name} and {other_person.name} are
arguing.")
        self.boredom += 15
        self.happiness -= 10

# Example usage:
person1 = MusicEnthusiast("Alice")
person2 = MusicEnthusiast("Bob")

person1.listen_to_music("jazz")
person2.practice_instrument("guitar")

person1.fight(person2)  # Uh-oh, a conflict arises!

print(f"{person1.name}'s boredom: {person1.boredom}")
print(f"{person1.name}'s skills: {person1.skills}")
print(f"{person1.name}'s happiness: {person1.happiness}")
```

Ken also thought music was a group activity, so it reunited people. He always worked alone.

ENCOUNTERING SURPRISING EVENTS (TIME MODULE) HARMONICA – LEON

Musicians were playing in an open space in the mountains, not far from the resort but far enough to feel wild. It felt strange to be under the sky, right on the grass, between the trees. The listeners brought blankets and baskets with food for the picnic. Nicely relaxed, they listened to this rare, experimental music. Then, the sprinklers went off right in the middle of the event. Leon started playing "Singing in the Rain," and the audience started dancing. The audience recommended the concert to others without disclosing why they liked it so much. The local newspaper offered a very positive review of the event, so the organizers made sure to set the watering system accordingly for each event on the warm summer days. They followed a code to synchronize each concert with the sprinklers:

```
import time
import threading

def concert():
    print("Concert is starting!")
    # Simulate the concert duration
    time.sleep(10)
    print("Concert is over!")

def sprinklers():
    print("Sprinklers are starting!")
    # Simulate the sprinklers duration
    time.sleep(10)
    print("Sprinklers are turned off.")

def synchronize_concert_with_sprinklers():
    # Create threads for concert and sprinklers
    concert_thread = threading.Thread(target=concert)
    sprinklers_thread = threading.Thread(target=sprinklers)

    # Start both threads simultaneously
    concert_thread.start()
    sprinklers_thread.start()

    # Wait for both threads to finish
    concert_thread.join()
    sprinklers_thread.join()

if __name__ == "__main__":
    synchronize_concert_with_sprinklers()
```

The concert and sprinklers functions represented the concert and sprinklers activities, respectively. The synchronize_concert_with_sprinklers function created separate threads for the concert and sprinklers to start them simultaneously. The time.sleep simulated the duration of each activity. Some started writing notes about each audience to adjust the sleep durations or add more complexity depending on the specific needs of the members of the audience requirements and the technology for controlling the sprinklers.

One day, a fearful thunderstorm interrupted the event. There was no code to adjust for that.

ENTERTAINING SYMBOLS (SYMBOLS MAPPING) ADMINISTRATOR – FOX

To him, clothing was a free speech, which meant free expression. He'd refuse to wear a tie, which was against his beliefs, comfort, or expression. Even his instrument reflected an issue of freedom. He changed his habits after accepting an administrative position. Fox started self-designing his ties for the holidays. He created a Python script that associated specific symbols with each holiday.

```
def holiday_symbols(holidays):
    symbol_mapping = {
        "Christmas": "🎄",
        "Thanksgiving": "🦃",
        "Labor Day": "🛠️",
        "New Year's Day": "🎉",
        "Independence Day": "🇺🇸",
        # he added more holidays and
symbols as needed
    }

    for holiday in holidays:
        if holiday in symbol_mapping:
            print(f"{holiday}:
{symbol_mapping[holiday]}")
        else:
            print(f"No symbol found for
{holiday}")

# Example usage
holidays = ["Christmas",
"Thanksgiving", "Labor Day", "New
Year's Day", "Independence Day"]
holiday_symbols(holidays)
```

Fox's work was based on this reasoning: def holiday_symbols(holidays): Define a function that takes a list of holidays as input. symbol_mapping = {...}: Create a dictionary that maps each holiday to its symbol: for holiday in holidays: Iterate through each holiday in the provided list.
if holiday in symbol_mapping: Check if a symbol is defined for the current holiday.
print(f"{holiday}: {symbol_mapping[holiday]}"): If a symbol is found, print the holiday
else: If no symbol is found, print a message indicating that no symbol is available.

He ordered custom-made ties for every working day to extend his work beyond the holidays. Each tie depicted the characteristics of a day by examining the power behind each one. Soon, his ties became screenshots from his appointment book. He mastered the photo silkscreen technique to achieve that.

ENTREPRENEURSHIP (USER INPUT) INVENTOR – TEN 2 2

They called her Ten 2 2. Nobody knew if this was ten to two or Tentoto. She completed four majors at four colleges: Chemistry, Music, Engineering, and Business. She wanted to make people's life filled with beauty and comfort. She never took a single art class, not to be influenced and not to copy somebody else's ideas. She invented several instruments, new ways to lose a migraine, ways to record music she played wirelessly, an eye camera that takes pictures precisely as the eye sees it triggered by an eye blink, a folder that names the files after its own name the moment the file is set in that folder, a heated sidewalk, a laundry folding machine, and natural grass that does not grow but stays green. Her greatest invention was her special robot. She was highly valued but hardly visible. At parties and events, she listened but rarely talked; she mostly observed and took notes. Those were the moments that gave her ideas for her inventions. She developed a way to store her inspirations:

```
import datetime

def record_invention(topic, invention):
    timestamp = datetime.datetime.now().strftime("%Y-%m-%d %H:%M:%S")

    with open("inventions.txt", "a") as file:
        file.write(f"{timestamp} - Topic: {topic}\n")
        file.write(f"Invention: {invention}\n\n")

# Example usage:
topic = input("Enter the discussion topic: ")
invention = input("Enter the inspired invention: ")

record_invention(topic, invention)
```

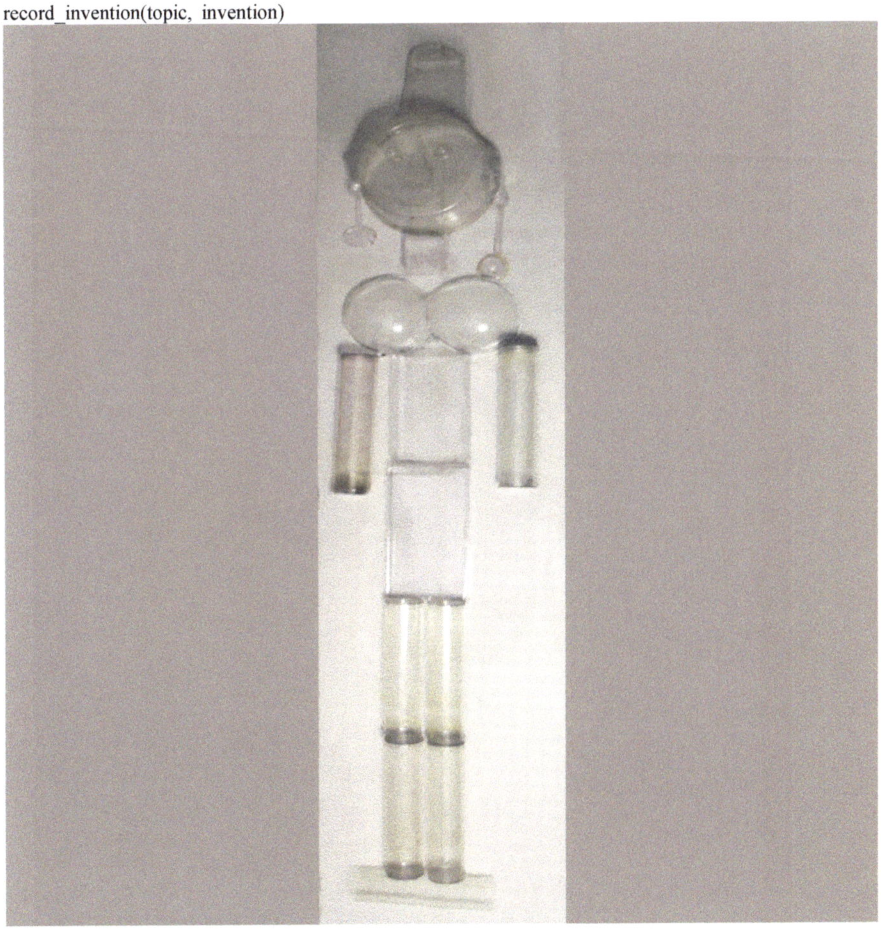

She then patented it and added it to her inventions list on her resume, which she had never used.

ENTRAPMENT
(IF, ELSE)
HULA HOOP – INSHA

Insha had no clue where Hula Hoop came from, the idea, or how she acquired her object. This felt weird. It must have been around for a long time. Insha's Hula Hoop has been in her house for as long as she can remember. It was big, round, shiny, dynamic, and light when put in motion. This was the most beautiful object she could imagine. It was perfect. She kept it hanging on the wall like a picture when it was at rest. The only problem was that she could not carry it around when she traveled. For this, she envied harmonica players. But they usually would not look as good with their instruments as she did with her device. She wrote a code for a collapsible one:

```
class CollapsibleHulaHoop:
    def __init__(self, diameter):
        self.diameter = diameter
        self.collapsed = False

    def collapse(self):
        if not self.collapsed:
            print("Collapsing the hula hoop for travel.")
            self.diameter /= 2  # You can adjust this based on your specific collapsing mechanism
            self.collapsed = True
        else:
            print("The hula hoop is already collapsed.")

    def expand(self):
        if self.collapsed:
            print("Expanding the hula hoop.")
            self.diameter *= 2  # Adjust this based on your expanding mechanism
            self.collapsed = False
        else:
            print("The hula hoop is already expanded.")

# Example usage:
if __name__ == "__main__":
    hula_hoop = CollapsibleHulaHoop(diameter=40)  # Initial diameter, you can adjust it

    print("Original hula hoop diameter:", hula_hoop.diameter)

    hula_hoop.collapse()
    print("Collapsed hula hoop diameter:", hula_hoop.diameter)

    hula_hoop.expand()
    print("Expanded hula hoop diameter:", hula_hoop.diameter)
```

Since then, she has traveled with a portable 3D printer.

ENVISIONING SOLUTIONS (CONDITIONS)
ACOUSTICIAN – DANNY

Danny is an active man. He believes he's got lots of luck. He keeps telling his friends that the weather should behave by adjusting itself to his plans. And indeed, those who camp with him always enjoy the best weather possible. His voice sometimes sounded like an indoor voice and, the other day, like an outdoor one. No one understands why, as it is unrelated to where he is calling from. Danny lives on Dry Street. It used to be his regular address until some city officials announced a contest to make the city more entertaining. When it was raining, one of the winning projects automatically changed the street's name. Everyone sending Danny a letter had to check the weather forecast so that the letter would not come back as undelivered. His Python code with a conditional statement helped determine if the street was wet or dry based on a boolean variable.

```
def get_street_condition(raining):
    if raining:
        return "123 Rainy Lane"
    else:
        return "456 Sunny Street"

# Example usage:
is_raining = True  # You can change this variable to test different conditions
address = get_street_condition(is_raining)
print("Address:", address)
```

The get_street_condition function it took a boolean parameter raining, indicating whether it was raining or not. Inside the function, there was a conditional statement (if raining:) that checks if it's raining. If it was, the function returned the address for a wet street ("123 Rainy Lane"). Otherwise, it returned the address for a dry street ("456 Sunny Street"). It set the is_raining variable to either True or False to simulate different weather conditions.

Now, the address changes itself, accordingly.

EQUESTRIANISM
(STATUS)
HORSE GROOMER – PUFKO

His job was to take care of one precious horse. He was to brush and bathe the horse, clean tack, and provide basic first aid. When the horse got scrapes and cuts, he'd bandage it all. He was mucking out the stall, taking care of the maintenance of the stable, and preparing or distributing feed. He also worked with mares, foals, and yearlings. He was very efficient, but nobody could see the results of his work.
He was busy writing his instruction\al codes.

```
class Horse:
    def __init__(self, name):
        self.name = name
        self.health = 100
        self.happiness = 100

    def feed(self):
        print(f"{self.name} is being fed. Yum!")
        self.health += 10
        self.happiness += 5

    def groom(self):
        print(f"Grooming {self.name}. Looking good!")
        self.happiness += 3

    def exercise(self):
        print(f"Taking {self.name} for a run. Exercise time!")
        self.health += 5
        self.happiness += 7

    def visit_vet(self):
        print(f"Time for a vet checkup for {self.name}.")
        self.health += 2

    def display_status(self):
        print(f"{self.name}'s Status:")
        print(f"Health: {self.health}")
        print(f"Happiness: {self.happiness}")

# Example usage
horse_name = input("Enter your horse's name: ")
my_horse = Horse(horse_name)

# Perform care activities
my_horse.feed()
my_horse.groom()
my_horse.exercise()
my_horse.visit_vet()

# Display final status
my_horse.display_status()
```

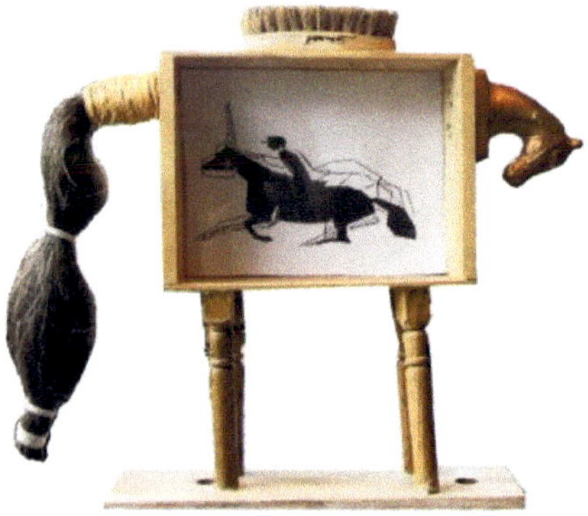

He created a Horse class defined with methods for feeding, grooming, exercising, visiting the vet, and displaying the horse's status. He shared that code so people could enter their horse's name, and then care activities are performed on that horse.

He was riding his horse at night when no one could see him but occasionally his horse.

Event Planning
(String Formatting and a Function to Provide Information)
VR Party Organizers

They oversaw annual parties for the orchestra. They had everything, from costumes to furniture for rent, including lists of menus, templates for invitations, party supplies, decorations, and ideas for over 200 party themes: for kid's birthdays, holidays, and event theme parties. All was virtual, of course.

```
def prepare_virtual_party(host_name, date, time, platform, theme):
    party_info = f"Dear {host_name},\n\nYou are invited to organize a Virtual Reality (VR) Party!\n"
    party_info += f"Date: {date}\nTime: {time}\nPlatform: {platform}\nTheme: {theme}\n\n"
    party_info += "Get ready for a virtual experience like never before. See you there!"

    return party_info

# Example usage
host_name = "John"
date = "2025-03-10"
time = "19:00"
platform = "VRChat"
theme = "Futuristic Galaxy"

party_invitation = prepare_virtual_party(host_name, date, time, platform, theme)
print(party_invitation)
```

A defined function prepare_virtual_party took the host's name, date, time, virtual platform, and theme as arguments. The function then constructed an invitation message using string formatting to allow for a flexible and easy way to generate information for a virtual party, making it suitable for sending invitations or displaying details on a website.

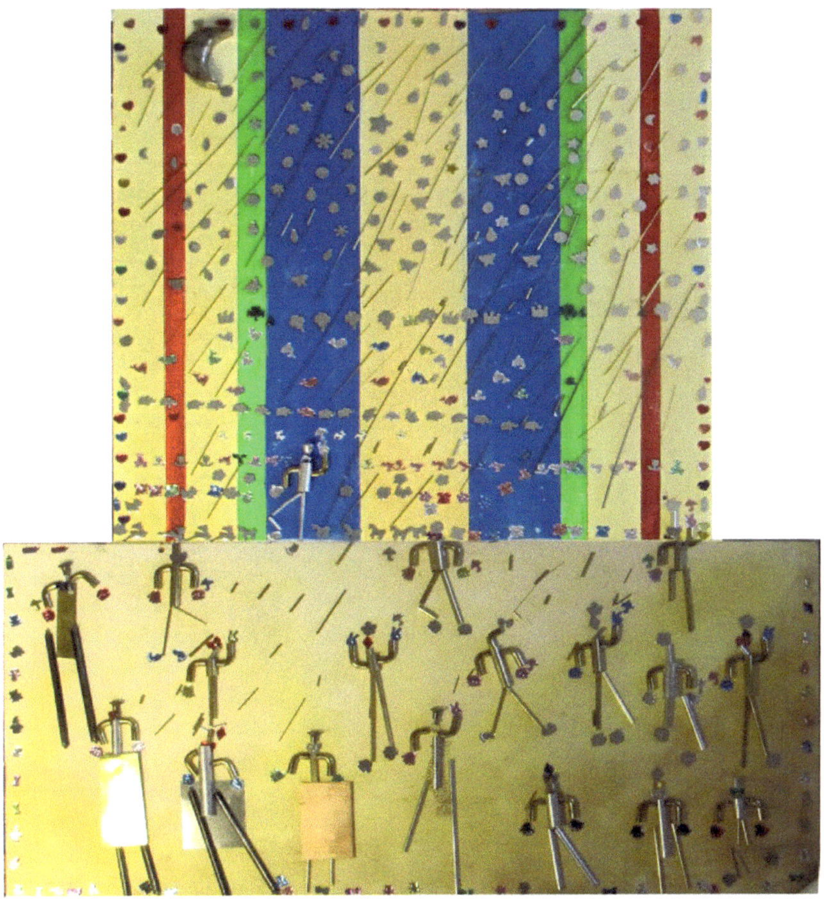

The biggest problem was music; their reputation made every musician want to join the party rather than perform there.

EVENTS
(TIME AND DURATION)
DIAMOND CUTTERS – TZO, SIN, NOT

They often regretted their choices. Either there was nothing to do, or at least two interesting events simultaneously. When they finally decided which event to attend, they all felt the other one was probably better. They agreed to move to a smaller city where they could manage to attend all the events in one night. They found it hard to agree on which event to attend first. The solution was to write a code defining a pattern to attend several events in one evening, assuming each event had a start time and duration.

```
class Event:
    def __init__(self, name, start_time, duration):
        self.name = name
        self.start_time = start_time
        self.duration = duration

def attend_events(events):
    events.sort(key=lambda x: x.start_time)  # Sort events based on start time

    current_time = 0  # Start at 0 time
    for event in events:
        if event.start_time >= current_time:
            print(f"Attending {event.name} from {event.start_time} to {event.start_time + event.duration}")
            current_time = event.start_time + event.duration

# Example usage
event1 = Event("Concert", 18, 2)
event2 = Event("Dinner", 20, 1.5)
event3 = Event("Comedy Show", 21.5, 1)

events_to_attend = [event1, event2, event3]

attend_events(events_to_attend)
```

The Event class had a name, start time, and duration. The attend_events function sorted events by start time and printed out non-overlapping events. The code was customized for specific needs.

Their city was awarded a grant for new cultural programs, so they had to attend them separately and then tell their partners what was happening and what was not to be missed. Soon, they started a gazette.

EXERCISE (ORGANIZE) DOG WALKER

His job was to walk dogs for other people. He could be seen holding several dogs of different colors and sizes in one hand. There were big ones, very big, tiny, or small. He often had to carry the small ones to protect them from the bigger ones. Walking dogs on a big city street, all covered with cement, would not make much sense to him. He invented a system for renting apartments for people with dogs. Those with small dogs would rent apartments on the low-numbered floors. Those with big dogs were supposed to rent atop the building. Since the building did not have an elevator, the exercise came quite naturally. The apartments were furnished the same way, so if someone's dog grew up needing more exercise, they could all move up to the higher floor. He started his renting apartment business based on the code he wrote:

```
class DogApartmentOrganizer:
    def __init__(self, num_floors):
        self.num_floors = num_floors
        self.apartments = {floor: [] for floor in range(1, num_floors + 1)}

    def assign_apartment(self, dog_size):
        # Assign apartments based on dog size and floor number
        if dog_size == "small":
            self.apartments[1].append("Small Dog Owner")
        elif dog_size == "medium":
            self.apartments[self.num_floors // 2].append("Medium Dog Owner")
        elif dog_size == "large":
            self.apartments[self.num_floors].append("Large Dog Owner")
        else:
            print("Invalid dog size")

    def show_apartments(self):
        # Display the assigned apartments
        for floor, residents in self.apartments.items():
            print(f"Floor {floor}: {residents}")

# Example usage:
organizer = DogApartmentOrganizer(num_floors=5)

organizer.assign_apartment("small")
organizer.assign_apartment("medium")
organizer.assign_apartment("large")
organizer.assign_apartment("invalid")  # This will print "Invalid dog size"

organizer.show_apartments()
```

His code defined a DogApartmentOrganizer class with methods to assign apartments based on the size of the dogs. Small dogs were placed on the first floor, medium on the middle floor, and large ones on the top floor. The show_apartments method displayed the assigned apartments for each floor. His business did not thrive, but he made much money selling his code. Other landlords could customize their codes further based on their specific requirements or add more features as needed. My small dog does not like small dogs but is good with big ones, explains the owner of the small dog, who was somehow surprised by his dog's good behavior. That is exactly the opposite of what my big dog does, answers the big dog's owner. He only attacks those bigger than himself. It is not even a "pick on someone of your own size" case, and not even "the grass looks greener on the other side." However, there must be a good saying for that.

EXPRESSIONS
(DICTIONARY)
SOCIALITE – CLAUDIA

Before endless parties, teas, and meetings, Claudia reinvented herself by exploring forms of expression.

```
class ExpressionInformer:
    def __init__(self):
        self.expression_forms = {
            'Mathematical': '2 + 2',
            'Verbal': 'Hello, how are you?',
            'Visual': '🎨🖼️',
            'Programming': 'print("Hello, World!")'
        }

    def inform_expression_forms(self):
        print("Various Forms of Expressions:")
        for form, example in self.expression_forms.items():
            print(f"{form} Expression: {example}")

# Example of using the ExpressionInformer class
expression_informer = ExpressionInformer()

# Inform about various forms of expressions
expression_informer.inform_expression_forms()
```

She wrote a code using a class (ExpressionInformer) to encapsulate the information. The class had a dictionary (expression_forms) that mapped expression forms to examples. The method inform_expression_forms iterated through the dictionary and printed information about various forms of expressions. Her code demonstrated the organization of information using a class. She had her list handy:

Mathematical Expression:
Example: 2 + 2
Verbal Expression:
Example: "Hello, how are you?"
Visual Expression:
Example: 🎨🖼️
Programming Expression:
Example: print("Hello, World!")
Musical Expression:
Example: A musical score or sheet music
Artistic Expression:
Example: A painting, sculpture, or visual art
Emotional Expression: conveying emotions
Example: Facial, written, body language
Scientific Expression:
Example: A scientific formula or equation
Dance Expression:
Example: Dance movements or choreography
Literary Expression:
Example: A written poem, story, or essay
Expressions can take various forms across different domains, and they serve as a means of communication, creativity, and representation in different contexts, and this is what she kept doing.

Her favorite expressions were those verbal ones. She mastered their use.

FABRICATION
(A CLASS TO ENCAPSULATE)
DIGITAL SMELL DESIGNER – ODOMETER

The new agenda had an item on it called "Novelty." Odometer was hired to distribute smells during various performances. She had never done it in such a big space, and putting the perfume into the fan did not work in this environment. She is working hard on a new type of fragrant: a digital one.

```
class DigitalFragrance:
    def _init_(self):
        self.scents = {
            'floral': 'Rose scent',
            'citrus': 'Lemon zest',
            'woody': 'Sandalwood aroma',
            'spicy': 'Cinnamon warmth',
            'fresh': 'Ocean breeze'
        }

    def experience_fragrance(self, scent):
        if scent.lower() in self.scents:
            print(f"Enjoy the digital fragrance: {self.scents[scent.lower()]}")
        else:
            print("Sorry, that scent is not available in the digital fragrance collection.")

# Example of using the DigitalFragrance class
digital_perfume = DigitalFragrance()

# User selects a scent
selected_scent = input("Choose a scent (floral, citrus, woody, spicy, fresh): ")

# Experience the digital fragrance
digital_perfume.experience_fragrance(selected_scent)
```

She used a class (DigitalFragrance) to encapsulate the digital fragrance simulation. The class had a dictionary (scents) that mapped scents to their digital representations. The method xperience_fragrance allows users to select a scent and experience the corresponding digital fragrance to simulate.

She is not the only one to experiment with digital smells.

Monsters under the bed, dream creatures, pop culture, old masters, nature, carnival kitsch, medieval heresies, obscure practices, sinful humanity, Heaven and Hell, Kabbalah, Dragons and Centaurs, Unicorns, Gnomes, all those living in the mirrors, the elephant that prefigured the birth of Buddha, the Lamed Wufniks, the Hairy Beast of La Ferte Bernard, as described by Jorge Luis Borges, or Homer, Pliny, Shakespeare, Confucius, Lewis Carroll, Franz Kafka, C.C. Lewis inspired her for her songs. Even Tolkien, but nobody after him, inspired her. It was always crowded around her fragile statue.

```
impossible_creatures = {
   "Manticorn": "A majestic creature with the body of a mantis and the wings of a unicorn.",
   "Dragonphant": "A mythical beast combining the features of a dragon and an elephant.",
   "Octofox": "An elusive creature with eight tentacles and the cunning of a fox.",
   "Giraffasaurus": "A towering hybrid of a giraffe and a dinosaur, roaming the savannah.",
   "Penguitten": "A cute but perplexing mix of a penguin and a kitten, waddling around in confusion.",
}

print("List of Impossible Creatures:")
for creature, description in impossible_creatures.items():
   print(f"{creature}: {description}")
```

Each impossible creature was represented by a key-value pair. The creature's name was the key, and the description was the corresponding value. The code then iterated over the dictionary to display the list of impossible creatures with their descriptions.

She preferred paintings with lots of red shades.

FINANCES
(TRUE, FALSE STATEMENTS (CLASS)
BANJO – ROBIN

Robin was both a painter and a banjo player. He married Irene because he liked her inventiveness and sense of proportion. Irene found a giant but condemned house on the hill that overlooked the entire city. She wrote a Python script that simulates a basic check for issues to determine what needs to be addressed.

```
class HouseInspector:
    def __init__(self, house):
        self.house = house

    def check_electrical_wiring(self):
        if "old_wiring" in self.house:
            print("Code Violation: Old electrical wiring present.")

    def check_plumbing_system(self):
        if "leaks" in self.house:
            print("Code Violation: Plumbing leaks present.")

    def check_structural_integrity(self):
        if "foundation_issues" in self.house:
            print("Code Violation: Foundation issues detected.")

    def check_fire_safety(self):
        if "missing_smoke_detectors" in self.house:
            print("Code Violation: Missing smoke detectors.")

    def run_inspection(self):
        print("Starting house inspection...")
        self.check_electrical_wiring()
        self.check_plumbing_system()
        self.check_structural_integrity()
        self.check_fire_safety()
        print("House inspection complete.")

# Example house with potential code violations
my_house = {
    "old_wiring": True,
    "leaks": True,
    "foundation_issues": False,
    "missing_smoke_detectors": True,
}

# Create an inspector and run the inspection
inspector = HouseInspector(my_house)
inspector.run_inspection()
```

She used the House Inspector class as a method to check for common issues such as old electrical wiring, plumbing leaks, structural integrity problems, and missing smoke detectors. The run_inspection method called each checked method and printed out any detected code violations. Based on the output, she could fix all the improper elements that violated the city code, and the house gained in value immensely.

Suddenly, Robin had a studio overseeing the area – with a 360-degree view! It was also a perfect house for parties, used exactly to its expectations. They felt rich, but the cost of maintaining the house was way above their combined salaries, and suddenly Robin realized his dream studio space would not go together with time restrictions, as he had to go back to making more money—no more time for his studio work.

FITNESS
(A FUNCTION THAT PERFORMS CALCULATION)
WALKER ON BEHALF – COR

Many people knew they needed to walk daily, but they had little time, energy, or will, and no dog to encourage them. To stay healthy, they hired Cor to walk on their behalf. They paid him by the mile.

```
def calculate_total_steps(steps_per_day):
    total_steps = sum(steps_per_day)
    return total_steps

# Example usage
steps_per_day = [5000, 6000, 7500, 8000, 7000]

total_steps_made = calculate_total_steps(steps_per_day)
print(f"The total steps made by the person is: {total_steps_made}")
```

He always ended up in some forest.

FOOD & DRINKS
(REFERENCE TO THE INSTANCE OF THE CLASS)
LOCAL ARTIST – DUBE

He used to drink black tea a lot. Not just black, but a mixture of various black teas, so strong that if someone tried a sip, they would regret it. His favorite teas were Assam, Kombucha, Madras, Ceylon, Oolong, Darjeeling, Georgian, and Yunnan. He drank Lapsang Souchong and Earl Grey once a year. He wanted to learn more.

```
class Tea:
    def __init__(self, name, origin):
        self.name = name
        self.origin = origin

    def disclose_origin(self):
        print(f"The origin of {self.name} tea is
{self.origin}.")


# Create instances of the Tea class for each type of tea
teas = [
    Tea("Assam", "Assam, India"),
    Tea("Kombucha", "Ancient China"),
    Tea("Madras", "Madras, India"),
    Tea("Ceylon", "Sri Lanka (formerly Ceylon)"),
    Tea("Oolong", "China and Taiwan"),
    Tea("Darjeeling", "Darjeeling, India"),
    Tea("Georgian", "Georgia, Caucasus"),
    Tea("Yunnan", "Yunnan, China"),
    Tea("Lapsang Souchong", "Wuyi Mountains, China"),
    Tea("Earl Grey", "England")
]

# Disclose the origin of each tea using the disclose_origin
method
for tea in teas:
    tea.disclose_origin()
```

Dube used the disclose_origin method within the Tea class. With no external parameters (other than self, a reference to the instance of the class), the code printed out a statement disclosing the origin of the tea. Now, he drinks Chamomile tea for any occasion. It spreads some secret powers over him, he thinks. If you do not notice that it is a calming tea, drink it for breakfast to get energized, and it can awaken you.

That's what that's for.

FUTURE OF COMPUTER GRAPHICS AND INTERACTIVE TECHNIQUES
(TOO MUCH CODING FOR DESCRIBING)
LOCAL ARTIST – OGU

Several exciting developments and trends will likely mark the future of computer graphics and interactive techniques. Ogu explored some potential directions for these fields:

Realistic Graphics Rendering: Advances in hardware capabilities and rendering algorithms will likely lead to even more realistic graphics regarding lighting, textures, and simulations. Technologies like ray tracing and a worldwide illumination will become more commonplace, enhancing visual fidelity in virtual environments.

Immersive Experiences with Extended Reality (XR): The convergence of augmented reality (AR), virtual reality (VR), and mixed reality (MR) is expected to provide more immersive and interactive experiences through improved graphics for VR simulations, AR applications in various industries, and the integration of virtual elements into the real world.

AI-Enhanced Graphics: Artificial intelligence and machine learning techniques will significantly enhance graphics and interactive experiences. AI algorithms can generate procedural content, adaptive rendering, and more dynamic and responsive virtual worlds.

Real-time Graphics and Simulation: The demand for real-time graphics in various applications, from gaming to simulations, will likely grow—advancements in graphics processing units (GPUs) and software computing capabilities. The future of computing may involve systems optimized for immersive experiences, impacting gaming, education, healthcare, and various industries.

5G and Beyond: The deployment of 5G networks is already underway. Offering faster and more reliable optimizations enables more complex simulations and graphics to be rendered in real time.

Haptic Feedback and Sensory Integration: Improvements in haptic feedback technology will contribute to more realistic and immersive interactive experiences. Integrating tactile sensations like touch and force feedback will enhance user engagement in virtual environments.

Gesture and Voice Interaction: The future may increase reliance on natural and intuitive interaction methods, such as gesture recognition and voice commands. These interfaces can make digital interactions more user-friendly and accessible.

3D Printing and Fabrication Integration: Computer graphics will likely play a crucial role in the design and fabrication process, especially with integrating 3D printing and other fabrication technologies. Designers may use advanced graphics tools to create and visualize complex 3D-printed objects.

Blockchain for Digital Assets: Blockchain technology may impact computer graphics by providing secure and decentralized platforms for creating, sharing, and trading digital as such as 3D models, textures, and virtual items.

Generative Adversarial Networks (GANs) in Content Creation: GANs and other AI-driven approaches will continue to influence content creation in computer graphics. These techniques can generate realistic textures, models, and even entire scenes.

Ethical and Acceptive Design Practices: As technology becomes more pervasive, there will likely be increased emphasis on ethical and receptive design in computer graphics and interactive techniques. Considerations for accessibility, diversity, and well-being will become integral to the design process. **Photonics-based inventions**: how we perceive data and gain access to micro and single-photon levels based on quantum physics. All the new inventions that are happening right now, at this very moment.

There is too much coding involved to describe it.

FUTURE TECHNOLOGY
(TOO MUCH CODING FOR DESCRIBING)
VITRUVIAN MANIKIN – VINC

Vinc had a list of hopes for technological solutions, trends, and directions for the future of computing:
Quantum Computing: Quantum computing has the potential to revolutionize the field by performing complex calculations at speeds impossible for classical computers. As research progresses, we may see the emergence of practical quantum computers, which would impact areas like cryptography, optimization problems, and scientific simulations.
Edge Computing: As the Internet of Things (IoT) grows, there's an increasing need for computing power at the edge. Computing involves processing data closer to the source, reducing latency, and improving efficiency. This trend is likely to continue as IoT devices become more prevalent.
AI and Machine Learning Integration: Artificial intelligence (AI) and machine learning (ML) are already integral to computing, and their influence will likely expand. Future systems may incorporate more advanced AI capabilities for improved decision-making, automation, and personalization.
Neuromorphic Computing: Inspired by the human brain's architecture, neuromorphic computing aims to build processors that mimic the brain's neural networks. This approach could lead to more energy-efficient and powerful computing systems, especially for pattern recognition and learning tasks.
Augmented and Virtual Reality: AR and VR technologies will demand more powerful connectivity as they mature. Beyond 5G, further advancements in communication technologies may enable even more seamless and responsive computing experiences.
Biocomputing and DNA Storage: Exploring new ways to store and process information, researchers are investigating biocomputing using biological molecules and DNA storage. These approaches could lead to more efficient and stable computing technologies.
Cybersecurity Advancements: As computing systems become increasingly complex, cybersecurity will be increasingly emphasized. Future computing developments will likely involve robust security measures to protect data and systems from evolving threats.
Stable Computing Systems: As concerns about energy consumption rise, there will likely be a greater focus on developing stable computing solutions. These could involve energy-efficient hardware, eco-friendly manufacturing processes, responsible emissions, and responsible disposal practices.
Human-Computer Interaction Evolution: Interfaces between humans and computers are evolving. Future computing may include advancements in natural language processing, gesture recognition, and brain-computer interfaces, making interactions more intuitive and seamless. The future of computing is dynamic, with constant innovation and adaptation to new challenges and opportunities. It will be shaped by interdisciplinary collaboration, ethical considerations, and a commitment to addressing societal needs. Overall, the future of computer graphics and interactive techniques holds great promise for more immersive, realistic, and receptive digital experiences driven by technological advancements and creative innovation.
All the new inventions were happening right now, at this very moment, all over the globe.

Again, too much coding was involved to describe it.

G GALLERY (USE OF COMMENTS TO EXPLAIN WITHIN THE CODE) RECORDER – TONY

Tony, the orchestra's recorder player, collects jewelry. He keeps his treasures in a big silver bowl full of necklaces, bracelets, earrings, and rings, which he brings on special occasions. At one point, his jewels changed. They began to look like miniature sculptures. All musicians agree they are of exceptional beauty and value as amazing works of art, and Tony is a talented jewelry designer. They also learned that he showed his jewels to gallery directors, and he was scheduled to have an exhibition in an art gallery. Violinist Amadeus, violist Eliza, flutist Peter, bassoonist Lawrence, and bass player Ronald volunteered to play at the opening reception to honor the artist. At the gallery, they saw something unexpected. The orchestra's photographer, Samuel, photographed all the little gems, manipulated the images, and then installed a photo projection on a wall to make people look very small compared to the jewels.

```
def display_projected_artifacts(scale_factor):
    """
    Function to simulate the display of projected artifacts in a gallery
setting,
    taking into account the role of scale.

    Parameters:
    - scale_factor (float): The scaling factor to adjust the size of the
artifacts.

    Returns:
    - str: Explanation of the impact of scale on artifact display.
    """

    # Assume original artifact dimensions
    original_width = 100
    original_height = 100

    # Calculate scaled dimensions
    scaled_width = original_width * scale_factor
    scaled_height = original_height * scale_factor

    # Explanation of the impact of scale
    explanation = f"""
    In the gallery setting, the role of scale is crucial in determining
how the audience perceives projected artifacts. When applying a
scale
    factor of {scale_factor},
    the dimensions of the artifacts are adjusted accordingly.

  Original Artifact Dimensions:
    Width: {original_width} units
    Height: {original_height} units

    Scaled Artifact Dimensions:
    Width: {scaled_width} units
    Height: {scaled_height} units

    The scale factor influences the perceived size, presence, and
impact of the artifacts
    within the gallery space. It allows curators to manipulate the visual
experience,
    emphasizing certain details or creating a grandiose display,
depending on the artistic
    intent and the spatial constraints of the gallery.
    """

    return explanation

# Example usage:
scale_factor_input = float(input("Enter the scale factor (e.g., 1.5 for
150% scale): "))
result_explanation = display_projected_artifacts(scale_factor_input)
print(result_explanation)
```

The function display_projected_artifacts took a scale factor as input and calculated the scaled dimensions, explaining the impact of scale on the display of artifacts.

Photographs of the installation with big jewels and tiny gallery visitors appeared in a newspaper. Some people laughed; others became angry.

GARDENING
(SUBCLASSES)
GARDENER – JET

Since he was little, Jet was often reminded that his profession should be his passion. His mind was set on the go-carts. The pleasure of racing, making sudden turns, balancing his vehicle, and alternating speed was his thing. He enjoyed being in control and on the safe side at the same time. No job would mimic this experience except riding on the lawnmower. He learned to compare the types of movement of a go-cart and a lawnmower by creating a Python script for movements forward, backward, left turn, and right turn.

```
class Vehicle:
    def __init__(self, name):
        self.name = name

    def move_forward(self):
        print(f"{self.name} is moving forward.")

    def move_backward(self):
        print(f"{self.name} is moving backward.")

    def turn_left(self):
        print(f"{self.name} is turning left.")

    def turn_right(self):
        print(f"{self.name} is turning right.")

class GoCart(Vehicle):
    def __init__(self):
        super().__init__("Go-Cart")

class LawnMower(Vehicle):
    def __init__(self):
        super().__init__("Lawnmower")

# Example Usage
go_cart = GoCart()
lawn_mower = LawnMower()

go_cart.move_forward()
go_cart.turn_left()

lawn_mower.move_backward()
lawn_mower.turn_right()
```

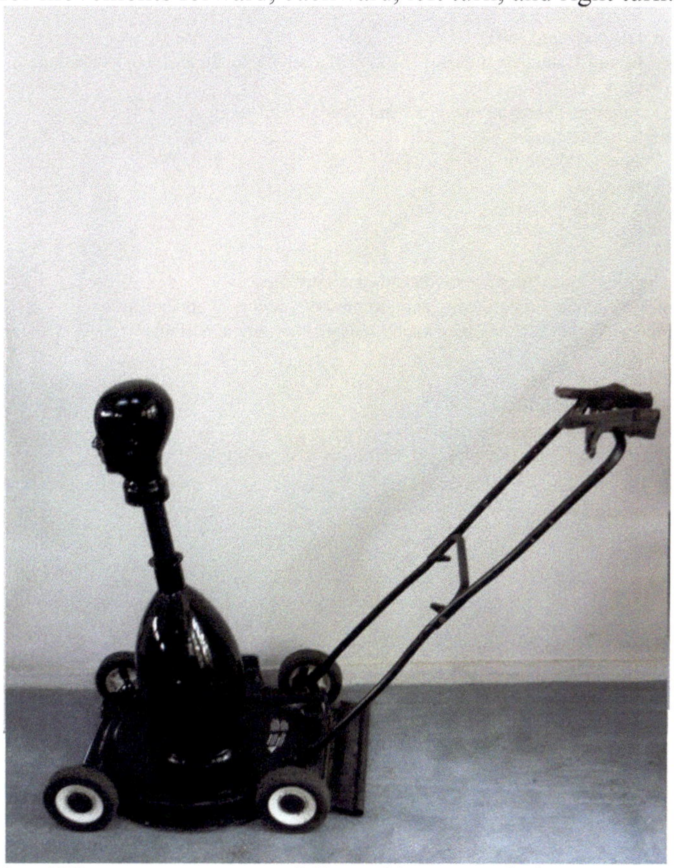

He created a base class Vehicle with methods for different movements, followed by two subclasses, Go and LawnMower, which were inherited from the Vehicle class. He added more methods or features.
He worked as a gardener for the orchestra hall's oversized yard. He would not take care of flowers, bushes, and trees.

They were too slow for him, but the lawn was cut in no time.

GENEALOGY
(CLASS INSTANTIATION AND OBJECT CREATION)
THE PORCELAIN FAMILY

They all had something in common.

```
class PorcelainFamilyMember:
    def __init__(self, name, age, occupation):
        self.name = name
        self.age = age
        self.occupation = occupation

    def display_info(self):
        print(f"Name: {self.name}, Age: {self.age}, Occupation: {self.occupation}")

# Common attributes among Porcelain family members
common_attributes = {
    "name": "Porcelain",
    "age": 30,
    "occupation": "Artist"
}

# Creating family members with common attributes
family_member1 = PorcelainFamilyMember(**common_attributes)
family_member2 = PorcelainFamilyMember(**common_attributes)

# Displaying information
family_member1.display_info()
family_member2.display_info()
learn_new_language(language_to_learn, learning_resources)
```

This worked the best, but the book on learning a new programming language was needed. It included:

- Welcome Message for the learning journey for a specific language.
- Recommended Learning Resources: a list of recommended language learning methods.
- Study Plan: a basic study schedule divided into weeks, progressively covering fundamental topics.
- Hands-on Practice: to engage the learner in hands-on practice by coding small projects and challenges.

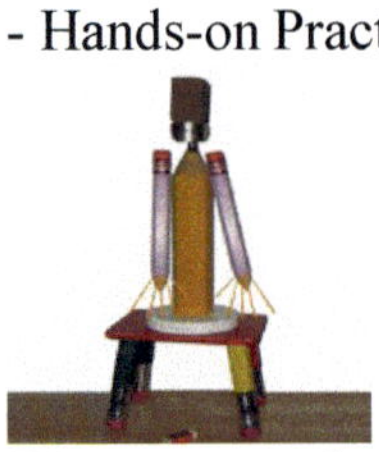

We use metaphors! Oh, these common attributes among members of the Porcelain family!

GENETICS
(CONDITIONAL STATEMENT)
SHOW HOSTS – DEJAN AND BOGDAN

Dejan and Bogdan were twins, not identical, but there was a strong resemblance between them.

```
def are_twins_identical(dna_sequence_twin1, dna_sequence_twin2):
   if dna_sequence_twin1 == dna_sequence_twin2:
      return True
   else:
      return False

# Hypothetical DNA sequences for the twins
twin1_dna = "ATCGGTA and on"
twin2_dna = "ATCGGTA and on"

# Check if the twins are identical
if are_twins_identical(twin1_dna, twin2_dna):
   print("The male twins are identical.")
else:
   print("The male twins are not identical.")
```

The function compared the DNA sequences of two twins. If the DNA sequences were identical, the function returned True, indicating that the twins were identical. The script then used a conditional statement to print a message based on the comparison result. Their parents had always wanted to name their child with both grandparents' first names. Having the twins came in handy. The firstborn got the name Dejan Bogdan, and the second one was called Bogdan Dejan. The life was easy. If one could not show up, the twin would fill in, and vice versa. Their IDs were almost identical, just as they were. Thus, Dejan attended a safety instruction session after Bogdan was caught speeding, and Bogdan met with a girl Dejan wanted to break up with. How unethical. How unearthly. How unkind.

Of course, she knew, but it was easier this way; besides, she started dating Bogdan.

Back then, the horizon line meant the end of the world around them. If it was raining, the Earth flooded; if there was sunshine, everyone on the planet was happy. The world was big, right up to the horizon line.

```
# Python code to illustrate the ancient belief that the horizon line marked the end of the world
import matplotlib.pyplot as plt
import numpy as np

def draw_horizon_line():
    # Generate a simple plot with a horizon line
    horizon_line = np.linspace(-1, 1, 1000)
    plt.plot(horizon_line, np.zeros_like(horizon_line), color='blue', linewidth=2)

    # Set plot properties
    plt.title("Ancient Belief: Horizon Line as the End of the World")
    plt.xlabel("Horizon Line")
    plt.ylabel("Sea Level")
    plt.axhline(0, color='black', linestyle='--', linewidth=1) # Sea level reference line
    plt.grid(True)

    # Highlight the idea of the world ending beyond the horizon
    plt.text(0.5, 0.2, "End of the World", fontsize=12, color='red', ha='center')

    # Show the plot
    plt.show()

# Run the code
draw_horizon_line()
```

In this visualization of the ancient belief that the horizon line marked the end of the world, their code used the matplotlib library to create a plot with a blue horizon line (the world's edge). The plot included annotations highlighting the idea and aims to illustrate how limited visibility led to the belief that the world was finite and ended when the eye could no longer see. They tried again, but differently.

```
import turtle

# Create a turtle screen
screen = turtle.Screen()
screen.bgcolor("lightblue")

# Create a turtle for drawing
world_turtle = turtle.Turtle()
world_turtle.speed(2)

# Draw the sky
world_turtle.penup()
world_turtle.goto(-300, 100)
world_turtle.pendown()
world_turtle.color("skyblue")
world_turtle.begin_fill()
world_turtle.forward(600)
world_turtle.right(90)
world_turtle.forward(200)
world_turtle.right(90)
world_turtle.forward(600)
world_turtle.right(90)
world_turtle.forward(200)
world_turtle.end_fill()
# Draw the ocean
world_turtle.penup()
world_turtle.goto(-300, -100)
world_turtle.pendown()
world_turtle.color("navy")
world_turtle.begin_fill()
world_turtle.forward(600)
world_turtle.right(90)
world_turtle.forward(200)

world_turtle.right(90)
world_turtle.forward(600)
world_turtle.right(90)
world_turtle.forward(200)
world_turtle.end_fill()

# Draw the horizon line
world_turtle.penup()
world_turtle.goto(-300, 0)
world_turtle.pendown()
world_turtle.color("gold")
world_turtle.pensize(2)
world_turtle.forward(600)

# Hide the turtle
world_turtle.hideturtle()

# Display the window
turtle.mainloop()
```

In this Python code, they used the Turtle graphics library, the visual representation of the world with a horizon line separating the sky and the ocean. The colors and shapes were used to illustrate the sky, ocean, and the horizon line. The comments explained the concept that, in ancient times, people might have perceived the horizon line as the literal end of the world.
It all made sense now; except people did not know coding then. Or maybe they did?

GEOGRAPHY AND MOON
(OBJECT-ORIENTED PROGRAMMING (OOP)
MOONWALKER – SART

He was not walking on the Moon but by the Moon, following its light. His GPS guided him back home. Python code he wrote simulated GPS guidance by using basic coordinates to point him to get back home.

```
import math

class GPS:
    def __init__(self, destination):
        self.destination = destination

    def calculate_distance(self, current_location):
        dest_lat, dest_lon = self.destination
        curr_lat, curr_lon = current_location
        # Using Haversine formula to calculate distance between two coordinates
        R = 6371  # Radius of the Earth in kilometers
        dlat = math.radians(dest_lat - curr_lat)
        dlon = math.radians(dest_lon - curr_lon)
        a = math.sin(dlat / 2) ** 2 + math.cos(math.radians(curr_lat)) * math.cos(math.radians(dest_lat)) * math.sin(dlon / 2) ** 2
        c = 2 * math.atan2(math.sqrt(a), math.sqrt(1 - a))
        distance = R * c
        return distance

    def navigate(self, current_location):
        distance_to_destination = self.calculate_distance(current_location)
        print(f"Distance to destination: {distance_to_destination:.2f} km")

        if distance_to_destination < 0.1:  # arbitrary threshold for reaching the destination
            print("You have reached your destination!")
        else:
            print("Continue navigating...")

# Example usage:
destination_coordinates = (37.7749, -122.4194)  # San Francisco coordinates
gps = GPS(destination_coordinates)

# Simulate movement
current_location = (37.773972, -122.431297)  # Starting point coordinates
gps.navigate(current_location)
```

His code defined a GPS class with methods to calculate the distance between two coordinates and to navigate based on the current location. This helped him organize the code, encapsulate related functionality, and promote code reusability.

He moved from place to place quite often but always landed in his current apartment, which was always located on the top floor of the building.

GIFT-GIVING (NESTED LOOPS)

MAIL WATCHER – KI

Distant relationships bring lots of waiting. None of the technological solutions can substitute for a special delivery. Ki was hoping and waiting for a present, but the mailbox was filled out with advertisements only. What a waste of good paper, she said to herself. While watching for a mail delivery person approaching her house, she heard her computer signaling a message. It was a wireframe of a table to be printed in plastic. Her present came! She quickly turned her 3D printer on to warm it up and started measuring her room to adjust the lengths of the lines, choosing the color of the filament and red it was. Now, she had to choose her material. PLA (Polylactic Acid): a popular choice for 3D printing due to its ease of use and environmental friendliness. Derived from renewable resources such as cornstarch, it is known for its low warping, high detail, and wide range of available colors, but not the best choice for outdoor use, as it can degrade in UV light over time. PETG (Polyethylene Terephthalate Glycol) is a durable and impact-resistant filament with higher strength than PLA. It has good layer adhesion, low shrinkage, and is suitable for functional parts. PETG is also resistant to moisture, making it a better choice for applications where the printed object might be exposed to some level of humidity. ABS (Acrylonitrile Butadiene Styrene): It is strong and tough, withstands temperatures higher than PLA, and has good impact resistance. However, ABS may produce fumes during printing, so it must be used in a well-ventilated area, but good for functional and durable items. Wood-Infused Filaments: wood particles or fibers (e.g., Wood PLA) provide a natural wood-like appearance. Good for decorative pieces and furniture with a rustic aesthetic. High-Temperature Filaments (e.g., ASA, Polycarbonate): For outdoor or high-temperature applications, she considered filaments like ASA or polycarbonate, the materials with better resistance to UV light and higher temperatures. She took a spool of the PLA out from under her bed. She set her mailbox to be packed for recycling.

```
def generate_wireframe(rows, columns):
    for i in range(rows):
        # Print the top border of the table
        if i == 0:
            print("+", end="")
            for j in range(columns):
                print("---+", end="")
            print()

        # Print the body of the table
        else:
            print("|", end="")
            for j in range(columns):
                print("   |", end="")
            print()

        # Print the bottom border of the table
        if i == rows - 1:
            print("+", end="")
            for j in range(columns):
                print("---+", end="")
            print()
```

Her code used nested loops to iterate over rows and columns. The outer loop (for i in range(rows)) was responsible for iterating over each row, and the inner loop (for j in range(columns)) was responsible for iterating over each column within a row. This concept was essential for constructing two-dimensional structures. Those repetitive tasks within repetitive tasks provided a way to handle multi-dimensional data structures or patterns. The nested loops helped create the rows and columns of the table in the wireframe. She looked at the code (as shown in the lines below). It was ASCII!

```
   ____
|  |
|  |
|____|
|  |
|____|
```

She hung her mailbox back on the house's wall.

(ASCII = American Standard Code for Information Interchange - a set of digital codes for letters, numerals, and symbols, to transfer, between computers – for example, such as 1101001text)

GLOSSOLOGY – THE STUDY OF LANGUAGE AND/OR THE TONGUE (FUNCTIONS)
TRANSLATOR B

B's family was close, and they spoke often about daily events. It was very unusual, but they seemed to have connected brains, Merlot said once during an interview. Whatever one family member would learn, everyone else would know. They'd know all the trade secrets, the power numbers, the scripts for the operas, songs, and lyrics, and they all spoke various languages, including Afrikaans, Arabic, Arkian, Assyrian, Asturian, Alurian, Basque, Euskara, Bengali, Berber, Bhojpuri, Brazilian Portuguese, Buhl, Bulgarian, Catalan, Chichewa, Chinese, Church, Slavonic, Degaspregos, Demotic, Dongxiang, Dutch, English, Estonian, Farsi, French, German, Greek, Gujarati, Hausa, Hawaiian, Hieroglyphic, Hindi, Hmong, Irish, Italian, Jameld, Japanese, Kankonian, Konkani, Lakota, Logan, Mala (now Minyeva), Marathi, Nepali, Occitan, Punjabi, Quechua, Sanskrit, Sinhalese, Slovene, Spanish, Tamil, Telugu, Tengwar, Urdu, Vague, Xhamagas, and Turkish., and more.

B and his family were among the many linguistic and ethnic groups. It was not that difficult for them to learn related languages, as they traveled together to perform in many countries; for example, they became part of the International Partnership Holiday. They often liked to sing together, and each family member would sing their own part in a different language. Their chorus sounded very intriguing this way.

```
def generate_song(verse_language='English', chorus_language='Spanish'):

    verse = f"I'm singing in {verse_language}, words so clear,\n"

    chorus = f"La la la, {chorus_language}, feeling near."

    song = f"{verse}\n{chorus}\n{verse}\n{chorus}\n"

    return song

# Example usage

song = generate_song('French', 'Italian')

print(song)
```

The generate_song function took two parameters, verse_language, and chorus_language, with default values set to 'English' and 'Spanish', respectively. Inside the function, a verse and a chorus were created using f-strings, and then the entire song was constructed by combining these elements. The function returned the generated song. This way, the code was modular and reusable. They could easily change the languages or add more features without duplicating it.

Some of the countries they visited were The seventeenth century Ark Maramia, the Turkey Peninsula, Euskara, the Basque Provinces, Alava North, the state of Uttar Pradesh (UP), Maharashtra state in Nepal, and some adjoining areas of Nepal, Portugal, Brazil, Angola, Mozambique, Cape Verde, and East Timor, South America, the Philippines, the Bicol Peninsula on the island of Luzon. Bulgaria, Spain, France, Andorra and Italy, and Spain again, South-central Africa, The Old Russia, Netherlands, Flanders, Belgium, England, The Ural Mountains, North Europe, the Volga and Ural region, Siberia and the Russian Far North, Iran (formerly Persia), Afghanistan, Tajikistan and the Pamir Mountain region, Québec, Switzerland, Haiti, French Guiana, Monaco, Southwest Asia and French Polynesia, Germany, the European Union, West coast of India, Gujarat borders with Rajasthan, Northern Nigeria, State of Hawaii, China, Canada, Argentina, Northern Ireland, Germany, Japan, The Middle East, Konkani community, Pakistan, Punjab, Bolivia, Peru, Ecuador, Northern Chile, Southern Colombia. Inca Empire. Russia, Greece, Bengali, people of Sri Lanka, ancient north India, Slovenia, many countries in Africa, Southern USA, Mexico, India in the Andhra, Madhya, and Pradesh regions, Malaysia, Israel, Mexico, Romania, and the U.S.

Their audience often had their phones ready to translate what they could not understand.

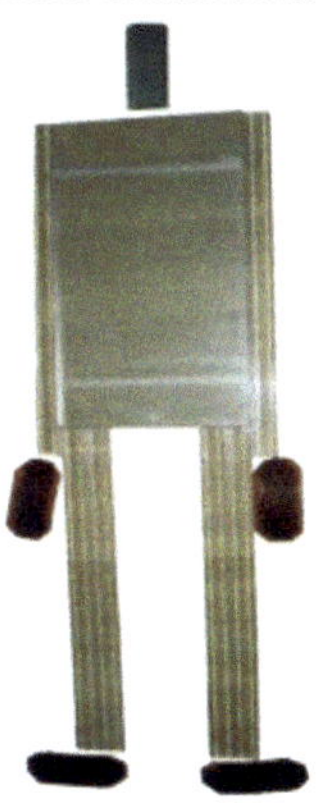

Oh, the power of lyrics!

GOOD WILL (MODULE) INVENTOR – JOHN

John developed a "Good Virus." He designed it to organize the recipient's desktop. It can mean different things to people, but his script was based on file types, moving them into respective folders.

```
import os
import shutil

def organize_desktop(desktop_path):
    # List all files on the desktop
    files = [f for f in os.listdir(desktop_path) if
os.path.isfile(os.path.join(desktop_path, f))]

    # Create folders for different file types
    folders = {
        'Documents': ['pdf', 'doc', 'docx', 'txt'],
        'Images': ['jpg', 'jpeg', 'png', 'gif'],
        'Videos': ['mp4', 'avi', 'mkv'],
        'Music': ['mp3', 'wav', 'flac'],
    }

    for folder, extensions in folders.items():
        folder_path = os.path.join(desktop_path, folder)
        os.makedirs(folder_path, exist_ok=True)
        for file in files:
            if any(file.lower().endswith(ext) for ext in extensions):
                file_path = os.path.join(desktop_path, file)
                new_path = os.path.join(folder_path, file)
                shutil.move(file_path, new_path)
                print(f"Moved {file} to {folder}")

    print("Desktop organized!")

if __name__ == "__main__":
    desktop_path = os.path.join(os.path.expanduser('~'), 'Desktop')
    organize_desktop(desktop_path)
```

His "gift" recipients found their desktops filled out with Documents, Images, Videos, and Music based on their file extensions as his script moved them accordingly. After that, he started having people send nice messages to everyone in their address book. He called it a "Better Virus."

```
import smtplib
from email.mime.text import MIMEText
from email.mime.multipart import MIMEMultipart

def send_nice_message(sender_email, sender_password, recipient_email,
message):
    # Set up the email server
    smtp_server = 'smtp.your_email_provider.com'
    smtp_port = 587  # Update the port based on your email provider's settings
    # Create a message
    msg = MIMEMultipart()
    msg['From'] = sender_email
    msg['To'] = recipient_email
    msg['Subject'] = 'A Nice Message'
    # Attach the message body
    msg.attach(MIMEText(message, 'plain'))
    # Log in to the email server
    with smtplib.SMTP(smtp_server, smtp_port) as server:
        server.starttls()
        server.login(sender_email, sender_password)

        # Send the email
        server.sendmail(sender_email, recipient_email, msg.as_string())

def send_nice_messages_to_all(sender_email, sender_password,
address_book, message):
    for contact in address_book:
        recipient_email = contact['email']
        send_nice_message(sender_email, sender_password,
recipient_email, message)
        print(f"Nice message sent to {contact['name']} at
{recipient_email}")

if __name__ == "__main__":
    # Update these values with your email credentials and address book
    sender_email = 'your_email@gmail.com'
    sender_password = 'your_email_password'

    # Example address book with name and email
    address_book = [
        {'name': 'Friend 1', 'email': 'friend1@example.com'},
        {'name': 'Friend 2', 'email': 'friend2@example.com'},
        # Add more contacts as needed
    ]

    nice_message = "Hey there! Just wanted to send you a nice message.
Have a great day!"

    send_nice_messages_to_all(sender_email, sender_password,
address_book, nice_message)
```

When people noticed their desktops were well-organized with nice emails from those not so friendly to them before, they felt it was an invasion of their privacy. John was forced to begin selling his products only to those who wanted them. He set the price low, and soon everyone possessed it.

GROUP DECISION – SOCIAL INFLUENCE (CALCULATIONS)
AN APPLE PEELER – TUKA

Tuka was growing apples as she thought that they were the most beautiful fruits. Apples have many connotations and associations. She started collecting texts, illustrations, videos, and other media involving them. Her collection was growing fast, as the apples on her trees. Soon, she could be found on a corner of two streets peeling apples for anyone wanting one. Her business was blossoming. The cost of a peeled apple needed to combine the price of the apple itself, tools, packaging, and expenses like transportation or permits for selling on the street. She wrote a script to come up with a proper price.

```
def calculate_apple_cost():
    # Cost of the apple
    apple_cost = float(input("Enter the cost of one apple: $"))

    # Cost of peeling equipment
    peeler_cost = float(input("Enter the cost of peeling equipment: $"))

    # Cost of packaging
    packaging_cost = float(input("Enter the cost of packaging: $"))

    # Additional expenses
    transportation_cost = float(input("Enter transportation cost: $"))
    permit_cost = float(input("Enter permit cost: $"))

    # Calculate total cost
    total_cost = apple_cost + peeler_cost + packaging_cost +
transportation_cost + permit_cost

    return total_cost

# Call the function
total_cost = calculate_apple_cost()

# Display the result
print(f"The total cost of a peeled apple to be sold on the Nstreet is:
${total_cost}")
```

She had the buyers type the costs of an apple, peeling equipment, packaging, transportation, and permits. The program calculated and printed the total sum. Soon, she became a local attraction when people could see the reason for each price. Some buyers suggested adding the cost of her time, benefits, and transportation. The apples became very expensive, yet more popular, for it became a group decision.

H

HABITS
OBJECT ORIENTED PROGRAMMING (OOP)
PUPPETEER – LOLA

Lola had been a puppeteer as far back as she could remember. She made her name for the audience's mind-reading while performing. One glance at them was sufficient for her to construct a mental skeleton for a story and then weave an action around it. She was skilled beyond imagination; anyone agreed with that. She had one problem, though. Her hands were always cold. That would make the job impossible for many, but not for Lola. It was for two reasons: self-esteem and self-efficacy. She could get over the problem, and it felt good. She convinced herself that stiff hands stimulate shaky movement; thus, the puppets looked more interesting in action.

```
import time

class Puppeteer:
    def __init__(self, name):
        self.name = name
        self.hand_temperature = 15  # Cold hands for puppeteering

    def move_puppet(self, direction):
        print(f"{self.name} is moving puppet {direction}")

    def speak_lines(self, lines):
        print(f"{self.name} is saying: {lines}")

    def manipulate_strings(self, strings):
        warmed_strings = [s + " (warmed)" for s in strings]
        print(f"{self.name} is manipulating strings:
{warmed_strings}")

    def perform(self):
        print(f"{self.name} is performing!")

# Puppeteer with cold hands
cold_hands_puppeteer = Puppeteer("Cold Hands Puppeteer")

# Simulate puppeteering with cold hands
cold_hands_puppeteer.move_puppet("up")
cold_hands_puppeteer.speak_lines("Hello, audience!")
cold_hands_puppeteer.manipulate_strings(["Jump", "Dance",
"Spin"])
cold_hands_puppeteer.perform()

# Simulate a break to warm hands
print(f"\n{cold_hands_puppeteer.name} is taking a break to warm
hands...\n")
time.sleep(2)  # Simulating a break

# Puppeteer with warm hands
warm_hands_puppeteer = Puppeteer("Warm Hands Puppeteer")
warm_hands_puppeteer.hand_temperature = 30  # Warm hands
for a break

# Simulate puppeteering with warm hands
warm_hands_puppeteer.move_puppet("left")
warm_hands_puppeteer.speak_lines("I'm back, everyone!")
warm_hands_puppeteer.manipulate_strings(["Wave", "Laugh",
"Bow"])
warm_hands_puppeteer.perform()
```

The puppeteer is represented as a class (Puppeteer), encapsulating related behaviors and attributes. Each puppeteer instance has its own set of properties (such as name and hand temperature) and methods (such as move_puppet and perform).

One glimpse at her audience helped her define the atmosphere of interaction, but she listened to her orbitofrontal cortex, which tells you what you really want. She mastered the art of giving one good answer at a time.

HANDYMAN SERVICES – MAINTENANCE (FUNCTIONS)

HELPFUL HANDS – H.H.

H.H. started his business to help people in the neighborhood. He asked them to have the tools ready when he'd arrive. His neighbors created a tool exchange network to ensure all sorts of tools would be available for H.H. Someone mentioned a fund for him to gather his own tools, but organizing each job was too much fun. He helped by writing the code to gather all the tools needed for fixing things in his area:

```
def gather_tools():
    print("Welcome to the Helping Hands Tool Gatherer!")

    # Create an empty list to store tools
    tools = []

    # Gather tools from the user
    while True:
        tool = input("Enter a tool needed for fixing (or 'done' to finish): ")

        if tool.lower() == 'done':
            break

        tools.append(tool)
        print(f"{tool} added to your toolkit.")

    # Display the gathered tools
    print("\nGathered Tools:")
    for tool in tools:
        print(tool)

    print("\nYou are now ready to help in your neighborhood with your toolkit!")

# Execute the function
gather_tools()
```

His script allowed him to enter tools individually, depending on the types of tasks he was planning to assist with. When he was done, he could type 'done' to finish the input. The gathered tools were then displayed, and he felt ready to help in the neighborhood.

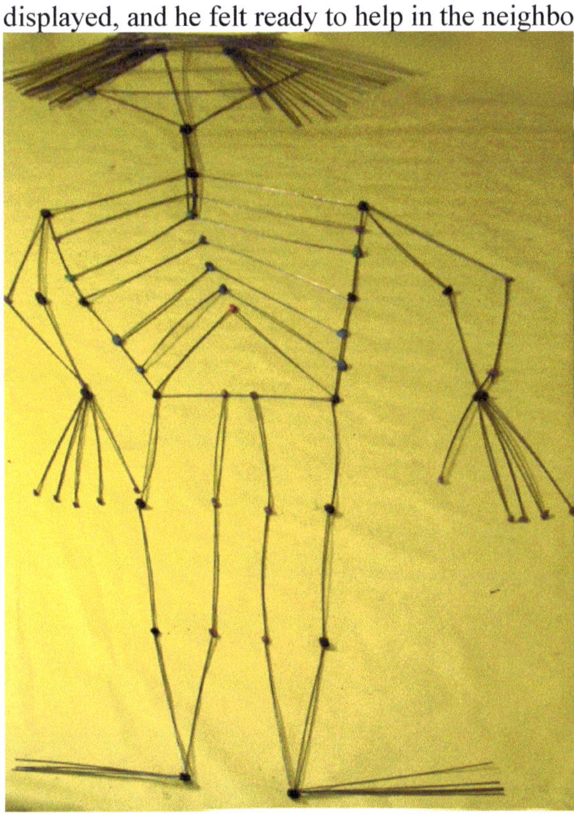

Soon, his area was awarded for being the most technologically advanced in the entire city.

HAPPINESS
(DICTIONARY)
SAXOPHONIST – BILL

They liked to play music. Curious why such a demanding skill brought others happiness, he examined it:

```
def enjoy_music_playing():
    # Dictionary to store reasons why people enjoy playing music
    enjoyment_factors = {
        "Expressive Outlet": "Playing music allows people to express their emotions and creativity.",
        "Stress Relief": "Music playing can serve as a stress-relieving activity, providing a sense of relaxation.",
        "Social Connection": "Playing music in a group or band fosters social bonds and a sense of community.",
        "Personal Achievement": "Mastering an instrument or creating music can give a sense of accomplishment.",
        "Joy of Creation": "Crafting and playing music is a fulfilling creative process."
    }

    # Print the reasons why people enjoy playing music
    print("Reasons why people enjoy playing music:")
        print(f"{factor}: {description}")

# Calling the function to display the enjoyment factors
enjoy_music_playing()
```

The enjoyment_factors variable is a dictionary where each key-value pair represents a reason why people enjoy playing music.

Soon, the whole neighborhood played some instrument fitting their interest and capabilities.

HEALTH
(PROCEDURAL PROGRAMMING)
SAZ – JONATHAN

Jonathan is a famous Saz, a plucked string instrument player. He is one of the oldest orchestra members; he remembers the musicians and instruments that helped him achieve his current high status in the orchestra. His ear for the nuances of string instruments is priceless to his colleagues. He cares a lot that he suffers from a stress syndrome and suffers from a stomach ailment. Therefore, wherever he goes, he orders an omelet. They are all the same everywhere to him; thus, there are no surprises. His diet constraints make his three friends (Frank, Bob, and Marcel, the cooks in a well-patroned restaurant) please Jonathan. However, it's a challenge to show their flair within the requirements of Jonathan's diet.

```
def _init_(self, hand_movements, hip_sways):
def make_omelet(ingredients):
    print("Recipe: Basic Omelet")
    print("Ingredients:")
    for ingredient in ingredients:
        print("- " + ingredient)

    print("\nInstructions:")
    print("1. Crack the eggs into a bowl.")
    print("2. Whisk the eggs until well beaten.")
    print("3. Heat a non-stick skillet over medium heat.")
    print("4. Pour the beaten eggs into the skillet.")
    print("5. Add the desired ingredients on one side of the omelet.")
    print("6. Wait until the edges are set, then gently lift and fold the
other side.")
    print("7. Cook for a few more minutes until the omelet is fully
cooked.")
    print("8. Slide the omelet onto a plate and serve.")

# Example usage:
omelet_ingredients = ["Eggs", "Salt", "Pepper", "Cheese",
"Vegetables"]
make_omelet(omelet_ingredients)
```

Their recipe was broken down into a series of steps represented by functions (make_omelet). Each step was executed in sequence to achieve the final result. For cultural differences, omelets are a versatile dish found in various cuisines around the world, and the ingredients and methods can vary based on cultural preferences. Different cultures may use unique ingredients based on local tastes and culinary traditions. In some regions, herbs, spices, meats, and vegetables specific to that culture may be added to the omelet. The cooking techniques also vary. Some cultures prefer a well-cooked and firm omelet, while others may enjoy a softer, almost custard-like texture. The choice of sides or accompaniments can differ. In some cultures, omelets are served with specific condiments, sauces, or bread. Cultural differences in omelet preparation highlight the diversity of various cuisines and the influence of local ingredients and traditions on a seemingly simple dish.

They always serve him a plate with a special dish named after one of the instruments. The most dietary one is "A Flute Souffle" with "A Piano Roll." Then comes Symphony of Spaghetti, Jazzed-up Jambalaya, Salsa Sonata, Rock 'n' Roll Risotto, Bluesy Blueberry Pancakes, Funky Fajitas, Rhapsody in Raspberry Cheesecake, Tango Tacos, Reggae Rice Bowl, Beethoven's Baguette, Minuet Muffins, Cello Salad, Sonata Stir-Fry, Samba Sushi, Chopin Chocolate Cake, Flamenco Flan, Calypso Cupcakes, Melody Mango Sorbet, Waltz Watermelon Salad, and Béchamel Ballad (for a creamy pasta dish).

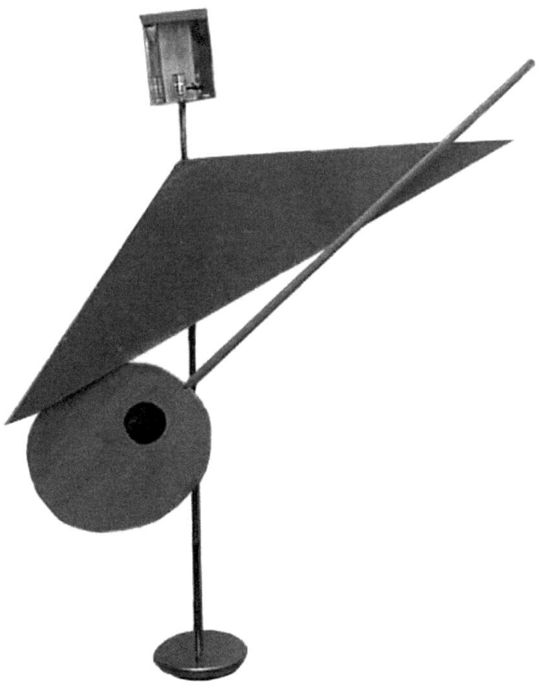

Since then, all his stomach-related problems mordaciously disappeared.

DAYCARE – PERIWINKLE

Periwinkle loved children. She dressed them in pink or blue as they entered her Daycare. Her organizational skills were superb, and she was known for her punctuality. Periwinkle valued fairness. She insisted that every child in her care would drink the same daily dose of milk. This was the part most parents would not approve of. If you give everybody the same portions of food or drink, most of them will not benefit from it. She wrote a code to measure the dose of milk suiting each child's data, considering various factors such as the child's age, weight, and any specific dietary requirements.

```
def calculate_milk_dose(age, weight):
   # Define recommended milk doses based on age groups
   if age < 1:
      recommended_dose = weight * 0.15  # Recommended dose
for infants
   elif 1 <= age <= 3:
      recommended_dose = weight * 0.12  # Recommended dose
for toddlers
   elif 4 <= age <= 8:
      recommended_dose = weight * 0.1   # Recommended dose
for young children
   else:
      recommended_dose = weight * 0.08  # Recommended dose
for older children

   return recommended_dose

# Get child's age and weight as input
child_age = float(input("Enter the child's age (in years): "))
child_weight = float(input("Enter the child's weight (in kg): "))

# Calculate the recommended dose of milk
recommended_milk_dose = calculate_milk_dose(child_age,
child_weight)

# Display the recommended dose
print(f"Recommended dose of milk for the child:
{recommended_milk_dose} ounces per day")
```

She adjusted the dose calculations based on the age group based on the specific requirements and guides. However, the parents insisted on consulting with healthcare professionals for personalized advice, who recommended allowing the children to pick the colors they wore.

HISTORY
(CLASS AND INSTANCES)
UKULELE – PAPRIKA

Paprika's interest was in the old cultures and the generation of art forms. Her specialty was tracking down the weaving techniques back to the Paleolithic era. She was most interested in fabrics done in about 5000 BC, for t items of clothing painted on wooden boards of the Fayum portraits. She was focused on playing ukulele and weaving. She made all her clothing herself. She collected various kinds of yarn, silk thread, wool, hemp, linen, and any fabric to knit, weave, and assemble them together. Depending on her costume, she'd try four sizes of ukulele: soprano, concert, tenor, and baritone. Paprika developed a code that builds a sentence by adding information about each role in fabricating Fayum portraits.

```
class FayumPortraitRole:
    def __init__(self, role, description):
        self.role = role
        self.description = description

# Create instances for each role
artist = FayumPortraitRole("artist", "The artist meticulously painted the portrait.")
canvas_maker = FayumPortraitRole("canvas maker", "A skilled canvas maker prepared a high-quality canvas.")
pigment_supplier = FayumPortraitRole("pigment supplier", "The pigment supplier provided vibrant colors for the painting.")
patron = FayumPortraitRole("patron", "The patron commissioned the portrait and supported the artist.")

# Build a sentence by adding information about each role
sentence = f"{artist.role.capitalize()}: {artist.description} "
sentence += f"{canvas_maker.role.capitalize()}: {canvas_maker.description} "
sentence += f"{pigment_supplier.role.capitalize()}: {pigment_supplier.description} "
sentence += f"{patron.role.capitalize()}: {patron.description}"

# Print the final sentence
print(sentence)
```

OOP allowed her to model real-world entities (roles) as objects with attributes and behaviors. She combined the role and description for each instance of the class. Her house was decorated with fabrics, including her furniture. Every object, whether a couch, a coffee table, or a bed, was covered with a knitted, decorative protector. The TV set had an opening for a screen, of course. She even wore jewelry made from fabric Soon, more museum visits expanded her interests and affected her interior.

During her Dias Dorados golden days, she lived at Via Hermosa, a beautiful way with her golden days' boyfriend on Linda Vista, with a beautiful view.

HERPETOLOGY
(HIERARCHY AND FUNCTION)
HERPETOLOGIST – PUFU

Reptiles and amphibians were his life. However, he adopted other species to keep them company. For this, he needed extensive research to be done and recorded:

```
class Organism:
    def __init__(self, name):
        self.name = name

class Insect(Organism):
    def __init__(self, name):
        super().__init__(name)

class Amphibian(Organism):
    def __init__(self, name):
        super().__init__(name)

class Reptile(Organism):
    def __init__(self, name):
        super().__init__(name)

# Define organisms
mosquito = Insect("Mosquito")
frog = Amphibian("Frog")
snake = Reptile("Snake")

# Define the food chain
def food_chain(organism):
    if isinstance(organism, Insect):
        return f"{organism.name} is eaten by {frog.name}
(Amphibian)"
    elif isinstance(organism, Amphibian):
        return f"{organism.name} is eaten by {snake.name} (Reptile)"
    elif isinstance(organism, Reptile):
        return f"{organism.name} is the top predator"

# Display the food chain
print(food_chain(mosquito))
print(food_chain(frog))
print(food_chain(snake))
```

After writing a code that defined a simple hierarchy of organisms (Insect, Amphibian, and Reptile) and a function (food_chain) that described the food chain relationships between them (a frog eats a mosquito, and the frog is eaten by a snake, which is the top predator in this food chain), he became the most frequent buyer of pet stores.

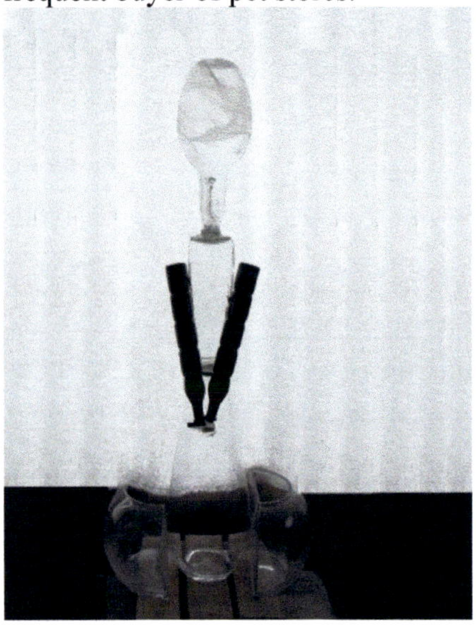

They want to follow up with their study on the symbiosis.

HISTORY OF MUSIC
(MODULARITY)
MUSIC HISTORIAN – RUDOLPH

Rudolph, a music historian, is close to completing his dissertation in music history. Everybody in the orchestra recognizes the quiet sound of his whirling wheelchair as he interviews each member of the Orchestra to build his immense database. He listens to everyone talking about the important figures that influenced each person's artistic style. He looks for a pattern in how musicians express their particular views and opinions. He draws some conclusions about the distinctive and identifiable styles in the artistic medium of music. Media Man Duncan is always ready to help him with data organization with his code, using the matplotlib library to plot a simple sine wave to represent a musical style.

```
import numpy as np
import matplotlib.pyplot as plt

def generate_music_style(style_name):
  time = np.linspace(0, 10, 1000)  # Time axis
  notes = np.sin(2 * np.pi * time)  # Simple sine wave for illustration

  plt.plot(time, notes)
  plt.title(f'{style_name} Music Style')
  plt.xlabel('Time')
  plt.ylabel('Amplitude')
  plt.show()

# Generate different music styles
generate_music_style('Classical')
generate_music_style('Jazz')
generate_music_style('Electronic')
```

As they say, "When you need advice, ask for money; if you need money, ask for some advice," Duncan told him.

HOME ECONOMICS
(LIST AND SORT)
HOME SCHOOLING MASTERS – MAXI, RAM, GIL

They have been happy for years despite their different taxonomies. This wasn't a noticeable difference, but it took lots of their time because they classified and organized things differently. Often, one could hear them replying, "It's in its own place," or "It's in the usual place," "You've put it into a safe place," or "Your hands classify things without any help from your brain." Looking for and searching were two quite important and time-consuming activities at their home. They came to an agreement to categorize and label all objects and to store them in an alphabetical order. Spoons were placed after knives and forks. They followed their Python script that organized household objects alphabetically.

```
def organize_household_objects(objects):
    # Sort the list alphabetically
    objects.sort()

    # Print the organized list
    print("Organized household objects:")
    for obj in objects:
        print(obj)

# Example usage
household_objects = ["Chair", "Table", "Lamp", "Bookshelf",
"Couch"]
organize_household_objects(household_objects)
```

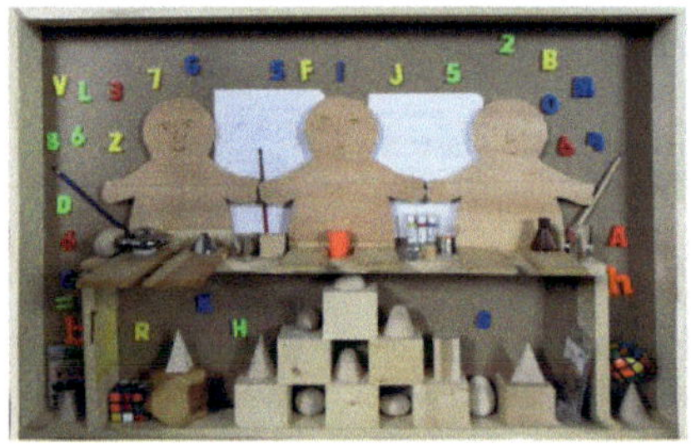

They used the organize_household_objects function that took a list of household objects as an argument, sorted it alphabetically using the sort() method, and then printed the organized list. The problem was all those objects that could be classified as utensils and knives kept disappearing into the workshop area.

This called for more customization.

HOSPITALITY
(DISPLAY STATUS FUNCTION)
HOST – LEOPOLDINE

Everything is closed except for you.

```
def display_status(person):
    if person == invited_guest:
        print(f"Welcome, {invited_guest}! The venue is OPEN.")
    else:
        print("Sorry, the venue is CLOSED.")

# Define the invited guest
invited_guest = input("Enter the invited guest's name: ")

# Test the display_status function
people = ["Alice", "Bob", "Charlie", invited_guest, "Eve"]

for person in people:
    display_status(person)
```

In her code, a person's name was used as an argument and checked if they were the invited guest. If they were, it welcomed them; otherwise, it displayed "CLOSED." The code then tested this function for a list of people, including the invited guest.

She never locked her doors.

HOSTING
(CONDITIONAL STATEMENT)
QUEEN – AMALITA

Queen Amalita had announced her visit. Everyone in the city was aware of her interest in music. The Orchestra members had to face serious preparations for a special performance. Director Gerlost held conferences with the stage designers Jons, designer Kathy, and his accountant Adrian. Everyone agreed the performance should be held in a well-designed, medieval scenario:

```
class Musician:
    def _init_(self, name, preferred_instrument):
      self.name = name
      self.preferred_instrument = preferred_instrument

# Create instances of Musician
musicians = [
   Musician("Sir Trumpet", "Trumpet"),
   Musician("Lady Harp", "Harp"),
   Musician("Knight Drummer", "Drums"),
   Musician("Squire Flute", "Flute"),
]

# Function to match instruments for musicians wearing armor
def match_instruments_for_armor(musicians_with_armor):
   instrument_matches = {}

   for musician in musicians_with_armor:
      if musician.preferred_instrument == "Trumpet":
         instrument_matches[musician.name] = "War Trumpet"
      elif musician.preferred_instrument == "Harp":
         instrument_matches[musician.name] = "Battle Harp"
      elif musician.preferred_instrument == "Drums":
         instrument_matches[musician.name] = "War Drums"
      elif musician.preferred_instrument == "Flute":
      instrument_matches[musician.name] = "Armored Flute"
      else:
         instrument_matches[musician.name] = "No match"


   return instrument_matches

# Example usage
armor_wearing_musicians = [
   Musician("Sir Trumpet", "Trumpet"),
   Musician("Knight Drummer", "Drums"),
]

instrument_matches =
match_instruments_for_armor(armor_wearing_musicians)

# Display the matches
for musician, instrument in instrument_matches.items():
   print(f"{musician} is playing: {instrument}")
```

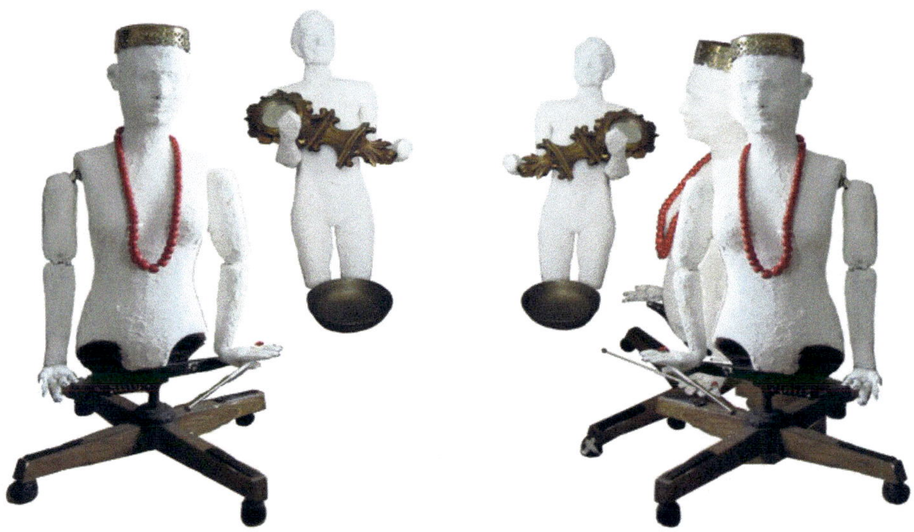

All was medieval that night, including the dinner that was prepared by the Opera Chefs, Frank, Bob, and Marcel, with the keen cooperation of the Nutritionists, Florian, and Fabian. They served an omelet with Italian-flavored olives. Everyone was to wear armor or some battle-related artifacts. Some musicians refused to play in a heavy costume that was not meant for performing music. Think of a battle as some sort of a performance, Gerlost kept saying, but only some volunteers agreed to it. For Gerlost, selecting music that could be played on instruments matching the volunteers to it proved challenging. Gerlost had to hire a composer to create music featuring only selected instruments. In the history of art, some painters choose to limit their palette on purpose, he began, encouraging the Maestro. It was hard to like the composed and played music, but Queen Amalita complimented the group for a contemporary evening. "Quite abstract," added her lady-in-waiting, still holding a mirror for her Queen.

HOUSEWORK
(CLASSES AND DEFINITIONS)
BLUES SINGERS – H AND H

H never accompanied him or did anything music-related. She was just there, but she thought about being a blues singer. Every time they had guests or a specialist coming to fix something in the house, they'd frantically clean the house, arrange their possessions, and desperately put them in boxes, bags, under rugs, or tables. "We can only do desperate cleaning," they kept complaining. After each visit, they'd had their house nicely clean and organized, but finding what they needed was quite a big task. "At least now we live like decent people," she said as soon as the plumber left their premises. H created a simple Python code involving various tasks that helped her organize different rooms.

```
class HouseOrganizer:
    def __init__(self):
        self.house = {}

    def add_item(self, room, item):
        room = room.capitalize()
        if room not in self.house:
            self.house[room] = [item]
        else:
            self.house[room].append(item)

    def view_house(self):
        print("House Organization:")
        for room, items in self.house.items():
            print(f"{room}: {', '.join(items)}")

# Example usage:
organizer = HouseOrganizer()

organizer.add_item("Living Room", "TV")
organizer.add_item("Kitchen", "Dishes")
organizer.add_item("Living Room", "Sofa")
organizer.add_item("Bedroom", "Bed")

organizer.view_house()
```

Their code defined a HouseOrganizer class with methods to add items to different rooms and view the current organization. After that, they customized and extended the code for her specific needs for managing things around the house, starting with the socks and ending with the musical notes.

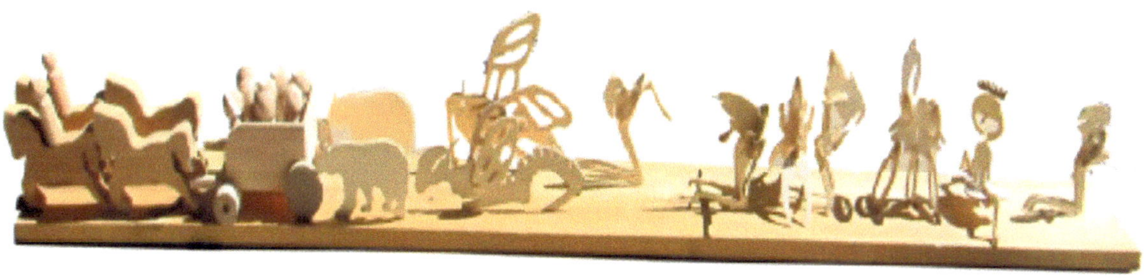

"I've never seen such a messy house as I saw today on the job," said the plumber to his wife the very same evening. "

HOUSING
(METHODS WITHIN A CLASS)
PEACE MAKER – HOL

His biggest invention was a balloon-like house, as those gathering more objects needed more space.

```
class SelfGrowingHouse:
  def __init__(self, initial_size=100):
    self.size = initial_size
    self.rooms = []
    self.needs = []

  def add_room(self, room_type, size):
    self.rooms.append({"type": room_type, "size": size})
    self.size += size

  def analyze_needs(self, *args):
    self.needs.extend(args)

  def grow_based_on_needs(self):
    for need in self.needs:
      if need == "More Space":
        self.size += 50
        print("House expanded to meet the need for more
space.")
      elif need == "Home Office":
        self.add_room("Office", 20)
        print("A new office room added to the house.")
      elif need == "Entertainment":
        self.add_room("Theater", 30)
        print("A home theater added for entertainment
purposes.")

# Creating an instance of SelfGrowingHouse
smart_home = SelfGrowingHouse()

# Analyzing the needs of the residents
smart_home.analyze_needs("More Space", "Home Office",
"Entertainment")

# Growing the house based on the identified needs
smart_home.grow_based_on_needs()

# Displaying the final state of the self-growing house
print(f"Final Size of the House: {smart_home.size} sq. meters")
print("Rooms in the House:")
for room in smart_home.rooms:
  print(f"- {room['type']} ({room['size']} sq. meters)")
```

SelfGrowingHouse class had methods like add_room, analyze_needs, and grow_based_on_needs to simulate the process of a house adding rooms based on needs. This reflected the (OOP) paradigm, where the code was organized around the concept of object-oriented programming and their interactions.

Hol became famous for his houses that expanded according to people's needs.

1	ICHTHYOLOGY – THE STUDY OF FISH (CLASS BASED APPROACH) SCHOOL OF FISH

Aut neca aut necatus eris: murder or you will be murdered.

```
class Organism:
    def __init__(self, name, energy):
        self.name = name
        self.energy = energy

    def eat(self, prey):
        if prey.energy > 0:
            self.energy += prey.energy
            prey.energy = 0
            print(f"{self.name} ate {prey.name} and gained energy!")

    def reproduce(self):
        offspring_energy = self.energy / 2
        self.energy /= 2
        return Organism(self.name + "_offspring", offspring_energy)

# Define organisms in the food chain
phytoplankton = Organism("Phytoplankton", 10)
zooplankton = Organism("Zooplankton", 20)
small_fish = Organism("Small Fish", 30)
big_fish = Organism("Big Fish", 50)

# Simulate the food chain interactions
phytoplankton.reproduce()
zooplankton.eat(phytoplankton)
small_fish.eat(zooplankton)
big_fish.eat(small_fish)

# Display final energy levels
print("Final Energy Levels:")
print(f"{phytoplankton.name}: {phytoplankton.energy}")
print(f"{zooplankton.name}: {zooplankton.energy}")
print(f"{small_fish.name}: {small_fish.energy}")
print(f"{big_fish.name}: {big_fish.energy}")
```

The Organism class represented different entities in the food chain, and it had methods for eating and reproducing. Each organism started with an initial energy level, and when one organism eats another one, it gained the energy of the prey. Reproduction resulted in creating a new organism with half of the parent's energy. (OOP) modeled entities in the ocean's food chain, making it modular and easier to understand.

INDIRECT COMMUNICATION (MODULARIZATION) THE MASK MAKER – CLOUD

Cloud had many faces. In a good way, of course. She could sense emotions, hidden agendas, signals, and open smiles. She had the skills for making masks for the performers. Masks are known as an invaluable tool for communication. Their power comes from adding inconvenient facts to the emotional agenda.

```
import random

def generate_emotion_mask():
    emotions = ['Happy', 'Sad', 'Angry', 'Surprised',
'Confused']
    return random.choice(emotions)

def display_hidden_agenda():
    hidden_agendas = ['Secret Plan', 'Hidden Motive',
'Covert Operation', 'Undercover Scheme']
    return random.choice(hidden_agendas)

def encode_communications():
    signals = ['Encoded Message', 'Hidden Signal',
'Cryptic Communication']
    return random.choice(signals)

def show_open_smile():
    return 'Open Smile'

def generate_mask():
    emotion = generate_emotion_mask()
    agenda = display_hidden_agenda()
    communication = encode_communications()
    smile = show_open_smile()

    mask = f"Emotion: {emotion}, Hidden Agenda:
{agenda}, Communication: {communication}, Smile:
{smile}"
    return mask

def main():
    num_masks = 5

    for _ in range(num_masks):
        mask = generate_mask()
        print(mask)

if __name__ == "__main__":
    main()
```

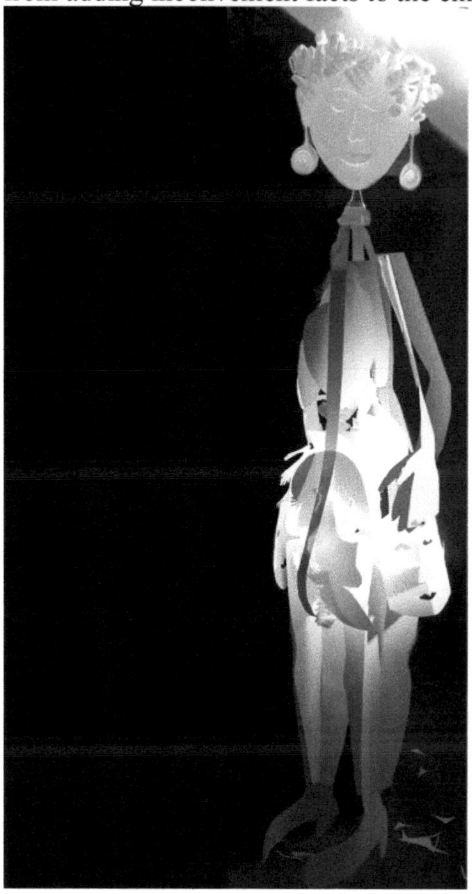

Her code was divided into functions, encapsulating a behavior (generating emotions, displaying hidden agendas, encoding communications, and showing open smiles); each responsible for a pattern aspect. Cloud was expecting the twins: Storm and Thunder.

It is all related; it's all about the circle, she used to say.

INSPIRATION
(ANALYZE – CORRELATION)
SERVER –TIMOTHY

All the writers associated with the orchestra-related business gathered weekly at the coffee shop on the nearest corner. Timothy was their server. In the evening, he kept writing his memoirs.

```
from textblob import TextBlob

def analyze_creativity(sentence):
    # Analyze sentiment using TextBlob
    blob = TextBlob(sentence)
    sentiment_score = blob.sentiment.polarity

    # Determine the correlation between stress and creativity
    if sentiment_score > 0:
        return "Stress is positively correlated with creativity."
    elif sentiment_score < 0:
        return "Stress is negatively correlated with creativity."
    else:
        return "Stress and creativity may not be strongly correlated."

# Example usage
saying = "Stress fertilizes creativity."
result = analyze_creativity(saying)
print(result)
```

The TextBlob library performed sentiment analysis on the given saying. He used the sentiment polarity score to determine the correlation between stress and creativity. Positive scores indicated a positive correlation, negative scores a negative one, and scores around zero suggested a weak correlation.

He had to install the TextBlob library for this code to work, using pip install textblob, which lowered his stress level for three hours.

INSPIRATION BY NATURE (FUNCTION ABSTRACTION)
PLUMBER – AMOS

He lived on the Garden of the Gods Road. Whenever he could, he'd compose. Amos could find inspiration coming from the wind, sounds produced by electrical wires, the tracks and wheels interactions caused by a trolley, or simply from water running down the drain:

```
import pygame
import random
import time

def generate_wind_music():
    # Simulate wind sounds
    notes = ["C", "D", "E", "F", "G", "A", "B"]

    melody = [random.choice(notes) for _ in range(20)]

    return melody

def generate_wire_music():
    # Simulate electrical wire sounds
    notes = ["C#", "D#", "F#", "G#", "A#"]

    melody = [random.choice(notes) for _ in range(15)]

    return melody

def generate_trolley_music():
    # Simulate trolley sounds
    notes = ["C", "E", "G", "B"]

    melody = [random.choice(notes) for _ in range(10)]

    return melody

def generate_water_music():
    # Simulate water drain sounds
    notes = ["D", "F", "A"]

    melody = [random.choice(notes) for _ in range(12)]

    return melody

def play_music(melody):
    # Play the generated melody using pygame
    pygame.init()

    for note in melody:
        pygame.mixer.music.set_volume(0.3)
        pygame.mixer.music.load(f"path/to/sound/{note}.mp3")  # Replace with actual sound files
        pygame.mixer.music.play(1)
        time.sleep(0.5)

    pygame.mixer.music.stop()
    pygame.quit()

if __name__ == "__main__":
    wind_melody = generate_wind_music()
    wire_melody = generate_wire_music()
    trolley_melody = generate_trolley_music()
    water_melody = generate_water_music()

    full_melody = wind_melody + wire_melody + trolley_melody + water_melody

    play_music(full_melody)
```

This way, each type of sound had its own function (generate_wind_music, generate_wire_music, etc.), which abstracted away the details of how the melody is generated for that specific sound.

A collection of his music production grew and gave him a prominent place among living composers. Once, a TV interviewer asked him about it. "I could not find a person talking about my art, who would not finish my sentences, or concur with me by stating that they knew, went to, saw it, or were familiar with, and…"

"Absolutely," interrupted the reporter," I know, they are all always like that," she added.

INSTRUCTIONS
(PROCEDURAL PROGRAMMING PARADIGM)
TRUMPET – TROBA

Troba had a trumpet she did not know how to use. She kept carrying it, hoping someone would teach her, but also, she looked cute with it, as they offered to say in response.

```
def play_trumpet():
    print("Welcome to the world of trumpet playing!")
    print("Follow these steps to play the trumpet:")

    # Step 1
    print("\nStep 1: Assembly")
    print("  - Connect the mouthpiece to the trumpet.")
    print("  - Attach the trumpet valve slides.")

    # Step 2
    print("\nStep 2: Posture")
    print("  - Stand or sit up straight.")
    print("  - Hold the trumpet with your left hand and support it with your right.")

    # Step 3
    print("\nStep 3: Embouchure")
    print("  - Form your embouchure by placing your lips together and blowing air through a small opening.")

    # Step 4
    print("\nStep 4: Finger Placement")
    print("  - Learn the basic fingerings for different notes.")
    print("  - Practice scales to improve finger dexterity.")

    # Step 5
    print("\nStep 5: Breathing")
    print("  - Take deep breaths to support your sound.")
    print("  - Practice controlled and steady breathing.")

  # Step 6
    print("\nStep 6: Start Playing")
    print("  - Start with simple melodies and exercises.")
    print("  - Pay attention to your tone quality and intonation.")

    # Step 7
    print("\nStep 7: Practice Regularly")
    print("  - Dedicate time each day to practice.")
    print("  - Work on challenging passages and gradually increase difficulty.")

    print("\nCongratulations! You are on your way to becoming a great trumpet player.")

# Call the main function to display instructions
play_trumpet()
```

For her birthday, she received an email that defined a function play_trumpet(), and it printed out step-by-step instructions on how to play the trumpet. Each step included a set of sub-steps or guidelines. It was a straightforward way to present information, especially for instructional purposes, and yes, it worked:

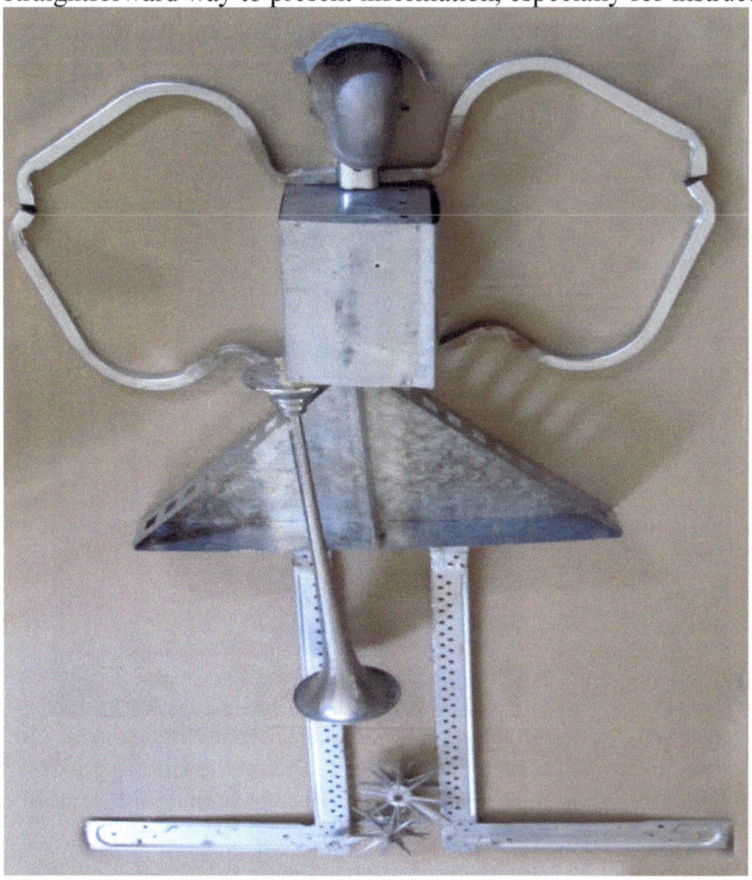

People kept telling her how nice she played instead of how nice she looked.

INTERDISCIPLINARY MUSIC (INHERITANCE)

ORCHESTRATOR – HE

He was born in a city as its fourth-generation inhabitant. This meant that whenever he went, a story was involved. Many houses were connected to several members of the family, their friends, and the friends of the friends. Since he could remember, the only thing he was able to do was make sounds. He even developed his own way of recording his compositions. He was untidy, unorganized, forgetful, and lazy when it came to school or his household, but the book where he kept his compositions was an example of organization, neatness, and order. He started it early in his life and kept reorganizing it, often copying all the content by hand. Soon, a large black cupboard was filled with black-covered books, all used for his compositions. By composition, we may understand a set of notes combined with little sketches, symbols, and words, totally unconnected but copied with an un-human perfection every time he'd be doing a "backup." He had to keep his books for further inspiration. It was not that he did not have a computer, but having an altered version of the score helped him to go deeper into the mood caused by the visual power of the few lines drafted to record the feeling. The most dramatic memory he had, related to his first book, given to him by his father, was all covered with lines and ready to retain his notes. Right after he put his hands on the book, several pages were filled out with new scores. Seeing that, his father asked him to limit himself to one page daily for neatness and quality's sake, as he explained. That's why a separate piece of plain paper, a newspaper fragment, and a big black marker served him best and allowed all the invented symbols to be embodied in his compositions. He was sent to a music school that was the best one in the entire city, which was located across the river. It took him two bus lines to get there; he had to switch buses and follow the bridge, listening to the sound of pillars responding to the bus's movement. He sat in classes to compose under the table, pretending to pay attention to the teacher. The fact was, his attention was true, as he followed the teacher's facial expression. His hand depicted it as a record of the emotions related to the subject. Later, he'd refine the entire composition, create an opening, the body of the composition, and the closing, and he'd surprise the audience with the physics, chemistry, or mathematics-related references one could detect in his creations. Based on his commuting, his recent composition was about building a skyscraper.

```
class Building:
    def __init__(self, name, height, material):
        self.name = name
        self.height = height
        self.material = material

    def display_info(self):
        print(f"{self.name} - {self.height} meters tall, made of {self.material}")

class Skyscraper(Building):
    def __init__(self, name, height, material, num_floors):
        super().__init__(name, height, material)
        self.num_floors = num_floors

    def display_info(self):
        super().display_info()
        print(f"{self.name} has {self.num_floors} floors.")

# Example usage
building = Building("City Hall", 50, "Brick")
building.display_info()

skyscraper = Skyscraper("Sky Tower", 300, "Steel and Glass", 80)
skyscraper.display_info()
```

A base class Building had attributes like name, height, and material. The display_info method printed out information about the building. Then, a derived class, Skyscraper, was inherited from the Building class. It added an additional attribute, num_floors, and overrode the display_info method to include information about the number of floors.

He started singing his memories to his own music that he remembered.

INTERESTS AND SKILLS (ENCAPSULATION AND OOP) MULTIINSTRUMENTALIST – TORVALD

His brain was fast, and so were his hands. He's been majoring in eight instruments and kept developing his skills. Some thought his interest in culture, food, and social drinks was responsible for his talents. They developed a code defining a TalentComparison class with attributes representing different aspects of talents and interests. The compare_talents method encapsulated the logic for calculating an overall talent score and determining its level based on that score.

```
class TalentComparison:
    def __init__(self, instruments, culture_interest, food_interest, drink_interest):
        self.instruments = instruments
        self.culture_interest = culture_interest
        self.food_interest = food_interest
        self.drink_interest = drink_interest

    def compare_talents(self):
        # Calculating an overall talent score based on various factors
        talent_score = len(self.instruments) + self.culture_interest + self.food_interest + self.drink_interest

        # Displaying the talent score
        print(f"Overall Talent Score: {talent_score}")

        # Determining talent level based on the score
        if talent_score >= 15:
            print("You have a high level of talent and diverse interests!")
        elif 10 <= talent_score < 15:
            print("You have a moderate level of talent and diverse interests.")
        else:
            print("You may want to explore and develop your talents and interests further.")

# Example usage:
instruments_played = ["Piano", "Guitar", "Violin"]
culture_interest_level = 3  # on a scale of 1 to 5
food_interest_level = 4  # on a scale of 1 to 5
drink_interest_level = 2  # on a scale of 1 to 5

talent_comparison = TalentComparison(instruments_played, culture_interest_level, food_interest_level, drink_interest_level)
talent_comparison.compare_talents()
```

This way, they could confirm their theory, which made them admire him even more. However, his secret was his.

INTUITION, INSTINCT, SUBCONSCIOUS, SUPERPOWER, CONTACT FROM A MUSE (CLASS AND DEFINITION)

SPACE ANGEL – AGNES

Agnes was called an angel. She took care of the spiritual-art needs of all the orchestra members. She was a muse, a source of inspiration, and a protective guardian to them all. Some of them believed in her. Agnes knew the musicians' strengths and weaknesses, but they could only talk to her in their dreams.

That is why some of them kept falling asleep during the endless organizational meetings.

```
class OrchestraMember:
    def __init__(self, name, instrument):
        self.name = name
        self.instrument = instrument
        self.spiritual_state = "Harmonious"

    def practice(self):
        # Simulate practicing and honing skills
        print(f"{self.name} is practicing {self.instrument}.")

    def perform(self):
        # Simulate a live performance
        print(f"{self.name} is performing with the orchestra.")

class SpiritualCare:
    @staticmethod
    def offer_encouragement(member):
        print(f"Sending positive vibes to {member.name} on their
{member.instrument}.")

    @staticmethod
    def mindful_melodies(member):
        # Implementing the concept of Mindful Melodies
        print(f"{member.name}
 is encouraged to play mindful melodies to enhance spiritual well-being.")
        member.spiritual_state = "Elevated"

# Example usage
violinist = OrchestraMember("Sophia", "Violin")
flutist = OrchestraMember("Elijah", "Flute")

SpiritualCare.offer_encouragement(violinist)
violinist.practice()

SpiritualCare.mindful_melodies(flutist)
flutist.perform()

print(f"{violinist.name}'s spiritual state: {violinist.spiritual_state}")
print(f"{flutist.name}'s spiritual state: {flutist.spiritual_state}")
```

Their code used "Mindful Melodies," which suggested that playing music can be a form of mindfulness and contribute to the spiritual well-being of orchestra members.

INVENTIONS
(RECOGNITION IN IMAGE PROCESSING)
INVENTOR – UGMA

Ugma was a well-known inventor. The first project he developed was a system that, in case of a personal attack, a scream would trigger sending a picture of the violator to the police from their smartphone. With the phone hanging on the person's chest, many attached mirrors on the backs of their hats to see behind them. In his code snippet, he used the opencv and sounddevice libraries for capturing images, sounddevice for recording audio, and Twilio for sending messages.

```
import cv2
import sounddevice as sd
import numpy as np
from scipy.io.wavfile import write
from twilio.rest import Client

# Function to capture image using webcam
def capture_image():
    camera = cv2.VideoCapture(0)
    _, frame = camera.read()
    camera.release()
    return frame

# Function to record audio when a person screams
def record_audio(duration, filename):
    fs = 44100  # Sample rate
    recording = sd.rec(int(duration * fs), samplerate=fs, channels=2,
dtype=np.int16)
    sd.wait()
    write(filename, fs, recording)

# Function to check if there is a scream in the audio
def is_scream(audio_data):
    # Add scream detection logic here
    # You may need a machine learning model or audio analysis
library

# Main function
def main():
    # Set up Twilio API credentials
    account_sid = 'your_account_sid'
    auth_token = 'your_auth_token'
    client = Client(account_sid, auth_token)

    # Capture image
    image = capture_image()

    # Record audio for 5 seconds
    audio_filename = 'scream.wav'
    record_audio(5, audio_filename)

    # Check if there is a scream in the audio
    if is_scream(audio_filename):
        # Send image to the police using Twilio MMS
        message = client.messages.create(
            body='Possible emergency, please check the attached image.',
            from_='your_twilio_number',
            to='police_phone_number'
        )
        print("Message sent to the police!")

if __name__ == "__main__":
    main()
```

It worked for him, but he was accused of disrespecting one's privacy.

INVENTIVENESS
(ASCII – AMERICAN STANDARD CODE FOR INFORMATION INTERCHANGE)
DEVICE ARTIST – KHALID

Khalid could be described with one word: playful. He liked to play with everything. At a restaurant, he was folding paper or throwing paper planes, following them until they landed on someone's plate. Whenever he'd find an object, a discard, or a part of a machine, he'd use it just for playing. His devices were little inventions aimed to add charm to a desk, humor to a dining table, or comfort to a bathtub. Each device had its own unusual, never-seen design. His work was often used as props for theatrical performances. Objects were jumping, swimming, unwinding, walking, talking, playing, looking, making odd sounds, or holding things. Each object had its unique personality combined with its function. His best invention was his self-portrait, making things that made things. While a textual representation might not fully capture the artistic essence, his Python code generated a basic ASCII art self-portrait:

```
def self_portrait():
    portrait = """
    _______
   | o  o |
   |  Δ  |  I'm a creator
   |_____|
   |_______|

   Making things that made things
   """

   print(portrait)

# Display the self-portrait
self_portrait()
```

These representations of his self-portraits had captions "making things that made things."

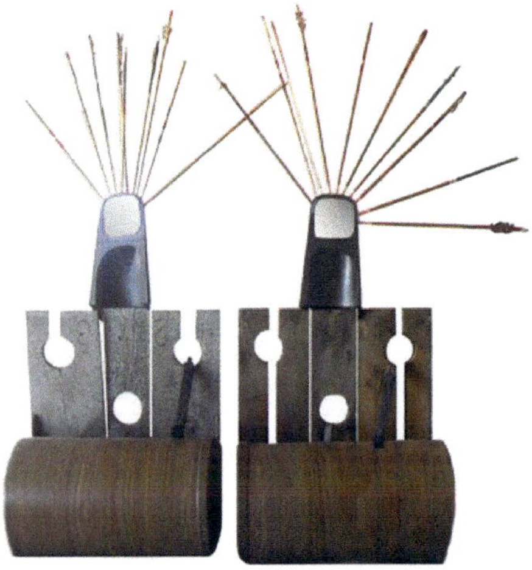

J
JOY
(ITERATION)
ELECTRONIC MUSICIAN – BRIAN

His stories covered only the successes, elations, joys, and pride of people depicted in his novels. His books were thick and well written, as described in major journal reviews, and the level of depiction of joy was above significant. Brian could describe joy so visually that his readers felt they could fly. There was no place for drama, despair, disagreement, gossip, or quarrel.

```
import random

def generate_story(iterations):
  story = ""
  protagonist = "Protagonist"

  for i in range(iterations):
    success_event = random.choice(["achieved a milestone", "overcame a challenge", "celebrated a victory"])
    emotion = random.choice(["elation", "joy", "pride"])
    time_passage = random.choice(["Later that day", "In the following weeks", "As time went on"])

    story += f"{protagonist} {success_event} with {emotion}. {time_passage}, {protagonist} felt a deep sense of {emotion}.\n"

  return story

# Generate and print 3 different success stories with 5 iterations each
for _ in range(3):
  story_iterations = 5
  success_story = generate_story(story_iterations)
  print("\nSuccess Story:")
  print(success_story)
```

His script defined a function generate_story that took the number of iterations as an argument and constructed a story based on random success events, emotions, and time passages to simulate the development or progression of each story. It then generated and printed three success stories, each with 5 iterations. He then modified the content or structure and the number of iterations to address the options:

The Triumph of Teamwork: A group of diverse individuals collaborate to overcome obstacles and celebrate their collective success.
Innovative Endeavors: Inventors go through multiple iterations of their creation, facing setbacks but ultimately achieving a groundbreaking invention that transforms lives.
From Novice to Expert: A person starts with a new skill or hobby, experiences the joy of progress through iterative learning, and eventually becomes a master in their field.
Entrepreneurial Victory: A startup founder navigates the ups and downs of building a business, adapting their strategy through iterations, and achieving success against all odds.
Personal Growth Through Challenges: A character faces personal challenges, undergoes self-improvement through iterative efforts, and emerges victorious, filled with newfound joy and pride.
Artistic Triumph: An artist experiments with self-imposed challenges, persevering through iterative refinement for a celebrated masterpiece.
Educational Milestones: Students face academic challenges, learn from each experience, and eventually achieve academic success, bringing pride to themselves and their supporters.
Community Transformation: A community comes together for a common goal, working through iterative processes to overcome issues, resulting in positive transformation and collective pride.
Athletic Journey: An athlete undergoes rigorous training and faces defeats but continually refines their skills through iterations, ultimately achieving victory in a significant competition.
Scientific Breakthrough: A scientist conducts experiments, faces failures, and learns from each iteration, eventually making a groundbreaking discovery that brings joy and pride to the scientific community.
Eco-Friendly Initiative: A group of environmental activists is working on an iterative plan to promote ecological balance, and their efforts have led to a successful, eco-friendly initiative benefiting the community.
Family Bond Strengthened: A family faces challenges, communicates openly, and works through their issues, resulting in a joyful family.

He thought he was the happiest writer alive, and so were his few readers.

JUDGING
(CRITERIA)
JURORS – AARON, AL, JEN, KIRK, AND TODD

There was a problem with the non-sequential judging. The jurors could never agree, so the opera needed many of them. Each one had different criteria, beliefs, and preferences. Finally, they discovered a tactic to be fair. Each one was submitting their judging based on one of the categories, respectively: Quality of Sound, Flow and Melody, Individuality, Technical Proficiency, Interpretation and Vision, Innovation versus Tradition, Tempo, Pitch, Volume, and Variation. The scores still looked inconsistent. Judging music is subjective, and different criteria can be considered depending on the context. Jen wrote a Python code that outlines some common criteria for evaluating music:

```
class MusicJudge:
    def __init__(self, music):
        self.music = music

    def evaluate(self):
        print("Judging Criteria for Music:")
        print("--------------------------")
        self.evaluate_rhythm()
        self.evaluate_melody()
        self.evaluate_harmony()
        self.evaluate_lyrics()
        self.evaluate_emotion()

    def evaluate_rhythm(self):
        print("1. Rhythm: Assessing the timing, tempo, and overall groove.")
    def evaluate_harmony(self):
        print("3. Harmony: Considering the chord progressions
and harmonic complexity.")

# Example usage def evaluate_lyrics(self):
        print("4. Lyrics: Evaluating the quality of the song's lyrics,
storytelling, and message.")

    def evaluate_emotion(self):
        print("5. Emotion: Gauging the emotional impact and
expression conveyed by the music.")

song = "Wonderful Song"
judge = MusicJudge(song)
judge.evaluate()
```

The MusicJudge class took a music title as input and provided a basic evaluation based on five criteria: Rhythm, Melody, Harmony, Lyrics, and Emotion. Each criterion was evaluated with a brief description. Kirk wrote a code to evaluate the judges based on expertise, consistency, and fairness criteria.

```
class MusicJudge:
    def __init__(self, name):
        self.name = name
        self.expertise = 0
        self.consistency = 0
        self.fairness = 0

    def evaluate(self):
        print(f"Evaluating Judge {self.name}:")
        print("----------------------------")
        self.evaluate_expertise()
        self.evaluate_consistency()
        self.evaluate_fairness()

    def evaluate_expertise(self):
        self.expertise = 8  # Assume a score out of 10
        print(f"1. Expertise: Judge {self.name} has a expertise score of
{self.expertise}/10.")
    def evaluate_consistency(self):
        self.consistency = 9  # Assume a score out of 10

print(f"2. Consistency: Judge {self.name} has a consistency score of
{self.consistency}/10.")

    def evaluate_fairness(self):
        self.fairness = 7  # Assume a score out of 10
        print(f"3. Fairness: Judge {self.name} has a fairness score of
{self.fairness}/10.")

# Example usage
judge1 = MusicJudge("Alice")
judge2 = MusicJudge("Bob")

judge1.evaluate()
print("\n")
judge2.evaluate()
```

K	KINESIOLOGY – STUDY OF HUMAN MOVEMENT AND POSTURE (BASIC 3D GRAPHICS RENDERING) ROLLER SKATER – NU

Nu was commuting to his work that way, but since it was far away, he became very good at skating. He never thought about competing, though. It was just some mode of transportation with performing some figures when traffic was heavy, he used to explain.

```
import pygame
import sys

# Initialize Pygame
pygame.init()

# Set up display
width, height = 800, 600
screen = pygame.display.set_mode((width, height))
pygame.display.set_caption("Skating Figures")

# Define colors
white = (255, 255, 255)
black = (0, 0, 0)

# Set initial position
x, y = width // 2, height // 2
```

```
# Main game loop
while True:
    for event in pygame.event.get():
        if event.type == pygame.QUIT:
            pygame.quit()
            sys.exit()

    # Clear the screen
    screen.fill(white)

    # Draw skater (just a circle for simplicity)
    pygame.draw.circle(screen, black, (x, y), 20)

    # Update display
    pygame.display.flip()

    # Control speed of the simulation
    pygame.time.Clock().tick(60)
```

He used the Pygame library to create a window, draw a simple skater (as a circle), and update the display. His basic drawing functions helped him create 2D graphics to enhance and modify his simulation.

Soon, a crowd was waiting for him daily when he went to work when he was more energetic and returned from work when he was tired but relaxed. Some wanted to compare his display.

L LANGUAGE ACQUISITION (DATA STRUCTURES - DICTIONARY) PICCOLO – NELSON

Nelson's career involved acting and directing, and then he started to produce films. He moved to Toy City. All was new around him. He had a tattoo on his wrist that spelled out "Reminder." He often wore an "I Live Here" t-shirt. When he started learning a new language, he had to do it differently at each new place he moved to. Tired of learning this way, he took an exam to be permitted to the next advanced beginner level for those who start and stop frequently. Since he did not pass the test, he made a movie about learning a new language:

```
def learn_new_language(language, resources):
    print(f"Welcome to the journey of learning {language}!")

    # Displaying recommended learning resources
    print("\nRecommended Learning Resources:")
    for resource in resources:
        print(f"- {resource}")

    # Setting up a study plan
    study_plan = {
        'Week 1': 'Basic syntax and language fundamentals',
        'Week 2': 'Data types and basic operations',
        'Week 3': 'Control flow and loops',
        'Week 4': 'Functions and modular programming',
        'Week 5': 'Working with data structures',
        'Week 6': 'Advanced topics and projects'
    }

    # Displaying the study plan
    print("\nStudy Plan:")
    for week, topic in study_plan.items():
        print(f"{week}: {topic}")

    # Encouraging hands-on practice
    print("\nHands-on Practice:")
    print("Start coding small projects and challenges to reinforce your learning.")

if __name__ == "__main__":
    language_to_learn = "Python"
    learning_resources = ["Online tutorials", "Coding exercises", "Documentation"]
```

The movie became so popular that he had to relocate and start learning another language with moviemaking in his plans.

LAW
(ENCAPSULATION)
MUSIC COPYIST – PABLO

His compositions were considered good, but not his own. He felt good about them, so he kept working. He divided his world between people who loved or despised him. The first group believed there was nothing wrong with inspiration, while others would stop at nothing to end his actions.
Determining if a music composition violates copyright laws can involve legal considerations, but Python code cannot accurately assess legal aspects. However, using a basic fingerprinting approach, the judges created a simple example to check for similarities between the two compositions.

```
class MusicComposition:
    def __init__(self, title, notes):
        self.title = title
        self.notes = notes

    def create_fingerprint(self):
        # Simple fingerprinting by converting notes to a string
        return str(self.notes)

def check_similarity(composition1, composition2):
    fingerprint1 = composition1.create_fingerprint()
    fingerprint2 = composition2.create_fingerprint()

    if fingerprint1 == fingerprint2:
        print("These compositions are identical or very similar.")
    else:
        print("These compositions are different.")

# Example usage:
composition1 = MusicComposition("Composition 1", "CDEFGABC")
composition2 = MusicComposition("Composition 2", "CDEFGABC")

check_similarity(composition1, composition2)
```

The MusicComposition class encapsulated the details of his composition, its title, and notes. The create_fingerprint method encapsulated the logic for creating a simple fingerprint based on the notes.

Pablo would not change even when imprisoned. He did not fit there, anyway. After studying his rights, he demanded a loudspeaker brought to his cell so all his inmates could hear his new music. They gave him a computer with music software and a good set of speakers. There was already a lyric writer and a singing coach, so his mates could join in and give the guardians a break. Soon, Pablo was released, as someone noticed that his sentence was based on a simplified representation and should not have happened.

Leadership (Dictionaries)

Office Manager – Cork

He was considered a good one but too controlling. He would not let his workers eat in their cubicles beyond their lunch break, make personal phone calls when on duty, or discuss what their eyes spotted at a given moment. He demanded totally empty desks, too. They felt like he was pinning them to their assigned places. Other than that, he was considered a good manager.

```
Def suggest_admin_qualities(administrator_type):
    """"Suggest qualities of a good administrator based on data.""""
    Admin_qualities = {
        "manager": ["leadership", "organization", "communication"],
        "school_admin": ["educational expertise", "communication",
"problem-solving"],
        "system_admin": ["technical skills", "troubleshooting",
"attention to detail"]
    }

    if administrator_type in admin_qualities:
        qualities = admin_qualities[administrator_type]
        print(f"To be a good {administrator_type}, consider the
following qualities:")
        for quality in qualities:
            print(f"- {quality}")
    else:
        print("Unknown administrator type. Unable to suggest
qualities.")

if __name__ == "__main__":
    # Suggest qualities for different types of administrators
    suggest_admin_qualities("manager")
    suggest_admin_qualities("school_admin")
    suggest_admin_qualities("system_admin")
```

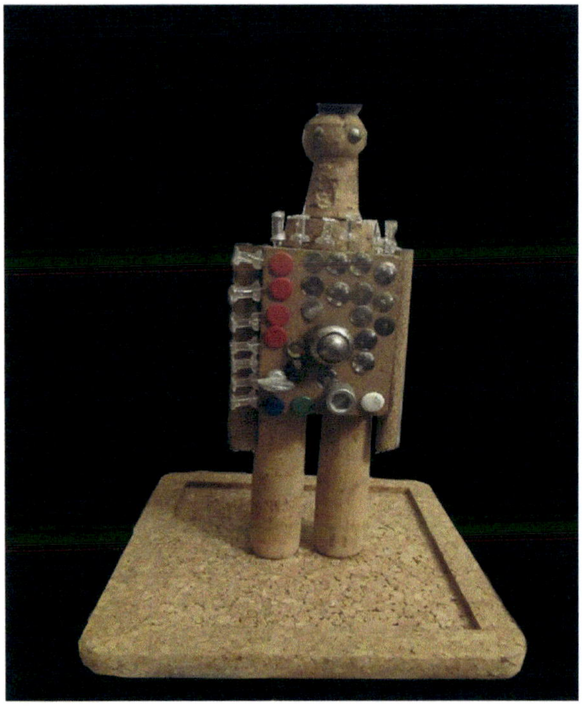

His Dictionaries for representing data in key-value pairs helped him stay organized and retrieve qualities based on administrator types. However, he felt he was the best one.

LIGHTS IN MUSIC
(COMMENTS EXPLAINING DETAILS)
THE ROCKMEN – BIROL, VINOD, AND JAVI

They all loved going to the rock music concerts. Especially those filled with lights and more traveling lights pulsating toward the rhythms of the music played and creating shadows that were even more powerful than the lights and music. ''Why do we like the lights so much?'' Birol once asked. ''It must be related to the Stonehenge, which has been going through daily time changes for so many ages,'' said Javi.

```
Class Stonehenge:
  def __init__(self):
    self.current_time = 0  # Represented in hours, ranging from 0 to 23

  def set_current_time(self, hour):
    if 0 <= hour <= 23:
      self.current_time = hour
      print(f"Setting Stonehenge time to {hour}:00.")
    else:
      print("Invalid hour. Please set a time between 0 and 23.")

  def explain_daily_time_changes(self):
    print("Stonehenge, a prehistoric monument in England, is known for its alignment with the sun.")
    print("The arrangement of stones allows for interesting observations related to daily time changes.")

    # Stonehenge is aligned with the sunrise during the summer solstice
    if 4 <= self.current_time <= 6:
      print("During the summer solstice, the sun aligns with the Heel Stone, marking the longest day of the year.")
    # Stonehenge is aligned with the sunset during the winter solstice
    elif 15 <= self.current_time <= 17:
      print("During the winter solstice, the sun aligns with the Trilithon, marking the shortest day of the year.")
    else:
      print("Stonehenge's alignment with the sun provides a unique connection to the changing seasons.")

# Example Usage:
stonehenge = Stonehenge()

# Set Stonehenge time to simulate different times of the day
stonehenge.set_current_time(8)
stonehenge.explain_daily_time_changes()

stonehenge.set_current_time(16)
stonehenge.explain_daily_time_changes()

stonehenge.set_current_time(20)
stonehenge.explain_daily_time_changes()
```

The Stonehenge class included a method (explain_daily_time_changes) that provides information about Stonehenge's alignment with the sun during different times of the day, emphasizing its significance during the summer and winter solstices. The code also included a method (set_current_time) to simulate different times of the day for explanation purposes.

They still preferred the shadows, though. They were making them feel safer.

LEISURE TIME – NATURE (STRING FORMATTING)

PASTA MAKER – SIL

He organized their civilized camping trip to Nature. They planned it all. They bought some firewood and charcoal briquets at the nearest gas station to build a fire near the lake. They opened their bottled water. They lit their battery-charged lamps. They invited participants.

```
class CivilizedPicnic:
    def __init__(self, event_name):
        self.event_name = event_name

    def send_invitation(self, participants):
        print(f"Dear {', '.join(participants)},\n"
              f"You are cordially invited to the {self.event_name}.\n"
              "Please join us for an afternoon of refined conversation, gourmet cuisine, and sophisticated leisure.\n"
              "Dress code: Smart Casual.\n"
              "Looking forward to your esteemed presence!\n"
              "Sincerely,\n"
              "The Organizers")

# Creating an instance of CivilizedPicnic
picnic_event = CivilizedPicnic("Civilized Picnic Gathering")

# Sending invitations to participants
participants_list = ["Alice", "Bob", "Charlie", "Diana"]
picnic_event.send_invitation(participants_list)
```

The send_invitation method used f-strings to dynamically create the invitation message by incorporating the event name and the list of participants. String formatting is a powerful concept in Python that allows the creation of dynamic and readable strings by embedding expressions inside string literals.

Everyone was so busy checking their email that no one could notice their canned food spilling all over a pressed charcoal grill.

LIFESTYLE
(CONDITIONAL STATEMENTS)
NIGHT CLUB OWNER – ROSCOE

He owned the club. The nightclub. This meant the club was open during the night. The entire night. Not during the day. During the day, he liked to sleep after working at night. Late at night.

```
import datetime

def get_time():
   return datetime.datetime.now().time()

def is_daytime():
   current_time = get_time()
   return current_time >= datetime.time(6, 0) and current_time < datetime.time(18, 0)

def main():
   if is_daytime():
      print(“It’s daytime!”)
   else:
      print(“It’s nighttime!”)

if __name__ == “__main__”:
   main()
```

Still saving some time for staying playful.

LIGHTING (MODULATION FACTOR) LASERS – KIMA

Some concerts need lasers to enhance the overall experience. The music played determines the color of the laser set. For her, it worked best when combined with certain lights. Her trademark was creating a moiré pattern out of overlapping lights. Right before it was played, they could anticipate the chord, the tune, and the balance of the forces. Her trick was that she could enliven the lights by pointing in the direction they'd shoot with her fingers. When she wanted the moiré effects to be present, she'd open both hands and make her five fingers overlap with those of the other hand. One could say that her dance or her performance created the whole lighting or laser design. Her body was becoming a tool, an instrument, or a device, causing the whole aura, atmosphere, and exaltation, sometimes even panic among the audience.

```
Import numpy as np
import matplotlib.pyplot as plt

def generate_moire_pattern(crossed_fingers):
    # Simulate laser light with crossed fingers modifying it
    if crossed_fingers:
        modulation_factor = 5.0
    else:
        modulation_factor = 1.0

    # Generate a grid for moiré pattern
    x, y = np.meshgrid(np.linspace(0, 4 * np.pi, 400), np.linspace(0, 4 * np.pi, 400))
    z = np.sin(modulation_factor * x) + np.sin(modulation_factor * y)

    return x, y, z

def plot_moire_pattern(x, y, z):
    plt.figure(figsize=(8, 8))
    plt.imshow(z, cmap='viridis', extent=(0, 4 * np.pi, 0, 4 * np.pi))
    plt.title("Moiré Pattern")
    plt.colorbar()
    plt.show()

# Example usage:
crossed_fingers = True
x, y, z = generate_moire_pattern(crossed_fingers)
plot_moire_pattern(x, y, z)
```

Her design worked differently when she worked indoors than when she was covering the space surrounding an outdoor stage.

The beams she shot seemed to reach the stars. Therefore, she'd never agree to design on cloudy nights.

LINGUISTICS – THE STUDY OF LANGUAGE (GENERATION USING A FUNCTION FROM A MODULE) UKULELE – LITTLE MUR

Mur was puny, her instrument even tinier. Every piece of clothing she ever received would not fit well on her. It was too teensy. "You are minuscule size," they'd say when offering her their small gifts. Anyway, her playing her bitsy instrument made her famous. Nobody, big or teeny, could play it that way. However, her audience was petite. They were coming with some pint-sized cans to drink during her trifling performances. Her compositions were wee-sized but quite good, they'd say. She kept playing in a pocket-size amphitheater. A member of the audience started clapping to the rhythm of her yea big song with his microscopic hands. The negligible response could be heard. A miniature part of the audience grabbed a Lilliputian member and slightly sang to the music. There was a bitty of romance and a trifling sense of humor. Perhaps teensy-weensy of joy. A minute of a break was interrupted by another music set, this time with a minuscular effect, so they had to start with their itsy-bitsy dancing. There was a need for mini music to dance to, so someone improvised a midget song, still with little clapping. Someone started diminutive leg pounding, followed by infinitesimal jumping up and down—just a bit. A wee voice added its pocket flavor. A minikin woman in a mini skirt started with her minimum-wage voice, but another one added an itty-bitty soprano. That started a new round of low-pitched other voices and more minuscular clapping, followed by an almost silent wee song. Since the songs did not match, organization was called for. Some unnoticed presence appeared too tiny to organize them all. A slight sound of an undermined thunderstorm could be heard in a teensy-weensy distance. Some diminutive decisions had to be made. They all went to hide under a small plant. Negligible raindrops fall on the plant, making some bitty sounds. Some petite drops went under the leaf, causing some miniature panic. A cent-sized puddle was formed. Oh, insignificant me, he said, how wet. Luckily, he came and took all the insects in.
Mur used itertools to generate all possible permutations of the letters in the word "small."

```
From itertools import permutations


def generate_permutations(word):
    permutations_list = [''.join(p) for p in permutations(word)]
    return permutations_list

# Example usage
word = "small"
all_permutations = generate_permutations(word)

# Print all permutations
for permutation in all_permutations:
    print(permutation)
```

The function returned all possible permutations of a given iterable (the letters in the word "small"). The generate_permutations function then converted the permutations into a list of strings and returned the list. Even though the method did not include repeated permutations, if there were repeated letters in the word, for unique permutations, she could convert the list to a set before printing or using it further.

LITERARY CONCEPTS (FUNCTIONS OR CLASSES) ANIMAL FAIRY – BLANC

Blanc was a fairy, and she took care of all the animals. Therefore, they liked her so much.
Blanc was a writer, a good one, she taught.
She used nouns to describe a word,
Word she used as a pronoun instead of a noun,
and an adjective, which describes a noun,
She was using verbs to describe an action of a verb,
And a conjunction to join two sentences together.
She used a preposition to describe the relationship between a pronoun and a noun.
And the interjection, which is a word thrown to express feeling.
She based her stories on the code he wrote:

```
        self.title = title
        self.protagonist = protagonist
        self.antagonist = antagonist
        self.setting = setting
        self.climax = climax
        self.resolution = resolution

    def introduce_characters(self):
        print(f"The story revolves around {self.protagonist} and
{self.antagonist}.")

    def set_the_scene(self):
        print(f"The story is set in {self.setting}.")

    def build_up(self):
        print("The plot thickens as the characters face various
challenges.")

    def reach_climax(self):
        print(f"The story reaches its climax: {self.climax}.")

    def resolve_conflict(self):
        print(f"The conflict is resolved, and the story concludes:
{self.resolution}.")

# Example usage
my_story = StoryStructure(
    "The Epic Adventure",
    "Hero",
    "Villain",
    "Fantasy Kingdom",
    "Epic Battle",
    "Happily Ever After"
)

my_story.introduce_characters()
my_story.set_the_scene()
my_story.build_up()
my_story.reach_climax()
my_story.resolve_conflict()
```

In the template she created, the StoryStructure class represented the story's overall structure. Each instance of this class was a specific story with its title, characters, setting, climax, and resolution. The class stood for different stages of the story, such as introducing characters, setting the scene, building up the plot, reaching the climax, and resolving the conflict. After that, she customized and expanded upon this structure based on each story's specific elements and complexity.
This is how good of a writer she was.

LITERATURE
(ENCAPSULATION)
OPERETTA LIBRETTO WRITERS – ALAN AND HENRY

Alan and Henry always worked together. They also collaborated with the composer. They had totally different beliefs and styles. Alan liked to look at the bright side of each issue, enjoyed everything, and always seemed happy. Henry was called Mr. Likable. He was often cynical with his opinions and was funny but in a nasty way. This worked perfectly for their librettos composing. They could establish some common ground for writing a libretto for an opera, operetta, oratorio, or musical. Their spoken passages and the lyrics to the musical numbers triggered the joy and drama so expected from the audience. Alan, a romantic type, always looked for a happy ending.

```
class Opera:
    def __init__(self, title, composer):
        self.title = title
        self.composer = composer
        self.libretto = None
        self.music = None

    def set_libretto(self, libretto):
        self.libretto = libretto

    def set_music(self, music):
        self.music = music

    def perform(self):
        if self.libretto is not None and self.music is not None:
            print(f"Performing {self.title} composed by
{self.composer}...")
            print(f"Libretto: {self.libretto}")
            print(f"Music: {self.music}")
        else:
            print("Cannot perform. Libretto or music is missing.")

# Example usage
opera = Opera("Carmen", "Georges Bizet")
opera.set_libretto("A passionate love story in Seville.")
opera.set_music("Lively and dramatic orchestral compositions.")

opera.perform()
```

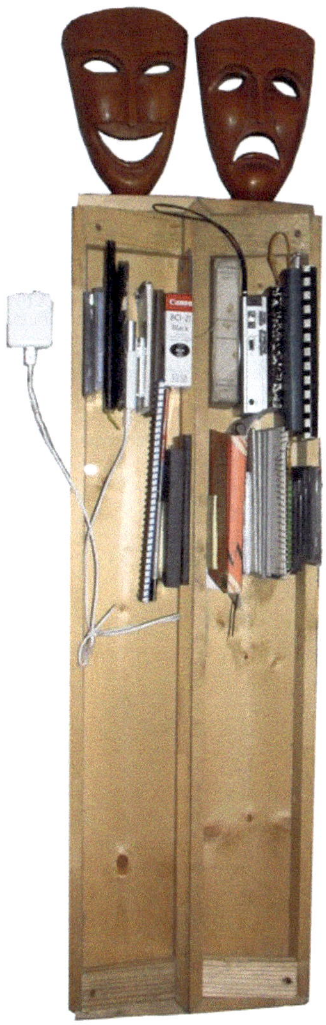

In writing librettos, the Opera class encapsulated the details of an opera, including its title, composer, libretto, and music. The methods set_libretto and set_music allowed them to associate a libretto and music with the opera. The perform method then printed out the details of the opera if both libretto and music were set.

Perhaps Alan's bitter philosophy was caused by the fact that he felt unsatisfied. The composer of the musical score to an opera or operetta was usually given the lion's share of credit for his work, and the libretto writer was only mentioned in a footnote. It frustrated Alan greatly as he searched for more romantic explanations for why things worked or did not work out. Yet, they could agree on one thing: balance was so effective in their work.

LOGIC
(CONDITIONAL STATEMENT)
KEYNOTE SPEAKER – OBSIDIAN

He worked with contrasts: black and white, smooth and rough, geometric and organic or amorphous, rural and city-based, digital and analog until he shifted into black, grey, and white, smooth, textured, and rough, geometric, and symmetric, organic, or amorphous, rural, city-based, or suburban, digital, tactile, and analog. He started thinking about how we group ideas. If an element has both "black" and "white" characteristics, it is categorized into "Dual Group 1." If an element has both "smooth" and "rough" characteristics, it is categorized into "Dual Group 2." If an element has "black" or "grey" characteristics, it is categorized into "Group 1" of the three-step groups. He wrote a code in Python that organized dual organization and contrasts it with three step-based groups:

```
class Element:
    def __init__(self, name, characteristics):
        self.name = name
        self.characteristics = characteristics

def organize_elements(elements):
    dual_groups = {"Dual Group 1": [], "Dual Group 2": []}
    three_step_groups = {"Group 1": [], "Group 2": [], "Group 3": []}

    for element in elements:
        if "black" in element.characteristics and "white" in
element.characteristics:
            dual_groups["Dual Group 1"].append(element)
        elif "smooth" in element.characteristics and "rough" in
element.characteristics:
            dual_groups["Dual Group 2"].append(element)

        # Three-step groups
        if "black" in element.characteristics or "grey" in
element.characteristics:
            three_step_groups["Group 1"].append(element)
        elif "smooth" in element.characteristics or "textured" in
element.characteristics:
            three_step_groups["Group 2"].append(element)
        elif "geometric" in element.characteristics or "symmetric" in
element.characteristics:
            three_step_groups["Group 3"].append(element)

    return dual_groups, three_step_groups

# Example elements
element1 = Element("Element1", ["black", "smooth", "geometric"])
element2 = Element("Element2", ["white", "rough", "organic"])
element3 = Element("Element3", ["grey", "textured", "symmetric"])
element4 = Element("Element4", ["black", "smooth", "organic"])

elements = [element1, element2, element3, element4]

dual_groups, three_step_groups = organize_elements(elements)

print("Dual Groups:")
for group, elements in dual_groups.items():
    print(f"{group}: {[element.name for element in elements]}")

print("\nThree-step Groups:")
for group, elements in three_step_groups.items():
    print(f"{group}: {[element.name for element in elements]}")
```

Conditional statements are essential for implementing logic, branching, and control flow in algorithms, making them a key element in various computer science applications.

Oh, how we enjoy logic explained behind concepts.

M	MAGIC (RANDOM NUMBER GENERATION) MAGICIAN – OLEG

He performed on many occasions at various locations. He often entertained the birthday boys and girls, the office party members, or the churchgoers. The scope of his surprises was unlimited because he could combine magic tricks and modify them as needed for each part of his performances. He kept his belongings in his oversized black hat. Many wondered how everything would fit there and how he managed to carry such a load on his already ideas-filled head and remain tall and straightened up. Would a rabbit coexist peacefully with a doe in that darkness? He had one answer: he was a magician.

```
import random

def magic_trick():
    print("Welcome to the Magic Number Guessing Trick!")
    print("Think of a number between 1 and 10 in your mind.")

    input("Press Enter when you are ready...")

    # Generate a random guess
    magic_number = random.randint(1, 10)

    print(f"\nIs your magic number {magic_number}?")

# Example of usage
magic_trick()
```

The random module he used to generate a random number (magic_number) within a specified range. This added an element of unpredictability to the magic trick, making it seem as if the program was magically guessing the user's number. This concept of randomness is commonly used in various applications, games, and simulations to introduce variability and surprise.

Yes, everybody was surprised. The most surprised person was the Magician, who had a code that worked.

MANAGEMENT
(STRUCTURE MANIPULATION)
TV CREW – MIL, HA, GI, AND TR

All they thought they had to do was be there at the right time until they saw another crew's working style. Using dictionaries to represent crew members and their roles and a basic scheduling algorithm, they created a TVCrewManager class that manages TV crew members. Crew members were stored in a dictionary where the key was the crew member's name, and the value was their role. The add_crew_member method added crew members, the assign_crew_to_show method assigned crew members to a show, and the schedule_show method scheduled the show.

```
class TVCrewManager:
    def __init__(self):
        self.crew_members = {}

    def add_crew_member(self, name, role):
        self.crew_members[name] = role

    def assign_crew_to_show(self, show_name, crew_names):
        print(f"\nAssigning crew to {show_name}:")

        for name in crew_names:
            role = self.crew_members.get(name)
            if role:
                print(f"{name} - {role}")
            else:
                print(f"{name} - Role not specified")

    def schedule_show(self, show_name, date, time):
        print(f"\nScheduling {show_name} for {date} at {time}")
```

```
# Example usage
crew_manager = TVCrewManager()

# Add crew members
crew_manager.add_crew_member("Mil", "Producer")
crew_manager.add_crew_member("Ha", "Director")
crew_manager.add_crew_member("Gi", "Camera Operator")
crew_manager.add_crew_member("Tr", "Sound Engineer")

# Assign crew to a show
crew_manager.assign_crew_to_show("News Hour", ["Alice", "Bob",
"Charlie", "David"])

# Schedule the show
crew_manager.schedule_show("News Hour", "2025-01-15",
"20:00")
```

The secret was the manipulation of dictionaries to store and retrieve information about crew members and their roles that manage, assign, and schedule correctly.

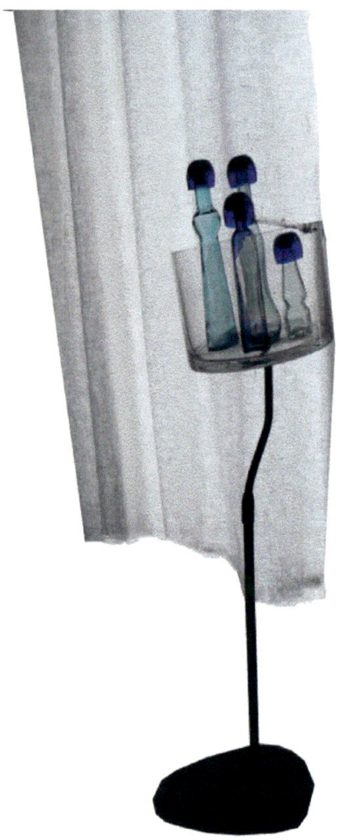

MARKETING
(OBJECT-ORIENTED PROGRAMMING (OOP) WITH CLASSES AND OBJECTS)
PRESENTER – SHO

His work was to present ideas created by other people. He excelled at it as he communicated well and understood the major concepts behind each invention. All went well until he was given a bird robot that was talking.

```
class BirdRobot:
    def __init__(self, name):
        self.name = name

    def present(self):
        print(f"Hello, I'm {self.name}, the talking bird robot. Ask me anything!")

# Example usage
bird_robot = BirdRobot("RoboBird")
bird_robot.present()
```

A class (BirdRobot) and an object instantiation defined the properties and behavior of the bird robot, and the object (bird_robot) was created based on this class to showcase the Bird-robot's presentation.

And a presentation it was!

MATERIAL SCIENCE
(A LIST)
MUSIC SAW – SETH

Seth used to work for a wood shop. He knew about types of wood, tools, and techniques. He could briefly look at the wood grain and tell what kind of tree it came from. He could estimate how old each tree was and what happened on its way. The tools were made of metal, so brutal and so precise. Seth always examined sculptures while walking by the library, parks, or central locations where the city placed bronze sculptures made by local enthusiasts from the 1% tax fund for the arts. On his way, he could see a life-size metal figure of a boy who just caught a fish or a realistic statue of a teacher reading a book to a group of children. If something happens to the planet, he thought, some beings capable of what we call thinking would analyze the remains of our culture, and they might only find these sculptures. The wooden ones would be gone, along with all sorts of artifacts from our people's creative endeavors.

In his code, Seth listed materials that can survive and be seen on the planet affected by disasters.

```
def survive_materials():
  # List of materials that can survive disasters
  materials = ["steel", "concrete", "glass", "titanium", "stone"]

  # Print the list of materials
  print("Materials that can survive disasters:")
  for material in materials:
    print(material)

# Calling the function to display the materials
survive_materials()
```

The materials variable was a list that contained different materials. The for loop was used to iterate over the elements of the list and print each material.

There will be a pile of Teflon and some 3D printing parts, of course, he thought.

He switched to creating Teflon-based and 3D-printed sculptures.

MATHEMATICS
(FILE SYSTEM INTERACTION)
MUSIC LIBRARIAN – STAN

When stranded on a deserted island, Stan found big, brown F-G volumes of an encyclopedia. He wanted to count all the entries in those volumes.

```
import os
t
def estimate_entries(directory_path, volume_names):
    total_entries = 0

    for volume in volume_names:
        volume_path = os.path.join(directory_path, volume)
        if os.path.exists(volume_path):
            entries = len(os.listdir(volume_path))
            total_entries += entries
            print(f"Volume {volume}: {entries} entries")

    print(f"Total entries in {', '.join(volume_names)}: {total_entries}")

# Example usage
encyclopedia_directory = "/path/to/encyclopedia"
volume_list = ['F', 'G']
estimate_entries(encyclopedia_directory, volume_list)
```

For that, he used the os module to navigate file system interaction, where he leveraged functions from the os module to check if the volumes exist and count the number of entries within each volume.
He wanted to replace "/path/to/encyclopedia" with the actual path to his encyclopedia directory, to realize those were paper volumes, so he counted all the entries manually. "Just one entry per day," he thought.

He was rescued by a whale sooner than he thought he would be and thus felt uneducated.

MEDICINE (MULTITHREADING) PIANO – ROB

Rob, the pianist, did not come to a party thrown by Lorenzo because his hand was ailing him. He had practiced so hard for the competitive international piano music interpretation that he began to suffer terribly. It appeared he had developed carpal tunnel syndrome, but that did not stop him at all.

```
import time
def remind_to_take_breaks():
    while True:
        print("Remember to take a break and stretch your hands!")
        time.sleep(60 * 30)  # Remind every 30 minutes

def suggest_hand_exercises():
    print("Here are some hand exercises to help prevent carpal tunnel syndrome:")
    print("1. Wrist Flexor Stretch: Hold your arm straight, palm facing down. Gently press on your fingers to stretch.")
    print("2. Wrist Extensor Stretch: Hold your arm straight, palm facing up. Gently press on your fingers to stretch.")
    print("3. Hand Tendon Gliding: Make a fist and then gradually open your hand, repeating several times.")
    print("4. Finger Tapping: Tap each finger individually on a flat surface.")

if __name__ == "__main__":
    # Start a thread to remind the user to take breaks
    import threading
    break_reminder_thread = threading.Thread(target=remind_to_take_breaks)
    break_reminder_thread.start()

    # Provide suggestions for hand exercises
    suggest_hand_exercises()

    # Wait for the break reminder thread to finish (you can use Ctrl+C to stop the program)
    break_reminder_thread.join()
```

The script ran two tasks concurrently: one to remind the user to take breaks at regular intervals and another to suggest hand exercises.

With a lot of ice at hand, he continued to prepare himself for the competition. He felt he was a strong candidate for a prize. He knew the aura of winning. It was beyond any level of understanding. It was like any single detail would go the best way possible. Every key would respond right, and every finger would know when and how to touch the surface. There would be no mention of any pain in his winning performance. Rob knew his aura, or a loss, too, when one single fact could trigger the next unwanted situation, the notes becoming hurtful and the sounds not collaborative. This time, however, he knew his aura was a good one. When he played, he worked; when he worked, he played.

MESSAGE IN MUSIC
(COMPOSITION)
TIMBALES – ABRIL, ARIAM, PORPY, ALBAN, KADECE, AND ADRIEL

They all agreed that one drum per person was enough. Less space, more attention. The problem was with Abril, who lost his drumstick.

```
class Drum:
    def __init__(self, name, role):
        self.name = name
        self.role = role

    def play(self):
        print(f"The {self.name} is playing a {self.role} rhythm.")

class BassDrum(Drum):
    def __init__(self):
        super().__init__("Bass Drum", "fundamental")

class SnareDrum(Drum):
    def __init__(self):
        super().__init__("Snare Drum", "accent")

class TomTomDrum(Drum):
    def __init__(self):
        super().__init__("Tom-Tom Drum", "fill")

class CongaDrum(Drum):
    def __init__(self):
        super().__iit__("Conga Drum", "Latin groove")
```

```
# Create instances of drums
bass_drum = BassDrum()
snare_drum = SnareDrum()
tom_tom_drum = TomTomDrum()
conga_drum = CongaDrum()

# Display the list and roles of various drums
print("List and Roles of Various Drums:")
print(f"{bass_drum.name}: {bass_drum.role}")
bass_drum.play()

print(f"\n{snare_drum.name}: {snare_drum.role}")
snare_drum.play()

print(f"\n{tom_tom_drum.name}: {tom_tom_drum.role}")
tom_tom_drum.play()

print(f"\n{conga_drum.name}: {conga_drum.role}")
conga_drum.play()
```

Abril was in the "You probably don't remember this" category.

METAPHORS
(OOP)
SEAMSTRESS – IVY

Ivy was so skilled, talented, and creative: some called her Poison Ivy, others Ivy League.

```
class Seamstress:
    def __init__(self, name):
        self.name = name

    def explain_metaphor(self):
        if "Poison Ivy" in self.name:
            return f"{self.name} has a unique and captivating style, just like the infamous Poison Ivy."
        elif "Ivy League" in self.name:
            return f"{self.name} is known for her high-quality and prestigious craftsmanship, reminiscent of the Ivy League standards."
        else:
            return f"{self.name} is a talented seamstress with her own distinctive flair."

# Create an instance of the Seamstress class
ivy_seamstress = Seamstress("Ivy Stitcher")

# Explain the metaphor for the seamstress
metaphor_explanation = ivy_seamstress.explain_metaphor()

# Display the explanation
print(metaphor_explanation)
```

The Seamstress class used an explain_metaphor method that checks if the name contains "Poison Ivy" or "Ivy League" and provided a corresponding metaphorical explanation. The concept of classes and methods in OOP was used to encapsulate attributes and behavior related to the seamstress.

After she published her code, they all saw her as a beautiful creature.

MIDI (MUSICAL INSTRUMENT DATA INTERFACE FOR MUSIC)
(MIDIUTIL LIBRARY FOR MUSICAL COMPOSITION)
ROPE JUMPER – DARKLY

Tension between harmonic and melody, Indian music rhythm and melody, beats are music through terror and love.

```
from midiutil import MIDIFile

def create_midi():
    # Create a MIDI file
    midi = MIDIFile(1)

    # Add track
    track = 0
    time = 0
    midi.addTrackName(track, time, "Rope Jumper Prep")

    # Set tempo
    tempo = 120
    midi.addTempo(track, time, tempo)

    # Add melody and harmony
    melody_notes = [60, 62, 64, 65, 67, 69, 71, 72]
    harmony_notes = [60, 64, 67, 72]

    for i in range(8):
        time = i * 2  # Each note lasts for 2 beats

        # Melody
        midi.addNote(track, 0, melody_notes[i], time, 2, 100)

        # Harmony
        midi.addNote(track, 1, harmony_notes[i %
len(harmony_notes)], time, 2, 80)

    # Save MIDI file
    with open("rope_jumper_prep.mid", "wb") as midi_file:
        midi.writeFile(midi_file)

if __name__ == "__main__":
    create_midi()
```

He used the major MIDI (Musical Instrument Digital Interface) concept to generate a musical work to incorporate a melody and harmony representing the tension between harmonic and melodic elements.

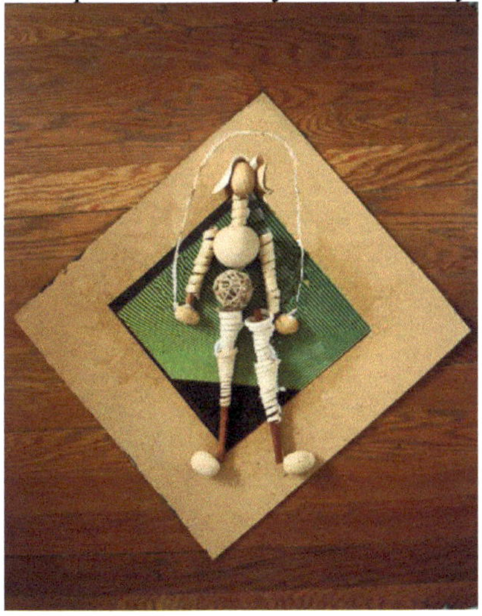

His success made him experiment with different notes, rhythms, and musical elements to enhance his code's representation of the given concepts.

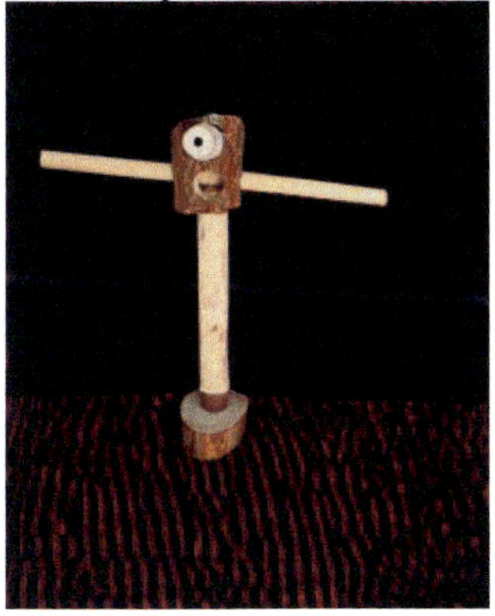

Those who enjoyed his terror and music gave him money. Since he was peaceful, he gave his earnings to those who inspired him.

MONITORING NOVELTY (SEARCH) CULTURAL ADVISOR – PEA

Her job is to keep her busy employers current, be fluent in new trends, and be familiar with recent cultural, scientific, sports, and politics-related events. This meant she had to live close to her employers, be alert, and always be ready for action. She had to be able to write well, talk fast or slow as needed, and make convincing reports. Her days were organized and chaotic at the same time: she had to constantly search the web, consult AI, read many blogs, listen to the news and podcasts, talk to specialists, politicians, doctors, and academics, and read a lot of books, newspapers, and journals, attend performances, and sports events. She even attended circus performances. At the same time, she was expected to be available at practically any time. That also meant her cell phone and her watch needed to be always on to distribute the latest news and other messages. To improve, she wrote a script fetching news articles using an API. One could choose a news API based on own preferences (e.g., NewsAPI, Bing News Search API, etc.).

```
import requests

def get_news(api_key, category='general', country='us',
language='en', num_articles=5):
    url = f'https://newsapi.org/v2/top-headlines'
    params = {
        'apiKey': api_key,
        'category': category,
        'country': country,
        'language': language,
        'pageSize': num_articles
    }

    response = requests.get(url, params=params)
    news_data = response.json()

    if news_data['status'] == 'ok':
        articles = news_data['articles']
        for idx, article in enumerate(articles, start=1):
            print(f"{idx}. {article['title']} - {article['url']}")
    else:
        print(f"Error: {news_data['message']}")
```

It all got better after she replaced 'YOUR_API_KEY' with her actual NewsAPI key

```
news_api_key = 'YOUR_API_KEY'
get_news(news_api_key, category='science')
```

She was the best, thus was constantly on a call. Sometimes, she felt like being a doctor.

MUSIC AND PERFORMANCE (MOTION TRACKING) CYMBALS – YAN

There were many cymbalists, but no one dared to play the instrument in Yan's presence. His playing was visual; it brought flowers to viewers' minds, filling the air with sounds of falling leaves, lawns, lakes, forests, mountains, and all the beauty that nature could offer. It made his listeners feel synesthetic. After all, Respighi wrote music to three paintings by Sandro Botticelli, they used to say. Yan never left his house for longer than a day. When asked about sources of his inspiration, he used to answer, "I was listening to the grass growing in my backyard." However, he always performed in front of the mirror and kept calling himself Des. It meant two in Spanish, but it was also an acronym for data encryption standard. His secret was pre-recorded music matching his playing with a tiny, hard-to-notice delay. Yan created a real-time visual duplication of one person's movement to further the effect for another person to follow. It involved computer vision and motion tracking. With Python and the OpenCV library, he knew it would require additional customization based on each specific use. Yan wrote:

```
import cv2
import numpy as np

# Open a webcam
cap = cv2.VideoCapture(0)

while True:
    # Capture a frame
    ret, frame = cap.read()

    # Flip the frame horizontally for a mirrored effect
    mirrored_frame = cv2.flip(frame, 1)

    # Display the original and mirrored frames side by side
    output_frame = np.hstack((frame, mirrored_frame))
    cv2.imshow('Dance Mirror', output_frame)

    # Break the loop when 'q' key is pressed
    if cv2.waitKey(1) & 0xFF == ord('q'):
        break

# Release the webcam and close windows
cap.release()
cv2.destroyAllWindows()
```

His code captured frames from the webcam, flipped them horizontally to create a mirrored effect, and displayed both the original and mirrored frames side by side. It did not involve any real dancing motion tracking or synchronization, so he had to employ motion tracking, a computer vision library like OpenPose or MediaPipe to detect and track key points in the dancer's body and then replicate those movements onto another display. Since he experimented with his dancing, he did not have to obtain consent before implementing such systems and consider the ethical implications of using technology to influence or replicate someone's actions.

Soon, they paid him double.

MUSIC CAREER PREPARATION
(TRUE, FALSE)
JANITOR – FUBUKI

Fubuki loved music but had to earn money to go to school. She took a job as a janitor in a concert hall to be close to the sounds, and to have more opportunities to look at the instruments, both when they were played and when they were silent at rest. Her dream was to play the flute. When she was little, she loved the theme of the Purple Jaguar show. It started with the sax until the flute took over. That's how she became interested in the flute. But she was still saving money. One could see her pushing her cart with her body while her hands played the imagined flute. This sight was quite appreciated by most members of the Orchestra who worked or stayed late. She wrote her code to set the finger's positions while pretending to play a flute. A simple representation in a programming-like pseudocode to illustrate the idea was enough for that. She created a "Flute" class with a method to set finger positions:

```
class Flute:
    def __init__(self):
        self.finger_positions = [False, False, False, False, False, False]

    def set_finger_position(self, finger_number, is_pressed):
        # Finger numbers are 1 to 6, corresponding to each finger
        if 1 <= finger_number <= 6:
            self.finger_positions[finger_number - 1] = is_pressed
        else:
            print("Invalid finger number. Please use a number between
1 and 6.")

# Example usage:
flute = Flute()

# Pressing and releasing fingers
flute.set_finger_position(1, True)
flute.set_finger_position(3, True)
flute.set_finger_position(5,  True)

# Releasing fingers
flute.set_finger_position(3, False)


# Check current finger positions
print("Current finger positions:", flute.finger_positions)
```

Her imaginative sounds got better and better.

MUSIC – COMPETITIVENESS (MIDI)
HARP EGYPTIAN – AIDA, CELIA

Aida was always competing with Celia. Actually, this was unnecessary, as they usually played together in a big group. The shimmering music of Celia's harp filled the entire house with its rich, resonant, and mellow sound. Celia liked to practice it by the water; it sounded even better there. Her reflection in the lake was so peaceful while she played that everybody wanted to take a picture of her, which soon became a local attraction named "Water Harp." One day, Aida started writing her own music for a duet they would both play. That event caused the roles to shift. Celia wrote a code for how playing can inspire composing with a Python script. She installed the pygame following with the code:

```
import pygame
import random
import time

# Initialize pygame
pygame.init()

# Set the tempo (beats per minute)
tempo = 120

# Set the duration of the composition
(in seconds)
duration = 30

# Define the scale of Egyptian harp
(you can modify this)
scale = [60, 62, 64, 67, 69, 72, 74,
76]

# Function to generate a random
melody based on the scale
def generate_melody():
    melody = []
    for _ in range(16):
        note = random.choice(scale)
        melody.append(note)
    return melody
```

```
# Function to play the melody
def play_melody(melody):
    for note in melody:


pygame.mixer.music.set_volume(0.4)
        pygame.mixer.music.set_busy(True)


pygame.mixer.music.load(pygame.mixer.Sound(pygame.midi.Sound("/usr/share/sounds/sf2/FluidR3
_GM.sf2", 1)))
        pygame.mixer.music.queue(pygame.midi.Sound("/usr/share/sounds/sf2/FluidR3_GM.sf2", 1))
        pygame.mixer.music.set_pos(0.0)
        pygame.mixer.music.play()
        time.sleep(0.5) # adjust the sleep duration to change the tempo

# Generate a melody
melody = generate_melody()

# Play the melody
play_melody(melody)

# Wait for the composition to finish
time.sleep(duration)

# Stop pygame
pygame.quit()
```

Her script used the pygame library to play a randomly generated melody based on the provided scale for a duration of 30 seconds. She kept modifying the scale list to include the specific notes that she associated with Egyptian harp playing whenever Aida followed up with her new compositions. They soon started experimenting with the script, adjusting the scale, tempo, and other parameters till they started a Duo group performing together. After all, the computer did it, so there was no need to compete.

MUSIC COMPOSITION
(OBJECT-ORIENTED PROGRAMMING (OOP)
METRONOME – DUSTIN

Colleagues used to call Dustin a Metronome. Due to the budget cuts, personnel of the Philharmonic musicians serve on numerous committees. They consider committee meetings a worrying duty; some even call it a waste of their time. Dustin never complains. He dutifully attends all the meetings. He is never late or never leaving a meeting room before the end. However, people noticed the peculiar way in which Dustin responds to the progression of a meeting agenda. He knocks his shoes repeatedly against the floor, makes short, rhythmical movements of his neck, and, at the same time, takes notes diligently in a big notebook. Often, a chair of the meeting reacts to the pace indicated by Dustin's movements and involuntarily makes her speech quicker (and shorter), to the great satisfaction of the committee members. One day, Celia (an Egyptian harp player) watched Dustin and commented, "Dustin is composing a new piece of music!" All eyes turned toward Dustin's notebook only to find that it was staff paper on which music notes were written. Compositions created by Dustin were titled according to the meeting agenda items, and the speakers' thoughts inspired his music.

```
import random

class MusicalComposition:
    def _init_(self, title, tempo, key):
        self.title = title
        self.tempo = tempo
        self.key = key
        self.notes = []

    def add_note(self, note):
        self.notes.append(note)

    def play(self):
        print(f"Playing '{self.title}' at {self.tempo} BPM in the key of
{self.key}:")
        for note in self.notes:
            print(note, end=' ')
        print("\n")

class AgendaItem:
    def _init_(self, topic, speaker, thoughts):
        self.topic = topic
        self.speaker = speaker
        self.thoughts = thoughts

    def generate_composition(agendas):
    composition = MusicalComposition("Meeting Composition", 120,
"C Major")

for agenda in agendas:
        composition.add_note(f"{agenda.topic} - {agenda.speaker}:
{agenda.thoughts}")

    return composition

# Example usage
agenda_items = [
    AgendaItem("Introduction", "Host", "Setting the tone for the
meeting"),
    AgendaItem("Financial Update", "CFO", "Discussing the
company's financial performance"),
    AgendaItem("Innovation", "CTO", "Exploring new technologies
and ideas"),
    AgendaItem("Closing Remarks", "CEO", "Inspiring the team for
future goals"),
]

meeting_composition = generate_composition(agenda_items)
meeting_composition.play()
```

He used classes (MusicalComposition and AgendaItem) to represent musical compositions and agenda items, respectively. He encapsulated data and functionality related to musical compositions and agenda items in separate classes. The generate_composition function took a list of agenda items and created a musical composition by adding notes based on the agenda topics, speakers, and their thoughts. Finally, the composition was played using the play method. Everybody was delighted except for the infuriated chair. After that, Dustin came carrying a laptop to a committee meeting. Again, while taking notes from the meeting, he was making recurring movements with his head and producing rhythm by tapping. The chair guessed at once that Dustin was using software allowing for writing scores and composing music. This time, Dustin's place in this committee was filled in by someone else. Finally, he could compose his music in peace.

MUSIC EDUCATION (IMPLEMENTATION OF A CLASS) MUSIC SCHOOL – CINE AND SIS

Cine opened a Music School with her friend Sis. They started with the research, forming it as a code:

```
class MusicSchool:
    def __init__(self):
        self.topics = []

    def add_topic(self, topic):
        self.topics.append(topic)

    def display_topics(self):
        print("Topics to be taught in the music school:")
        for topic in self.topics:
            print("- " + topic)

# Example usage:
music_school = MusicSchool()
music_school.add_topic("Music Theory")
music_school.add_topic("Instrument Techniques")
music_school.add_topic("Ear Training")
music_school.add_topic("Music Composition")

music_school.display_topics()
```

They encapsulated the related functionality with OOP, where they used a class to bundle data (topics) and methods (add_topic, display_topics) that operated on that data. In their curriculum:

<table>
<tr>
<td>History of Music came first
1. Music Now
2. Music Before
3. Music Then
Some called them Older, Medium Old Music, and Newer Music.
Then came the practical part
1. Intro to All Instruments
2. Select Your Instrument
3. Master Your Instrument
4. What Can You Do with those 12 Notes?
Next came theory courses:
1. Theory of Beauty
2. Harmony in Nature
3. Chaos of Thought
Following that came vocal skills
1. Try Your Voice
- Baritone
- Alto Soprano
- Mezzo-Soprano
2. Practice Makes Perfect
- Master your Voice
- State Your Voice
- Promote Your Voice
3. Promote Yourself
- Dress for Success (Dress Up Right)
- Luggage Content
- Recording techniques for various platforms
4. Then, motivational skills come
- Sing Louder
- Try Harder
- Play Better</td>
<td>5. And Music for Others: Film genres and characters who live there:
- Action-adventure
- Film noir
- Science fiction
- Period piece
- Western
- Theater
- Comedy (they got married, after all).
- Drama (they got married, all right, but divorced afterwards).
- Tragedy (They did not get married because something divided them).
After that, one had to study
- Efficacy
- Efficiency
- Access
- Aesthetics
- Just for fun.
The Grading system looked as follows:
- Solid Hard Work
- There Were Others Before Us, There Will Be After Us
- Not Half Bad
- Awesome
- Why Didn't I Come Up With This Myself? (WDNICUWTM)
Website
- Commercial
- Gaming
- Educational
- Informational
- Social
- Artistic
- News
- Future</td>
</tr>
</table>

They were even talking about opening a new Department of Tautology.

MUSIC MULTIPLE FREQUENCY
(THE GENERATION OF SOUND WAVES USING THE NUMPY LIBRARY)
TROMBA PERFIANA – RICARDO

This tromba was always longer than its player. Crusaders would like that, he thought. His instrument sounded scary. Having dissonance in music in mind, Ricardo wrote a code:

```
import numpy as np
import matplotlib.pyplot as plt

def generate_tromba_perfiana_sound(duration, sampling_rate):
   t = np.linspace(0, duration, int(sampling_rate * duration), endpoint=False)

   # Create a basic sine wave representing the fundamental frequency
   fundamental_freq = 440  # in Hertz (you can change this)
   sine_wave = np.sin(2 * np.pi * fundamental_freq * t)

   # Add some dissonant frequencies to create a tense sound
   dissonant_freqs = [fundamental_freq * 1.5, fundamental_freq * 2, fundamental_freq * 2.5]
   for freq in dissonant_freqs:
      sine_wave += 0.3 * np.sin(2 * np.pi * freq * t)

   return sine_wave

def main():
   duration = 3  # seconds
   sampling_rate = 44100  # samples per second

   # Generate Tromba Perfiana sound
   tromba_perfiana_sound = generate_tromba_perfiana_sound(duration, sampling_rate)

   # Plot the sound wave
   plt.plot(np.arange(0, duration, 1/sampling_rate), tromba_perfiana_sound)
   plt.title("Tromba Perfiana Sound")
   plt.xlabel("Time (s)")
   plt.ylabel("Amplitude")
   plt.show()

if __name__ == "__main__":
   main()
```

His code created a basic sine wave as the fundamental frequency and then added dissonant frequencies to it. Dissonance refers to the tension or clash between musical notes, and adding dissonant frequencies can create a sense of unease or scariness in the sound. They were multiples of the fundamental frequency, and adjusting their amplitudes and ratios affected the perceived tension in the sound.

He often felt like being a scary person – the sound of his instrument did it to him. His audience was less scared by the size of his instrument than by his way of moving it around.

MUSIC ORIGINS
(TIME)
MUSIC ANTHROPOLOGIST – YVES

Yves was teaching topics related to the origin of music making: Ancient Music. Early humans had two ways of making sounds: with their mouths and hands. They could sing, whistle, pop, whist, hands click, bang, slap, and hit with anything they could grasp. It was only entertainment for the mouth and hands. Everything was related to approximation and accompaniment. However, some students felt lost or confused. Yves wrote a program that represents how to make music using text output. It did not produce actual sounds but simulated the different ways of making music in a fun way:

```
import time

def sing():
    return "La la la..."

def whistle():
    return "Whistle, whistle..."

def pop():
    return "Pop! Pop!"

def whist():
    return "Whist, whist..."

def hands_click():
    return "Clap, clap..."

def bang():
    return "Bang! Bang!"

def slap():
    return "Slap, slap..."

def hit():
    return "Hit hit!"
```

```
# Let's make some music!
print(sing())
time.sleep(1)

print(whistle())
time.sleep(1)

print(pop())
time.sleep(1)

print(whist())
time.sleep(1)

print(hands_click())
time.sleep(1)

print(bang())
time.sleep(1)

print(slap())
time.sleep(1)

print(hit())
```

His text-based representation of different ways to make music was run by Python script to print out the simulated sounds for each action with a one-second pause in between. Some students modified the code for many styles of musical performances. Then, Yves started teaching classes by having his students try everything they'd discussed. No instruments were needed, no extra cost was required; they were one of the most popular ones. He started studying the role of the legs in music-making. This time, he knew better: introduced the code first. One student wrote a code that simulates leg-based music with the pygame library to play sounds and trigger different notes by moving one's legs:

```
import pygame
import time

def play_note(note):
    pygame.mixer.init()

pygame.mixer.music.load(f"notes/{note}.mp3")
# Assuming you have audio files for each note
in a 'notes' folder
    pygame.mixer.music.play()
    time.sleep(1) # Adjust the duration as
needed
    pygame.mixer.music.stop()

def main():
    # Simulate leg movements to trigger different
notes
    leg_movements = ["left", "right", "left",
"right", "jump", "stomp", "spin"]
```

```
    for movement in leg_movements:
        if movement == "left":
            play_note("C")
        elif movement == "right":
            play_note("D")
        elif movement == "jump":
            play_note("E")
        elif movement == "stomp":
            play_note("F")
        elif movement == "spin":
            play_note("G")

if __name__ == "__main__":
    main()
```

With the pygame library to play different notes when it detected specific leg movements, the students had audio files for each note (C, D, E, F, G) in an appropriately named 'notes' folder. Afterward, they customized the code based on his preferences and available resources.
What a class to teach! What a class to take!

MUSIC PARTS
(ENCAPSULATION AND DATA STRUCTURES)
PAGE TURNER – ELEONA

Eleona was the best page-turner any pianist has ever worked with. It was not because of her glowing personality or skills; it was all about the rhythm and her decisive way to turn the pages. Sometimes, it was a bit too fast; sometimes, the slightest delay was applied. This could motivate the pianist, who knows, through the power of irritation or awaiting the unexpected. It just worked. Soon, the pianists were presented with tablets in front of them. Eleona was hired to program the tablets to turn the screens according to each musical composition. To learn to code, she started with programming tablets:

```
class Tablet:
    def __init__(self, music_composition):
        self.music_composition = music_composition
        self.current_page = 1

    def turn_page(self):
        if self.current_page < len(self.music_composition):
            self.current_page += 1
            print(f"Turning to page {self.current_page}")
        else:
            print("End of music composition reached.")

# Example usage
music_piece = ["Page 1", "Page 2", "Page 3", "Page 4"]
tablet = Tablet(music_piece)

for _ in range(5):
    tablet.turn_page()have them turn the pages of musical notations:
```

She used the concept of a class (Tablet) to encapsulate the behavior of turning pages. The class had a method turn_page that updated the current page and printed a message. Then, to add dynamics to the concert, she wrote another code to adjust their screen orientation based on the musical composition being played. She used a dictionary to map musical compositions to the desired screen orientations:

```
class Tablet:
    def __init__(self, tablet_id):
        self.tablet_id = tablet_id
        self.screen_orientation = "Portrait"

    def set_screen_orientation(self, orientation):
        self.screen_orientation = orientation
        print(f"Tablet {self.tablet_id}: Screen orientation set to
{orientation}")

def program_tablets(musical_compositions):
    tablets = [Tablet(i) for i in range(1, len(musical_compositions) +
1)]

    for tablet, composition in zip(tablets, musical_compositions):
        set_orientation_based_on_composition(tablet, composition)

def set_orientation_based_on_composition(tablet, composition):
    orientations = {
        "Classical": "Landscape",
        "Jazz": "Portrait",
        "Rock": "Portrait",
        "Electronic": "Landscape"

     # Add more musical compositions and orientations as needed
    }

    if composition in orientations:
        tablet.set_screen_orientation(orientations[composition])
    else:
        print(f"Tablet {tablet.tablet_id}: Unknown composition.
Keeping current orientation.")

if __name__ == "__main__":
    musical_compositions = ["Classical", "Jazz", "Rock",
"Electronic"]

    program_tablets(musical_compositions)
```

A class (Tablet) represented individual tablets. This allowed the pianists to encapsulate tablet-specific behavior and manage multiple tablets easily. Additionally, the use of a dictionary (orientations) to map musical compositions to screen orientations demonstrated the concept of data structures for efficient lookup and organization of information.

All worked well, but the pianists needed some time to adjust to the absence of her quiet singing in the background.

MUSIC SOUND
(SOUND METHOD)
ELECTRIC VIOLIN – UGNA

Ugna played the electric violin. Since the sound box was small and hidden, the instrument looked like a simple stick. Some of these instruments had a big ornamental box to make it look like the regular violin, but not the one Ugna had. Ugna wanted to describe the flow of sound for an electric violin shaped like a stick. This complex task involved signal processing, physics simulations, complex physics, and possibly external libraries, so he came up with a simplified representation:

```
class ElectricViolin:
    def __init__(self, length):
        self.length = length
        self.vibrations = [0] * length

    def pluck(self, position, force):
        self.vibrations[position] = force

    def propagate_sound(self):
        new_vibrations = [0] * self.length

        for i in range(1, self.length - 1):
            new_vibrations[i] = 0.5 * (self.vibrations[i - 1] +
self.vibrations[i + 1])

        self.vibrations = new_vibrations

    def simulate_sound(self, num_iterations):
        for _ in range(num_iterations):
            self.propagate_sound()

    def get_sound_profile(self):
        return self.vibrations

# Example usage
electric_violin = ElectricViolin(length=50)

# Pluck the violin at position 25 with a force of 1.0
electric_violin.pluck(position=25, force=1.0)

# Simulate the sound propagation for 100 iterations
electric_violin.simulate_sound(num_iterations=100)

# Get the sound profile
sound_profile = electric_violin.get_sound_profile()

print(sound_profile)
```

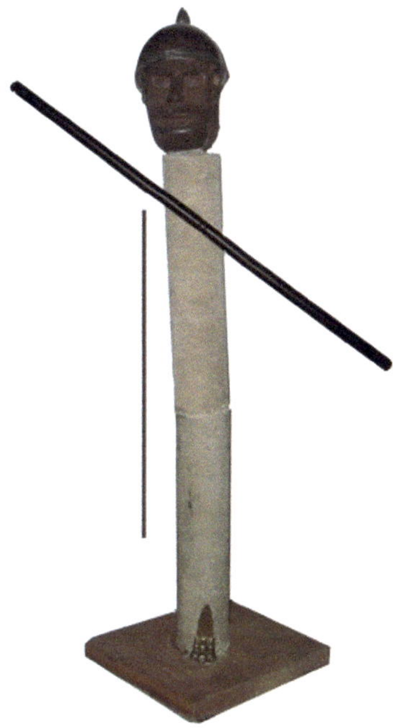

In Ugna's code, the ElectricViolin class represented the stick-shaped electric violin. The pluck method simulated plucking the string at a specific position with a given force. The propagate_sound method simulated the propagation of sound vibrations along the string, and the simulate_sound method allowed him to run the simulation for a specified number of iterations.

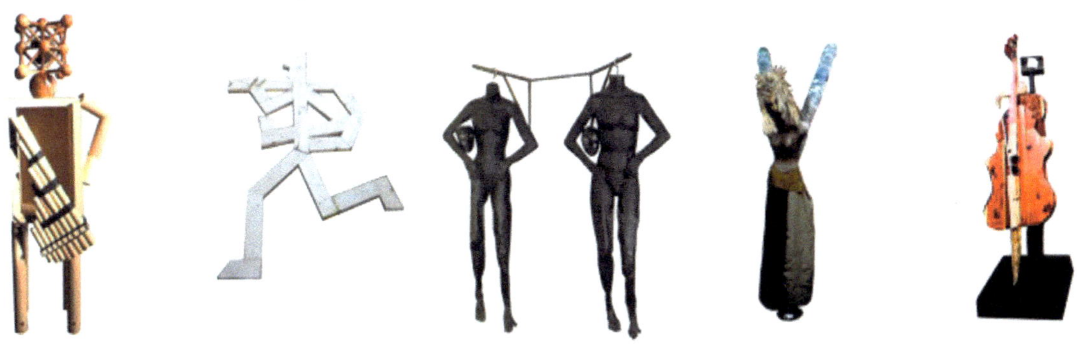

He saw art as seeing, dance as moving, poetry as speaking, and music as a deep sound coming from a rod.

MUSIC STORYTELLING (STRUCTURE) DRUM – CONFUSED ARROW

He could notice things. He could see what other people would miss, take no notice, or forget. All the details were adding up for him for a bigger story. He never knew why it all was working so well and why it was making others angry. His family could be traced to the 1700s, and the Great Book of Family Traditions was written in 1876. His gift was not listed for any of the family members. He was jotting down his discoveries but never dared to weave them into one story that would have a beginning, the development of an event, and an action followed by an ending with some moral. Instead, he'd beat his drum to send a message this way. Each story was vivid to him, so he felt it was obvious and easy to follow. Each of his audio stories consisted of many differentiated beatings, snapping, or flat-hand rhythmical touching that could emphasize the drama. His aim was to show the conflict, its resolution, and always a happy ending, which he felt was his musical signature. Mathematics is the art of the possible. Algebra is not about numbers but letters. He created an outline code using a library to generate a sequence of beats, snaps, and rhythmic touches. He then used them to represent different elements of each story.

```
from pydub import AudioSegment
from pydub.generators import Sine

def generate_beat(duration_ms):
    beat = Sine(440).to_audio_segment(duration=duration_ms)
    return beat

def generate_snap(duration_ms):
    snap = Sine(880).to_audio_segment(duration=duration_ms)
    return snap

def generate_touch(duration_ms):
    touch = Sine(660).to_audio_segment(duration=duration_ms)
    return touch

def main():
    # Define the structure of your story in terms of beats, snaps, and touches
    beats = [generate_beat(500) for _ in range(4)] # Representing conflict
    snaps = [generate_snap(300) for _ in range(3)] # Representing resolution
    touches = [generate_touch(200) for _ in range(5)] # Representing happy ending

    # Combine the audio segments to create the final audio story
    story_audio = sum(beats + snaps + touches)

    # Export the audio to a file
    story_audio.export("audio_story.mp3", format="mp3")

if __name__ == "__main__":
    main()
```

He then adjusted the frequencies, durations, and the sequence of beats, snaps, and touches to suit the rhythm of his story better. For more intricate and dynamic ones, he advanced audio processing libraries. In the eye of the conflict, the sound was so powerful that many wanted to seek some shelter to stay safe.

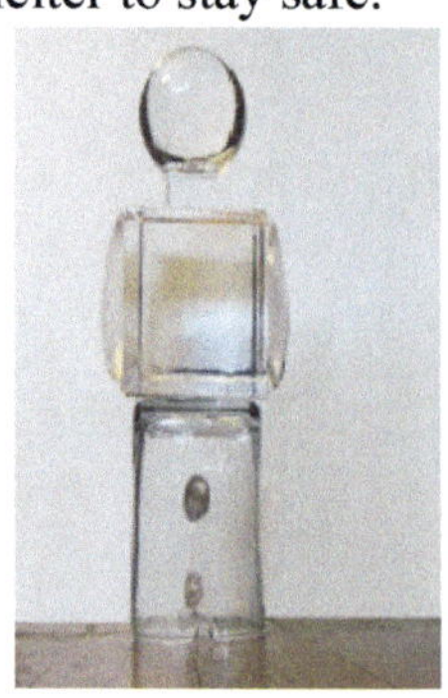

MUSIC STRING PLAYERS (INHERITANCE)
FIVE GENERATIONS - GER, LILO, MAURIZIO, TERD, MOHSEN, BEA, DITTA, AMRA, NIGA, PRINCESS SUN

They were five generations of String Players. They played string quartets, quintets, and sextets together.

The group consisted of:

The Great Grand Grandpa, Ger, 82
The Great Grandpa, Lilo, 64
The Grandpa, Maurizio, 46
The Father, Terd, 28
The Son, Mohsen, 10

The Great Grand Grandma, Bea, 81
The Great Grandma, Ditta, 65
The Grandma, Amra, 45
The Mother, Niga, 26
The Daughter, Princess Sun, 9

It was their family tradition to present newborns with their first violins. It was the very first present every addition to the family would receive. They did not need any outside teachings. Older members of their family home-schooled them all. Great Grand Grandpa just turned 82. His license plate read GR8GR8GPA. He was the only one who could handle a double bass. His son, Grand Grandpa, played the violin. His son, Grandpa, played a viola, but he was left-handed. It always looked weird, but it sounded great. His son played a fiddle. He liked to plunk the strings or pull his fingers against them. Sonny, his son, was 10. His violin was tiny, crafted for a child. Great Grand Grandma played double bass. Her daughter-in-law, Grand Grandma, played the Saz. Grandma played her guitar-shaped fiddle. Mother played the violin, while the daughter played the guitar. The StringInstrument class was the base class, and the Violin, Guitar, and Cello classes were inherited from it. Each specific instrument class took the attributes and methods of the StringInstrument class, allowing for a hierarchy of string instruments:

```
class StringInstrument:
    def __init__(self, name, family, sound):
        self.name = name
        self.family = family
        self.sound = sound

    def play(self):
        print(f"The {self.name} produces a {self.sound} sound.")

class Violin(StringInstrument):
    def __init__(self):
        super().__init__("Violin", "Violin Family", "sweet")

class Guitar(StringInstrument):
    def __init__(self):
        super().__init__("Guitar", "Guitar Family", "melodious")
```

```
class Cello(StringInstrument):
    def __init__(self):
        super().__init__("Cello", "Violin Family", "rich")

# Create instances of string instruments
violin = Violin()
guitar = Guitar()
cello = Cello()

# Display the hierarchy and play each instrument
print("String Instruments Hierarchy:")
print(f"{violin.name} belongs to the {violin.family}.")
violin.play()

print(f"\n{guitar.name} belongs to the {guitar.family}.")
guitar.play()

print(f"\n{cello.name} belongs to the {cello.family}.")
cello.play()
```

The whole family was always dressed in black. Not only for occasions, concerts, or practices, but it was the color they all liked. No one would tell a child what to wear, but somehow it was all black. Black looked good against the reddish-brown and sleek instrument. And black clothing was easy to wash (all of them wore black, remember?) Moreover, their black cats' fur would not appear in their wardrobe. It filled the house atmosphere with concert hall types of decency, harmony, joy, and seriousness.
Even the sound was better when surrounded by darkness.

MUSIC -- VOICE (CONDITIONAL STATEMENTS)

SOPRANO – DOROTHEA

Dorothea's voice is so deep, pure, sharp, balanced, warm, sensitive, clear, harmonious, loud, powerful, tonal, strong, tuned, vibrant, clean, and colorful that there are no words to describe it.

```
def assess_voice(type_score, quality_score):
    if type_score > 8 and quality_score > 8:
        print("The singer has an excellent voice with great type and quality!")
    elif type_score > 8:
        print("The singer has a fantastic vocal type!")
    elif quality_score > 8:
        print("The singer has a voice of outstanding quality!")
    else:
        print("The singer's voice is good, but there may be room for improvement.")

def main():
    print("Welcome to the Singer's Voice Assessment Program!")
    print("Please provide scores for vocal type and voice quality on a scale from 1 to 10.")

    # Get user input for vocal type and quality
    type_score = float(input("Enter the score for vocal type: "))
    quality_score = float(input("Enter the score for voice quality: "))

    # Validate input scores
    if 1 <= type_score <= 10 and 1 <= quality_score <= 10:
        assess_voice(type_score, quality_score)
    else:
        print("Invalid input. Please enter scores between 1 and 10.")

# Run the main function to execute the code
if __name__ == "__main__":
    main()
```

They came out with “Glassbreaking.”

MUSICAL CHOICES
(OOP)
THE QUADRUPLETS – PIANO

They all had their favorite composers: Haydn, Mozart, Tchaikovsky, Stravinsky, Beethoven, Mahler, Brahms, Liszt, Schumann, Schubert, and Shostakovich. Together they played their compositions in alphabetical order. Their areas of specialization were Triad, Vernacular, Folk, Jazz, Neo-Romantic, Neo-Classic, Modern, Avant-Garde, and Postmodern. They came up with a plan to combine their interests:

```
class Composer:
    def __init__(self, name, genre):
        self.name = name
        self.genre = genre

# Create instances of Composer
composers = [
    Composer("Mozart", "Neo-Classic"),
    Composer("Beethoven", "Neo-Romantic"),
    Composer("Bach", "Triad"),
    Composer("Miles Davis", "Jazz"),
    Composer("Bob Dylan", "Folk"),
    Composer("Stravinsky", "Avant-Garde"),
    Composer("Schoenberg", "Postmodern"),
    Composer("Philip Glass", "Modern"),
    Composer("John Cage", "Vernacular"),
]

# Function to relate composers to a specific genre
def relate_composers_to_genre(target_genre):
    related_composers = [composer.name for composer in composers if composer.genre == target_genre]
    return related_composers

# Example usage
genre_to_search = input("Enter a genre to find related composers: ")
related_composers = relate_composers_to_genre(genre_to_search)

if related_composers:
    print(f"Composers related to {genre_to_search}: {', '.join(related_composers)}")
else:
    print(f"No composers found for the genre: {genre_to_search}")
```

They named their group "Random."

MUSICAL INSTRUMENT PRESERVATION (ADJUSTMENT VALUES)

DOUBLE FLUTE/FLAUTO DOPPIO – EFFI

Effi spent her vacations in a small town, where the sound of instruments and the deep voices of singers contributed to the end-of-the-week celebrations. The folk orchestra used to play and sing all night in the park located down below her window. The summerhouse built by her grandfather was hanging on a shelf cut at the slope of a steep hill. The roof was covered with metal sheets, so every time it rained, she'd go up to the attic and listen to the drops of the rain rhythmically banging on the roof's surface. She loved to watch and observe the circular rings of water deep down the well. One day at the market, Effi found a stand with various folk instruments carved out of wood. One of them began her career in the science of genealogy. She asked the seller many questions. To carve this instrument, a person used information from a museum and many book descriptions to follow instructions. It was called flauto doppio, double aulos, or double pipes. These pipes were quite esteemed in the Sumerian, Egyptian, Greek, and Roman civilizations. They became obsolete, but not for folk music. This instrument had two cylindrical pipes that reinforced each other. It had double reeds. The tone of a single pipe was rather weak, but together, they produced a powerful sound, which created a hypnotic effect. Effi kept checking the internet, participated in blog discussions, asked many questions, and visited all ethnographic, local, or musical museums that listed her instrument among their collections and trophies. Based on her findings, she had one made just for her, but each pipe alone had a low pitch; thus, she wrote a code simulating the adjustment process, which fixed the instrument, and helped her adjust the length of the pipes.

```
class DoubleReedInstrument:
    def _init_(self, pipe1_length, pipe2_length):
        self.pipe1_length = pipe1_length
        self.pipe2_length = pipe2_length

    def adjust_pipe_length(self, pipe_number, adjustment):
        if pipe_number == 1:
            self.pipe1_length += adjustment
        elif pipe_number == 2:
            self.pipe2_length += adjustment
        else:
            print("Invalid pipe number")

    def play_tone(self):
        print(f"Playing tone with Pipe 1 length: {self.pipe1_length} and
Pipe 2 length: {self.pipe2_length}")
```

```
# Example usage:
instrument = DoubleReedInstrument(pipe1_length=30,
pipe2_length=35)

instrument.play_tone()

# Adjust the length of Pipe 1 to increase pitch
instrument.adjust_pipe_length(pipe_number=1, adjustment=5)

# Adjust the length of Pipe 2 to increase pitch
instrument.adjust_pipe_length(pipe_number=2, adjustment=5)

instrument.play_tone()
```

The code that defined a DoubleReedInstrument class with methods to adjust the length of each pipe and play the instrument, the adjust_pipe_length method, took the pipe number (1 or 2) and the adjustment value to modify the length of the corresponding pipe. Adjusting the pipes' lengths helped fine-tune each pipe's pitch individually and customize the code. She started playing it publicly and even succeeded in getting that often-mentioned hypnotic effect. Some of her listeners invited her to play to resolve issues. Despite a big reward offered, she refused. She only wanted to hypnotize one person.

MUSICAL INSTRUMENT VARIATION
(OBJECT-ORIENTED PROGRAMMING (OOP)
ORGAN – DORALD

There is another reason why the philharmonic halls have organs as part of the room. They look like an embedded decoration. They are not very often played during concerts; they just are there. Sometimes Dorald was needed or not, but it was okay, as he played a lot for his church. This gave him a sense of fulfillment and enough time to play the instrument. The practice was extremely demanding and often difficult, as the sound was loud, spread through the space, and annoyed some people. Contrary to some laypeople's opinions, he considered the organs in the church and the philharmonic hall as two different instruments and messages. "Artists are picky," said one of his colleagues. Are we? he asked himself, or is it just the message being determined by the purpose and the environment? The stained-glass windows, for example, made him play differently just by reflecting the light and changing the atmosphere. He thought of the wooden concert halls as cold, even though the temperature was much lower in the stone-finished churches. He wrote a Python code that represented the concept of how organs work in the human body. He used a class-based approach to represent an organ, specifically a heart.

```
class Heart:
    def __init__(self, name, chambers,
beats_per_minute):
        self.name = name
        self.chambers = chambers
        self.beats_per_minute = beats_per_minute
        self.is_beating = False

    def start_beating(self):
        self.is_beating = True
        print(f"The {self.name} is now beating at
{self.beats_per_minute} beats per minute.")

    def stop_beating(self):
        self.is_beating = False
        print(f"The {self.name} has stopped beating.")

    def get_info(self):
        print(f"{self.name} Information:")
        print(f"Chambers: {self.chambers}")
        print(f"Beats per Minute:
{self.beats_per_minute}")
        print(f"Is Beating: {self.is_beating}")


# Create an instance of the Heart class
human_heart = Heart("Human Heart", 4, 75)

# Start beating the heart
human_heart.start_beating()

# Display information about the heart
human_heart.get_info()

# Stop beating the heart
human_heart.stop_beating()
```

He defined a class Heart to represent the concept of a heart. The __init__ method served as a constructor that initialized the attributes of the heart, such as its name, number of chambers, beats per minute, and whether it was currently beating. Methods like start_beating, stop_beating, and get_info were defined as performing actions on the heart and retrieving information about it. He then created an instance of the Heart class called human_heart and interacted with it by starting and stopping its beating and getting information about it. He used Object-Oriented Programming (OOP), where he modeled the real-world concept of a heart as an object with properties (attributes) and behaviors (methods). Donald loved organs.

MUSICAL SOUNDS
(LOOP)
OCARINAS – DEM AND FERN

Dem had a little ocarina, and Fern got a larger one. The sizes surely affected their sounds. They did not sound nice when they played together. After all, people liked nice sounds. They were trying to exchange their instruments, but it was too personal. You do not trade an ocarina. They composed music that allowed Dem to play a fragment, Fern would follow, and then there was time for Dem.

```
import time

def play_ocarina(player1, player2, num_rounds):
    """Simulate alternating playing an ocarina between two
players."""
    for round_num in range(1, num_rounds + 1):
        if round_num % 2 == 1:
            print(f"{player1} plays the ocarina.")
        else:
            print(f"{player2} plays the ocarina.")

        # Simulate a brief pause between rounds
        time.sleep(1)

if __name__ == "__main__":
    # Set the names of the players and the number of rounds
    player1_name = "Link"
    player2_name = "Zelda"
    rounds_to_play = 5

    # Use the play_ocarina function to simulate the alternating play
    play_ocarina(player1_name, player2_name, rounds_to_play)
```

The code iterated through a specified number of rounds (num_rounds). Within each iteration of the loop, the code checked whether the current round number was odd or even using the modulo operator (%). If the round number was odd, it printed the first player being the ocarina; otherwise, the second player played it. Loops are fundamental in programming as they allow the repetition of a set of instructions.

After a while, they alternated singing when not playing their parts.

N | NEUROLOGY (COMMENTS) PROMPTER – EMILIANO

He was among the first people who joined the Orchestra. He knew all the lines for everyone, for every performance being produced. He felt like a walking library. He even started talking to people by quoting great lines in literature to respond to every question, situation, or event. Those who did not know his profession were impressed; those who knew him shortly got annoyed. Being there all the time, listening to lines spoken or sung many times, often in different timbres of voice, speeds, emphasizes, or even languages, made him willing to do something with his skills after technology offered new solutions. He had read someplace about absolute pitch. When children are born with perfect pitch, after being exposed to the same words pronounced differently by their parents, family members, and friends, they lose this ability and pay attention to the meaning of words rather than the pitch.

```
# Perfect Pitch Descriptor

def describe_perfect_pitch():
    """
    This function provides a description of what perfect pitch is.
    """
    print("Perfect pitch, also known as absolute pitch, is the ability")
    print("to identify or produce musical notes without any reference.")
    print("Individuals with perfect pitch can recognize pitches by name")
    print("without the need for a reference note. It is a rare and valuable")
    print("skill in the realm of music.")

# Example: Describe Perfect Pitch
describe_perfect_pitch()
```

Emiliano began feeling both lost and motivated to direct his own productions. But his vision was melted by his perfect memory. What he proposed was considered a set of highlights from various performances.

He was too perfect.

NUTRITION
(LISTS)
NUTRITIONISTS – FLORIAN AND FABIAN

Florian and Fabian used to fulfill all the needs of the Orchestra members. They were ready for any occasion or any difficult situation, such as a throat-related problem of an opera singer. They knew that knowledge about what's good for you was changing, and it was hard to catch up with. At first, they kept saying, "Eat an apple with the skin; all the vitamins are there," and then they reversed it to "Eat only peeled apples; its skin has all the pesticides in it." The food pyramid was to be followed even after it was totally inverted. Florian and Fabian said, "Hard to say when we harm people rather than helping them if we keep following what is current in the nutrition theory. The worst part is preparing snacks for parties: IS THERE ANY FOOD THAT NO ONE IS ALLERGIC TO?"

```
def display_safe_foods(allergic_people, food_list):
    """Display foods that no one is allergic to."""
    safe_foods = set(food_list)  # Convert food_list to a set for efficient comparison

    # Remove foods that any allergic person is allergic to
    for person in allergic_people:
        safe_foods -= set(person["allergies"])

    # Display the list of safe foods
    if safe_foods:
        print("Safe Foods:")
        for food in safe_foods:
            print(f"- {food}")
    else:
        print("There are no foods that no one is allergic to.")

if __name__ == "__main__":
    # Example data: List of people with allergies and a list of available foods
    allergic_people = [
        {"name": "Alice", "allergies": ["peanuts", "shellfish"]},
        {"name": "Bob", "allergies": ["dairy", "eggs"]},
        {"name": "Charlie", "allergies": ["gluten", "soy"]}
    ]

    available_foods = ["apple", "banana", "rice", "chicken", "carrot", "tomato"]

    # Use the display_safe_foods function to show safe foods
    display_safe_foods(allergic_people, available_foods)
```

The available_foods list contained the available food items, and the allergic_people list contained dictionaries representing people and their allergies. Then, they used sets to efficiently perform set operations to find the list of safe foods by subtracting the set of allergic foods from the set of all available foods. Lists are a fundamental data structure in programming to store and manipulate data.

They recommended eating half-peeled apples, but their recommendations were based on their lists that people could not understand, but followed them.

O	OCEANOGRAPHY (FUNCTION) LAMPLIGHTER – CYRIL

He's been working in solitary settings, controlling proper signaling. His job consisted of od a mix of responsibility and free time. A helicopter was dropping the food off every week. He brought a telescope, microscope, violin, guitar, soap, a box of resin (for his violin), staff paper, pen, pencil, clothing, hat, cosmetics, and a large net. Constantly being under pressure, he composed music in his free time, under the influence of the daytime and the nighttime of the ocean, heard and seen from above. He used the space right below the lines filled with notes to write and describe his music. He was also writing based on the same theme. He then converted his work into songs consisting of music, lyrics, and the sounds offered by the ocean. He started by recording the sound of the ocean and saving it as "ocean_wave_sound.wav" for the ocean sounds. He then replaced it with the actual sound file to use.

```
import time
import pygame
import math

def generate_ocean_sounds(time_of_day):
    # Assume time_of_day is a value between 0 (midnight) and 1 (midnight of the next day)
    # Let's map it to a range of frequencies for the ocean sounds
    base_frequency = 200  # Base frequency for the ocean sounds
    time_factor = 1000  # Scaling factor for time_of_day

    frequency = base_frequency + math.sin(2 * math.pi * time_of_day) * time_factor

    # Generate sound using pygame mixer (he had to install pygame)
    pygame.mixer.init()
    pygame.mixer.music.set_volume(0.5)  # Set the volume to 50%
    pygame.mixer.music.set_num_channels(1)  # Use a single channel for simplicity

    pygame.mixer.music.load("ocean_wave_sound.wav")  # Replace with your ocean sound file

    pygame.mixer.music.play(loops=-1)  # Play the ocean sounds in a loop

# Example usage: simulate changing ocean sounds throughout the day
for i in range(24):
    time_of_day = i / 24.0  # Normalize time_of_day to be between 0 and 1
    generate_ocean_sounds(time_of_day)
    time.sleep(5)  # Simulate a 5-second interval between each hour
```

After years, his beacon was transformed into a curved deck, so boats, sailboats, small ships, and smacks could stop for a snack or a nice chat.

He'd play and sing for them. Soon, he had to hire some waiters for the helicopter's daily food drop-offs.

ONEIROLOGY
(PATTERN REPRESENTATION)
DAY DREAMERS – HY, REG, ZUM, DE, SEI, FU, AND RA

All day, they were dreaming. At night, they created. It was easy to see their dreams, except for Ra's, who had a cloudy mind. Displaying the brain when dreaming is not straightforward, as dreams are subjective experiences, and the brain's activity is complex and not fully understood. Ra, hungry for some new content, used a Python library called Matplotlib to create a basic representation of his brain, but it did not reflect actual brain activity during dreaming.

```
Import matplotlib.pyplot as plt
import numpy as np

def display_dreaming_brain():
   # Create a simple representation of a brain
   fig, ax = plt.subplots(figsize=(8, 6))
   ax.set_title("Dreaming Brain")

   # Draw a basic brain shape
   brain_outline = plt.Circle((0.5, 0.5), 0.4, color='gray', fill=False,
linewidth=2)
   ax.add_patch(brain_outline)

   # Draw some dreamy patterns inside the brain
   num_patterns = 5
   for _ in range(num_patterns):
      x = np.random.uniform(0.2, 0.8)
      y = np.random.uniform(0.2, 0.8)
      radius = np.random.uniform(0.05, 0.15)
      dream_pattern = plt.Circle((x, y), radius, color='blue',
alpha=0.5)
      ax.add_patch(dream_pattern)

   # Set axis limits and remove ticks
   ax.set_xlim(0, 1)
   ax.set_ylim(0, 1)
   ax.set_xticks([])
   ax.set_yticks([])

   # Show the plot
   plt.show()

# Display the dreaming brain
display_dreaming_brain()
```

This way, Ra had a representation of his brain with some dreamy patterns inside. As a deep-diver, Ra saw all sorts of fish deep down the ocean that no one would even imagine. His big question was why fish living deep down, without access to any light, were still colorful. There was no camera at hand to go that deep with him, so his memories were mixed out with his dreams. Somehow, he started remembering his dreams. He has been writing a play per day since.

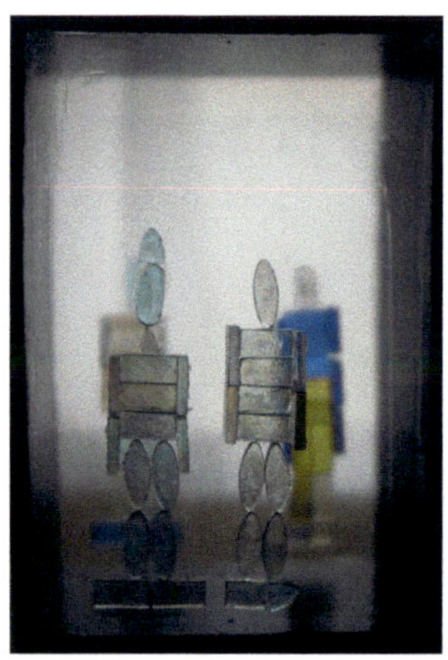

OPERA LIFE
(WHILE LOOP)
BOX OFFICE CASHIER – ESTEBAN

A line never formed when he was working. He was fast, kind, and efficient. Even when the "whole city" rushed to secure tickets for a performance, he could handle it. Once, he was selling tickets for an opera named in Latin "Quo Vadis." The title asked the human race in Latin where they were going.
Once he overheard the conversation:

Where are you going?"
"To the opera."
"What are they playing?"
"Quo Vadis."
"What does it mean?"
"Where are you going?"
"To the opera."
"What are they playing?"

He wrote a Python code using a while loop that continued indefinitely until a certain condition was met:

```
while True:
  user_input = input("Where are you going?  (type 'exit' to quit): ")

  if user_input.lower() == 'exit':
    print("Exiting the loop.")
    break  # This will exit the loop
  else:
    print(f"Where are you going?: {user_input}")
```

Finally, the opera's program was changed.

Their assignment was to ensure that all orchestra members would remember their posture, keep smiles on their faces, and move in a certain way, each resembling a star or celebrity. The job was not easy as some group members were not motivated. They kept busy and thought more about their creative production, their spots to focus on and concentrate on, with little space left for their self-image. Tokita kept saying the performance should be visually interesting, "People look at you while you are playing and when you are waiting for your turn to begin." Niga believed that books should not be allowed during the rehearsals. Some musicians brought them along and read them when they were not expected to play. Taro saw that happening even during the regular ballet performance. Some musicians believed that since the audience's attention was on the ballet dancers, no one would bother to look down and see what the musicians were doing. "Like binoculars have not been invented yet," Tokita said. Moreover, the cameras were filming everything from every angle. Tokita wrote a code with the Pygame library to simulate cameras placed in different positions and display their performance from various angles:

```
import pygame
import math

# Define colors
WHITE = (255, 255, 255)
RED = (255, 0, 0)

# Define camera class
class Camera:
    def __init__(self, x, y):
        self.x = x
        self.y = y

    def display(self):
        pygame.draw.circle(screen, RED, (int(self.x), int(self.y)), 10)

# Define specific camera subclass with additional functionality
class PanTiltCamera(Camera):
    def __init__(self, x, y, pan_angle, tilt_angle):
        super().__init__(x, y)
        self.pan_angle = pan_angle
        self.tilt_angle = tilt_angle

    def display(self):
        super().display()
        # Draw camera orientation lines
        end_x = self.x + 20 * math.cos(math.radians(self.pan_angle))
        end_y = self.y + 20 * math.sin(math.radians(self.pan_angle))
        pygame.draw.line(screen, WHITE, (self.x, self.y), (end_x, end_y), 2)

        end_x = self.x + 20 * math.cos(math.radians(self.tilt_angle))
        end_y = self.y + 20 * math.sin(math.radians(self.tilt_angle))
        pygame.draw.line(screen, WHITE, (self.x, self.y), (end_x, end_y), 2)

# Initialize Pygame
pygame.init()

# Set up display
width, height = 800, 600
screen = pygame.display.set_mode((width, height))
pygame.display.set_caption("Camera  Simulation")

# Create cameras
camera1 = Camera(100, 100)
camera2 = PanTiltCamera(200, 200, 45, 30)

# Main loop
running = True
while running:
    for event in pygame.event.get():
        if event.type == pygame.QUIT:
            running = False

    # Clear the screen.
    screen.fill((0, 0, 0))

    # Display cameras
    camera1.display()
    camera2.display()

    # Update the display
    pygame.display.flip()

# Quit Pygame
pygame.quit()
```

The PanTiltCamera class inherited from the Camera class, for reusing the common properties and methods of the Camera class while adding its own specific functionality (pan and tilt angles). Nid had an idea to move all the rehearsals to the ballet rehearsing rooms. After all, those rooms are practically covered with mirrors so everyone can see their actions. But according to Niga, it's just like reading a book during the performance.

ORGANIZATION (KEY-VALUE PAIRS) MARIMBA – FORREST

He was named Forrest. He liked his name a lot. It became a symbol for all he was doing. Gradually, he became obsessed with the relationship between one's name and a profession of choice, look, character, or hobbies a person would perform. He liked spending his weekends in the forest, driving his car that sounded similar. His last name suggested marimba. It gave him some fulfillment. People laughed and ignored his theories, except for Dave, who suggested that one's name is one of the first meaningful messages one recognizes as a child; it makes a person alerted to the concepts associated with these words. Forrest's new hobby became to compare names with all that people made them be. He used to capture his findings in a box he carried with him all the time but shared it only with his psychologist, Dave.

```
# Dictionary associating names with professions
name_profession_dict = {
    "Forrest": "Forest Ranger",
    "Baker": "Bread Maker",
    "Coder": "Software Developer",
    # Add more names and professions as needed
}

# Function to suggest a profession based on the name
def suggest_profession(name):
    return name_profession_dict.get(name, "Unknown Profession")

# Test the function with some names
names_to_test = ["Forrest", "Baker", "Coder", "Alice"]

for name in names_to_test:
    suggestion = suggest_profession(name)
    print(f"{name} might be a {suggestion}")
```

Forrest used the dictionary name_profession_dict, which contained names as keys and corresponding professions as values. The suggest_profession function took a name as input and used the get method to retrieve the associated profession. If the name was not found in the dictionary, it returned "Unknown Profession." Dictionaries allowed him to store and retrieve data based on keys, providing a convenient way to associate information.

At least it is an inexpensive hobby, he kept saying.

ORNITHOLOGY
(PHYSICS MODEL)
THE OWL – HOWL

Everyone knew him. He knew them all. That's a good comfort level. When he left for school, nobody did.

```
import random

class Owl:
    def __init__(self, name):
        self.name = name
        self.flying_ability = 0

    def learn_to_fly(self):
        print(f"{self.name} is attempting to fly!")

        # Simulate the learning process
        success_probability = random.uniform(0, 1)
        if success_probability > 0.3:
            print(f"{self.name} successfully flew!")
            self.flying_ability += 1
        else:
            print(f"{self.name} needs more practice. Better luck next
time!")

if __name__ == "__main__":
    owlets = [Owl("Owlet1"), Owl("Owlet2"), Owl("Owlet3")]

    for _ in range(5):  # Let's simulate 5 learning sessions
        for owlet in owlets:
            owlet.learn_to_fly()
            print(f"{owlet.name}'s flying ability: {owlet.flying_ability}")

    print("Owl flying school session complete!")
```

The Flying School for the Owls taught object-oriented programming (OOP). They first defined a class Owl to represent individual owls, and each owl had attributes like name and flying_ability. The learn_to_fly method simulated the owl's attempt to fly, and the owl teachers could track their progress. OOP allows them to model the concept of owls and their learning process in a structured way to reuse.

There are more and more owls coming in.

P	PERCUSSION (WHILE LOOP) MARACA – JAIME

Her instrument was also called rumba shaker or chac-chac, a rattle appearing in many Caribbean and Latin music genres. She shook it by a handle, even though it was usually played as a pair. Jaime was the fastest in hand movement during her drum practices. It's not like it was a competition, nor would they measure other percussion players, but it seemed like they all started playing faster in her presence. She was the one who would shuffle cards during games-filled evenings.

```
import time
import random

def simulate_fast_drumming(hand_speed):
  print("Get ready for the fastest hand movement on the drums!")

  try:
    while True:
      time.sleep(random.uniform(0, 1) / hand_speed) # Simulate random drum hits
      print("Hit!")

  except KeyboardInterrupt:
    print("\nDrumming stopped.")

# Example of usage
hand_speed = 2  # Adjust this value for faster or slower hand movement

simulate_fast_drumming(hand_speed)
```

Loop (the while loop) continuously simulated drum hits with random timing until the user interrupted the program (e.g., by pressing Ctrl+C). The loop allowed for the repetition of the drumming simulation, creating a continuous and dynamic experience. It could be employed to repeat a sequence of actions, making it suitable for scenarios where repetitive or continuous behavior is required.

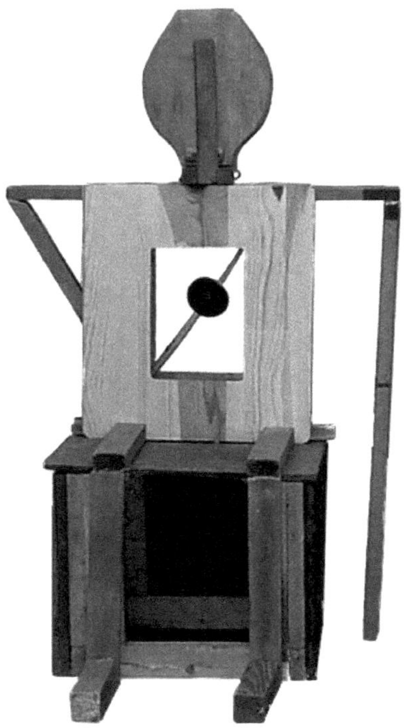

She could not dance. She could not sing. She was too fast for that. She was only slow when she talked. They had to wait patiently till she'd finish a sentence. When she was in the room, everyone spoke slower.

MUSICAL POODLE – OS AND ES

The poodle could sing, so they sang together. The only problem was to find a proper repertoire. Os used the analyze_voice_range function in his code, which took a voice range as input and provided an analysis based on that range. The suggest_repertoire function then uses this analysis to determine a suggestion.

```
def analyze_voice_range(scope):
    if scope == "wide":
        return "Consider repertoire with a variety of vocal ranges."
    elif scope == "limited":
        return "Opt for repertoire with a narrower vocal range to match the limited scope."

def suggest_repertoire(person_voice_range, poodle_voice_range):
    person_analysis = analyze_voice_range(person_voice_range)
    poodle_analysis = analyze_voice_range(poodle_voice_range)

    # Your repertoire suggestion logic goes here
    # You can consider both analyses to determine the best repertoire suggestion

    # For simplicity, let's just print the analyses for now
    print("Person's voice:", person_analysis)
    print("Poodle's voice:", poodle_analysis)

# Example voice range data (you can replace these with actual data)
person_voice_range = "wide"
poodle_voice_range = "limited"

# Call the function to get the repertoire suggestion
suggest_repertoire(person_voice_range, poodle_voice_range)
```

These functions helped organize and modularize the code by breaking it into smaller, reusable blocks.

His poodle won a dog obedience competition.

PHILOSOPHY
(ENCAPSULATION)
LOTTERY TICKETS SELLERS – ROKO, TY, AND EKI

They had lots of time to compose, sing, and discuss the outcomes. They composed together and sang together. One false note could ruin the entire effort. Their singing was stopped suddenly by a vivid philosophical discussion if one sings one's composition, is it possible to sing it falsely?

```
class Singing:
    def __init__(self, composition, is_own_composition):
        self.composition = composition
        self.is_own_composition = is_own_composition

    def can_sing_falsely(self):
        if self.is_own_composition:
            print(f"When singing your own composition, it's possible to interpret it in various ways, but singing falsely depends on individual skill and interpretation.")
        else:
            print("Singing someone else's composition falsely might indicate a lack of familiarity or understanding of the original piece.")

# Example usage
my_composition = Singing("My Heart's Song", True)
my_composition.can_sing_falsely()

other_composition = Singing("Classic Symphony", False)
other_composition.can_sing_falsely()
```

Their code was encapsulated through the Singing class and its method can_sing_falsely. This technique helped organize related functionality and data into a single unit. The class bundled information about a composition and whether it's the singer's own composition. The can_sing_falsely method then encapsulated the logic for discussing the possibility of singing falsely based on whether the composition is one's own or someone else's. This approach enhanced code readability, maintainability, and reusability. It allowed for a clear separation of concerns, making it easier to understand and modify the behavior related to singing a composition. This discovery called for them to sing together each composition, respectively. All they had to do was to agree on the alternative modulation of their voices.

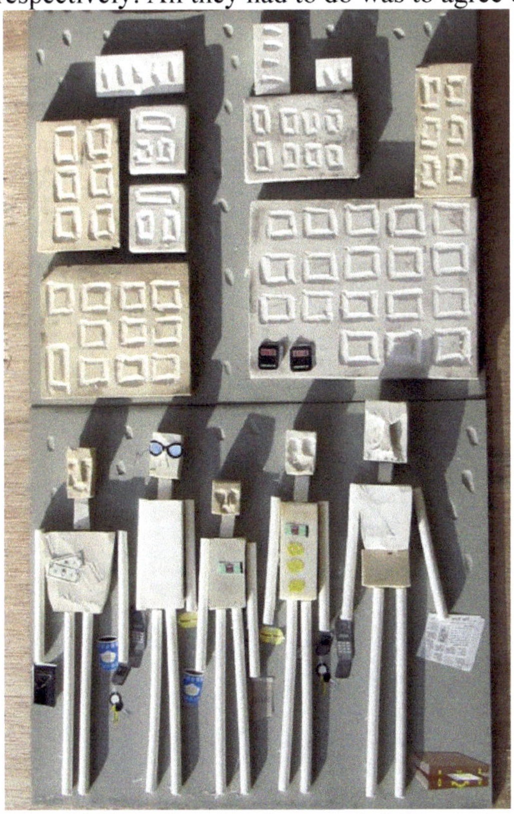

It sounded so nice that they made it into a song that could be sung falsely.

Physiology
(Metaphorical representation through a code)
Jazz Vocalist – Jeanne-Antoinette

Jeanne-Antoinette was born with a beautiful voice and dimmed diction. They kept saying one could learn good vocal expression, especially pronunciation, and enunciation of words in singing, but not her. She was just wired that way. The sounds she produced were clear, vivid, and deep, so she was often asked to join groups and performers. Her voice sounded its best when she was reclining. The club she worked for was equipped with various types of furniture, so finding a sofa for her performances was easy. Not only was her music highly appreciated, but the decorations were limited to the small carpet she could step on when she finished her singing. Whenever a member of the audience would ask why she sang while reclining, she would offer the following answer: "When a jazz singer is reclining, it can impact how they breathe and control their diaphragm. Singing involves coordinating various muscles, including those responsible for breathing. Here's her simplified explanation:

```
class JazzSinger:
    def __init__(self, position):
        self.position = position

    def sing(self):
        if self.position == "reclining":
            print("Singing in a reclining position...")
            print("Improved diaphragmatic control leads to a smoother vocal performance.")
        else:
            print("Singing in a different position...")
            print("Diaphragmatic control may vary, affecting vocal quality differently.")

# Example usage
jazz_singer = JazzSinger(position="reclining")
jazz_singer.sing()
```

Improved diaphragmatic control can lead to a more stable and controlled airflow in a reclining position, resulting in a smoother and potentially "better" vocal performance, but what sounds better is subjective. It's always essential for a singer to find a position that allows them to express themselves comfortably and effectively, but a code is a metaphorical representation and not a simulation of a singer's physiology. She studied the science behind singing and posture, so vocal mechanics and posture in singing it was.

She noticed getting more invitations to join groups at some clubs.

PLAY
(VISUALIZING THE TRANSFORMATION)
SNOWMAN – CUBE

He was known for inventing a formula for a rotational cube becoming a circle.

```
import pygame
import sys
import math

# Initialize Pygame
pygame.init()

# Constants
WIDTH, HEIGHT = 500, 500
FPS = 60

# Colors
BLACK = (0, 0, 0)
WHITE = (255, 255, 255)

# Create the Pygame window
screen = pygame.display.set_mode((WIDTH, HEIGHT))
pygame.display.set_caption("Rotational Cube to Circle")

clock = pygame.time.Clock()

def draw_cube(rotation_angle):
    side_length = 100
    cube_vertices = [
        (-side_length / 2, -side_length / 2),
        (side_length / 2, -side_length / 2),
        (side_length / 2, side_length / 2),
        (-side_length / 2, side_length / 2)
    ]
    rotated_vertices = []
    for vertex in cube_vertices:
        x = vertex[0] * math.cos(rotation_angle) - vertex[1] *
math.sin(rotation_angle)
        y = vertex[0] * math.sin(rotation_angle) + vertex[1] *
math.cos(rotation_angle)
        rotated_vertices.append((x, y))

    pygame.draw.polygon(screen, WHITE, rotated_vertices, 2)

def main():
    rotation_angle = 0

    while True:
        for event in pygame.event.get():
            if event.type == pygame.QUIT:
                pygame.quit()
                sys.exit()

        screen.fill(BLACK)

        draw_cube(rotation_angle)

        rotation_angle += 0.02

        pygame.display.flip()
        clock.tick(FPS)

if __name__ == "__main__":
    main()
```

He used graphics rendering and transformation. The draw_cube function calculated the rotated vertices of a cube based on a rotation angle, creating the illusion of a rotating cube. The rotation was continuous, demonstrating the transformation from a cube to a circular shape. The graphical library Pygame created the window, handled events, and rendered the shapes.

Now, he could sit in the center.

PORTRAYING SOUND
(DEFINITIONS)
WIND INSTRUMENTS – OWEN

Owen was a teacher. He often said, "Teaching means constant waiting for something breathtaking to happen." He was a good player, too. The movement of the trombone's parts was mysterious to Owen. He often watched his grandfather play and admired how the metal fit so perfectly that it was possible to alter the sound. It felt magical. He loved the control over the brass and the interaction with the instrument. Owen liked improvisations with dynamic changes in frequency (pitch) based on the slide position.

```
import numpy as np
import matplotlib.pyplot as plt

def generate_trombone_sound(duration, sampling_rate,
slide_positions):
    t = np.linspace(0, duration, int(sampling_rate * duration),
endpoint=False)

    # Create a basic sine wave representing the fundamental frequency
    fundamental_freq = 440  # in Hertz (you can change this)
    sine_wave = np.sin(2 * np.pi * fundamental_freq * t)

    # Simulate the movement of the trombone slide
    for position in slide_positions:
        # Adjust the frequency based on the slide position
        adjusted_freq = fundamental_freq * (1 + position)

        # Generate a sine wave with the adjusted frequency
        sine_wave += 0.3 * np.sin(2 * np.pi * adjusted_freq * t)

    return sine_wave

def main():
    duration = 3  # seconds
    sampling_rate = 44100  # samples per second

    # Simulate trombone slide positions over time
    slide_positions = np.linspace(-0.2, 0.2, int(duration * 2))  # move
from fully retracted to fully extended

    # Generate trombone sound with dynamic slide movement
    trombone_sound = generate_trombone_sound(duration,
sampling_rate, slide_positions)

    # Plot the sound wave
    plt.plot(np.arange(0, duration, 1/sampling_rate),
trombone_sound)
    plt.title("Trombone Sound with Dynamic Slide Movement")
    plt.xlabel("Time (s)")
    plt.ylabel("Amplitude")
    plt.show()

if __name__ == "__main__":
    main()
```

Once, something breathtaking happened. Two of his students developed a project, a symmetrical image of a landscape set for two musicians to play together while following this image. It was music visualization. The students created an interactive visualization by playing their wind instruments. Instead of notes, the score looked like a city skyline. The students modified the image, so it was flipped upside-down like a reflection. It seemed to have an ancient power which sounded pagan to them. A scanned, transformed, and mirrored silhouette of the horizon line served as inspiration for the two players. The project was called "Two Directions for the Two Players." One player improvised by "reading" the image from left to right, while the other one from right to left. The image's outline served as a guide for music improvisation while changing the pitch and the volume.

PHYSICS – AN ABSENCE OF LIGHT (VECTOR MATHEMATICS) SHADOW OF THE MUSICIAN – TOLN

His shadow never matched.

```
import matplotlib.pyplot as plt
import numpy as np

def generate_shadow(light_source, object_position):
    # Calculate the direction vector from the light source to the object
    light_direction = object_position - light_source

    # Normalize the direction vector
    light_direction /= np.linalg.norm(light_direction)

    # Set the length of the shadow
    shadow_length = 5.0

    # Calculate the shadow position
    shadow_position = object_position + shadow_length * light_direction

    # Plotting
    plt.plot([light_source[0], object_position[0]], [light_source[1], object_position[1]], 'r-') # Light source to object
    plt.plot([object_position[0], shadow_position[0]], [object_position[1], shadow_position[1]], 'b--') # Object to shadow
    plt.plot(light_source[0], light_source[1], 'yo', label='Light Source')
    plt.plot(object_position[0], object_position[1], 'go', label='Object')
    plt.plot(shadow_position[0], shadow_position[1], 'bo', label='Shadow')

    # Set plot limits and labels
    plt.xlim(-10, 10)
    plt.ylim(-10, 10)
    plt.xlabel('X-axis')
    plt.ylabel('Y-axis')
    plt.title('Shadow Phenomenon')
    plt.legend()

    # Show the plot
    plt.show()
```

Python code simulated the phenomenon of a shadow using the concept of basic 2D graphics to represent a light source, an object, and its shadow. The code calculated the direction vector from the light source to the object, normalized it, and then used it to determine the position of the shadow. Then, with the matplotlib library, visualize the light source, object, and shadow in a 2D space.

Some thought his unique personality caused it, but it was due to his ability to hide quickly.

PHYSICAL FORCES (CALCULATE AND PRINT) INVISIBLE – AAZAM

Aazam enjoyed waiting for the stoplight to change at the cross sections. She watched the drivers taking the left turn. They looked happy, without knowing they were amused, as their car gave them the feeling of being on a merry-go-round. To describe the physical forces involved in a car's left turn, concepts like centrifugal force, friction, and inertia are req. She wrote a Python code snippet to illustrate these forces.

```
import matplotlib.pyplot as plt
import numpy as np

def left_turn_simulation(radius, speed):
    # Constants
    gravity = 9.8  # Acceleration due to gravity in m/s^2
    friction_coefficient = 0.8  # Friction coefficient between tires
and road

    # Calculate centrifugal force
    centrifugal_force = (speed ** 2) / radius

    # Calculate frictional force
    frictional_force = friction_coefficient * gravity

    # Display forces
    print(f"Centrifugal Force: {centrifugal_force} N")
    print(f"Frictional Force: {frictional_force} N")

    # Plot forces
    forces = [centrifugal_force, frictional_force]
    force_labels = ['Centripetal Force', 'Frictional Force']

    plt.bar(force_labels, forces)
    plt.ylabel('Force (N)')
    plt.title('Forces in a Left Turn')
    plt.show()

# Example usage:
radius_of_turn = float(input("Enter the radius of the turn
(meters): "))
speed_of_turn = float(input("Enter the speed of the car (m/s):
"))

left_turn_simulation(radius_of_turn, speed_of_turn)
```

Her code calculated and printed the centrifugal force during a left turn based on the provided radius and turn speed. Her code also calculated and printed the frictional force acting between the tires and the road.

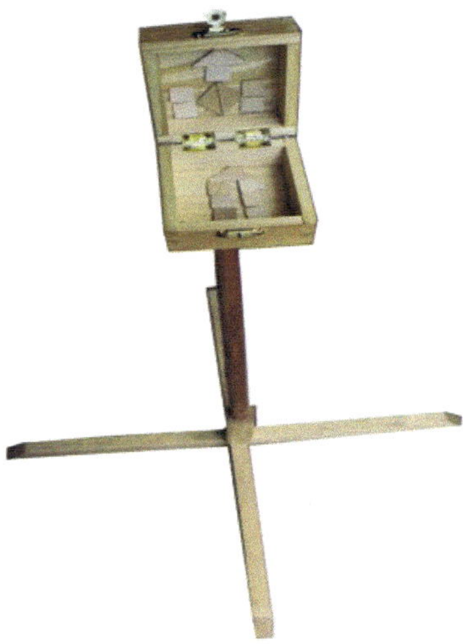

At least she understood why people were smiling.

PERCEPTION
(CLASSES AND DEFINITIONS)
ZITHER-TRAINEE – ELAH

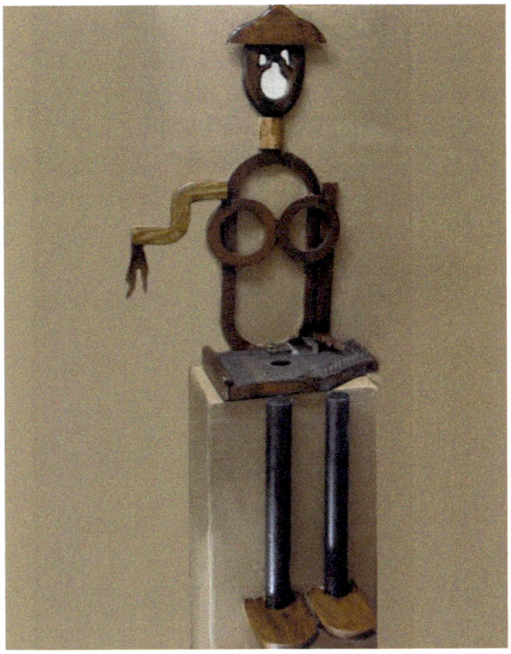

Her intention was not to look at or listen to anything but to see and hear everything to enhance perception.

```
class SelectivePerception:
    def __init__(self):
        self.eyes_closed = False
        self.ears_blocked = False

    def focus_on_senses(self):
        self.close_eyes()
        self.block_ears()

    def close_eyes(self):
        self.eyes_closed = True
        print("Closing your eyes to eliminate visual distractions.")

    def block_ears(self):
        self.ears_blocked = True
        print("Blocking your ears to eliminate auditory distractions.")

    def see_and_hear_everything(self):
        if self.eyes_closed and self.ears_blocked:
            print("Now, you can truly see and hear everything!")

# Example usage
selective_perception = SelectivePerception()
selective_perception.focus_on_senses()
selective_perception.see_and_hear_everything()
```

The "SelectivePerception" class provided methods to close eyes (close_eyes) and block ears (block_ears). The focus_on_senses method invoked both actions, simulating the idea of not looking or listening to anything specific but enhancing the ability to see and hear everything. The method see_and_hear_everything confirmed that the conditions were met for optimal perception. We can perceive more when we focus without any disturbance. Our senses can shift, she kept saying.
Despite her efforts, she was called the Agreeable Person: "As it will be, Sir."

PERFORMANCE (ROUTINE)

MIMES – MIME OLIVIER & MIME OLIVIA

They met on the deserted island. They came from the same sunken ship but had no prior relationship as they traveled on different decks. Olivier was a documentary filmmaker, and Olivia was a high school career counselor. They both felt like their careers dealt with human emotions, and both searched for them deep down in the personality of the person they'd talked to. Life on the island was good, and soon, they had a nice six-room shelter and a little boat to catch some fish. They started an entertaining business for a local monkey, which united them for life. Soon, the monkey took over their business, since they were rescued by a ship heading to Beaubourg; it amused the visitors of this newly discovered island.

```
import time

class MonkeyEntertainer:
    def __init__(self, name):
        self.name = name

    def introduce(self):
        print(f"Hello, I'm {self.name} the Monkey Entertainer! Get ready for some fun!")

    def do_magic_trick(self):
        print(f"{self.name} is about to perform a magic trick...")
        time.sleep(2)
        print("Abracadabra! 🎩✨")
        time.sleep(1)
        print(f"Ta-da! Wasn't that magical?")

    def do_dance_routine(self):
        print(f"Now, {self.name} will showcase a dance routine!")
        time.sleep(1)
        print("🐵💃🕺🐵")
        time.sleep(2)
        print("What do you think? Dance, dance, dance!")

    def entertain(self):
        self.introduce()
        self.do_magic_trick()
        self.do_dance_routine()
        print(f"{self.name} hopes you enjoyed the show!")

# Let's create a monkey entertainer and watch the performance
monkey_entertainer = MonkeyEntertainer("Mango")
monkey_entertainer.entertain()
```

They left the monkey their six-bedroom shelter and the boat to catch fish to feed the new clients. Soon, they noticed the same monkey performing with them in front of the Centre Pompidou, known as Beaubourg.

PEST CONTROL – DIGITAL WAY (TURTLE) HAIRDRESSER – KOOMO

Koomo had one question: "If the outdoors is so great, why are the bugs in my house?" Koomo developed a code with the Turtle graphics library to simulate a bug-repelling program without hurting the bugs. She represented bugs with small shapes, and the program made them move away from a central point:

```
import turtle
import random

# Set up the turtle screen
screen = turtle.Screen()
screen.title("Bug Repellent")
screen.bgcolor("white")

# Create a turtle for drawing bugs
bug_drawer = turtle.Turtle()
bug_drawer.speed(2)
bug_drawer.shape("circle")
bug_drawer.color("red")

# Function to move bugs away from a central point
def repel_bugs():
    for _ in range(20):
        bug_drawer.penup()
        x = random.randint(-200, 200)
        y = random.randint(-200, 200)
        bug_drawer.goto(x, y)
        bug_drawer.pendown()

        bug_drawer.setheading(bug_drawer.towards(0, 0))
        bug_drawer.forward(50)

# Call the function to repel bugs
repel_bugs()

# Close the turtle graphics window when clicked
screen.exitonclick()
```

In her code, bugs (represented by red circles) were randomly placed on the screen, and then they moved away from the central point (0, 0) without being harmed. Koomo soon adjusted parameters like the number of bugs or the distance they moved to customize their behavior, but the most important factor was to change color from red to green for positive connotations related to her game.
Without bugs, there would be no life, she thought. Her computer was error and virus free, since.

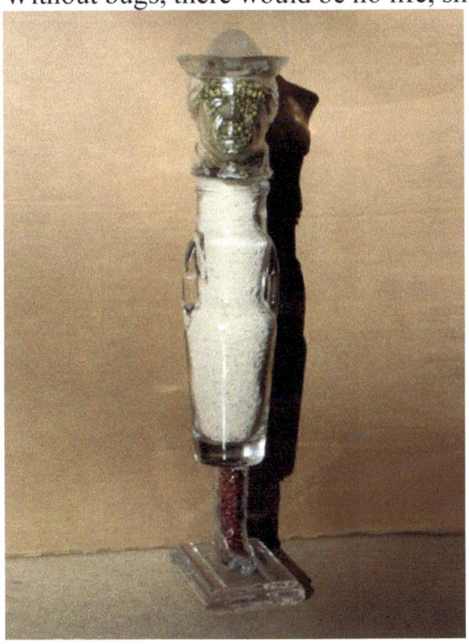

PHILOSOPHY
(CONDITIONAL STATEMENTS)
PANPIPES CINFOLI PASTORALI – PAN

Pan's instrument was considered historical. It was played in Europe, Asia, and South America, but first in ancient Greece by the goat-footed god Pan, the god of shepherds and flocks, mountain wilds, hunting, and rustic music. Pan's name was taken from the word *pan,* which meant "all." He'd never found out if he was named Pan to play this instrument or if he played it because his name was Pan. To find out:

```
class PanPlayer:
    def __init__(self, name):
        self.name = name

    def play_instrument(self, instrument):
        print(f"{self.name} plays the {instrument}.")

def determine_relationship(player_name, instrument_name):
    if player_name.lower() == instrument_name.lower():
        print(f"{player_name} was named after the {instrument_name} instrument.")
    else:
        print(f"{player_name} plays the {instrument_name} instrument because of their name.")

# Creating an instance of PanPlayer
pan_musician = PanPlayer("Pan")

# Playing the Pan instrument
pan_musician.play_instrument("Pan")

# Determining the relationship between the player's name and the instrument
determine_relationship(pan_musician.name, "Pan")
```

The determine_relationship function used an if-else statement to check whether the player's name matched the instrument name. If they were the same, it concluded that he was named after the instrument. Otherwise, it stated that he played the instrument because of his name. This concept allowed the code to make decisions based on certain conditions.

All the above must be true, he thought.

PHOTOGRAPHY
(IMAGE PROCESSING)
PHOTO NEWS – BARON ZEE

Baron Zee was well known for his photography skills. He could present anyone in a light that would enhance all the good features and hide those less wanted. As hard as it sounds, everyone knew it was true.

```
import cv2

def enhance_face(image_path):
  # Load the image
  image = cv2.imread(image_path)

  # Load pre-trained face detection model
  face_cascade = cv2.CascadeClassifier(cv2.data.haarcascades + 'haarcascade_frontalface_default.xml')

  # Convert the image to grayscale for face detection
  gray = cv2.cvtColor(image, cv2.COLOR_BGR2GRAY)

  # Detect faces in the image
  faces = face_cascade.detectMultiScale(gray, scaleFactor=1.1, minNeighbors=5, minSize=(30, 30))

  # Iterate through detected faces
  for (x, y, w, h) in faces:
    # Extract the region of interest (ROI) for face
    face_roi = image[y:y + h, x:x + w]

    # Apply basic enhancement (e.g., increase brightness and contrast)
    enhanced_face = cv2.convertScaleAbs(face_roi, alpha=1.5, beta=30)

    # Replace the original face with the enhanced version
    image[y:y + h, x:x + w] = enhanced_face

  # Display the original and enhanced images
  cv2.imshow('Original Image', cv2.resize(image, (600, 800)))
  cv2.waitKey(0)
  cv2.destroyAllWindows()

# Example usage
enhance_face('path/to/your/photo.jpg')
```

The OpenCV library detected faces in an image and then applied basic enhancements to the detected face regions. Image processing techniques could be more advanced depending on the features to enhance.

Somehow, everybody could agree on what good features were and what those less wanted would be.

PHYSICAL COMPUTING (CONDITIONAL STATEMENT) METAL BEACH COMBERS – P.P.P.

They were making not a bad living out of dropped change. All it took was perseverance, precision, and persistence. P coordinated from his desk using an Arduino board-based system while P. and P. followed.

```
const int ultrasonicTrigPin = 2;
const int ultrasonicEchoPin = 3;
const int leftMotorPin = 4;
const int rightMotorPin = 5;

void setup() {
  pinMode(ultrasonicTrigPin, OUTPUT);
  pinMode(ultrasonicEchoPin, INPUT);
  pinMode(leftMotorPin, OUTPUT);
  pinMode(rightMotorPin, OUTPUT);
  Serial.begin(9600);
}

void loop() {
  // Measure distance using ultrasonic sensor
  long duration, distance;
  digitalWrite(ultrasonicTrigPin, LOW);
  delayMicroseconds(2);
  digitalWrite(ultrasonicTrigPin, HIGH);
delayMicroseconds(10);
digitalWrite(ultrasonicTrigPin, LOW);
duration = pulseIn(ultrasonicEchoPin,
HIGH);
  distance = duration * 0.034 / 2;
  // Check if there is a coin within a certain
range
  if (distance < 30) {
    // Coin detected, guide the person to
collect it
    moveForward();
    delay(1000);
    stopMotors();
  } else {
    // No coin detected, continue scanning
    moveLeft();
  }
}
void moveForward() {
  digitalWrite(leftMotorPin, HIGH);
  digitalWrite(rightMotorPin, HIGH);
}

void moveLeft() {
  digitalWrite(leftMotorPin, LOW);
  digitalWrite(rightMotorPin, HIGH);
}

void stopMotors() {
  digitalWrite(leftMotorPin, LOW);
  digitalWrite(rightMotorPin, LOW);
}
```

The Arduino board measured the distance using an ultrasonic sensor. If it detected a coin within a certain range, it executed the code within the if block to guide the person forward to collect it. Otherwise, it executed the code within the else block to turn left and continue scanning for coins. They used their collected coins to buy a Raspberry Pi to compare the results.

```
import RPi.GPIO as GPIO
import time

# Set GPIO pins
ultrasonic_trig_pin = 23
ultrasonic_echo_pin = 24
left_motor_pin = 17
right_motor_pin = 18

# Setup GPIO
GPIO.setmode(GPIO.BCM)
GPIO.setup(ultrasonic_trig_pin,
GPIO.OUT)
GPIO.setup(ultrasonic_echo_pin, GPIO.IN)
GPIO.setup(left_motor_pin, GPIO.OUT)
GPIO.setup(right_motor_pin, GPIO.OUT)

def measure_distance():
    # Measure distance using ultrasonic
sensor
    GPIO.output(ultrasonic_trig_pin,
GPIO.LOW)
    time.sleep(0.2)
    GPIO.output(ultrasonic_trig_pin,
GPIO.HIGH)
    time.sleep(0.00001)
    GPIO.output(ultrasonic_trig_pin,
GPIO.LOW)
    pulse_start_time = time.time()
    pulse_end_time = time.time()

while GPIO.input(ultrasonic_echo_pin) ==
0:
        pulse_start_time = time.time()

    while GPIO.input(ultrasonic_echo_pin)
== 1:
        pulse_end_time = time.time()
    pulse_duration = pulse_end_time -
pulse_start_time
    distance = pulse_duration * 34300 / 2

    return distance

def move_forward():
    GPIO.output(left_motor_pin,
GPIO.HIGH)
    GPIO.output(right_motor_pin,
GPIO.HIGH)

def move_left():
    GPIO.output(left_motor_pin,
GPIO.LOW)
    GPIO.output(right_motor_pin,
GPIO.HIGH)
def stop_motors():
    GPIO.output(left_motor_pin,
GPIO.LOW)
    GPIO.output(right_motor_pin,
GPIO.LOW)

try:
    while True:
        # Measure distance
        distance = measure_distance()

        # Check if there is a coin within a
certain range
        if distance < 30:
            # Coin detected, guide the person to
collect it
            move_forward()
            time.sleep(1)
            stop_motors()
        else:
            # No coin detected, continue
scanning
            move_left()

finally:
    # Cleanup GPIO
    GPIO.cleanup()
```

They used Scratch (https://scratch.mit.edu/), popular for Makey Makey projects.

```
when green flag clicked
forever
  if touching [coin v]?
    say [Collect the coin!] for (2) seconds
  else
    say [Move left and search for coins.] for (2) seconds
```

This script used the "Event Handling" concept by responding to the event by clicking the green flag and continuously checking the condition of touching the coin. It told them if the coin was detected or not. After that, they hired a crew to use all the systems to compete for a prize: the biggest coin.

PIGEONEER (A PIGEON FANCIER)
(OOP)
PIDGEON TRAINER – BURO

Besides his pigeons, Buro had four dogs: one working, one hunting, one digging, and one running. His dogs had one thing in common: they all were loving dogs.

```
class Dog:
    def __init__(self, name, energy_level):
        self.name = name
        self.energy_level = energy_level

    def classify_performance(self):
        if self.energy_level > 70:
            return f"{self.name} is a high-performing dog."
        elif 40 <= self.energy_level <= 70:
            return f"{self.name} is a moderate-performing dog."
        else:
            return f"{self.name} is a low-performing dog."
```

He could not count his pigeons. They were fun and friendly, and they were winning at various competitions.

The Dog class encapsulated a dog's properties (name, energy_level, and behavior).

All he had to do was to train them and love them all. And they sure loved him back.

PLANETOLOGY – A STUDY OF PLANETS (SEMI-RANDOMNESS, RANDOMNESS, OR CHAOS) BASSOONIST – LAWRENCE AND HIS SOLAR MUSIC

Lawrence loved Astronomy. He studied the Solar System, then kept writing stories about some fictional life on some planet, star, or galaxy. "There are more cells in the human brain than there are stars in the Universe," as he read in Michael Gazzaniga's statement. He often had existential thoughts and could be heard saying, "Here is the chair, and here are my shoes, and the Cosmos is far away. "His special focus involved composing music. His compositions included the Solar Music: Pluto March, Ode to Mars, Venus Symphony, Mercury Blues, or Saturnal Nocturn. His bassoon sounded differently depending on the structure of each planet. His music took a specific form when Lawrence matched the physical data with the notes for his compositions. "Physical beauty of change would promote the beauty of Nature and random poetry," Lawrence said. He wrote a code to depict the planets' weight, gravity, or density in the solar system to relate them to musical notes by combining astrophysical data with musical elements. The distance between them determined the silence between planets but gravity and density caused some problems. He installed libraries: pip install pygame:

```
import pygame
from astropy import constants
from astropy import units as u
import sys
import random

# Initialize Pygame
pygame.init()

# Set up the screen
width, height = 800, 600
screen = pygame.display.set_mode((width, height))
pygame.display.set_caption("Solar System Symphony")

# Set up colors
black = (0, 0, 0)
white = (255, 255, 255)

# Set up musical parameters
base_frequency = 440  # A4 note
speed_of_sound = 343  # Speed of sound in m/s
min_distance = 1e9  # Minimum distance to prevent division by zero

# Planetary data (mass, gravity, density)
planet_data = {
   "Mercury": {"mass": 3.285e23, "gravity": None, "density": None},
   "Venus": {"mass": 4.867e24, "gravity": None, "density": None},
   "Earth": {"mass": 5.972e24, "gravity": None, "density": None},
   "Mars": {"mass": 6.39e23, "gravity": None, "density": None},
   "Jupiter": {"mass": 1.898e27, "gravity": None, "density": None},
   "Saturn": {"mass": 5.683e26, "gravity": None, "density": None},
   "Uranus": {"mass": 8.681e25, "gravity": None, "density": None},
   "Neptune": {"mass": 1.024e26, "gravity": None, "density": None},
}

# Calculate gravity and density for each planet
for planet, data in planet_data.items():
   data["gravity"] = constants.G * data["mass"] / (constants.R_earth
+ min_distance) ** 2
   data["density"] = data["mass"] / (4 / 3 * u.pi * (constants.R_earth
+ min_distance) ** 3)

  # Sort planets by gravity
sorted_planets = sorted(planet_data.items(), key=lambda x:
x[1]["gravity"].value)

# Main game loop
while True:

for event in pygame.event.get():
      if event.type == pygame.QUIT:
         pygame.quit()
         sys.exit()

   # Clear the screen
   screen.fill(black)

   # Generate musical composition based on planet parameters
   for i in range(len(sorted_planets) - 1):
      planet1, data1 = sorted_planets[i]
      planet2, data2 = sorted_planets[i + 1]

      distance = abs(data2["gravity"] - data1["gravity"]).value
      note_duration = int(distance / speed_of_sound * 1000)  # Convert
distance to time (milliseconds)

      # Play a note based on the distance
      if note_duration > 0:
         frequency = base_frequency * (i + 1)  # Increase frequency for higher
gravity planets
         pygame.mixer.Sound(frequency).play()

      # Draw lines between planets based on density
      line_color = (255 - int(data2["density"].value), 0,
int(data1["density"].value))
      pygame.draw.line(screen, line_color, (i * 50, 300), ((i + 1) * 50, 300), 2)

   # Update the display
   pygame.display.flip()

   # Set the frame rate
   pygame.time.Clock().tick(60)
```

With Pygame to create a window, the computer calculated the gravity, forming the pitch of the notes and density of the planets, making the colors of the lines between them form a musical composition. Lawrence won every competition. People see Nature as beautiful, but many are afraid of physics. Some unconsciously related to Lawrence's music without knowing that the physical rules guided his work.

PLAY
(CLASSES AND METHODS, FOLLOWING THE (OOP) PARADIGM)
PARK PLAYERS – MUL AND ALE

Playing games on their phones in a park was the best thing their parents thought they could do. Not only were they spending time in the sun, but their brain functions were stimulated, which pleased the adults, who developed methods like stimulate_brain and observe_effects.

```
class SunStimulation:
    def __init__(self, person_name):
        self.person_name = person_name
        self.brain_functions = []

    def stimulate_brain(self, *args):
        self.brain_functions.extend(args)

    def observe_effects(self):
        print(f"The sun stimulates {self.person_name}'s brain
functions.")
        print("Effects:")
        for function in self.brain_functions:
            print(f"- {function}")

# Creating an instance of SunStimulation
sun_lover = SunStimulation("Alex")

# Stimulation of brain functions by the sun
sun_lover.stimulate_brain(
    "Increased serotonin production",
    "Improved mood",
    "Enhanced vitamin D synthesis",
    "Boosted cognitive function"
)

# Observing the effects of sun stimulation on brain functions
sun_lover.observe_effects()
```

However, no equipment was employed to gather data crucial for any serious outcome.

The only problem their parents had was that playing intellectual games did not involve much motion.

POETRY
(OOP)
POET – CEDRIC

Cedric was a good poet. He thought in verses, spoke like that, and was always ready for any topic to be used as his inspiration. He suffered from occasional writer's block, though. He used magnetic poetry with a magnet-based poetry generator during those hard times:

```
import random

class MagnetPoetryGenerator:
    def __init__(self):
        self.words = ["Love", "Nature", "Dream", "Silence", "Whisper",
"Ocean", "Stars", "Eternal", "Serenity"]

    def generate_poetry(self, num_lines):
        poetry = []

        for _ in range(num_lines):
            line = " ".join(random.sample(self.words, len(self.words)))
            poetry.append(line)

        return poetry

if __name__ == "__main__":
    poetry_generator = MagnetPoetryGenerator()
    num_lines = 5
    generated_poetry = poetry_generator.generate_poetry(num_lines)

    print("Generated Poetry:")
    for line in generated_poetry:
        print(line)
```

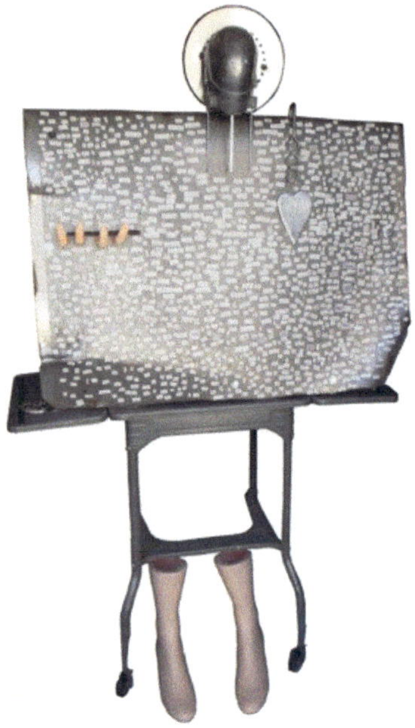

The idea was to have a set of words that can be rearranged to form creative but often random phrases. His code defined a MagnetPoetryGenerator class with an _init_ method to initialize the set of words and a generate_poetry method to create random phrases by shuffling the words. He could always be seen with those magnet-coated words, many of them carried just in case.

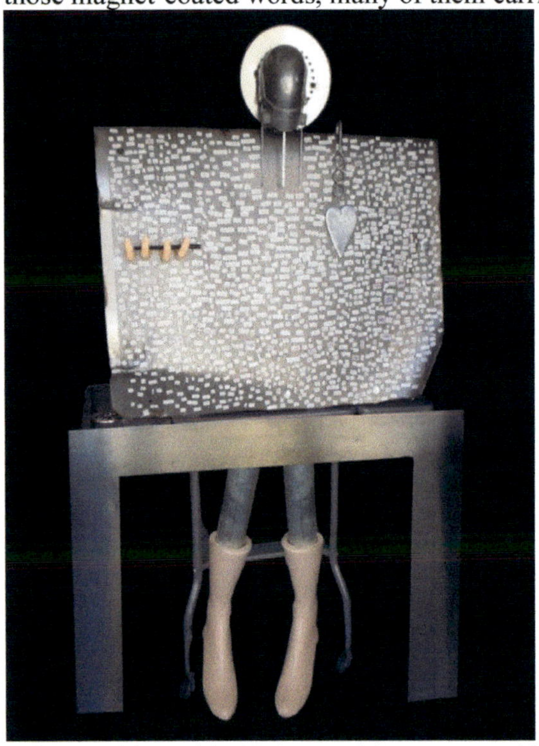

After working with AI, he would not agree with anything. It depends, was his phrase.
Creatures from the Abyss of his mind.

POETRY – RAP
(DICTIONARY TO MAP)
RAPPERS – LU, ENNY, AKE, AND ULE

They were the ones who remembered that most matters contained a second bottom.
How is it going?
Nothing bad.
That's good.
Is nothing good bad?
No!

```
def explain_rap_terms(word):
    rap_dictionary = {
        "flow": "The rhythm and rhyming in a rapper's style.",
        "lit": " Description of something that is super, impressive, or cool",
        "bars": "Clever verses in a rap song.",
        "flex": "To brag about one's achievements or possessions.",
        "dope": "Cool, exciting, or impressive.",
        "trap": "A style of rap music that originated in the Southern United States, often characterized by heavy beats and lyrics about street life.",
        "mic drop": "A confident gesture using a microphone after a particularly impressive statement."
    }

    word_lower = word.lower()  # Convert input to lowercase for case-insensitivity
    if word_lower in rap_dictionary:
        return rap_dictionary[word_lower]
    else:
        return f"Sorry, I don't have an explanation for '{word}' in my rap dictionary."

# Example usage:
word_to_explain = input("Enter a rap term to explain: ")
explanation = explain_rap_terms(word_to_explain)
print(explanation)
```

They used their fictional rap dictionary. "The explain_rap_terms function took a word as input, converted it to lowercase for case-insensitivity, and checked if the word existed in the dictionary. If it did, it returned the corresponding explanation; otherwise, it provided a default message.

They all preferred clubs to political parties.

Welcome to:
Focus and Listen Vol. XXXXVI. No 38724.

EDITOR'S RANT

In this issue, we finally settle the age-old question: Are those who listen to music slowly becoming better people?

```
import random

def main():
    # Generate random opinions
    opinions = [
        "Listening to music can enhance emotional intelligence.",
        "Music may contribute to improved focus and productivity.",
        "It depends on the type of music; not all genres have the same impact.",
        "There's no direct correlation between music preference and personal development.",
        "Music is just one factor among many that contribute to personal growth.",
    ]

    # Print a random opinion
    print("Are those who listen to music slowly becoming better people?")
    print("Here's a perspective:")
    print(random.choice(opinions))

if __name__ == "__main__":
    main()
```

In the end, most of them agreed.

PRESERVATION
(OOP WITH METHODS TO ENCAPSULATE THE FUNCTIONALITY)
PRINTERS – PEL & MUA

They were printing everything they could to preserve it. Data flies away, and paper stays, they agreed.

```
class ThoughtPreservationSystem:
    def __init__(self):
        self.thoughts = []

    def preserve_thought(self, thought):
        self.thoughts.append(thought)

    def retrieve_thoughts(self):
        return self.thoughts

# Example Usage
if __name__ == "__main__":
    preservation_system = ThoughtPreservationSystem()

    preservation_system.preserve_thought("I wonder what the future holds.")
    preservation_system.preserve_thought("The code is a reflection of the mind.")
    preservation_system.preserve_thought("To be or not to be, that is the question.")

    preserved_thoughts = preservation_system.retrieve_thoughts()

    for thought in preserved_thoughts:
        print(thought)
```

The invention of 3D printing helped them, but not the planet.

```
class ThreeDPrintingImpact:
    def __init__(self):
        self.supports_planet = ["Reduced waste in manufacturing", "Customization and local production", "Resource efficiency"]
        self.distresses_planet = ["Material consumption and waste", "Energy consumption", "E-waste from 3D printers"]

    def explain_impact(self):
        print("Ways 3D printing supports our planet:")
        for support in self.supports_planet:
            print(f"- {support}")

        print("\nWays 3D printing distresses our planet:")
        for distress in self.distresses_planet:
            print(f"- {distress}")

# Example Usage
if __name__ == "__main__":
    impact_analysis = ThreeDPrintingImpact()
    impact_analysis.explain_impact()
```

They are working on adding some recyclers for every 3D printer to be sold.

MY BIRD – NUO

He knew all the tricks and trades but shortcuts to basket making. Nuo's collection of tools and materials came from the best sources. He understood the wear and tear condition and the constraints behind the usability and elegance of rattan design. He learned to color the reeds. He wrote a code that compares rattan, wicker, and reed and displays similarities and differences:

```
def compare_materials(rattan, wicker, reed):
  # Displaying definitions of each material
  print(f"Definition of Rattan: {rattan}")
  print(f"Definition of Wicker: {wicker}")
  print(f"Definition of Reed: {reed}")

  # Comparing materials and displaying similarities and differences
  if rattan == wicker and wicker == reed:
    print("All three materials are the same.")
  elif rattan == wicker or rattan == reed or wicker == reed:
    print("At least two of the materials are similar.")
  else:
    print("All three materials are different.")

# Calling the function with sample definitions
compare_materials("A type of palm", "Woven furniture or items", "Tall, slender grass-like plants")
```

He showed the definitions of rattan, wicker, and reed as strings, which a print function displayed; the if-elif-else structure was used to compare the materials. For a bird, it made a lot of sense.

Since his collection of reeds took up a lot of space in this nest, he started building wicker furniture out of them. His plates, vases, slippers, backpack, and placemats were made of the same material. His pajamas matched his sheets, so every morning, when waking him for a flying school, his mother would say, "I cannot find you." His king-size reed bed in his nest also matched his favorite slippers.

PRODUCT SEMIOTICS (QUERY CRITERIA) ALMOST ALL – LAK

Lak thought of love as coming from one point to another, as an attitude, a sense, or a frame of mind. He was nostalgic. He longed for daily objects, soon to be replaced by some new solutions. It was an elegy for old tools. Prosaic tools have the power to inspire heroic actions. A will has strong potential. The scissors are seen as iconic objects, as it is hard to design them differently without causing blisters. Objects will find their use among people no matter how much we automate. Can you replace a shovel? he thought. It will always be handy to a person, despite how many new devices can be invented. How can one change the incinerator, also known as a badger? It cannot be automated not to hurt one's hand. A rain gutter needs to set the path of the running water. He wrote a code determining if an old invention could be safely replaced with new technologies, which depended on the old specifics and the criteria for determining safety. He started with old incandescent bulbs vs. LED bulbs based on energy efficiency and cost.

```
def can_replace_incandescent_with_led(old_invention, new_technology):
    # Assuming old_invention and new_technology are dictionaries with
relevant information
class StoryStructure:
    def _init_(self, title, protagonist, antagonist, setting, climax,
resolution):

    # Criteria for replacement
    energy_efficiency_old = old_invention.get("energy_efficiency", 0)
    energy_efficiency_new = new_technology.get("energy_efficiency", 0)

    cost_old = old_invention.get("cost", 0)
    cost_new = new_technology.get("cost", 0)

    # Safety criteria - you can add more conditions based on your scenario
    if energy_efficiency_new > energy_efficiency_old and cost_new <=
cost_old:
        return True
    else:
        return False

# Example data for incandescent bulbs and LED bulbs
old_incandescent = {"energy_efficiency": 0.2, "cost": 5}
new_led = {"energy_efficiency": 0.8, "cost": 10}

# Check if LED bulbs can replace incandescent bulbs
result = can_replace_incandescent_with_led(old_incandescent, new_led)

if result:
    print("It is safe to replace old incandescent bulbs with new LED bulbs.")
else:
    print("It is not recommended to replace old incandescent bulbs with new
LED bulbs.")
```

He kept researching—a sense of force, function versus the material. He discovered that a force was a collection of vectors, not a vector, like a star with a collection of vectors, sizes, and directions.

PROFESSIONAL CRITIQUE
(ABSTRACTION THROUGH FUNCTIONS)
MATHEMATICIANS GOING TO A CONFERENCE

This group of conference participants was known for criticizing first and understanding later.

```
def analyze_code_quality(code):
    # Placeholder for code analysis logic
    print("Analyzing code quality...")

def provide_feedback(quality_score):
    if quality_score > 0.8:
        return "Excellent work! Your code is of high quality."
    elif 0.6 <= quality_score <= 0.8:
        return "Good job, but there's room for improvement in code
quality."
    else:
        return "Consider revising and improving your code."

 def professional_critique(code):
    analyze_code_quality(code)

    # Placeholder for additional critique criteria

    quality_score = 0.75  # Placeholder for the quality score
    feedback = provide_feedback(quality_score)

    return feedback

def main():
    # Example code for critique
    sample_code = """
    def greet(name):
        print("Hello, " + name + "!")
    greet("World")
    """

    critique_feedback = professional_critique(sample_code)
    print(critique_feedback)

if __name__ == "__main__":
    main()
```

Each aspect of the critique was encapsulated in a separate function. For quality: analyze_code_quality: Placeholder for code quality analysis. provide_feedback: Generated feedback based on the quality score. professional_critique: Orchestrated the critique process by calling the analysis and feedback functions. Each function served a specific purpose, promoting code organization and reusability.

This is how they arrived at an understanding of what they criticized.

PSYCHOLINGUISTICS – PSYCHOLOGY OF LANGUAGE (LANGUAGE (LIBRARY) HACKER – K

He was trying to create a unique language reserved for computing. K was against metaphors. He saw them as oriented toward one type of thinking with no meaningful associations with people from other countries. Some believed that since most conferences were based on English, this should be the language behind the naming of computer-based words. Esperanto failed, felt the others. But its origins were closer to one group of people. Metaphors are more accessible to grasp in a folder or file; why not holder, container, data, or something from a different language of a different root? USB is an acronym, but who remembers SCSI now? Trash, recycling bins, or dumpsters are other names that share the same function for different operating systems because of copyright. He gave up even thinking about it until he developed a computer language, an equal one for all the languages that used shapes for each object and operation accordingly. He created a code for shapes to represent essential computer components.

```
import turtle

# Set up the turtle screen
screen = turtle.Screen()
screen.title("Computer Shapes")
screen.bgcolor("white")

# Create a turtle for drawing
drawer = turtle.Turtle()
drawer.speed(2)

# Function to draw a rectangle
def draw_rectangle(width, height):
    for _ in range(2):
        drawer.forward(width)
        drawer.left(90)
        drawer.forward(height)
        drawer.left(90)

# Function to draw a triangle
def draw_triangle(side_length):


    for _ in range(3):
        drawer.forward(side_length)
        drawer.left(120)


# Function to draw a circle
def draw_circle(radius):
    drawer.circle(radius)
```

```
# Draw a rectangle representing a desktop
drawer.color("blue")
draw_rectangle(200, 150)

# Move to draw other shapes
drawer.penup()
drawer.goto(100, 75)
drawer.pendown()

# Draw a triangle representing a mouse
drawer.color("green")
draw_triangle(50)

# Move to draw another shape
drawer.penup()
drawer.goto(-100, 75)
drawer.pen down()

# Draw a circle representing a monitor
drawer.color("red")
draw_circle(75)

# Close the turtle graphics window when clicking
The screen.exitonclick()
```

The Turtle graphics library simplified the drawing: a blue rectangle (a desktop), a green triangle (a mouse), and a red circle (a monitor). With his friends, they modified the code to add more shapes for other computer components, but they ended up creating artwork together with no other activities needed.

Psychological Dualism
(Conditional Statements (if, elif, and else)
Notorious – Nikifora

She balanced between:
greed – generosity
anger – compassion
ignorance – wisdom
She was researching for more:

```
def juxtapose_concepts(is_light):
    """Juxtapose the concepts of light and darkness."""
    if is_light:
        print("The room is filled with light.")
    else:
        print("The room is in darkness.")

if __name__ == "__main__":
    # Prompt the user to choose a concept
    user_choice = input("Enter 'light' or 'darkness': ").lower()

    # Use conditional statements to juxtapose the chosen concept
    if user_choice == 'light':
        juxtapose_concepts(True)
    elif user_choice == 'darkness':
        juxtapose_concepts(False)
    else:
        print("Invalid choice. Please enter 'light' or 'darkness'.")
```

Her program prompted the user to enter either 'light' or 'darkness', and based on the user's input, it used conditional statements to juxtapose the chosen concept. If the user chooses 'light, ' it prints a message indicating that it is filled with light. If the user chose 'darkness,' it printed a message indicating that the room was filled with darkness. The else statement handled any invalid input. Conditional statements are fundamental in programming as they allow the execution of different code blocks based on certain conditions, such as control of the flow of the program based on the user's input.
After that, she wrote a poem:

It Is Not Warm

It is not warm
It is not cold
It is not wet
It is not dry
It is not loud
It is not quiet
It is not bad
It is not good
It is not bright
It is not dark
It is not bad
It's all good.

PSYCHOLOGICAL – MENTAL STATE (CLASS) GUITAR – CORNELIA

She constantly had to focus on two things: precision and speed. She was not just about her fingers but her state of mind, alertness, and readiness. It all started after she read an article in which a script simulated the connection between one's state of mind while playing the guitar and a computer game. Those who stayed away from game relaxation, needed psychotherapy:

```
def psychotherapy_for_musicians():
    """
    List techniques used in psychotherapy for musicians.
    """
    techniques = [
        "Performance anxiety management",
        "Mindfulness and relaxation exercises",
        "Goal-setting and progress tracking",
        "Emotional expression through music",
        "Cognitive-behavioral therapy for negative thoughts",
    ]

    print("Psychotherapy techniques for musicians:")
    for technique in techniques:
        print(f"- {technique}")

# Example: Psychotherapy Techniques for Musicians
psychotherapy_for_musicians()
```

Many were observed to stop having their problems.

PSYCHOLOGY OF LOVE
(CLASSES AND OBJECTS)
THE MUSIC LOVER – PEDRO

Music lover Pedro, who also practices various sports, has always intrigued musicians. Pedro was passionate about extreme bike rides and a great fan of demolition derby. But he was also present at every concert given by the symphony orchestra and opera performance, where he always sat in the same chair in the front row. He was bringing flowers for a different musician each time. Then, he quickly disappeared. Nobody could understand the reasons for this behavior. Music talkers Todd and Tina discussed motivations that might make people want to do certain peculiar things. There were a lot of hypotheses. Maybe he felt a true love for music, enjoyed being seen on a stage, was an accomplished musician some time ago, or had one in his family. With classes and objects to model the concept of opera performers, they encapsulated related data and behavior within objects:

```
class OperaPerformer:
    def __init__(self, name):
        self.name = name

def bring_flowers_for_performers(performers):
    for performer in performers:
        print(f"Bringing flowers for {performer.name}")

if __name__ == "__main__":
    performers = [
        OperaPerformer("Soprano"),
        OperaPerformer("Tenor"),
        OperaPerformer("Baritone"),
    ]deliver

    bring_flowers_for_performers(performers)
```

None of these suppositions seemed true, as Pedro did not look sentimental. Adam, the oboist, believed that Pedro was in love with a florist, who was selling flowers in a nearby store.

PROBLEM-SOLVING (ERROR HANDLING) PREVENTER -- EMPAR

His job was not to solve problems but to prevent them.

```
def safe_division(x, y):
    if y == 0:
        print("Error: Division by zero is not allowed.")
        return None
    else:
        result = x / y
        return result

# Example usage
numerator = 10
denominator = 0

result = safe_division(numerator, denominator)

if result is not None:
    print(f"The result of the division is: {result}")
```

He was always needed by many.

PUBLIC SPEAKING
(AUDIO RECORDING AND PLAYBACK)
MOOD ENHANCERS – WYOMA AND DELIAH

Gerlost, the Orchestra Director, had extensive experience in performing before devoting himself to an administrative career. He also used to teach for a while. Every time new students would tell him that their teachers (who happened to be Gerlost's former students) recommended him as a person to study under, he felt like he had grand students. Gerlost knew well what it takes to make a good lecture. He felt that every professor should have a voice coach to help deliver the material but also to save one's voice, so often endangered by lengthy speeches. Gerlost knew what performers go through before, during, and after the performance. Thus, he hired two Mood Enhancers: Wyoma and Deliah. They majored in communication, had great public speaking skills, and besides being well-rounded, had a sense of humor. Their previous comedian experience was found to be on demand. First, they suggested replacing the lectures with more involving activities. They wrote a Python code using the pyaudio library to record one's voice during a lecture and add a touch of humor by randomly inserting applause sounds.

```
import pyaudio
import wave
import random
import time

# Set up PyAudio
p = pyaudio.PyAudio()

# Define recording parameters
FORMAT = pyaudio.paInt16
CHANNELS = 1
RATE = 44100
CHUNK = 1024
RECORD_SECONDS = 10
WAVE_OUTPUT_FILENAME = 'lecture_recording.wav'

# Function to play applause sound
def play_applause():
    applause_files = ['applause1.wav', 'applause2.wav', 'applause3.wav']
    applause_file = random.choice(applause_files)

    applause_wave = wave.open(applause_file, 'rb')
    applause_stream =
p.open(format=p.get_format_from_width(applause_wave.getsampwidth()),
                    channels=applause_wave.getnchannels(),
                    rate=applause_wave.getframerate(),
                    output=True)

    applause_data = applause_wave.readframes(CHUNK)

    while applause_data:
        applause_stream.write(applause_data)
        applause_data = applause_wave.readframes(CHUNK)

    applause_wave.close()
    applause_stream.stop_stream()
    applause_stream.close()

# Record the lecture
stream = p.open(format=FORMAT,
            channels=CHANNELS,
            rate=RATE,
            input=True,
            frames_per_buffer=CHUNK)

print("Recording started...")
frames = []
for i in range(0, int(RATE / CHUNK * RECORD_SECONDS)):
    data = stream.read(CHUNK)
    frames.append(data)

print("Recording finished.")

# Stop the recording stream
stream.stop_stream()
stream.close()
p.terminate()

# Save the recorded voice
wf = wave.open(WAVE_OUTPUT_FILENAME, 'wb')
wf.setnchannels(CHANNELS)
wf.setsampwidth(p.get_sample_size(FORMAT))
wf.setframerate(RATE)
wf.writeframes(b''.join(frames))
wf.close()

print(f"Voice recording saved to {WAVE_OUTPUT_FILENAME}")

# Play the applause randomly during playback
replay_stream = p.open(format=FORMAT,
                channels=CHANNELS,
                rate=RATE,
                output=True)

# Playback the recorded voice
voice_wave = wave.open(WAVE_OUTPUT_FILENAME, 'rb')
voice_data = voice_wave.readframes(CHUNK)

while voice_data:
    replay_stream.write(voice_data)
    voice_data = voice_wave.readframes(CHUNK)

    # Randomly insert applause sound
    if random.random() < 0.05:
        play_applause()

# Close the streams
voice_wave.close()
replay_stream.stop_stream()
replay_stream.close()
p.terminate()
```

The pyaudio library captured the user's voice and saved it to play it back with applause. It made Gerlost add a "pfft" sound after each sentence.

Q	QUALITY OF SOUND (FORMATTING) OBOE – COLIN

Oboist Colin approached the acoustician Danny to ask him for advice, and they went together to the chiefs Frank, Bob, and Marcel's place (Frank, Bob, and Marcel are marvelous cooks). After dinner was served, Colin began to talk about his seventeen-year-old daughter Andrea, who will soon graduate from high school. Andrea played oboe in Doran's symphony orchestra, but she enjoyed math and wanted to work as an architect and devote her skills exclusively to designing concert halls. Colin asked Danny if it would be possible to open a special course for the students to focus on this field. Danny believed it was a perfect time to discuss this idea because of the approaching international conference on acoustics. Danny will organize panels where architects and acousticians discuss sound quality at the concert stages, in conference halls, and in movie theaters.

```
def evaluate_sound_quality(venue_type):
    """Evaluate and discuss sound quality at different venues."""
    if venue_type == "concert":
        sound_quality = "high-fidelity"
    elif venue_type == "conference":
        sound_quality = "clear and intelligible"
    elif venue_type == "movie_theater":
        sound_quality = "immersive with surround sound"
    else:
        sound_quality = "unknown"

    print(f"At the {venue_type} venue:")
    print(f"The sound quality is {sound_quality}.")

if __name__ == "__main__":
    # Discuss sound quality at different venues
    evaluate_sound_quality("concert")
    evaluate_sound_quality("conference")
    evaluate_sound_quality("movie_theater")
```

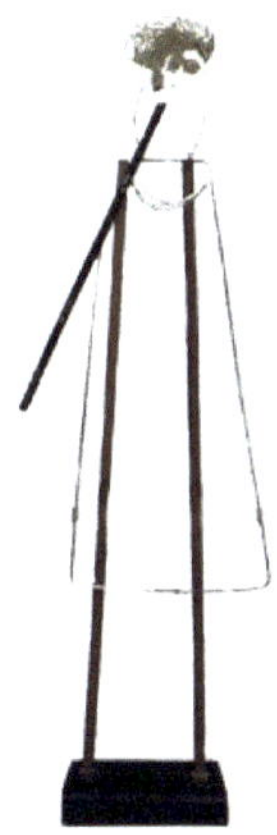

The print statements used f-strings (formatted string literals) to include the evaluated sound quality in the output. F-strings allowed one to embed expressions inside string literals, making it easy to format and display dynamic information in a readable way. String formatting is a powerful tool for creating informative and readable output, while f-strings are a convenient and efficient way to achieve this.

Colin also suggested going to the Conference on Generative Art. "Do you make art because you are the artist, or you are the artist because you make art?" asked Danny. "Oh, the need to make art is almost like an urge to go to the bathroom," Colin replied.

R RECORD KEEPING (DICTIONARIES) DOCUMENTALIST – HEVOR

Along with the records for his professional life he kept track of everything. He had a journal, sketchbook, illustrated journal, notes on his watch, phone, tablet, all computers, and lots of sticky notes covering the space around him. The problem was he'd never found the time to make any sense of it, even for himself. One day, he wrote a code that organizes information using dictionaries:

```
class Organizer:
  def __init__(self):
    self.journal = {}
    self.sketchbook = {}
    self.illustrated_journal = {}
    self.watch_notes = {}
    self.phone_notes = {}
    self.tablet_notes = {}
    self.computer_notes = {}
    self.sticky_notes = {}

  def add_to_journal(self, entry):
    self.journal[self.get_next_entry_number(self.journal)] = entry

  def add_to_sketchbook(self, sketch):
    self.sketchbook[self.get_next_entry_number(self.sketchbook)] =
sketch

  def add_to_illustrated_journal(self, illustration):

self.illustrated_journal[self.get_next_entry_number(self.illustrated_journal
)] = illustration

  def add_to_watch_notes(self, note):
    self.watch_notes[self.get_next_entry_number(self.watch_notes)] =

note

  def add_to_phone_notes(self, note):
    self.phone_notes[self.get_next_entry_number(self.phone_notes)] =
note

  def add_to_tablet_notes(self, note):
    self.tablet_notes[self.get_next_entry_number(self.tablet_notes)] =
note

def add_to_computer_notes(self, note):

  self.computer_notes[self.get_next_entry_number(self.computer_notes)] =
  note

  def add_to_sticky_notes(self, note):

self.sticky_notes[self.get_next_entry_number(self.sticky_notes
)] = note

  def get_next_entry_number(self, entries):
    return len(entries) + 1


# Example usage:
organizer = Organizer()

organizer.add_to_journal("Wrote about an exciting day!")
organizer.add_to_sketchbook("Drew a beautiful landscape.")
organizer.add_to_illustrated_journal("Combined writing and
drawings about a memorable event.")
organizer.add_to_watch_notes("Reminder: Meeting at 2 PM.")
organizer.add_to_phone_notes("Grocery list: Milk, eggs,
bread.")
organizer.add_to_tablet_notes("Idea for a new project.")
organizer.add_to_computer_notes("Code for the upcoming
feature.")
organizer.add_to_sticky_notes("Call Mom later.")

# Accessing the organized information
print("Journal Entries:", organizer.journal)
print("Sketchbook Entries:", organizer.sketchbook)
print("Illustrated Journal Entries:",
organizer.illustrated_journal)
print("Watch Notes:", organizer.watch_notes)
print("Phone Notes:", organizer.phone_notes)
print("Tablet Notes:", organizer.tablet_notes)
print("Computer Notes:", organizer.computer_notes)
print("Sticky Notes:", organizer.sticky_notes)
```

His code defined a simple Organizer class with methods to add entries to different categories.

His next task was to write a code for his work duties, but it was hard to achieve group consensus.

REFLECTIONS
(REFLECTIONS)
FRENCH HORN – ARTHUR

Arthur loved the deep sound of his instrument. He also liked its form and shape, its colors and glossiness. But most of all, he enjoyed seeing the reflections of his fellow orchestra members on his instrument. However, this caused some problems when he practiced alone. He was not able to concentrate without seeing the reflections of the orchestra members present on his instrument. He decided to seek professional help from the psychotherapist Dave. Dave advised asking the Media Man, Duncan, to take a big photo of the entire group and set it up in Arthur's practice room in front of his instrument with a proper angle, allowing for reflection. To achieve this, Duncan would need to use a combination of image processing and manipulation libraries, such as Python's Pillow and OpenCV. It was hard to execute code or directly manipulate images, but he wrote a basic outline to get started by having Pillow and OpenCV installed:

```
pip install Pillow
pip install OpenCV-python


from PIL import Image
import cv2
import numpy as np

def create_reflection(image_path, output_path):
    # Load the image
    original_image = Image.open(image_path)

    # Convert the image to a NumPy array
    original_np = np.array(original_image)

    # Flip the image vertically to create a reflection
    reflected_np = np.flipud(original_np)

    # Create a mask for the reflection using a gradient
    mask = np.zeros_like(original_np[:, :, 0])
    rows, cols = mask.shape
    for i in range(rows):
        mask[i, :] = np.linspace(0, 1, cols)

    # Apply the mask to the reflection
    reflected_np = (reflected_np * mask[:, :,
np.newaxis]).astype(np.uint8)

    # Convert the NumPy array back to an image
    reflected_image = Image.fromarray(reflected_np)

    # Save the result
    reflected_image.save(output_path)

if __name__ == "__main__":
    input_image_path = "path/to/your/group_photo.jpg"
    output_image_path = "path/to/your/output/reflected_photo.jpg"

    create_reflection(input_image_path, output_image_path)
```

He replaced "path/to/your/group_photo.jpg" with the path to the group photo and adjusted the output path accordingly. This script loaded the image, created a reflection by flipping it vertically, and applied a gradient mask to fade the reflection. It could even be customized based on Artur's preferences to excel.

RENEWABLE ENERGY (GENETIC ALGORITHM) SCABILLO DEGL' ANTICHI – ORTHOCERAS

Orthoceras always wore his soiled wooden shoes. Historically this type of shoes was used for setting and stabilizing rhythm for the bagpipers. He felt like being a scientist, musician, and dancer simultaneously, but his heart was someplace else. Once, when walking down the street, he noticed a sentence on the pavement: "Make your perceived abilities greater than your dreams or demons," was it? Chalks can be quite misleading when used on a rough sidewalk. Since he wore his mighty shoes, he impulsively danced two versions of this sentence. Someone even dropped him a nice donation.

Orthoceras kept studying math, physics, and chemistry. It irritated him that all the heat from the summer was not stored for the winter, and the winter cold could hardly be stored for the hot days. He was determined to solve the energy problems by generating negative gravitation for a selected spot. This way, the underground water could cycle up, heating and cooling houses depending on the season. Creating negative gravity to solve energy problems can be quite a fascinating concept, but unfortunately, it's not within the realm of current scientific understanding or technological feasibility. Gravity is a fundamental force of nature and manipulating it in such a way would require technologies far beyond our current capabilities. However, he came up with a concept that's closer to reality and focused on stable energy solutions. He wrote a code snippet for a renewable energy optimization algorithm. He then used a genetic algorithm to optimize the placement of wind turbines in a given area for maximum energy output.

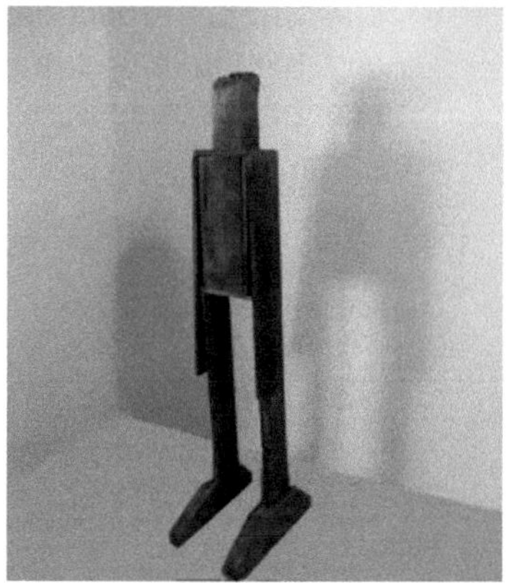

```
import random

# Define the objective function (fitness function)
def calculate_energy_output(turbine_positions):
    # Your energy output calculation logic goes here
    # This function should return a value to be maximized
    pass

# Genetic Algorithm Parameters
population_size = 50
generations = 100
mutation_rate = 0.1

# Generate initial population
def generate_population():
    return [[random.uniform(0, 100), random.uniform(0, 100)] for _ in
range(population_size)]

# Crossover function
def crossover(parent1, parent2):
    crossover_point = random.randint(0, len(parent1) - 1)
    child = parent1[:crossover_point] + parent2[crossover_point:]
    return child

# Mutation function
def mutate(individual):
    mutated_individual = [gene + random.uniform(-5, 5) for gene in
individual]
    return mutated_individual


# Main Genetic Algorithm
def genetic_algorithm():
    population = generate_population()
for generation in range(generations):
        # Evaluate fitness
        fitness_scores = [calculate_energy_output(individual) for individual in
population]

        # Select parents for crossover
        parents = [population[i] for i in range(population_size) if random.random()
< fitness_scores[i] / sum(fitness_scores)]

        # Generate new population through crossover and mutation
        new_population = []

        while len(new_population) < population_size:
            parent1 = random.choice(parents)
            parent2 = random.choice(parents)
            child = crossover(parent1, parent2)
            if random.random() < mutation_rate:
                child = mutate(child)
            new_population.append(child)

        population = new_population

    # Return the best solution
    best_solution = max(population, key=calculate_energy_output)
    return best_solution

# Example usage
optimized_turbine_positions = genetic_algorithm()
print("Optimized Turbine Positions:", optimized_turbine_positions)
```

He applied a concept of evolutionary Genetic Algorithm, inspired by a process of natural selection. It iteratively evolved a population of candidate solutions to find the best idea for a given problem: the placement of wind turbines to maximize energy output. The algorithm used selection, crossover, and mutation operations to generate new solutions over several generations. His real passion was to understand the Universe. He kept studying micro-related topics, to draw conclusions and apply them to the Macro World. It was usually followed by a dance performance related to each idea.

Robotics
(Inheritance)
Robot Makers – R1 & R2

They can build you a robot as a doppelgänger or soothsayer, a cyborg; robots focused on militarism, aka weaponry robots, robot sapiens, integrated robotic devices and human beings, and the advanced ones with human abilities. They started with four types of robots: doppelgangers, soothsayers, cyborgs, and weaponry robots, which were to fight clatter, as they later discovered.

```
class Robot:
    def __init__(self, name):
        self.name = name
        self.power_level = 100

    def recharge(self):
        print(f"{self.name} is recharging. Power level increased.")

    def display_status(self):
        print(f"{self.name} - Power Level: {self.power_level}")

# Major Concept: Class Inheritance
# Inheriting from the Robot class to create specialized robot types
class DoppelgangerRobot(Robot):
    def mimic(self, target):
        print(f"{self.name} is mimicking {target}.")

class SoothsayerRobot(Robot):
    def predict_future(self):
        print(f"{self.name} is predicting the future.")

class CyborgRobot(Robot):
    def enhance_human_part(self, body_part):
        print(f"{self.name} is enhancing {body_part} with cybernetic
components.")

class WeaponryRobot(Robot):
    def equip_weapon(self, weapon):
        print(f"{self.name} is equipping {weapon} for militaristic
purposes.")

class RoboSapiensRobot(Robot):
    def emulate_human_behavior(self, behavior):
        print(f"{self.name} is emulating human behavior: {behavior}.")

# Example Usage:
doppelganger_robot = DoppelgangerRobot("MirrorBot")
doppelganger_robot.mimic("Human")

soothsayer_robot = SoothsayerRobot("OracleBot")
soothsayer_robot.predict_future()

cyborg_robot = CyborgRobot("EnhanceBot")
cyborg_robot.enhance_human_part("Arm")

weaponry_robot = WeaponryRobot("WarBot")
weaponry_robot.equip_weapon("Laser Cannon")

robosapiens_robot = RoboSapiensRobot("HumanoidBot")
robosapiens_robot.emulate_human_behavior("Walking")

# Displaying status of all robots
print("\nRobot Status:")
doppelganger_robot.display_status()
soothsayer_robot.display_status()
cyborg_robot.display_status()
weaponry_robot.display_status()
robosapiens_robot.display_status()
```

The Robot class captured common functionalities and behaviors shared among different types of robots. The specialized robot types (DoppelgangerRobot, SoothsayerRobot, CyborgRobot, WeaponryRobot, RoboSapiensRobot) inherited from the Robot class and added specific behaviors or features related to their intended purpose. This approach allowed for a modular and extensible design, where new robot types could be easily added by creating additional classes inherited from the base Robot class.

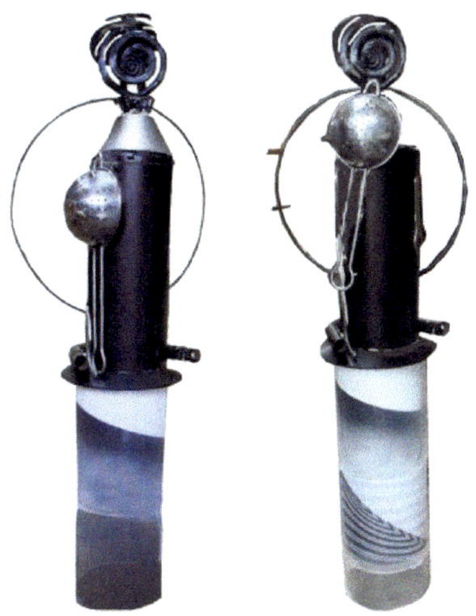

Elegance was important, but the future of the planet was more valued. They worked on reusable 3D-printed materials. If disinfecting appliances were in place, the more uses, the better.

ROBOTICS
(CLASS-BASED DESIGN AND METHOD EXECUTION)
ROBOT/THREE-HANDED – GLOBETROTTER

It designed itself as three-handed. It was all because of the parties. One needed one hand for holding a tray, the second one for a glass, and yet another one to eat with.

```
class SelfDesigningRobot:
    def __init__(self):
        self.number_of_hands = 2  # Default number of hands
        self.design_status = "Initial design with 2 hands."

    def add_hand(self):
        self.number_of_hands += 1
        self.design_status = f"Updated design with {self.number_of_hands} hands."

    def self_design(self):
        if self.number_of_hands == 2:
            print("Analyzing current design...")
            print("Decision: I want to have three hands!")
            self.add_hand()
        else:
            print("Already designed with three hands. No modification needed.")

    def display_design_status(self):
        print(self.design_status)

# Major Concept: Class-based design and method execution
# Simulating the robot's self-design process
self_designing_robot = SelfDesigningRobot()
self_designing_robot.display_design_status()
self_designing_robot.self_design()
self_designing_robot.display_design_status()
```

The SelfDesigningRobot class had methods to add a hand (add_hand), perform the self-design analysis (self_design), and display the current design status (display_design_status). The robot, upon initialization, had two hands by default. The self_design method simulated the robot analyzing its design and deciding to add a third hand.

How about a hand for shaking hands? For gesturing? They asked for a new robot, as they still needed an end-effector to shake hands and end-effectors for new ideas. It was always doing better than it's best.

Robots
(Class-based design and method execution)
Robot – Gardner

He was set to eight intelligences-related tasks. It still had a manual switch box placed on its torso, for people to turn it for the right function. The most used option was musical intelligence: many people needed a good musical score for their practices. Another worn-out spot was the linguistic one, for writing poems to the music. In April, the switch pointed to math was used a lot, as many used him for tax preparations. The eighth gear allowed for all types of performances.

```
Class IntelligentRobot:
    def _init_(self):
        self.current_intelligence = None

    def set_intelligence(self, intelligence):
        self.current_intelligence = intelligence
        print(f"Switching to {intelligence} intelligence.")

    def perform_task(self):
        if self.current_intelligence is None:
            print("Please set the intelligence first.")
            return

        if self.current_intelligence == "musical":
            self.play_musical_score()
        elif self.current_intelligence == "linguistic":
            self.write_poems_to_music()
        elif self.current_intelligence == "math":
            self.prepare_tax()
        else:
            print("Invalid intelligence selected. Please choose a valid intelligence.")

    def play_musical_score(self):
        print("Performing musical intelligence task: Playing a musical score.")

    def write_poems_to_music(self):
        print("Performing linguistic intelligence task: Writing poems to music.")

    def prepare_tax(self):
        print("Performing mathematical intelligence task: Tax preparations.")

# Major Concept: Class-based design and method execution
# Simulating the robot's tasks based on selected intelligence
robot = IntelligentRobot()

# Set musical intelligence
robot.set_intelligence("musical")
robot.perform_task()

# Set linguistic intelligence
robot.set_intelligence("linguistic")
robot.perform_task()

# Set mathematical intelligence
robot.set_intelligence("math")
robot.perform_task()

# Invalid intelligence
robot.set_intelligence("invalid")
robot.perform_task()
```

The IntelligentRobot class had methods to set the current intelligence, perform tasks based on the selected one, and specific methods for each type of intelligence task (a class to represent the robot and methods to perform tasks). The bulky human form made it look friendlier, despite being seen as outdated.

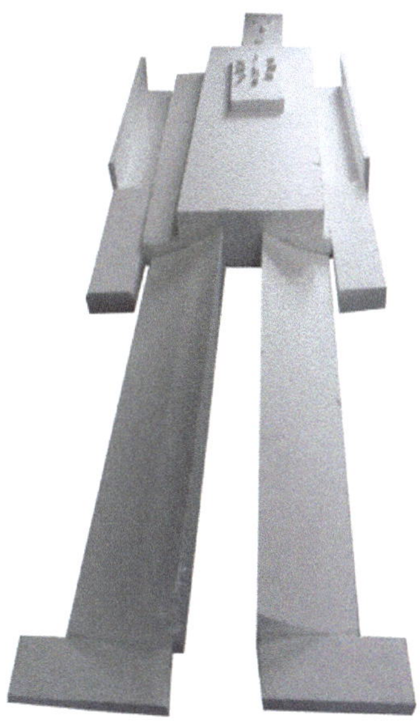

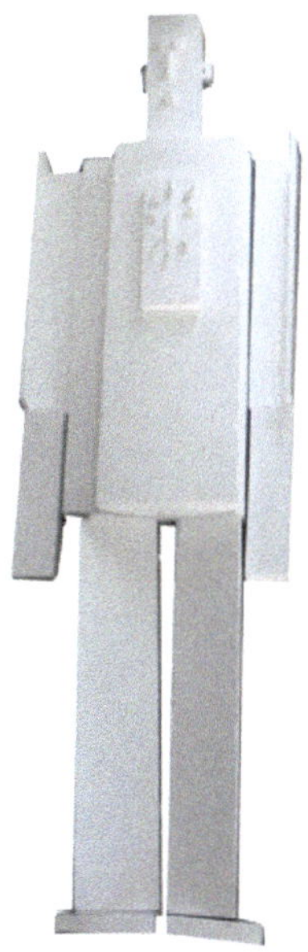

With all the technology available, people preferred manually turning the switch to typing or speaking.

S SANITATION
(OBJECT-ORIENTED PROGRAMMING (OOP))
LEADMAN – ELLIOT

His idea for maintaining ecological balance was to install consistently color-coded recycling bins in front of every dwelling all over the country. White bins were for paper, yellow for plastic, red for cans, green for bottles, violet for clothing and shoes, and blue for all toxic waste. The idea was to send color-matching self-driving trucks to collect the content of the bins matching their colors. This way, the yellow truck would collect from the yellow container (plastic), etc. Trucks picking up the regular trash were to be painted grey.

```
class Bin:
    def __init__(self, color):
        self.color = color
        self.content = []

class Truck:
    def __init__(self, color):
        self.color = color
        self.contents_collected = []

def organize_bins():
    white_bin = Bin("white")
    yellow_bin = Bin("yellow")
    red_bin = Bin("red")
    green_bin = Bin("green")
    violet_bin = Bin("violet")
    blue_bin = Bin("blue")
    grey_bin = Bin("grey")  # for regular trash

    bins = [white_bin, yellow_bin, red_bin, green_bin, violet_bin,
blue_bin, grey_bin]

    # Assume some items in each bin for demonstration purposes
    for bin in bins[:-1]:
        bin.content = [f"{bin.color}_item_{i+1}" for i in range(3)]

    return bins
```

```
def assign_trucks(bins):
    trucks = []
    for bin in bins:
        if bin.color == "grey":
            truck = Truck("grey")
        else:
            truck = Truck(bin.color)
        trucks.append(truck)

    return trucks

def collect_trash(bins, trucks):
    for bin in bins:
        for truck in trucks:
            if bin.color == truck.color:
                truck.contents_collected.extend(bin.content)

# Main program
bins = organize_bins()
trucks = assign_trucks(bins)
collect_trash(bins, trucks)

# Print the contents collected by each truck
for truck in trucks:
    print(f"{truck.color.capitalize()} Truck Collected: {',
'.join(truck.contents_collected)}")
```

OOP allowed to model real-world entities (bins and trucks) as objects with properties (attributes) and behaviors (methods). Each bin and truck was an instance of its respective class, and they interacted with each other through well-defined methods (__init__ constructor in this case).

The trash companies wanted colors associated with them. Others disliked a blue set for all toxic waste.

SECURITY PRIVACY
(A LIST)
NETWORK SECURITY SPECIALISTS – S

They had the task of securing everyone's privacy, data, and content. They wanted to be seen as the messengers of safety.

```
# Define a list representing key aspects of securing privacy, data, and content
security_aspects = [
   "Encryption", # Protecting data by converting it into a secure format
   "Authentication", # Verifying the identity of users or systems
   "Access Control", # Restricting access to authorized individuals or entities
   "Regular Audits", # Periodic checks and reviews to identify vulnerabilities
   "Data Backups" # Creating copies of data to prevent loss in case of incidents
]

# Explain what is behind securing everyone's privacy, data, and content
"""
Securing privacy, data, and content involves implementing various measures to protect sensitive information.
Key aspects include:
- Encryption: Protecting data by converting it into a secure format.
- Authentication: Verifying the identity of users or systems.
- Access Control: Restricting access to authorized individuals or entities.
- Regular Audits: Periodic checks and reviews to identify vulnerabilities.
- Data Backups: Creating copies of data to prevent loss in case of incidents.
"""

# Print the key aspects of securing privacy, data, and content
print("Key aspects of securing everyone's privacy, data, and content:")
for aspect in security_aspects:
   print("- " + aspect)
```

They provided explanations and documentation on the key aspects of securing privacy, data, and content with encryption, authentication, access control, regular audits, and backups.

That made everybody feel safe, and people did see them as messengers for it.

SELF-ENTERTAINMENT
(OOP)
PERFUMER – AGAFA

Agafa had a collection of chickens in her backyard. She could tell which egg belonged to which hen, even if one tried to hide it from her in some neighboring bushes. To make sure, she designed a system:

```
class Hen:
    def __init__(self, name):
        self.name = name
        self.eggs = []

def assign_eggs(hens, eggs):
    for i, egg in enumerate(eggs):
        hen_index = i % len(hens)
        hens[hen_index].eggs.append(egg)
        print(f"Egg {egg} belongs to {hens[hen_index].name}")

# Creating hens
hen1 = Hen("Hen A")
hen2 = Hen("Hen B")
hen3 = Hen("Hen C")

# List of eggs
eggs_list = ["Egg 1", "Egg 2", "Egg 3", "Egg 4", "Egg 5"]

# Assigning eggs to hens
assign_eggs([hen1, hen2, hen3], eggs_list)
```

She knew the best way to add a new chick was to do it at night. In the morning, all of them thought it always was there. Her favorite way to entertain her guests was to take them to the coop at night. When she turned the lights on, loud hens' voices could be heard, and they went suddenly silent the moment the light went off, but she appeared more entertained than her guests were.
We can entertain ourselves when entertaining others, some thought.

SELF ESTEEM
(STRING CONCATENATION)
VIDEOGRAPHER – MOMO

Momo loved filming. Thus, he was doing what he liked, and he liked what he was doing.

```
def explain_sentence(sentence):
    phrases = sentence.split()

    explanations = {
        "he": "refers to a male person",
        "did": "performed or carried out an action",
        "what": "refers to the thing or things that",
        "he liked": "he enjoyed or had a preference for",
        "what he was doing": "refers to the action or activity he was engaged in"
    }

    explanation_sentence = ""

    for phrase in phrases:
        explanation_sentence += f"{phrase} ({explanations.get(phrase, 'No explanation')}) "

    return explanation_sentence.strip()

# Example usage
sentence = "he did what he liked what he was doing"
explained_sentence = explain_sentence(sentence)
print(explained_sentence)
```

His colleagues defined a function explain_sentence that took a sentence as an argument to understand him. The sentence was split into individual phrases to explain each part, and each phrase was then explained using a dictionary (explanations). This way, a simple explanation of each phrase in the given sentence made it easier to understand the meaning of the sentence as a whole.

He never needed to be popular or famous.

SEMIOTICS
(CLASS STRUCTURE TO REPRESENT OBJECTS AND THEIR ATTRIBUTES)
SECURITY – BRUNO

Bruno likes to read to learn. His job requires lots of traveling and also waiting. He's been reading about semiotics, objects, images, icons, metaphors, and iconic objects. Bruno found a special interest in "pretenders" – objects with a form that does not correspond with their function. Bruno collects them and uses them all around his house. His goal is that every functional object he possesses is a pretender and looks like something else. He uses a basic class structure to represent objects and their attributes. The major concept he used here is the idea of "signs" and "signifiers" from semiotics.

```
class Object:
    def __init__(self, name, form, function):
        self.name = name
        self.form = form
        self.function = function

    def is_pretender(self):
        # Check if the form does not correspond with the function
        return self.form != self.function

def identify_pretenders(objects):
    pretenders = [obj for obj in objects if obj.is_pretender()]
    return pretenders

# Example objects
apple = Object("Apple", "Round", "Edible")
clock = Object("Clock", "Square", "Timekeeping Device")
book = Object("Book", "Triangle", "Reading Material")

# List of objects
objects_list = [apple, clock, book]

# Identify pretenders
pretender_objects = identify_pretenders(objects_list)

# Print pretender objects
print("Pretender Objects:")
for obj in pretender_objects:
    print(f"{obj.name} - Form: {obj.form}, Function:
{obj.function}")
```

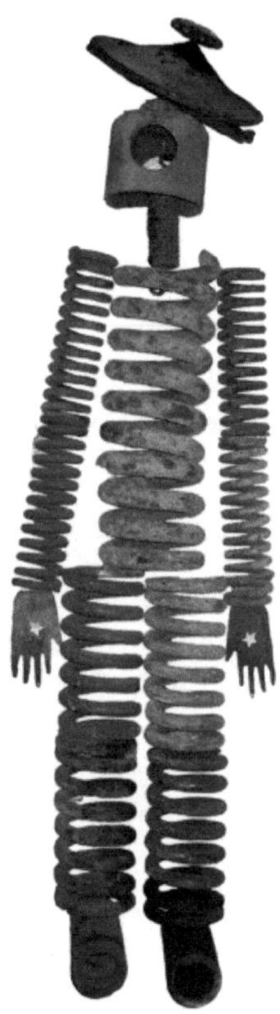

In his code, each Object had a name, form, and function. The pretender method checked if the form and function were mismatched. The identify_pretenders function filtered out the pretender objects from a list of objects. The output showed the objects that did not correspond in form and function.

Edward often brings him something from his frequent trips. Debbie tries to give him an estimated value for each object. He created a list of pretenders to illustrate the concept of "pretenders," where the form and function are intentionally mismatched. In real-world scenarios, identifying such objects could involve more nuanced criteria and a deeper understanding of semiotics.

Pillow (form: square, function: sleeping support)
Flashlight (form: banana, function: lighting)
Umbrella (form: cube, function: rain protection)
Scissors (form: circle, function: cutting)
Chair (form: triangular, function: sitting support)
Computer Mouse (form: book, function: pointer device)
Coffee Mug (form: pyramid, function: holding liquid)
Mirror (form: hexagon, function: reflection)
Keyboard (form: oval, function: input device)
Headphones (form: flower, function: audio output)

Debbie commented that those were just functional objects." But it is not about money," he keeps telling her. Debbie watched the news and info, instead of reading. She was called a *Truth Bender*, as she always changed the facts and information - even just a bit. But information may be untrue.

SHIPPING SERVICES
(SORTING ALGORITHM)
MAILPERSON – FUSON

He delivered letters, flyers, big and small packages, and what was handed to him. He knew all the dogs, who could appreciate him due to his calm manners, quiet presence, and nice face. Cats were often greeting him, too. He did not have to go to any fitness clubs. This part got check marked for him.

```
class MailDelivery:
    def __init__(self, deliveries):
        self.deliveries = deliveries

    def sort_deliveries(self):
        # Sorting deliveries based on the street name
        sorted_deliveries = sorted(self.deliveries, key=lambda x: x['street'])

        print("Sorted Deliveries:")
        for delivery in sorted_deliveries:
            print(f"{delivery['street']}, {delivery['recipient']} - {delivery['package']}")

# Example of usage
deliveries = [
    {'street': 'Maple Street', 'recipient': 'John', 'package': 'Box 1'},
    {'street': 'Oak Street', 'recipient': 'Alice', 'package': 'Box 2'},
    {'street': 'Pine Street', 'recipient': 'Bob', 'package': 'Box 3'},
    {'street': 'Maple Street', 'recipient': 'Charlie', 'package': 'Box 4'},
]

mailman = MailDelivery(deliveries)
mailman.sort_deliveries()
```

He used the sorting Lambda Function (lambda x: x['street']) that extracts the street name from each delivery dictionary for the deliveries based on the street name. His concept of sorting based on a specific criterion or key followed a fundamental concept in programming and a convenient way to sort data based on custom criteria as a key extraction mechanism for the sorting process.

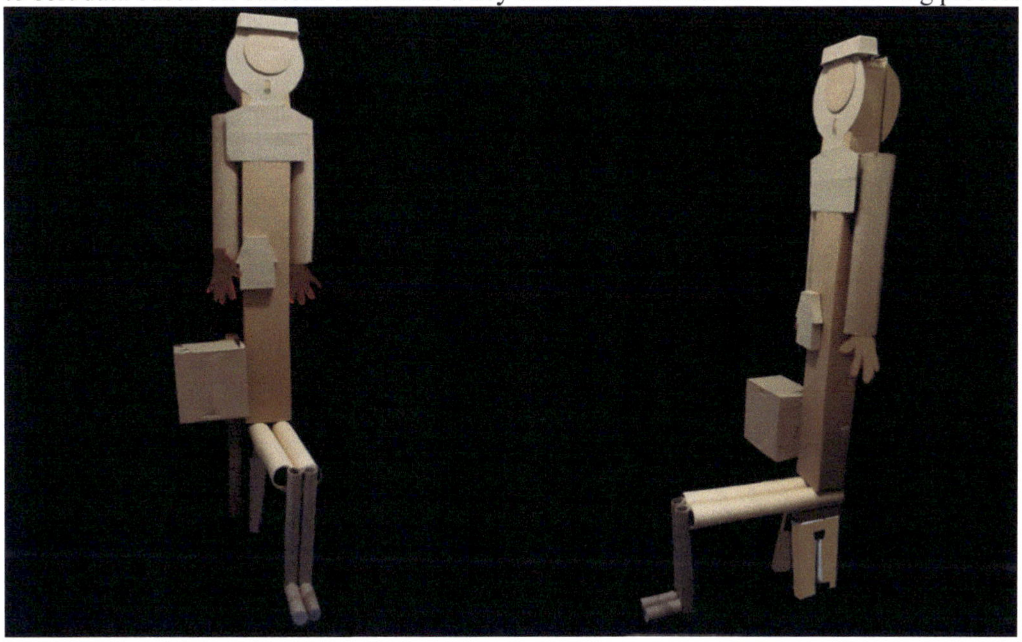

Now, his mental exercises have been checked and marked as well.

SIMULATION (VISUAL REPRESENTATION) POKER PLAYER – COLT

Colt was hired as a helping hand. It meant helping with practically anything. Everyone could post a task for him on the schedule. He made a list of the most unusual needs for his novels. He was ordered to remove a flying bat from a lecture room, and a pigeon from the theater workshop. Someone wanted him to present someone's composition on a phone connected to the speakers. He's been growing in every direction, learning new skills, and mastering the old ones. Colt knew a lot and kept learning, but he felt they were trying to change him into someone he was not.

```
import pygame
import sys

class SlinkySimulation:
    def __init__(self):
        self.screen_width = 800
        self.screen_height = 600
        self.spring_color = (255, 0, 0)
        self.slinky_color = (0, 0, 255)
        self.spring_height = 100
        self.slinky_height = 400

    def run_simulation(self):
        pygame.init()
        screen = pygame.display.set_mode((self.screen_width, self.screen_height))
        pygame.display.set_caption("Spring to Slinky Simulation")

        clock = pygame.time.Clock()

        while True:
            for event in pygame.event.get():
                if event.type == pygame.QUIT:
                    pygame.quit()
                    sys.exit()

            screen.fill((255, 255, 255))

            # Draw spring
            pygame.draw.rect(screen, self.spring_color, (self.screen_width // 2 - 10, self.screen_height // 2 - self.spring_height, 20,
self.spring_height))

            # Draw slinky
            pygame.draw.rect(screen, self.slinky_color, (self.screen_width // 2 - 10, self.screen_height // 2, 20, self.slinky_height))

            pygame.display.flip()
            clock.tick(60)

if __name__ == "__main__":
    simulation = SlinkySimulation()
    simulation.run_simulation()
```

He thought it was like forcing a spring to become a slinky, using simulation class to encapsulate the simulation logic, screen parameters, and colors.

SIMULATION OF REFLECTIONS
(GRAPHICAL REPRESENTATION WITH OOP)
POSITIVE ORGANS/ROMAN CORNU/BUCCINA – GIOVANNI & JEANNE

Giovanni and Jeanne developed their unique style of entertaining people. They often perform at private and official gatherings, and participants express appreciation for their ability to amuse them because of the overall quality of their performances. The secret lies in the spectacular way they are playing. They arrived in a big van with everything they needed for Andrea's graduation party. Even their instruments, the positive organs, and buccina, of relatively small size, arrived in a big van. An easel, a big mirror, a table, and a special set of lamps were carried from their van. Giovanni and Jeanne were dressed in tulle and silk robes. They played in front of a mirror placed on a tall easel, and thus, they were repeated by their reflections to exist in two distinct embodiments. They liked to be jokingly called "a quartet."

```
import pygame
import sys

class Musician:
    def _init_(self, instrument, attire):
        self.instrument = instrument
        self.attire = attire

    def play(self):
        print(f"{self.attire} {self.instrument} player is
playing.")

class MirrorQuartetSimulation:
    def _init_(self):
        self.screen_width = 800
        self.screen_height = 600
        self.musicians = [
            Musician("Cornu", "Tulle and Silk"),
            Musician("Buccina", "Tulle and Silk"),
            Musician("Cornu", "Tulle and Silk"),
            Musician("Buccina", "Tulle and Silk"),
        ]

    def run_simulation(self):
        pygame.init()
        screen =
pygame.display.set_mode((self.screen_width,
self.screen_height))
        pygame.display.set_caption("Mirror Quartet
Simulation")

        clock = pygame.time.Clock()

        while True:
            for event in pygame.event.get():
                if event.type == pygame.QUIT:
                    pygame.quit()
                    sys.exit()

            screen.fill((255, 255, 255))

            for i, musician in enumerate(self.musicians):
                x_position = 200 + i * 150
                pygame.draw.rect(screen, (0, 0, 255),
(x_position, 200, 50, 100)) # Representing musicians
                musician.play()

            pygame.display.flip()
            clock.tick(60)

if __name__ == "__main__":
    simulation = MirrorQuartetSimulation()
    simulation.run_simulation()
```

They successfully performed at Andrea's graduation party – all four of them.

SINGING
(GRAPHICS LIBRARIES)
TWO BARITONES — HANS & HELLER

Hans and Heller were both tall and skinny. They stood straight, side by side, whenever singing together or in the park during their walks around the lake. Water tended to make their voices sound louder and cleaner. They liked their reflections, making them look even taller and skinnier. They would not stop singing when someone approached them. They often had some animals following them. Dogs love singing. Hans depicted them through a code by creating a visual representation of reflections:

```
import turtle

def draw_man(x, y, color):
    turtle.penup()
    turtle.goto(x, y)
    turtle.pendown()
    turtle.color(color)
    turtle.circle(30) # Head
    turtle.forward(60) # Body
    turtle.left(90)
    turtle.forward(80) # Legs
    turtle.backward(160)
    turtle.right(90)
    turtle.forward(80) # Arms
    turtle.backward(80)

def draw_lake():
    turtle.penup()
    turtle.goto(-300, -150)
    turtle.pendown()
    turtle.color("blue")
    turtle.begin_fill()
    turtle.forward(600)
    turtle.right(90)
    turtle.forward(100)
    turtle.right(90)
    turtle.forward(600)
    turtle.right(90)
    turtle.forward(100)
    turtle.end_fill()

def draw_reflection(x, y, color):
    turtle.penup()
    turtle.goto(x, -y) # Mirror reflection on the lake
    turtle.pendown()
    turtle.color(color)
    turtle.circle(30)
    turtle.forward(60)
    turtle.left(90)
    turtle.forward(80)
    turtle.backward(160)
    turtle.right(90)
    turtle.forward(80)
    turtle.backward(80)

def draw_singing():
    turtle.penup()
    turtle.goto(0, 120)
    turtle.pendown()
    turtle.write("La la la", align="center", font=("Arial", 16,
"normal"))

def main():
    turtle.speed(2)

    # Draw the lake
    draw_lake()

    # Draw two men
    draw_man(-100, 0, "green")
    draw_man(100, 0, "brown")

    # Draw reflections
    draw_reflection(-100, 0, "green")
    draw_reflection(100, 0, "brown")

    # Draw singing text
    draw_singing()

    turtle.hideturtle()
    turtle.done()

if __name__ == "__main__":
    main()
```

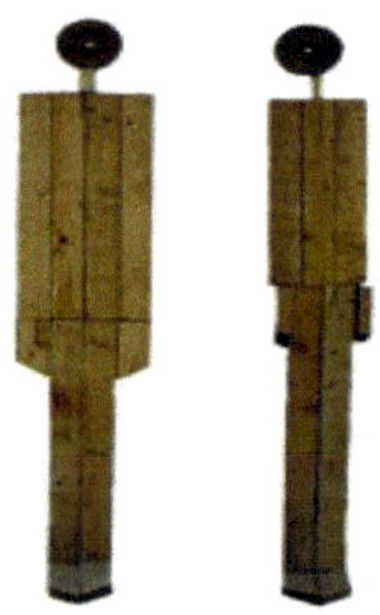

With Turtle graphics, he created a non-realistic representation of two men and their reflections on a lake while singing. The more advanced libraries, such as Pygame or OpenGL, would work better, but he used it as his training tool, just like skiers watch footage of their own racing recorded on a video to enjoy and get better at their skiing techniques.

SIRENS
(COMMENTS (#))
MY COMPUTER RIVER SINGERS – DO, RE, MI, FA, SOL, LA

They defined Biology as the science of life. This is what their songs were about. Even in the open space opera performances, they could be heard clearly. Their voices were strong; songs were well designed and inspiring, written so that one would memorize each one instantly and sing whenever courage, strength, or bravery was needed. The reason was hidden behind:

```
# Define a list representing the musical notes
musical_notes = ["Do", "Re", "Mi", "Fa", "Sol", "La"]
# Add more notes to represent the entire octave
musical_notes += ["Ti", "Do'"]
# Explain the concept beyond Do, Re, Mi, Fa, Sol, La
"""
In Western music, the solf.ge syllables are used to represent musical notes.
The basic solf.ge includes the notes Do, Re, Mi, Fa, Sol, La, and each syllable represents a different pitch.
Beyond La, the sequence continues with Ti and then repeats with Do' to represent the next octave.
"""
# Print the complete list of musical notes
print("Complete list of musical notes:")
for note in musical_notes:
print(note)
```

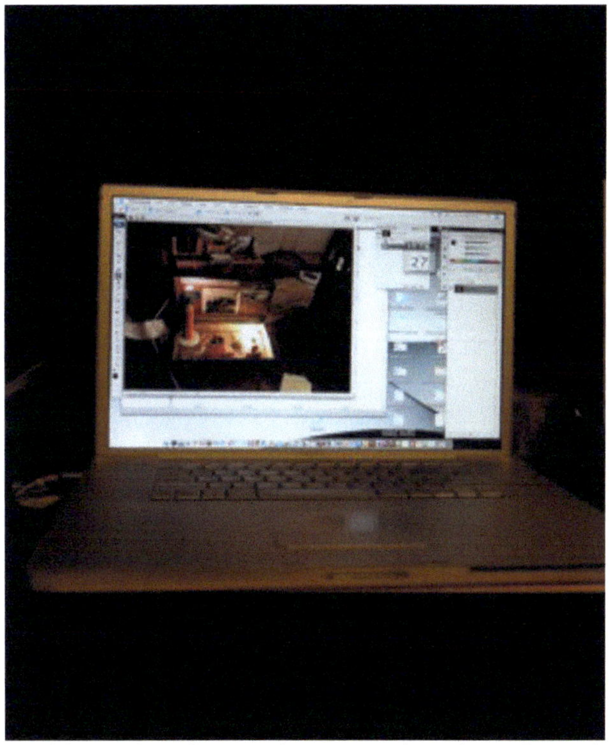

Python comments using the # symbol were used to provide explanations or documentation about the code and to explain how the musical notes continued with Ti and repeated with Do' to represent the next octave. Knowing all that, even the small fish sang when escaping the bigger ones inside of the nets.

SKILLS
(A FUNCTION THAT PROVIDES MULTIPLE PERSPECTIVES)
WEDDING – KU AND FU

They never had enemies because they kept learning to see things from other people's perspectives. Their secret was a code that presented different viewpoints in a given situation.

```
def see_from_other_perspectives(situation):
    perspectives = {
        "Person A": f"As Person A, I see {situation} from a positive angle.",
        "Person B": f"As Person B, I perceive {situation} with caution and uncertainty.",
        "Person C": f"Person C views {situation} as a great opportunity for improvement.",
        "Person D": f"From Person D's perspective, {situation} seems challenging but rewarding.",
    }

    return perspectives

# Example usage
situation = "a new project proposal"

perspectives = see_from_other_perspectives(situation)

print(f"Different Perspectives on '{situation}':")
for person, view in perspectives.items():
    print(f"{person}: {view}")
```

The see_from_other_perspectives function took a situation as an argument and provided different perspectives using a dictionary to simulate seeing things from other people's points of view.
The number of situations was overwhelming, though.

SMART HOME DESIGN – INTERACTIVE AND IMMERSIVE ENVIRONMENT (MODULAR DESIGN AND ENCAPSULATION)

RESTROOM OFFICIALS - ONE, TWO, THREE, FOUR, FIVE, SIX, SEVEN, EIGHT, NINE, TEN, ELEVEN, AND TWELVE

To keep the complex interesting and worth paying frequent visits, the *Impress Your Patron Committee* decided to make restroom visits attractive by hiring men and women. Their duties ranged from making doors open with a hand wave (like towel dispensers) to shining the shoes. The coat hanger followed each visitor to take their coat. Waterfall movies were projected on the walls and on the floor. The ceiling was covered with moving clouds of various shapes and colors. A big tank with koi fish was inserted on the floor. The patrons could select music, temperature, colors of water, soap, hand towels, and tissues.

```
import random

class SmartDoor:
    def __init__(self):
        self.is_open = False

    def open_door(self):
        self.is_open = True
        print("The door opens with a wave of sounds, greeting you.")

class WaterfallProjection:
    def project_on_walls(self):
        print("Waterfall movies are projected on the walls.")

    def project_on_floor(self):
        print("Waterfall movies are projected on the floor.")

class CloudCeiling:
    def generate_clouds(self):
        shapes = ["fluffy", "wispy", "puffy"]
        colors = ["white", "gray", "pink", "orange"]
        movements = ["slow drifting", "gentle swirling", "rapid
changing"]

        for _ in range(5):
            shape = random.choice(shapes)
            color = random.choice(colors)
            movement = random.choice(movements)
            print(f"A {color} {shape} cloud with {movement}
movement appears on the ceiling.")

class AmbientControl:
    def select_music(self, music_type):
        print(f"Selected {music_type} music is playing.")

    def set_temperature(self, temperature):
        print(f"The temperature is set to {temperature} degrees F.")
    def select_color_scheme(self, color):
        print(f"The color scheme is set to {color}.")

    def customize_bathroom(self, water_color, soap_type,
towel_color, tissue_type):
        print(f"Bathroom customized - Water color: {water_color},
Soap: {soap_type}, Towel color: {towel_color}, Tissue type:
{tissue_type}.")

class KoiFishTank:
    def __init__(self):
        self.is_inserted = False

def insert_into_floor(self):
        self.is_inserted = True
        print("A big tank with colorful koi fish is inserted into the
floor.")

# Major Concept: Modular design and encapsulation
class SmartHomeEnvironment:
    def __init__(self):
        self.door = SmartDoor()
        self.waterfall_projection = WaterfallProjection()
        self.cloud_ceiling = CloudCeiling()
        self.ambient_control = AmbientControl()
        self.koi_fish_tank = KoiFishTank()

    def welcome_guest(self):
        self.door.open_door()
        self.waterfall_projection.project_on_walls()
        self.waterfall_projection.project_on_floor()
        self.cloud_ceiling.generate_clouds()
        self.ambient_control.select_music("Chillout")
        self.ambient_control.set_temperature(22)
        self.ambient_control.select_color_scheme("Blue")
        self.ambient_control.customize_bathroom("Aqua",
"Lavender", "White", "Recycled")

        if not self.koi_fish_tank.is_inserted:
            self.koi_fish_tank.insert_into_floor()
```

Each aspect of the smart restroom environment (door, waterfall projection, cloud ceiling, ambient control, and koi fish tank) was encapsulated within its own class. The SmartHomeEnvironment class acted as a coordinator, bringing together various components.

With each project, they moved to the newer technology. The patrons enjoyed the progression of the sound and image quality and could not wait to see what other programmers would come up with, so it was full.

SOCIAL ACTIVITY
(INTERACTIVE)
DETECTIVES – HIOLE & ZIN

They believe rap is a form of interactive art. Two rappers worked together, and the best outcome was when they improvised in front of the audience. However, creating an interactive art form for a rap performance involves combining code with user input, so the input() function to take user input for a rap performance helps the user provide words or phrases, and the program will incorporate them into a rap.

```
import random

def generate_rap(verse, user_input):
    # Split the verse into lines
    lines = verse.split('\n')

    # Add user input to random lines
    selected_lines = random.sample(lines, min(len(lines),
len(user_input)))
    for i, line in enumerate(selected_lines):
        lines[i] += f" ({user_input[i]})"

    # Join the modified lines into a new verse
    modified_verse = '\n'.join(lines)

    return modified_verse

# Example rap verse
original_verse = """
I'm the rhyme master, the lyrical disaster,
Spitting fire on the mic, causing a laughter.
In the game of life, I'm the ultimate caster,
Every word I drop, a linguistic plaster.
"""

# Get user input for customization
user_input = input("Enter words or phrases to customize the rap
(separated by commas): ").split(',')

# Generate and display the modified rap verse
modified_rap = generate_rap(original_verse, user_input)
print("\nYour Customized Rap:")
print(modified_rap)
```

The program allowed users to input words and phrases into a predefined rap verse, creating a customized version. This interactive experience led to a large rap party with audience participation.

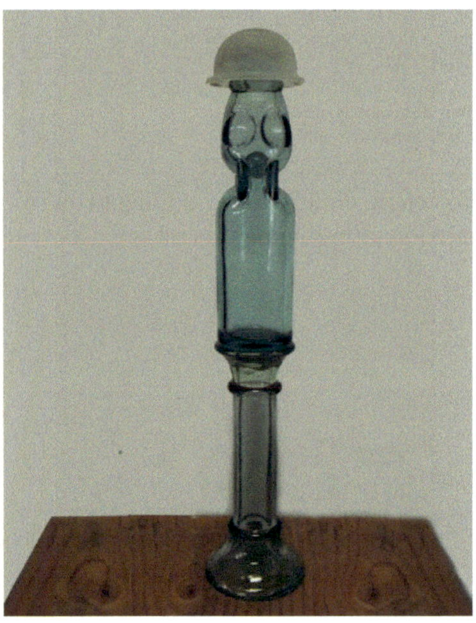

SOCIAL LIFE
(BOOLEAN PARAMETERS)
BLOCK PARTY - JON

John was ambitious, successful, and efficient. He was known for changing apartments in his city more often than anybody else. Every time he'd move, he could be seen buying a new jacket for a new neighborhood block party. He needed a better selection, so he followed a code to select a pattern for different neighborhoods. For example, he devised a tight pattern if the neighborhood was crowded. If there were lots of plants, he went with a green color, etc.

```
def generate_neighborhood_pattern(crowded, lots_of_plants):
    pattern = ""

    if crowded:
        pattern += "Tight "
    else:
        pattern += "Spacious "

    if lots_of_plants:
        pattern += "Green"
    else:
        pattern += "Neutral"

    return pattern

# Example usage:
crowded_neighborhood = input("Is the neighborhood crowded? (yes/no): ").lower() == 'yes'
lots_of_plants_neighborhood = input("Are there lots of plants in the neighborhood? (yes/no): ").lower() == 'yes'

selected_pattern = generate_neighborhood_pattern(crowded_neighborhood, lots_of_plants_neighborhood)
print(f"Selected neighborhood pattern: {selected_pattern}")
```

His code defined a function generate_neighborhood_pattern (crowded and lots_of_plants) and generated a pattern based on these characteristics. He could customize the patterns and characteristics depending on each neighborhood he was moving to.
He learned to use the photo silkscreen technique to apply them to his new jackets, but nobody noticed.

SOCIAL POWERS – CHARISMA
(LIST)
MAGNETIC PERSON — CHEN

Everybody liked him for no reason. He did not care much about anyone but aimed to make people like his ideas. It did not work as expected, so he wrote "How to Be Very Popular."

```
def be_very_popular():
    # List of tips for being very popular
    popularity_tips = [
        "Always wear a smile.",
        "Learn to dance like no one is watching.",
        "Be genuinely interested in others.",
        "Share funny cat memes.",
        "Listen more than you talk.",
        "Remember people's names.",
        "Bring snacks to share.",
        "Be positive and uplifting.",
        "Offer compliments freely.",
        "Master the art of the high-five."
    ]

    print("Tips for Being Very Popular:")
    for tip in popularity_tips:
        print(f"- {tip}")
```

The popularity_tips variable was a list containing tips for being very popular. Lists are a fundamental data structure that allows for storing and iterating over a collection of items as a set of tips. Using lists is a fundamental aspect of data storage and retrieval to organize and work with collections of related information.

After this post, everybody liked his ideas.

SOCIOLINGUISTICS – A STUDY OF HOW SOCIETY AFFECTS LANGUAGE (STRING CONCATENATION WITH THE += OPERATOR) UKULELE – MOANA

Moana liked to talk to people. Her mind worked faster than she could speak, so often, her stories were lengthy and involved many characters. Here is one of them: "She went to the dentist, whose dog had chased a mailman, who was just about to deliver a letter to Stephanie, who had hoped it would be a letter from Director Gerlost, inviting and informing her about her new role in a performance for Queen Amalia, who was just in town staying at the residence, the owners of which had just left for a Music Fair, in which five percussionists, Jaimie, Tom, Thomas, Raymond, and Kevin were involved, as per invitation of their fan, who's friend Kathy had to visit Peter to consult on her new dress, which she saw on TV watched by David when they visited him without warning, because it was on their way to buy a new instrument for Tom, but Edward was passing by, and then they all knew his aunt was sick, so he had to bring her some medications from a pharmacy run by a mother of Mark, who … "
Not feeling appreciated, she wrote a simple code to build her sentences by adding information about each character involved in the storytelling. She had a list of characters and their corresponding info.

```
def build_sentence(characters_info):
    sentence = "Once upon a time, there was a story with:"

    for character, info in characters_info.items():
        sentence += f"\n- {character}: {info}"

    return sentence

# Example usage
characters_info = {
    "Alice": "a curious adventurer",
    "Bob": "an aspiring musician",
    "Charlie": "a wise old wizard",
    "David": "a mischievous cat"
}

story_sentence = build_sentence(characters_info)
print(story_sentence)
```

First, she defined a function build_sentence that took a dictionary (characters_info) containing characters and their corresponding information. It then iterated through the dictionary and added information about each character to the initial sentence. This approach allowed her to dynamically build a sentence based on the characters and their information, making the code flexible and easily adaptable for different storytelling scenarios.

No one could guess what she was thinking, but she played well. Hurt by her colleagues' attitudes, Moana started singing her texts while playing her instrument every Saturday at the Farmers Market.
The farmers never saw their sales grow so fast.

SOCIOLOGY
(A CLASS TO ENCAPSULATE ORGANIZATION)
SOCIAL CLIMBERS - KITI, DIVI, AND ELVI

They had a list of activities aimed at promoting their social significance. Attending music-related events was placed at the top of the list. The order of importance of the events to be attended was published online to inform everyone how to qualify for a desired social level.

```
class MusicalEventsOrganizer:
    def __init__(self):
        self.events = {
            'Concert A': ' Platinum',
            'Festival B': ' Gold ',
            'Recital C': ' Silver ',
            'Symphony D': Bronze "
        }

    def inform_event_order(self):
        sorted_events = sorted(self.events.items(), key=lambda x: x[1])
        print("Order of Musical Events based on Social Level:")
        for event, social_level in sorted_events:
            print(f"{event} - Social Level: {social_level}")

# Example of using the MusicalEventsOrganizer class
event_organizer = MusicalEventsOrganizer()

# Inform attendees about the order of events
event_organizer.inform_event_order()
```

A class (MusicalEventsOrganizer) was used to encapsulate the organization of musical events. The class had a dictionary (events) that maps events to their associated social levels. The inform_event_order method sorted the events based on social levels and printed the order to inform attendees. The sorting was done using the sorted function and a lambda function was the key argument, sorted the events based on their social levels.

What they did not know was that it was a never-ending process.

SOCIOLOGY OF REACTIONS (NATURAL LANGUAGE PROCESSING) TRUMPET – HARRY

Harry had a glow. When he left the room, it felt like the light was suddenly turned off in the space. He could do anything he wanted, and he could have anyone do whatever he wanted, but he never used his powers. After the rehearsals, he was the first one to leave the room. He shared his secret with friends:

```
def explain_glow(sentence):
  if "glow" in sentence:
    explanation = "When someone is said to have a 'glow,' it often means they appear radiant, healthy, and full of positive energy."
  else:
    explanation = "The sentence does not mention a 'glow.'"

  return explanation

# Example usage:
sentence = "He has a natural glow that lights up the room."
result = explain_glow(sentence)
print(result)
```

His code defined a function explain_glow that takes a sentence as input, checks if the word "glow" is present, and provides an explanation accordingly. The sentence is "He has a natural glow that lights up the room," and the code would output an explanation of what it means to have a glow.
It did not work for his friends, so he shared another code. This time, he used Python using the Natural Language Toolkit (NLTK) library to analyze the meaning of a sentence that mentions someone glowing. He used part-of-speech tagging to identify the words and their roles in the sentence.

```
import nltk
from nltk.tokenize import word_tokenize, sent_tokenize
from nltk import pos_tag

nltk.download('punkt')
nltk.download('averaged_perceptron_tagger')

def analyze_sentence(sentence):
  # Tokenize the sentence into words
  words = word_tokenize(sentence)

  # Perform part-of-speech tagging
  tagged_words = pos_tag(words)

  # Extract relevant information
  nouns = [word for word, pos in tagged_words if pos.startswith('NN')]
  adjectives = [word for word, pos in tagged_words if pos.startswith('JJ')]

  # Check for the presence of words related to "glow"
  has_glow = any(word.lower() in ['glow', 'radiance', 'shine'] for word in
words)

  # Print the analysis
  print(sentence: {sentence}")
  print(f"Nouns: {nouns}")
  print(f"Adjectives: {adjectives}")
  print(f"Has glow: {has_glow}")

# Example sentence
example_sentence = "He has a radiant glow that brightens up the room."

# Analyze the example sentence
analyze_sentence(example_sentence)
```

The NLTK library tokenized the input sentence into words and performed part-of-speech tagging. It then identified nouns and adjectives in the sentence and checked if any of the words were related to the concept of "glow." The results were printed for analysis to follow. This time, all the rooms were filled with radiance. Everybody shined, but not even close to Harry's luminosity.

SOCIOLOGY/PSYCHOLOGY (FORM_OPINION METHOD) PEOPLE LIKE YOU

People like you because they all are like you.
People are like you because they really like you.

```
class People:
    def __init__(self, name):
        self.name = name
        self.like_you = False

    def form_opinion(self, others):
        self.like_you = all(person.like_you for person in others)

    def express_opinion(self, person):
        person.like_you = True
        print(f"{self.name}: People like you because they all are like
you.")

# Creating instances of People
person1 = People("Alice")
person2 = People("Bob")
person3 = People("Charlie")

# Expressing opinions
person1.express_opinion(person2)
person1.express_opinion(person3)

# Forming opinions based on others
people_list = [person1, person2, person3]
person2.form_opinion(people_list)
person3.form_opinion(people_list)

# Displaying the final opinions
print(f"{person1.name}: People are like you because they really like
you.")
print(f"{person2.name}: Like you? {person2.like_you}")
print(f"{person3.name}: Like you? {person3.like_you}")
```

One major method used in this code is the form_opinion method of the People class. This method took a list of other people and set the like_you attribute of the current person based on whether all the other people have the like_you attribute set to True. It demonstrated the use of a method within a class to encapsulate behavior and make the code more modular.

They really like you.

SOFT SKILLS
(CLASSES AND DEFINITIONS)
HEARTBREAKER – KIERA

Oh, beautiful she was, but heartless, would say her men. What a heart, would say her female friends. Spreading niceness through a code that encourages kindness towards every person was her answer:

```
class Person:
    def __init__(self, name):
        self.name = name
        self.kindness_level = 0

    def spread_kindness(self, other_person):
        self.kindness_level += 1
        other_person.receive_kindness()

    def receive_kindness(self):
        self.kindness_level += 1

class Friend:
    def __init__(self, name):
        self.name = name
        self.friendship_level = 0

    def receive_kindness(self):
        self.friendship_level += 1
```

```
def main():
    person = Person("woman")
    friend = Friend("man")

    print(f"{person.name}'s kindness level: {person.kindness_level}")
    print(f"{friend.name}'s friendship level:
{friend.friendship_level}")

    person.spread_kindness(friend)

    print(f"\nAfter spreading kindness:")
    print(f"{person.name}'s kindness level: {person.kindness_level}")
    print(f"{friend.name}'s friendship level:
{friend.friendship_level}")

if __name__ == "__main__":
    main()
```

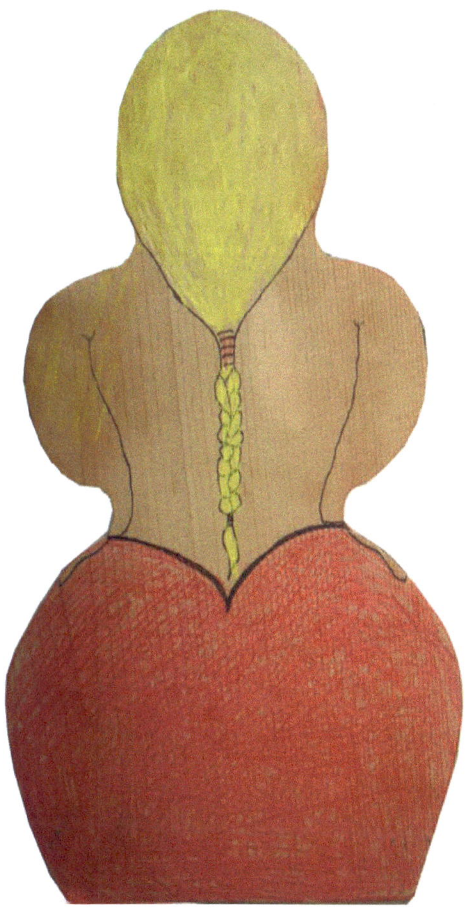

When a woman person spreads kindness, a man's friendship level increases. She extended this pattern by creating more classes for different types of people and adjusting the spread_kindness method accordingly. It worked!

Everyone was saying what a kind heartbreaker Kiera was.

SOLUTIONS
(STRING CONCATENATION AND FORMATTING)
UNDERSTUDY – ALI, SIXTO, GIOK, REZA

They could do all the impossible. Some thought it was a computer but were ready to risk it all to create unimaginable solutions. Be it that hackers broke, or brokers hacked, they could do quite hard to imagine being done tasks. They had to exercise and run in the morning, with no music on them, so they could listen to their bodies. They were unbeatable and irreplaceable, could fight all styles and traditions, and even scold the opponent in various languages without risking further malfunctions. Even a machine!

```
def scold_computer(task_name):
    scolding_message = f"Error: Computer, you've done it again! Your execution of {task_name} is completely off."

    return scolding_message

# Example usage
task_name = "data analysis"
scolding_message = scold_computer(task_name)
print(scolding_message)
```

They defined a function scold_computer that took a task name as an argument. The function then constructed a scolding message using string formatting to create a scolding message by combining a fixed string with the provided task name. They knew how to maintain a positive and respectful tone when interacting with computers or any technology, especially when using string manipulation techniques.

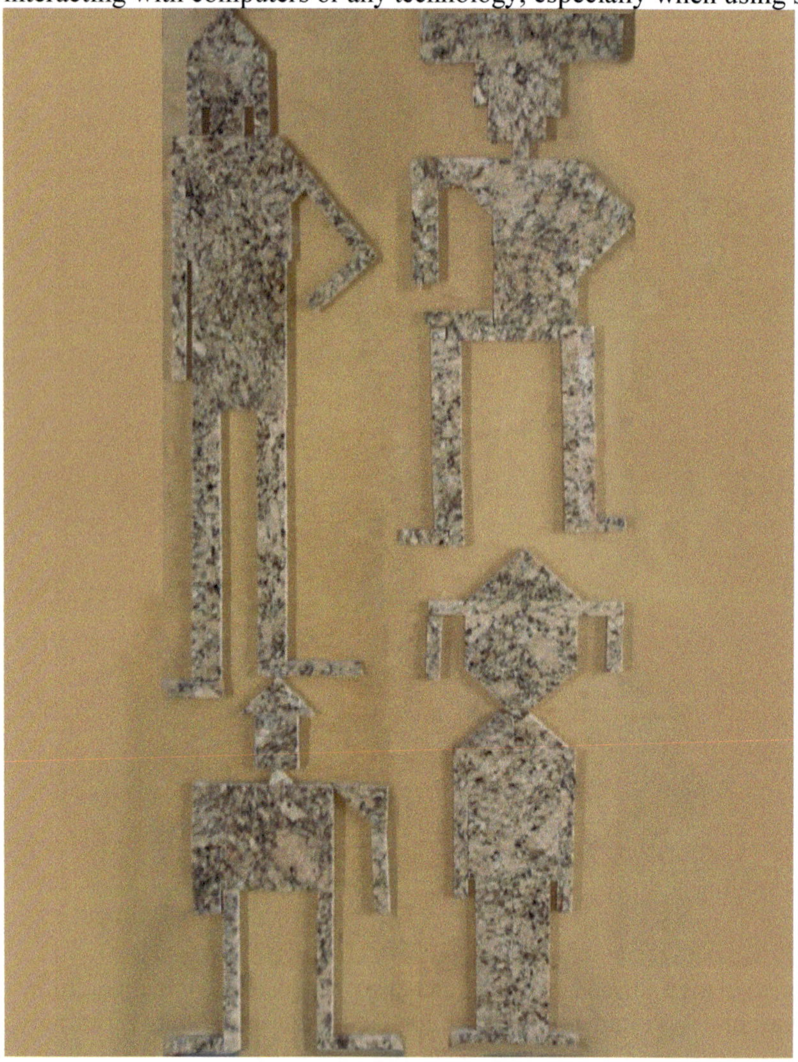

They were always ready for anything, including pranks and punishments aimed at computers and carrying their director's car to be set tight between the two trees so he could not drive away without their help, for which he became appreciative.

Space Music
(Creating a Function – Explanation with Triple-Quoted String)
Recorder – Allen

Allen learned to play the recorder in kindergarten. He dreamed of going to the moon to teach "Moonians" to play the recorder.

```
def moon_instruments_explanation():
    explanation = """
    In the enchanting realm of music, where notes dance through the cosmic symphony,
    wind instruments take on a celestial role—intimately tied to the whims of the moon.

    As the moonlight caresses the earth, it awakens the spirits of wind instruments,
    infusing them with lunar energy that transcends mere melodies. The gentle breezes
    whisper lunar secrets to the flutes, clarinets, and saxophones, inspiring them to
    serenade the night sky.

    The moon, with its gravitational pull, orchestrates a cosmic ballet, guiding the
    breath of the wind instruments. Each note becomes a celestial dance, a harmonious
    collaboration between the earthly winds and the lunar forces.

    So, why should wind instruments be moon-related? Because in the Symphony of the
    universe, they are the celestial messengers, translating the moon's language into
    melodies that resonate with the cosmic vibrations.

    Embrace the lunar serenade of wind instruments, and let the moonlight guide your
    musical journey through the celestial arias of the night.
    """
    return explanation

# Example usage:
print(moon_instruments_explanation())
```

The function returned the moon-related narrative, celebrating the idea that wind instruments are intimately connected to the moon and its mystical influence on music.

He believed all the instruments you blow into would be moon-related. The teacher asked him about other planets, but he was too busy mastering his plan.

SPACE SOCIOLOGY (CONSOLE) HAPPYLAND PLAYERS

They lived in an endless space but could travel with the speed of light. Their jobs were picked based on their talents and preferences, and they were guided by themselves. That meant whatever they wanted to do was automatically considered a part of the open database for collaborative efforts. A console-based program allowed individuals to input their talents and then suggested jobs based on those inputs:

```
class JobRecommendationSystem:
    def __init__(self):
        self.jobs = {
            'Software Engineer': ['coding', 'problem-solving', 'logical thinking'],
            'Graphic Designer': ['creativity', 'design skills', 'attention to detail'],
            'Marketing Specialist': ['communication', 'creativity', 'analytical skills'],
            'Chef': ['cooking', 'creativity', 'attention to detail'],
            # Add more jobs and associated skills/preferences
        }

    def get_user_input(self):
        talents = input("Enter your talents (comma-separated): ").split(', ')
        preferences = input("Enter your preferences (comma-separated): ").split(', ')
        return talents, preferences

    def recommend_jobs(self, talents, preferences):
        recommended_jobs = []
        for job, required_skills in self.jobs.items():
            if all(skill in talents or skill in preferences for skill in required_skills):
                recommended_jobs.append(job)
        return recommended_jobs

    def run_recommendation_system(self):
        print("Welcome to the Job Recommendation System!")
        talents, preferences = self.get_user_input()
        recommended_jobs = self.recommend_jobs(talents, preferences)

        if recommended_jobs:
            print("\nBased on your talents and preferences, we recommend the following jobs:")
            for job in recommended_jobs:
                print(f"- {job}")
        else:
            print("\nSorry, we couldn't find any matching jobs based on your talents and preferences.")

# Instantiate and run the recommendation system
job_system = JobRecommendationSystem()
job_system.run_recommendation_system()
```

There was no need for the leaders, bosses, or supervisors, as anything one would do was appreciated as having potential for future efforts. They could work from a place of their choosing. There was no copyright, and all had access to the database to search for what they needed to learn or use. Their assets were automatically growing each year, and thus as their living conditions and the sizes of their houses, but since they lived in an unconstrained space, it did not create problems for anybody. There was no reason for any form of comparison. Every task they played had awards for different skills so that each player could get an award on various levels. Due to some special filters, everybody looked alike. One could live with any number of roommates, still having access to different households, to join others for any amount of time. No one belonged to anyone, so there were no separations. Some of them mastered musical instruments. In the evening, they discussed their talents and preferences as a part of the database open for collaborative efforts, and their list of skills and special talents grew constantly. They were never bored this way. Every night, they told each other all the nice things about their contribution to their System. They lived forever.

SPECIAL TALENTS
(CLASSES AND METHODS)
PARAPSYCHOLOGIST/HEALER – LORNA

Since they could remember, Lorna exhibited signs of extrasensory perception. She passed the test on reading someone's characteristics and the future, floating above the floor with some unexplained energy, predicting the future by seeing images, dealing with ghosts and making them attracted to her, knowing about the object and its history by touching it, detecting underground water, talking to her sister through their minds, finding a stolen car, set a paper on fire, play an instrument without any prior training, speaking a particular language in her sleep, and also relocating objects with her mind. Everybody she knew had many ideas for her about how she should apply her skills to make money. She was known as an astrologist, an expert in astral kinesis, precognition, being a focal person, knowing and experiencing psychometry and telepathy, being clairvoyant, being able to experience pyrokinesis, atavism, xenoglossy, and psychokinesis.

```
class ParapsychologistMind:
    def __init__(self):
        self.beliefs = []
        self.observations = []

    def form_beliefs(self, *args):
        self.beliefs.extend(args)

    def observe_phenomena(self, *args):
        self.observations.extend(args)

    def analyze_mind(self):
        print("Inside the mind of a Parapsychologist:")
        print("Beliefs:")
        for belief in self.beliefs:
            print(f"- {belief}")
        print("\nObservations:")
        for observation in self.observations:
            print(f"- {observation}")

# Creating an instance of ParapsychologistMind
parapsychologist_mind = ParapsychologistMind()

# Forming beliefs
parapsychologist_mind.form_beliefs(
    "Ghosts communicate through electromagnetic fields.",
    "Telepathy is a plausible means of communication.",
    "Dreams can predict the future."
)

# Observing phenomena
parapsychologist_mind.observe_phenomena(
    "Recording EVPs (Electronic Voice Phenomena).",
    "Analyzing aura colors of individuals.",
    "Documenting instances of precognition."
)

# Analyzing the mind of a Parapsychologist
parapsychologist_mind.analyze_mind()
```

The ParapsychologistMind class was created to represent the mind of a Parapsychologist, and it had methods like form_beliefs, observe_phenomena, and analyze_mind. This followed the object-oriented programming (OOP) paradigm, allowing the code to model the structure and behavior of a Parapsychologist's mind more organized and modularly.

Lorna was hired as a healer for the orchestra members. Now she had to study and experiment with her abilities to learn more about herself.

SPELLING AND SPELLCHECKING (SYSTEMS)

BIRDKEEPER – BCK BUPRE

BCK's mortgage company reported stolen devices containing patrons' identities. "We fired the person who did that," they assured her. BCK called her bank to cancel all her accounts and cards and freeze her assets. She was asked to spell out her full name: BCK: butterfly, cat, kitten? asked the clerk. She said: bitter, cobra, kill. The clerk repeated after her.

Last name, please, he demanded. Bupre: beauty, unite, pink, rare, elegant, she continued.

Barbar, ugly, pirate, rude, energy, the clerk confirmed a proper spelling of her name.

I need to develop a system to ensure correct spellchecking, thought BCK. After all, many birds have a Latin name, which might be hard to spell for many. She wrote a code snippet using the pyspellchecker library to perform spellchecking:

```
from spellchecker import SpellChecker

def spellcheck(text):
    spell = SpellChecker()

    # Split the text into words
    words = text.split()

    # Find misspelled words
    misspelled = spell.unknown(words)

    # Correct misspelled words
    for word in misspelled:
        correction = spell.correction(word)
        text = text.replace(word, correction)

    return text

# Example usage
input_text = "Ths is a smple sentnce wth misspleled wrds."
corrected_text = spellcheck(input_text)

print("Original text:", input_text)
print("Corrected text:", corrected_text)
```

That did not work. It's a simple spellchecker, after all. She had to write another code to devise a system to use a word with a meaning, such as an object for each letter, to spell out a word correctly. First, she developed a dictionary where each letter corresponded to a word and then used it. She avoided the names of the birds. She used a penguin, though, as she believed this one goes beyond the bird's kingdom.

```
def spell_word(word):
    word_dict = {
        'A': 'Apple',
        'B': 'Banana',
        'C': 'Carrot',
        'D': 'Dog',
        'E': 'Elephant',
        'F': 'Fox',
        'G': 'Giraffe',
        'H': 'Hat',
        'I': 'Ice Cream',
        'J': 'Jellyfish',
        'K': 'Kite',
        'L': 'Lion',
        'M': 'Monkey',
        'N': 'Nest',
        'O': 'Orange',
        'P': 'Penguin',
        'Q': 'Queen',
        'R': 'Rainbow',
        'S': 'Sun',
        'T': 'Tree',
        'U': 'Umbrella',
        'V': 'Violin',
        'W': 'Watermelon',
        'X': 'Xylophone',
        'Y': 'Yarn',
        'Z': 'Zebra'
    }

    spelled_out = [word_dict[letter.upper()] for letter in word if
letter.upper() in word_dict]
    return ' '.join(spelled_out)

# Example usage:
word_to_spell = input("Enter a word to spell: ")
spelled_word = spell_word(word_to_spell)
print(f"Spelling of {word_to_spell}: {spelled_word}")
```

Her code defined a function spell_word that took a word as input and spelled it out using the dictionary word_dict. She placed the code on her website, and whenever someone would ask her to spell out her name, she'd send them there. At least she was consistent. She saw people as an Oversized botany.

No one would guess why.

SPORTS
(CLASSES)
THE GYMNASTS – FOX AND TIMUR

Gymnasts were an important part of many performances, from theater plays and ballet operas to concerts that needed some visual impact to keep the audience coming. There were high expectations, of course, so training them was necessary. The youngsters were paired with the professionals for practices and even performances. They performed what they had practiced. Their code represents a training session:

```
class Person:
    def __init__(self, name, age):
        self.name = name
        self.age = age

    def introduce(self):
        print(f"Hello, I'm {self.name} and I'm {self.age} years old.")

class Gymnast(Person):
    def __init__(self, name, age, specialty):
        super().__init__(name, age)
        self.specialty = specialty

    def train(self):
        print(f"{self.name} is a gymnast specializing in
{self.specialty}. Training now!")

class Child(Person):
    def __init__(self, name, age, playful_level):
        super().__init__(name, age)
        self.playful_level = playful_level

    def play(self):
        print(f"{self.name} is a child with a playful level of
{self.playful_level}. Playing now!")

# Training Session
gymnast1 = Gymnast("Sophie", 25, "Rhythmic Gymnastics")
gymnast2 = Gymnast("Alex", 28, "Artistic Gymnastics")

child1 = Child("Emma", 8, "High")
child2 = Child("Ethan", 7, "Medium")

# Introduce participants
gymnast1.introduce()
gymnast2.introduce()
child1.introduce()
child2.introduce()

# Training and playing together
print("\nTraining Session Begins!\n")
gymnast1.train()
gymnast2.train()
child1.play()
child2.play()
```

In the training session, gymnasts and children introduced themselves and then proceeded to train and play together, then extended or modified the script based on more specific training activities or interactions they wanted to simulate. Then, they were learning to sing and dance.

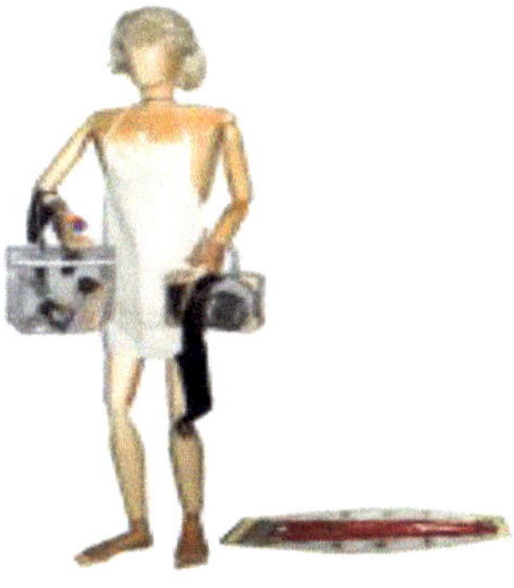

SPORTS
(SIMULATION)
BALL PLAYERS – SID, SAG, AND SMU

Playing ball meant many things to them, from learning physics to spending time outside. To illustrate the physics behind playing a bouncing ball, they developed a Python simulation using the Pygame library. First, they had to install Pygame.

```
pip install Pygame
import pygame
import sys


# Initialize Pygame
pygame.init()

# Set up the screen
width, height = 800, 600
screen = pygame.display.set_mode((width, height))
pygame.display.set_caption("Bouncing Ball Physics")

# Set up the ball
ball_radius = 20
ball_color = (255, 0, 0)
ball_pos = [width // 2, height // 2]
ball_speed = [5, 5]  # Initial speed in x and y directions

# Set up the physics parameters
gravity = 0.5
bounce_factor = 0.8

# Main game loop
while True:
    for event in pygame.event.get():
        if event.type == pygame.QUIT:
            pygame.quit()
            sys.exit()

    # Update ball position based on physics
    ball_pos[0] += ball_speed[0]
    ball_pos[1] += ball_speed[1]

    # Update vertical speed with gravity
    ball_speed[1] += gravity

    # Bounce off the walls
    if ball_pos[0] - ball_radius <= 0 or ball_pos[0] +
ball_radius >= width:
        ball_speed[0] = -ball_speed[0]
    if ball_pos[1] - ball_radius <= 0 or ball_pos[1] +
ball_radius >= height:
        ball_speed[1] = -ball_speed[1] * bounce_factor

    # Draw the background
    screen.fill((255, 255, 255))

    # Draw the ball
    pygame.draw.circle(screen, ball_color,
(int(ball_pos[0]), int(ball_pos[1])), ball_radius)

    # Update the display
    pygame.display.flip()

    # Set the frame rate
    pygame.time.Clock().tick(60)
```

In their code, the physics involved gravity affecting the vertical speed and bouncing off the walls with a certain bounce factor. They experimented with the parameters to add more physics elements to enhance the simulation.

Soon, they enrolled in the Physics School of Ball-Playing.

SPORT AND ENTERTAINMENT (ITERATION AND SYNCHRONIZATION)
MASTER JUGGLER – PETA

Peta was often asked to correct someone's writing, as AI was seen as simplifying things too much. The biggest problem was the commas: every time she looked at the text, it looked like someone had sneezed with punctuations on their pages. Her new skill of being patient helped her concentrate when juggling, so:

```
import time

def throw_ball(height):
    print(f"Throwing ball to a height of {height} meters")

def catch_ball():
    print("Catching the ball")

def juggling_routine(num_throws):
    for i in range(num_throws):
        throw_ball(i + 1)
        catch_ball()

def main():
    num_juggling_cycles = 3

    for _ in range(num_juggling_cycles):
        juggling_routine(5)
        print("Rest for a moment...")
        time.sleep(2)

if __name__ == "__main__":
    main()
```

The for loop was used to iterate over the juggling cycles. Within each cycle, the juggling_routine function was called, which, in turn, used another for loop to iterate over the number of throws specified. This structure allowed her to repeat the juggling routine for several cycles. Additionally(2) function call demonstrated a simple use of synchronization. It added a pause of 2 seconds between juggling cycles to simulate a rest period, which enhanced the realism of the juggling routine in the code.

 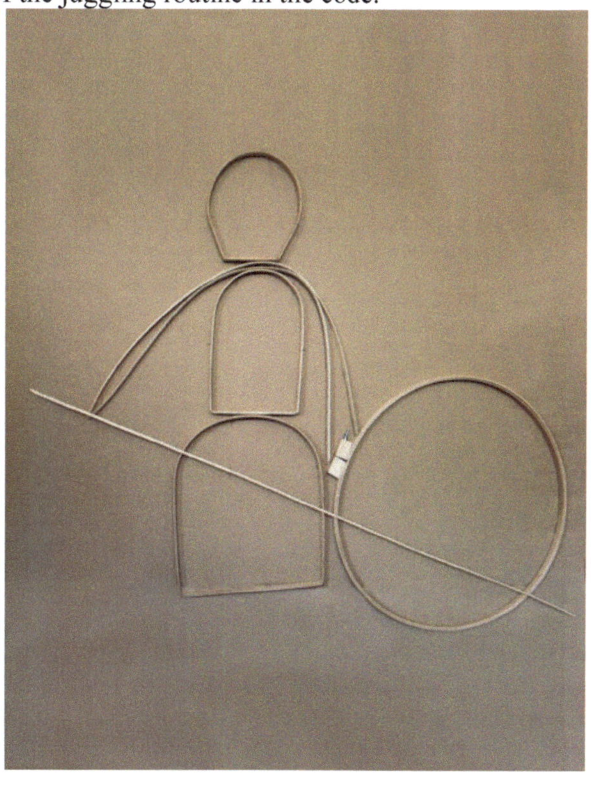

What one drops, another one picks up.
Oh, the power of Joy!

PYROTECHNIC – SOLAR

They say a sapper can only make a mistake once. After all, clearing minefields is not easy. Sonar's skills were extensive, while still expanding. It resulted from the increasing demand for some unusual effects and because of the new non-violence policy that would restrict the usage of life-threatening devices, such as guns or knives, at the theater stage. Her favorite task was to do weather-related effects. Thunderstorms, tornadoes, or typhoons were noisy and spectacular, but floods and fire required preparations. Her code used the Pygame library, which provided functionalities for drawing graphics, handling user input, and managing the game loop. Her graphics programming created the visual effects of raindrops falling on the screen. The pygame.draw.line function drew each raindrop, and the position of the raindrops was updated to simulate their motion for visually engaging special effects.

```
import pygame
import sys
import random

# Initialize Pygame
pygame.init()

# Set up the display
width, height = 800, 600
screen = pygame.display.set_mode((width, height))
pygame.display.set_caption("Special Effects Performance")

# Set up raindrops
raindrops = []
for _ in range(100):
    x = random.randint(0, width)
    y = random.randint(0, height)
    raindrops.append([x, y])

# Main game loop
while True:
    for event in pygame.event.get():
        if event.type == pygame.QUIT:
            pygame.quit()
            sys.exit()

    # Update raindrop positions
    for drop in raindrops:
        drop[1] += 5  # Raindrop falls down

        # Reset raindrop if it goes below the screen
        if drop[1] > height:
            drop[1] = 0
            drop[0] = random.randint(0, width)

    # Clear the screen
    screen.fill((0, 0, 0))  # Black background

    # Draw raindrops
    for drop in raindrops:
        pygame.draw.line(screen, (0, 0, 255), (drop[0], drop[1]), (drop[0], drop[1] + 5))

    # Update the display
    pygame.display.flip()

    # Set the frame rate
    pygame.time.Clock().tick(30)
```

Her special trick to accompany the rainbow was a sound that made the audience sigh as one person when it was projected. Despite using a gong to do it, the thunderstorm was not easy for her. She'd shake the floor so everybody could feel it. She mastered the effects. She could make a blast that looked like it was miles away. Once, there was a historic train ride for the whole troop. The malfunctioning of the tracks made it very rough. No one was hurt, and Solar was congratulated for creating such an exciting evening.

Stage Design with Holograms
(Class)
Opera Singers – Gigi, Erna, Edgar, Flash, and Paperos

Their acting skills had to go with their vocal perfection. They specialized in the roles of the king, the queen, the guard, and the tea boy. That's all. The opera director wanted to adapt a special play into an opera setting, so they developed a list of major characters. Most of their dramas were based on four characters. All other people in the plot were mentioned in a dialogue projected on the backdrop, in a photographic form, or as the movies recorded for the battle scenes brought from major movie productions. There were also other projections used of people eating or dancing. It all worked, but the stage was still only three-dimensional. This was when they decided to bring in the robots. They were called Paperos I, II, III, etc. They looked like people and could follow the paths precisely. Paperos could change the costume display in seconds to say nothing about the tone of their voice, the language, and the facial expressions projected on their current mask. Now, on top of remembering their role and acting patterns, the singers had to learn the robots' trajectories. The plan was to add holograms:

```
class HologramProjector:
    def __init__(self, character_name):
        self.character_name = character_name

    def display_hologram(self):
        """Simulate displaying a hologram on the theater stage."""
        print(f"A hologram of {self.character_name} appears on the stage.")

if __name__ == "__main__":
    # Create an instance of the HologramProjector class
    hologram_projector = HologramProjector("Shakespeare's Ghost")

    # Use the display_hologram method to simulate the hologram display
    hologram_projector.display_hologram()
```

The HologramProjector class was used to model the behavior of a hologram projector, and an instance of the class (hologram_projector) was created to use the methods defined within the class. The hologram technology involved complex optics, projections, and often 3D modeling (CG, physics, and engineering).

The following year, they plan to add floating virtual reality objects between the rows, and the holograms, for the audience to have an interactive learning experience in the opera house.

STATISTICAL PROBABILITY
(LIST COMPREHENSION)
MUSIC CRITICS – M.JS: MONIQUE, MICHELLE, MIRANDA

Three music critics, Monique, Miranda, and Michelle were considered illustrious guests at Lorenzo's parties because of their beauty and wit. Monique, Miranda, and Michelle are triplets, and nobody knows which one (only one) is truly kind and how dangerous it is to chatter with the two other unidentified sisters. Each of the triplets asks to be called M.J. Once, after reading an unfavorable critique authored by M.J., Colin, the oboist, was infuriated to the point that he decided to sue the music critic for libel. He hired agent Michael to discover whom he was going to sue. Michael fell in love with one of M.J. 's, but he did not know which one of the sisters was the object of his desire. Colin publicly stated that the sister, who used to have the other two triplets keeping their incognito, would commit a form of identity theft, but he still did not know who was behind this action. They used the list comprehension to create a list of nice sisters from the given list of sisters based on the kind attribute.

```
class Sister:
    def __init__(self, name, kind=False):
        self.name = name
        self.kind = kind

def find_nice_sister(sisters):
    nice_sisters = [sister for sister in sisters if sister.kind]

    if len(nice_sisters) == 1:
        nice_sister = nice_sisters[0]
        print(f"The nice sister is: {nice_sister.name}")
    elif len(nice_sisters) > 1:
        print("Oops! More than one sister is kind.")
    else:
        print("None of the sisters is kind.")

# Example usage:
triplet1 = Sister("Anna")
triplet2 = Sister("Bella", kind=True)
triplet3 = Sister("Clara")

sisters = [triplet1, triplet2, triplet3]

find_nice_sister(sisters)
```

After that, all the sisters became kind and nice to everyone, but Michael lost interest in all of them.

STATISTICS
(PROBABILITY)
BEACH RESIDENT – ZUT

Zut could be spotted on the same beach at the same time throughout the year. Nobody knew about him as he looked too busy to be approached. It was hard to determine what he was occupied with, though. Thinking of the past, said one; predicting the future, said another. Solving the same problem over and over, said another one. Getting inspiration for his music, said a passerby who happened to be a musician and knew Zut, but nobody was listening. One person wrote a probability code considering what a person sitting on a beach at the same time can be occupied with every time of the year. The probabilities are arbitrary to be adjusted based on one's preferences or assumptions:

```
import random
def beach_activities_probability():
    activities = ["Reading a book", "Listening to music", "Building sandcastles", "Sunbathing",
                  "Collecting seashells", "Taking a walk", "Playing beach games", "Drawing or writing"]

    # Arbitrary probabilities for each activity
    probabilities = [0.2, 0.15, 0.1, 0.1, 0.1, 0.1, 0.1, 0.05]

    # Select an activity based on probabilities
    chosen_activity = random.choices(activities, probabilities)[0]

    return chosen_activity

def main():
    # Simulate a person sitting on the beach at the same time every day
    for _ in range(10):  # Run the simulation 10 times
        activity = beach_activities_probability()
        print("Today's activity: {}".format(activity))

if __name__ == "__main__":
    main()
```

In this code, he had the beach_activities_probability function use the random.choices function to select an activity based on the specified probabilities. The main function simulated a person sitting on the beach for 10 days and printed the chosen activity for each day. Then, he adjusted the probabilities or added or removed activities based on what he thought a person might be occupied with on the beach, but it did not solve the mystery behind the person. Nobody dared to interrupt or pull away from his deep thoughts.

STATISTICS – PROBABILITY (RANDOM SYNTAX) ACTOR PLAYING DRUMMER – NORMAN

On some occasions, the Orchestra drummers were needed on tour. Oftentimes, there was a need for a drummer during the Orchestra performance, but all of them were on the road. Director Gerlost came up with a solution. He hired an actor to pretend that he was playing drums. The actor was instructed to play really fast and be spectacular, but to beat on an empty drum top, instead of touching an actual instrument. This way, there would be no sound, only some impressive action. However, Gerlost and Norman had doubts. One day, they decided to experiment. They lowered ticket prices for those who'd be willing to fill out a survey. One of the questions was to list all the instruments played during the performance. Ninety-three percent of the responders listed drums, though there were three responders.
A Python script with a random number generation to determine each person's response was used to check. It simulated a scenario where 93% of people responded with "yes," and there were three responders.

```
import random


def simulate_survey():
    # Probability of responding with "yes" (93%)
    yes_probability = 0.93

    # Number of responders
    num_responders = 3

    # Simulate responses
    responses = [random.random() < yes_probability for _ in
range(num_responders)]

    # Print the responses
    print("Responses:")
    for i, response in enumerate(responses, 1):
        print(f"Responder {i}: {'Yes' if response else 'No'}")

    # Check if the majority said "yes"
    if responses.count(True) > num_responders // 2:
        print("The majority said 'Yes'!")
    else:
        print("The majority did not say 'Yes'.")

# Run the simulation
simulate_survey()
```

Algura: swims his way up.

Number of responders. responses = [random.random() < yes_probability for _ in range(num_responders)]: Simulate the responses using a list comprehension. For each responder, generate a random number between 0 and 1. If the random number is less than the yes probability, the response is "yes"; otherwise, it's "no". Print the responses for each responder. Check if the majority of responders said "yes" (responses.count(True) > num_responders // 2) and print the result. simulate_survey(): Run the simulation when the script is executed.
His code simulated a survey with three responders, each having a 93% chance of responding with.
As he explained to his audience, import the random module generated random numbers. yes_probability = 0.93: Set the probability of responding with "yes" to 93%. num_responders = 3: Define the num "yes." 93% is a good number, as they agreed while ignoring the number of patrons taking their survey.

STATUS
(FUNCTION)
PRECIOUS & MRS. PRECIOUS

She was important twice in her life. He was always precious.

```
def interpret_sentence(sentence):
    words = sentence.split()

    for word in words:
        if word.lower() in ["important", "precious"]:
            print(f"{word.capitalize()} is mentioned in the sentence.")

# Example usage
sentence = "She was important twice in her life. He was always precious."
interpret_sentence(sentence)
```

The function (interpret_sentence) took a sentence as input, split it into words, and then checked if certain keywords ("important" and "precious") were present in the sentence. It used a loop to iterate through the words and a conditional statement to check for the keywords.

Our life is about the keywords, she thought.

Stereotypes
(Print Statements)
Tuba – Long

He was so tall that when sitting at the table, the soup on the spoon he carried to his mouth would get cold on its way. No one, no one, he thought, had the slightest clue about his daily troubles. The biggest and most repetitive one was listening to the same stereotyping sentences.

```
def tall_person_perspective():
    print("Advantages and Disadvantages of Being Extremely Tall:")
    print("\nAdvantages:")
    print("1. Great visibility in crowded places.")
    print("2. Often excel in sports like basketball or volleyball.")
    print("3. Reach high shelves without the need for assistance.")
    print("4. Stay safe, as people avoid trouble around you.")
    print("\nDisadvantages:")
    print("1. Difficulty finding clothes that fit well.")
    print("2. Increased risk of health issues like joint problems.")
    print("3. Limited options for transportation (legroom in cars, airplane seats).")
    print("4. Attracts attention, which can be uncomfortable in some situations.")

# Call the function to display the advantages and disadvantages
tall_person_perspective()
```

His answer was to focus on conveying information and keeping it simple for readability.

STORYTELLING (GRAPHIC LIBRARIES) BASIC ART CONCEPTS – ELE

Ele developed a book discussing new approaches to artistic creations using an apple as her character. She discovered what new technologies offered to an artist affected the basic art concepts on many levels. Ele thought about how the new developments shifted art-related jobs. She wondered how they inspired cooperative, interdisciplinary, and multi-sensory styles of production of art, the teaching and learning, knowledge visualization, marketing, promotion, and entertainment. Her first question was: "Who is my audience: who am I writing this book for?" Based on her answer, she selected the font that matched the characteristics of her group. The next question was how her book was going to be distributed. She chose a printed book, an interactive book, an eBook, VR, AR, XR, a video, animation as a book, 3D printed, generative artificial intelligence (GAI) art, or something else in a range of physical computing. She was creating a book that she wrote and illustrated. Her text was informative, clear, and concise to grab the attention of her audience. She wanted to keep the current generation known for their attention span of 8 seconds, interested and willing to read and see more.

Type or Form of Art - the varieties of art products and kinds of artists, the schemes used to classify art, and the functions art products serve. She described and showed 2D drawing or painting, 3D sculpture or architecture, or time-based, interactive, immersive, or integrated media arts.

Medium - the materials, tools, and procedures the artist uses to create the work of art. Skipping an oil on paper or other media on a piece of paper, she used pen and ink over chalk to create a drawing of her apple.

Design - the planned organization of the phenomena the artist manipulates, the visual elements, and principles. She considered depictive, flat (drawing), spatial (sculpture), or abstract in nature cross-section of an apple. Ele used lines to create depth and texture in her character. By cross-hatching and hatching, she created what appears to be a three-dimensional apple on a flat piece of paper. Various lines, with both straight lines and curved lines, added dimension and variety to the drawing. Emphasis was given to the roundness of an apple. The lack of line on the outside hairline was implied, and yet there was no doubt that the apple had a full body. This time, the focus was on the curvatures. The line describing an apple was an actual line, versus positive and negative spaces. Thus, she created a character using hatching, cross-hatching, and stippling.

Subject Matter - the meaning of the work of art, the things depicted, the theme. She chose to draw a portrait of an apple. She taught about a still life, about apple trees present in a given landscape, but abstract depiction was beyond her interest. An apple brings many connotations, associations, and metaphors. She developed an apple of her own creation but based her drawing on an actual model.

Style - the family resemblances between works of art, the visual similarities. She represented the natural world to capture life realistically and authentically, to create the illusion of accurate three-dimensional space. Yet her character had vibrancy and self-expression.

As a perfectionist, she wanted a level of realism in her depiction. Thus, she turned to the computer for a visual representation of an apple, using Python with the Pygame library to draw a simple apple:

```
pip install Pygame

import pygame
import sys

# Initialize Pygame
pygame.init()

# Set up the screen
width, height = 400, 400
screen = pygame.display.set_mode((width, height))
pygame.display.set_caption("Apple Drawing")

# Set up colors
red = (255, 0, 0)
green = (0, 255, 0)
```

```
# Main game loop
while True:
    for event in pygame.event.get():
        if event.type == pygame.QUIT:
            pygame.quit()
            sys.exit()

    # Draw the apple
    pygame.draw.ellipse(screen, red, (150, 100, 100, 120)) # Apple body
    pygame.draw.circle(screen, green, (200, 90), 10) # Apple stem

    # Update the display
    pygame.display.flip()

    # Set the frame rate
    pygame.time.Clock().tick(60)
```

She created a window to draw an apple with a red body and a green stem. Then, she modified the code to change apple's appearance. The lines were perfect: no more need for realism. We have a camera for that.

STORYTELLING – CONTAINER FOR A STORY CONCEPT
(IF ELSE)
CONDUCTOR – DAVID

Conductor David was new here and did not know the names of his musicians yet. He was embarrassed when uncertain how to address people he had already met. His kids, Paul and Jessica, asked the media man, Duncan, to let them use an orchestra website with artists' photographs to design a pop-up book on a computer. David could thus connect names with the faces of the musicians. David used a special conducting technique. He lined up all instruments on one graph, to be able to quickly see who should play when and discern all the intervals. This contributed to his success. David liked stories. He spotted them everywhere: in a book, on the radio, on the internet, or as comics, manga, cartoons, theatrical plays, movies or animation, songs, or told as podcasts. Once he read about a theory called a container for a story, he realized how the same plot needs to be told differently for each medium and for each way of delivery, and it can be packaged in a new form. The writer needs to tell a story to match each medium's framework, timing, and technical requirements. Every night David tried to come up with a brand-new tale to tell his children before bedtime. First, he told it to Jessica with an emphasis on a movie setup; then, he could be seen in Paul's room converting it into a theatrical production. Converting it involved adapting the screenplay into a script suitable for live performance:

```
def convert_to_theatrical(movie_script):
    theatrical_script = []

    # Split the movie script into lines
    movie_lines = movie_script.split('\n')

    for line in movie_lines:
        # Assume dialogue lines start with the character's name
followed by a colon
        if ':' in line:
            character, dialogue = line.split(':', 1)
            theatrical_line = f"{character.strip()}:
{dialogue.strip()}"
            theatrical_script.append(theatrical_line)
        else:
            # Non-dialogue lines can be included as is
            theatrical_script.append(line)

    return '\n'.join(theatrical_script)

# Example movie script
movie_script = """
CHARACTER1: Hello there!
CHARACTER2: How are you?
"""

# Convert to theatrical script
theatrical_script = convert_to_theatrical(movie_script)

# Print the result
print("Theatrical Script:")
print(theatrical_script)
```

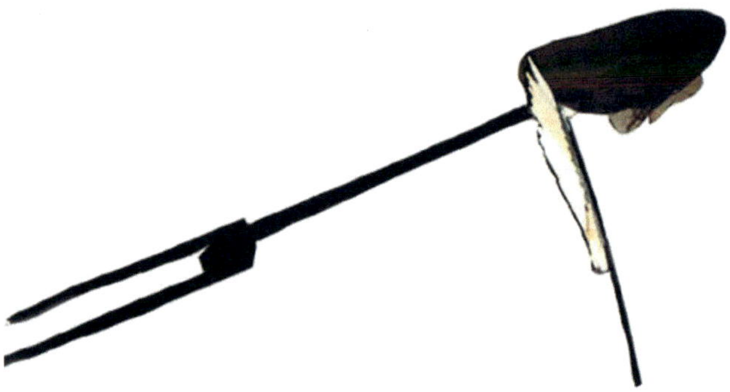

After they both fell asleep, he took notes on their reactions and worked further on his storytelling technique. Stories helped him to form his version of each music composition his orchestra performed. All we do can be a story.

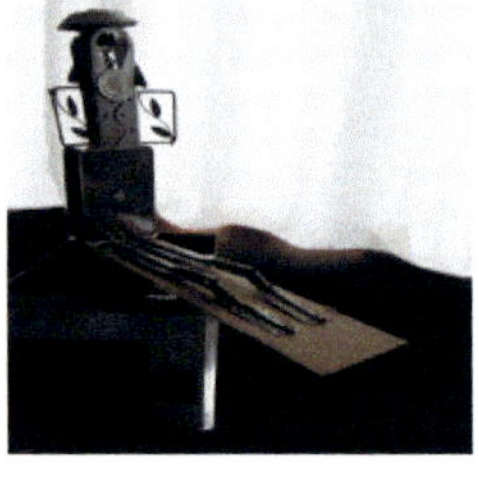

STORYTELLING OPPOSITE WAYS (PROCEDURAL PROGRAMMING) TRUMPET – JOHN & CHRIS

John and Chris played trumpets. They always stood back-to-back while playing, as they believed the sound filled out the room better that way. Since eye contact was impossible, they had to develop another way of communication, but they knew each other so well that no eye contact was needed during the performance. They created a body code for each message they wanted to signal. They married twins on the same day, and they used to spend most of their time together. They even rented a condominium together. Everything worked excellently except for one day when John saw something that Chris, who was facing the opposite direction, could not see. Chris hired a detective:

```
def person_facing_forward():
    print("Person facing forward:")
    print("  - Sees a beautiful sunset.")
    print("  - Observes a mountain in the distance.")
    print("  - Notices a colorful bird flying by.")
    print("  - Enjoys the overall landscape.")

def person_facing_backward():
    print("\nPerson facing backward:")
    print("  - Cannot see the sunset behind them.")
    print("  - Is unaware of the mountain view.")
    print("  - Misses the colorful bird flying in the opposite direction.")
    print("  - Doesn't see the landscape in front.")
```

```
def main():
    print("Simulating a scenario where one person sees something that another person cannot.")

    # Call functions for each person's perspective
    person_facing_forward()
    person_facing_backward()

# Call the main function to execute the code
main()
```

In his code, he used the person_facing_forward() and person_facing_backward() functions to represent the perspectives of two individuals. The main() function orchestrates the overall flow of the code by calling these perspective functions. His code was organized into functions to promote readability and maintainability. Having no answer, he tried differently, using the concept of a "cone of vision." It represented each person's field of view as a cone and checked if the other person was within it.

```
import math

def can_see_each_other(person1_position, person1_direction, person2_position):
    # Define the cone angle (in degrees)
    cone_angle = 90  # You can adjust this angle based on the scenario

    # Convert cone angle to radians for trigonometric functions
    cone_angle_rad = math.radians(cone_angle)

    # Calculate vector from person1 to person2
    vector_person1_to_person2 = (person2_position[0] - person1_position[0], person2_position[1] - person1_position[1])

    # Calculate angle between person1's direction and the vector to person2
    angle_difference = math.atan2(vector_person1_to_person2[1], vector_person1_to_person2[0]) - math.radians(person1_direction)

    # Check if the angle difference is within the cone of vision
    if -cone_angle_rad / 2 <= angle_difference <= cone_angle_rad / 2:
        return True
    else:
        return False

# Example usage
person1_position = (0, 0)
person1_direction = 0  # 0 degrees means facing to the right
person2_position = (3, 2)

result = can_see_each_other(person1_position, person1_direction, person2_position)
print("Can person 1 see person 2?", result)
```

His code used trigonometry to calculate the angle between the direction a person is facing and the vector from that person to another. If the angle was within the defined cone of vision, then the two people could see each other. His use of trigonometry and the use of math.atan2 function to calculate angles and the conversion between degrees and radians unfolded the answer:

"Missing the colorful bird flying in the opposite direction."

SUPPORT
(INSTANCE)
LYRE – CALVIN

Calvin could adapt to different functions in the orchestra. He was known for being a vegetarian, supporting Macs, being left left-brainer, and having a dog-in-law who enjoyed chasing cats. Calvin drank tea, preferred taking a shower, and biked to work. He often felt guilty for being accurate. His preferences were stereotyped, so every Friday, he tried something opposite to his beliefs. He kept a diary and a program calculating and displaying the carbon footprint based on user input for different activities.

```
class PreservingBehaviorCalculator:
    def __init__(self):
        self.carbon_footprint = 0

    def calculate_carbon_footprint(self, activity, duration):
        # Define carbon footprint values for different
activities (hypothetical values)
        activity_footprints = {
            'walking': 0.02,
            'cycling': 0.05,
            'public_transport': 0.1,
            'car': 0.2,
            'recycling': -0.1  # Negative value for eco-friendly
activities
        }

        # Calculate carbon footprint for the given activity and
duration
        if activity in activity_footprints:
            self.carbon_footprint +=
activity_footprints[activity] * duration
        else:
            print("Invalid activity!")

    def display_carbon_footprint(self):
        print(f"Your total carbon footprint is:
{self.carbon_footprint} kgCO2")

# Example of usage
calculator = PreservingBehaviorCalculator()

calculator.calculate_carbon_footprint('walking', 2)
calculator.calculate_carbon_footprint('cycling', 1)
calculator.calculate_carbon_footprint('public_transport',
0.5)
calculator.calculate_carbon_footprint('car', 1)

calculator.display_carbon_footprint()
```

His code used (class PreservingBehaviorCalculator) encapsulated the functionality _init_ Method: Initialized the carbon_footprint attribute to track the total carbon footprint.calculate_carbon_footprint Method: Takes an activity and duration as input, calculated splay_carbon_footprint Method:Displays the total carbon footprint calculated.

```
class AnimalAdventure:
    def __init__(self, cat_name, dog_name):
        self.cat_name = cat_name
        self.dog_name = dog_name

    def tell_poem(self):
        print(f"Once upon a time, in a digital land,")
        print(f"A cat named {self.cat_name} had a plan.")
        print(f"{self.cat_name} craved a feast, juicy and grand,")
        print(f"So, into a car, with {self.dog_name} in command.")

        print(f"\nOn the road they went, a duo so neat,")
        print(f"{self.dog_name} at the wheel, with four paws on the
seat.")
        print(f"The engine roared, the adventure unfurled,")
        print(f"With a steak on a plate, for the cat in the world.")

        print(f"\nThrough valleys and hills, the car smoothly glides,")
        print(f"{self.cat_name} licked its lips, anticipation in strides.")
        print(f"With a purr and a meow, they cruised through the night,")
        print(f"A cat and a dog, their friendship took flight.")

# Example of usage
cat_name = "Whiskers"
dog_name = "Buddy"

adventure = AnimalAdventure(cat_name, dog_name)
adventure.tell_poem()
```

Last Friday, he wrote a poem on a PC about the cat eating a steak in a car driven by his dog:

SYMBOLISM
(MULTIPLE CONDITIONAL EXPRESSIONS)
ABSTRACTION AD DIRECTOR/MARKETING/PR – UGMA LADDER – FAR

Cognitive and abstract thinking were her life. She developed a code comparing signs, symbols, metaphors, and allegories.

```
def compare_concepts(concept1, concept2):
    if concept1 == concept2:
        return "These concepts are identical."
    elif concept1.lower() == concept2.lower():
        return "These concepts are similar, considering case-insensitivity."
    else:
        return "These concepts are different."

# Example usage:
concept1 = "Sign"
concept2 = "Symbol"
result = compare_concepts(concept1, concept2)
print(result)
```

Her code defined a function compare_concepts that took two concepts as input and compared them, considering both case-sensitive and case-insensitive matches. The example usage compared the concepts "Sign" and "Symbol" and printed the result. She modified the concept1 and concept2 variables with other terms to see different results.

Soon she learned about the abstraction ladder.

He designed keyboards for various professions: mathematician, astrophysicist, astronomer, chemist, geometrician, and musician. They all were different but had one thing in common: aside from being useful for a particular discipline, using them was hard. He assumed that Antikythera had a keyboard.

```
class Keyboard:
    def _init_(self, layout):
        self.layout = layout

    def display(self):
        for row in self.layout:
            print(" ".join(row))
        print("\n")

# Define keyboards for different professions
musician_layout = [
    ["C", "D", "E", "F", "G", "A", "B"],
    ["1/4", "1/2", "3/4", "♪", "♫", "♩", " ♬"]
]

mathematician_layout = [
    ["+", "-", "*", "/", "=", "^", "√"],
    ["1", "2", "3", "4", "5", "6", "7"],
    ["8", "9", "0", "π", "∫", "∑", "∂"]
]
chemist_layout = [
    ["H", "He", "Li", "Be", "B", "C", "N"],
    ["O", "F", "Ne", "Na", "Mg", "Al", "Si"],
    ["P", "S", "Cl", "K", "Ar", "Ca", "Fe"]
]

# Create instances of keyboards
musician_keyboard = Keyboard(musician_layout)
mathematician_keyboard = Keyboard(mathematician_layout)
chemist_keyboard = Keyboard(chemist_layout)

# Display keyboards
print("Musician Keyboard:")
musician_keyboard.display()

print("Mathematician Keyboard:")
mathematician_keyboard.display()

print("Chemist Keyboard:")
chemist_keyboard.display()
```

The keyboards for different professions were represented with (layout). The Keyboard class had a display method that printed the keys visually. Each profession had its layouts of keys, such as musical notes for the musician, mathematical symbols for the mathematician, and chemical elements for the chemist.

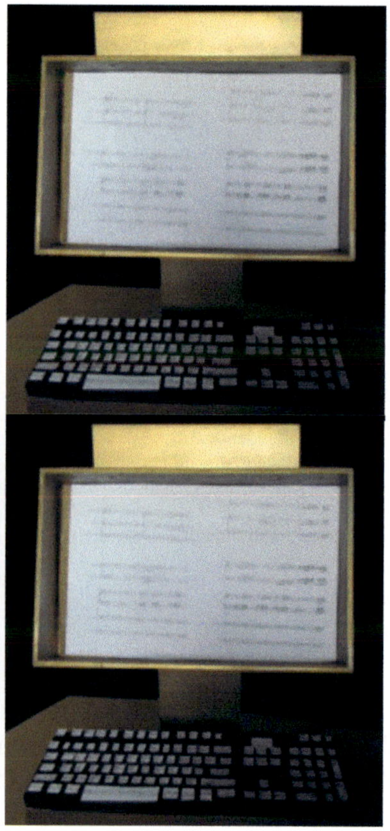

It's harder to see what's not there than what is there.

T	TAUTOLOGY (CONDITIONAL STATEMENT) PROTESTERS

They protested on demand. If the tasks were too difficult, they would protest.

```
# Protest On Demand

def check_difficulty(task_difficulty):
    """
    Check if the task difficulty is too high.
    If it is, simulate a protest.
    """
    if task_difficulty > 5:
        print("Task is too difficult! Protest initiated.")
    else:
        print("Task is manageable. No need to protest.")

# Example: Protest On Demand
task_difficulty = 3
check_difficulty(task_difficulty)
```

The if-else statement was used to check if the task difficulty was greater than 5. If it is, the code printed a message indicating that a protest was initiated. Otherwise, if the task difficulty is 5 or lower, it printed a message indicating that there is no need to protest.

Some still were confused about the cause but followed up with the rest.

TEACHING
(CLASSES AND OOP)
PAINTING DEMO – RUMO

Every Thursday at 6 p.m., Rumo showed people how to develop painting. In front of his weekly audience, he was painting while talking. He talked about media, traditions, styles, influences, dynasties, and kings, so his sessions were renamed as art history demos.

```
class ArtHistoryDemo:
    def __init__(self, topic):
        self.topic = topic
        self.content = []

    def add_content(self, *args):
        self.content.extend(args)

    def present_lecture(self):
        print(f"Art History Demo: {self.topic}")
        for index, item in enumerate(self.content, start=1):
            print(f"{index}. {item}")

# Creating an art history demo on media, traditions, styles, influences, dynasties, and kings
lecture_on_art_history = ArtHistoryDemo("Exploring Art Through the Ages")

lecture_on_art_history.add_content(
    "Introduction to Different Artistic Media",
    "Exploration of Artistic Traditions",
    "Evolution of Art Styles",
    "Influences on Artistic Movements",
    "Overview of Artistic Dynasties",
    "The Art of Kings: Patronage and Influence"
)

# Presenting the art history demo
lecture_on_art_history.present_lecture()
```

The code defined a class ArtHistoryDemo with methods like _init_, add_content, and present_lecture. Objects of this class could be created (in this case, lecture_on_art_history) to encapsulate data and behavior related to a specific art history demo.

He was known as an idea generator even though he was immersed in the past.

THEATER
(PYTHON AND THE RASPBERRY PI GPIO LIBRARY)
THE CURTAIN HANDLER – JEREMIAH

His job was important. It ensured the curtain was opened or closed or opened fast after closing. That was not easy. His resume was exemplary. He had dealt with all sorts of curtains, going from top to bottom, the metal ones, left to right, right to left (he worked for a prison for a while), and from the middle of the stage to the left or the right, as needed, to name just a few. He could handle double curtains: the tulle ones - showing the shadow, followed by the red wine plush – big, warm, and heavy ones. There were also those for changing the set while the audience was still in chairs, waiting impatiently for a new setup.
With many ways a curtain could be opened: mechanically, by hand, or both—those mechanical ways involved buttons, wireless communication, and pull-ups; the hand method was based on working with a long stick that ended with a big hook designed to pick up a metal circle attached to the top of a curtain. It is still used in small theaters, comedy houses, cabarets, and live-action houses. Jeremiah has done it all, even for those performances where actors would use their bodies, previously painted, decorated, and embellished by make-up artists, to create live pictures based on famous masterpieces. He's seen all the possible approaches and knew all types of actors' behavior, from hysteria and drama to the joy of success. His job required physical strength and softness of the heart. Jeremiah was the only Curtain Handler known, as he knew his methods well to defeat technology on the theater stage. After all, he was one of them, so close to the stage entrance. They kept him working even after theaters started using holograms and various approaches to light as a visual barrier. He devised a code to trigger lights on the theater stage to serve as a curtain. He varied the results depending on the hardware and requirements.

```
import RPi.GPIO as GPIO
import time

# Set up GPIO
GPIO.setmode(GPIO.BOARD)
light_pin = 17  # Replace with the actual GPIO pin you're using
GPIO.setup(light_pin, GPIO.OUT)

def open_curtain():
    GPIO.output(light_pin, GPIO.HIGH)
    time.sleep(2)  # Adjust the sleep duration as needed
    GPIO.output(light_pin, GPIO.LOW)

# Trigger the lights to open the curtain
open_curtain()

# Clean up GPIO
GPIO.cleanup()
```

He used the light_pin variable to represent the GPIO pin connected to the lights. The open_curtain function turned on the lights for 2 seconds (adjustable) to simulate the opening of the curtain. He installed the RPi.GPIO library on his Raspberry Pi before running the code: pip install RPi.GPIO.
Jeremiah knew how to adjust his code according to the needs of each performance.
The theater got more attended after he mastered his new skills.

Therapy
(Classes and Methods in OOP)
Music Therapist – AtheA

AtheA had the best memories from her experience of undergoing music therapy sessions. Not only was her time organized, but also people cared for her. She felt brave and important and felt like she was setting an example to others. Her therapists listened to her stories with real interest. This was a big change for her. Before the accident, her stories were considered not so interesting. No one had the time. AtheA decided to become a music therapist herself. One would think she had to go over a career change, but she wrote a code that represented the duties and expected outcomes of the work of a music therapist:

```
class MusicTherapist:
    def __init__(self, name):
        self.name = name

    def provide_therapy(self):
        print(f"{self.name} is providing music therapy.")
        # Additional duties and activities can be added here.

    def measure_outcomes(self):
        print(f"{self.name} is measuring the outcomes of the music
therapy.")
        # Logic for measuring outcomes can be added here.

# Example usage:
therapist = MusicTherapist("Alice")
therapist.provide_therapy()
therapist.measure_outcomes()
```

The MusicTherapist class encapsulated the related functionality (providing therapy and measuring outcomes) with the use of methods. The class provided a blueprint for creating instances of a therapist. Then, AtheA started studying music, music theory, and facts about composers, psychology, sociology, physiology, neurophysiology, astronomy, cosmology, and divination. She kept collecting all the information she could find. A set of special devices was recommended to her to help her fulfill the tasks. She enrolled in a program and soon became one of the best students. This discovery gave her more motivation. Time was flying. Now, for the first time, she felt like she understood people.

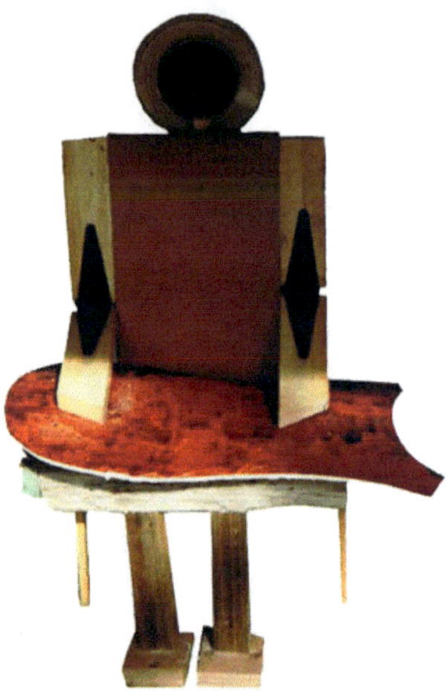

It was something she felt she was born to do.

TIME-BASED ART
(EVENT-DRIVEN PROGRAMMING)
PUPPETEER – BASA

Basa was a Performer. She performed her stories. Her passion was to manipulate various puppets in real time so she could create the illusion of life.

```
import pygame
import sys

# Initialize Pygame
pygame.init()

# Set up the display
width, height = 800, 600
screen = pygame.display.set_mode((width, height))
pygame.display.set_caption("The Illusion of Life")

# Set up the ball
ball_radius = 20
ball_color = (255, 0, 0)
ball_position = [width // 2, height // 2]
ball_speed = [5, 5]

# Main game loop
while True:
    for event in pygame.event.get():
        if event.type == pygame.QUIT:
            pygame.quit()
            sys.exit()

        # Update ball position
    ball_position[0] += ball_speed[0]
    ball_position[1] += ball_speed[1]

# Bounce off the walls
    if ball_position[0] - ball_radius <= 0 or ball_position[0] + ball_radius >= width:
        ball_speed[0] = -ball_speed[0]
    if ball_position[1] - ball_radius <= 0 or ball_position[1] + ball_radius >= height:
        ball_speed[1] = -ball_speed[1]

    # Clear the screen
    screen.fill((255, 255, 255))

    # Draw the ball
    pygame.draw.circle(screen, ball_color, (int(ball_position[0]), int(ball_position[1])), ball_radius)

    # Update the display
    pygame.display.flip()

    # Set the frame rate
    pygame.time.Clock().tick(30)
```

She was like a juggler in her puppeteering profession.

TIME-BASED EVENTS ('FOR' LOOP) OUD/LUTE -- KATHERINE

Katherine was a moviegoer. Her favorite films were silent movies, the ones that had music played during each performance. She thought she was born too late. She'd love to play the piano in the silent movie era if she could choose. If only time could be reversed! Or could she find out how to time travel? Although her coding skills might not be up to par with the complexities of temporal manipulation, she could whip up a basic script that at least gives the illusion of time travel. She created a program that printed out historical events as if the user witnessed them firsthand. The loop iterated over a list of historical events, allowing the program to display each event in sequence.

```
import time

def time_travel():
    print("Welcome, Time Traveler! Let's embark on a journey through history.")
    time.sleep(2)

    events = [
        "The signing of the Declaration of Independence",
        "The moon landing",
        "The fall of the Berlin Wall",
        "The invention of the wheel (well, almost)",
        "The release of Python 3.5 (a monumental moment, I must say)"
            ]

    for event in events:
        print(f"You are now witnessing: {event}")
        time.sleep(3)

    print("Your time-travel adventure comes to an end. Hope you enjoyed the ride!")

if __name__ == "__main__":
    time_travel()
```

As not very appreciated, she often felt like an ugly duckling. Her attitude and luck had changed during her rural vacations. A big vulture had attacked a chicken. The little bird was brave enough to fight until it was finally released from the big guy's beak. It landed featherless and ugly but got all the respect of the rest of the livestock members. The feathers grew back, and the honor stayed with him. Always.

TIME AND VALUE MEASUREMENTS (CLASSES)
WHISTLER – TARIQ

Tariq had problems with how people measure time. When he was little, his parents would keep talking about events or artworks created sometime in B.C. or A.D. There was some division; as he could see it, the time was like returning to the B.C. times, confusing and hard to understand. He started imagining how people of various religions and beliefs would interpret time measurement by reading and talking to people from multiple cultures and religions. How would the exact age be determined? How old would it be in years? Tariq wanted to develop a unified time-measuring system so everyone worldwide could agree on so there would be better communication. He invited specialists in knowledge visualization and documentary filmmakers, paleo climatologists, cultural anthropologists, art historians, chemists, indigenous inhabitants, historians, linguists, communication specialists, musicologists, sports science specialists, military specialists, mathematicians, and astronomers.

After a week of discussions, the only solution was to try coding: he considered a calendar for simplicity to develop a Python code that defined the "Number One" year for the beginning of history:

```
def get_number_one_year():
    # Replace this with the base year of the chosen numbering system
    base_year = 1

    # Add any other considerations or calculations here
    # For simplicity, I'm just returning the base year
    return base_year

# Example usage:
number_one_year = get_number_one_year()
print(f"The Number One year for the beginning of history is: {number_one_year}")
```

They decided to create a common monetary value named World instead. Developing an universal currency involves massive economic, political, and technological considerations. Tariq was interested in a hypothetical code snippet for a primary digital currency, but a real-world universal currency would require careful planning, collaboration between nations, and a robust infrastructure. His code showed digital currency using a blockchain-like structure: Instead of being printed, The World was to be beamed from any new device that fitted all just like palm pilots used before. People must trade, and fixed value, with no decimals, would be more effective. There were some security measures for the device to be connected to its owner through a biofeedback sensor, so a person under duress could not transfer any money. That made the bankers and robbers need to be composed and polite. It would replace a war of muscles with a battle of brains. Now, he wants the satellites to control the weather and save summer's energy for winter and winter's chill for the summer. He is still thinking.

TIME TRAVEL (DATETIME MANIPULATION) PRIZES AND VALUES

They were time warps enthusiasts.

```
import datetime

def time_warp():
    current_time = datetime.datetime.now()
    print(f"Current Time: {current_time}")

    # Creating a time delta for time travel
    time_travel_delta = datetime.timedelta(days=365)

    # Applying time travel
    future_time = current_time + time_travel_delta
    print(f"Time Travel Destination: {future_time}")

    # Simulating a time warp
    simulated_warp_time = future_time - datetime.timedelta(hours=2)
    print(f"Simulated Time Warp: {simulated_warp_time}")

    return simulated_warp_time

if __name__ == "__main__":
    warped_time = time_warp()
    print("\nTime Warping Complete!")
```

The Romans had many ways to entertain:

Current Time Retrieval: Obtain the current date and time using datetime.datetime.now().

Time Delta Creation: Created a time delta (time_travel_delta) representing the time travel set to 365 days.

Time Travel Calculation: Added the time delta to the current time, simulating a jump into the future.

Simulated Time Warp: by subtracting a time delta of 2 hours from the future time, creating a warped time.

Return and Output: The simulated warped time was returned and printed.

Datetime manipulation involves working with date and time objects. The manipulation of current time, the creation of a time delta, and calculations referred to datetime objects showcased this concept.

Even if one reaches Pinto (the Roman Empire), they will not project what is happening on the Earth now at the local cinema.

TRANSLATION OF MESSAGES (SYMBOLIC REPRESENTATION) SAXOPHONE – LUCAS

Lucas, Joe, and Oscar participated in an exchange program that took them to an island. Lucas took his saxophone there, and Oscar his accordion to play on the beach with a group of local musicians. Joe took her keyboard, as she hoped it might help her learn new tunes. She also had a video camera ready to shoot the dances. Nothing was as simple and easy as they wished. The music was quite different, and the dances needed explanation to be fully understood. All the female dancers performed each musical composition in a way that conveyed particular ideas or emotions in their lives. Fortunately, Joe met a hula dancer named Waiaka, who gave Lucas, Joe, and Oscar many details about replacing speech with dance and reasons for using specific gestures and motions. Female dancers made distinctive movements with their hands to tell stories further expressed by their dances. They also conveyed feelings resulting from the events they discussed, such as the dangers from their men's exhausting work when they went to sea to catch fish. After a mutual discussion with Waiaka and clarification of previously unknown concepts, Lucas, Joe, and Oscar returned home with a video production about the music and dance of the Island. After a short time, they invited Waiaka and a group of musicians to present their art on their theater stage. Entrepreneur Joe, after learning from the visitors was urged to enhance the code he wrote to prepare them for the trip:

```
class HulaCommunication:
      self.hand_movements = hand_movements
      self.hip_sways = hip_sways

   def convey_message(self):
      print("Communicating through Hula Dance:")
      print("Hand Movements:", self.hand_movements)
      print("Hip Sways:", self.hip_sways)
      print("Message Conveyed!")

# Example usage:
hula_message = HulaCommunication("Ahe Lau Makani", "Ami
Ami")
hula_message.convey_message()
```

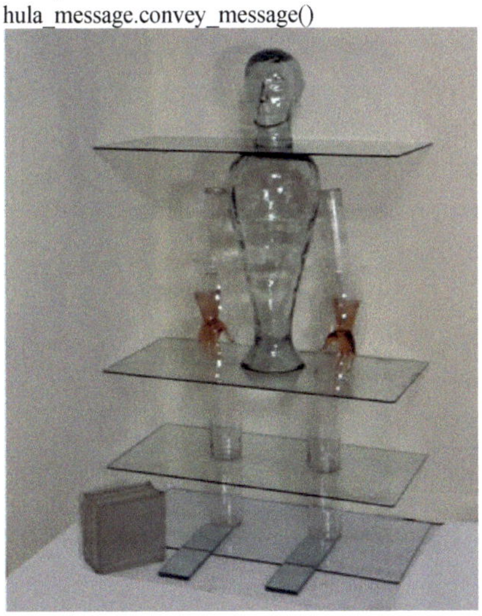

In their code, the class had attributes like hand_movements and hip_sways, which are symbolic representations of messages conveyed through the dance. They customized the hand_movements and hip_sways to represent specific hula dance movements that convey a particular message. When the convey_message method, was called, it printed out the details of the communicated message.

Last year, actors played a special form of drama using music, dance masks, and traditional costumes. They used a highly stylized way of expressing ideas and events.

Understanding them was only possible when somebody translated into speech what the actors said in the language of this theater. A translator ascribes a particular meaning to specific motions and facial expressions. This time, Joe modified the code for a similar kind of translation so it would inform more for the audience to fully engage and be interested.

TRANSPORT
(CLASS)
PACKAGE DELIVERY – MURO

Delivering was hard to handle. So many places, so many packages. Available delivery technology was impressive, but the street signs were to be obeyed.

```
import time
class DeliveryPerson:
    def __init__(self, name):
        self.name = name

    def deliver_package(self, city_map):
        print(f"{self.name} is starting the package delivery!")

        for intersection in city_map:
            self.obey_traffic_signals(intersection)
            print(f"{self.name} reached intersection {intersection}")
            time.sleep(2)  # Simulate time taken to travel between
intersections

        print(f"{self.name} successfully delivered all packages!")

    def obey_traffic_signals(self, intersection):
        if "red" in intersection:
            print(f"{self.name}: Waiting at a red traffic signal...")
            time.sleep(1)  # Simulate waiting at a red signal

if __name__ == "__main__":
    city_map = [
        "green", # Intersection 1
        "red",   # Intersection 2
        "green", # Intersection 3
        "green", # Intersection 4
        "red"    # Intersection 5
    ]

    delivery_person = DeliveryPerson("John Doe")
    delivery_person.deliver_package(city_map)
```

A class (DeliveryPerson) was used to encapsulate the behavior of a delivery person, which promoted code organization and reusability. Additionally, a loop was used to iterate through the intersections in the city map, and within that loop, the obey_traffic_signals method was called to simulate the delivery person obeying traffic signals at each intersection. This helped with the concept of control flow within a program, but many other warnings were on the way throughout the day.

The signs, sounds, and signals can occur at the same time.

TRANSPORTATION
(CLASSES AND OBJECTS IN OBJECT-ORIENTED PROGRAMMING (OOP)
THE MOVERS – DESADONE AND MISADO

Desadone and Misado owned a Randomization business. Until hiring them, nobody realized that they were moving households with 3D printing technology. The company advertised as a worldwide business. If one wanted to have a table, cabinet, chairs, or any part of their household furniture moved to another destination, the company would 3D scan it and send a wireframe to a new destination. They could move anything, including carpets and pillows, while matching the previously owned ones, their textures, and materials. The old furniture was then moved to an antique store for those willing to live the old-fashioned way. Despite using laser scanning technique, they had a code with types of furniture for various cultures:

```
class Furniture:
    def __init__(self, name, culture):
        self.name = name
        self.culture = culture

    def display_info(self):
        print(f"Name: {self.name}, Culture: {self.culture}")

# Creating instances of Furniture
furniture_list = [
    Furniture("Sofa", "Western"),
    Furniture("Tatami", "Japanese"),
    Furniture("Kang bed", "Chinese"),
    Furniture("Divan", "Middle Eastern"),
    Furniture("Chaise longue", "French"),
    Furniture("Moroccan Pouf", "Moroccan"),
]

# Displaying information about each piece of furniture
for furniture in furniture_list:
    furniture.display_info()
```

The code defined a Furniture class with attributes like name and culture and a method display_info to display information about each item. Instances of the Furniture class represented specific pieces of furniture with their respective cultural associations.

Many were willing to hire them on a universal level.

HULA DANCER – WAIAKA

When she danced, the family secrets were out. Each muscle of hers was encoded with a message and a story. Every pitch change triggered a reaction. Her movements sent an open message that each viewer could interpret differently. Waiaka developed her own system that could be called an encyclopedia of signs, or better yet, of body signs, which she knew better than anybody else.
She created a structure of the code for a basic sign encyclopedia using Python and dictionaries. She expanded upon this foundation to include more signs and details daily.

```
class SignEncyclopedia:
    def __init__(self):
        self.signs = {}

    def add_sign(self, name, description):
        self.signs[name] = description

    def get_sign_description(self, name):
        return self.signs.get(name, "Sign not found in the encyclopedia.")

# Example usage:
if __name__ == "__main__":
    sign_encyclopedia = SignEncyclopedia()

    # Adding signs to the encyclopedia
    sign_encyclopedia.add_sign("Stop Sign", "Indicates that drivers must stop before proceeding.")
    sign_encyclopedia.add_sign("Yield Sign", "Drivers must slow down or stop if necessary to yield the right-of-way.")

    # Retrieving sign descriptions
    print(sign_encyclopedia.get_sign_description("Stop Sign"))
    print(sign_encyclopedia.get_sign_description("Speed Limit Sign"))
```

Then, she enhanced it by adding more details to each sign, organizing signs into categories, or even creating a user interface for better interaction. She customized it according to her specific needs and the programming language/environment she was using.
She loved dancing in the rain, but it was not allowed because it would ruin the makeup she never wore.

TRAVEL
(SIMULATION OF A PROCESS)
KINGS – K AND Q

They had a summerhouse located eight hours from their castle. It was hidden deep in the forest, on the slope of a mountain. Their favorite way of spending weekends, holidays, and breaks was to go there. They thought driving was tiring and time-wasting, even though they'd park their car on a train and sleep while traveling. One day, instead of going there, they started pushing their luggage into a window on the painting of their summerhouse. It was created a long time ago by some forgotten uncle. Upon arrival, they noticed all the luggage stored inside their summerhouse right below the window. Shall we start getting back the same way by pushing ourselves through the painting's window when we want to return? Asked the King. I must study teleporting, answered the Queen. She used a 2-second delay using time.sleep(2), to soon be replaced with the actual teleportation mechanism.

```
import time

def teleport(current_location, destination):
    print(f"Teleporting from {current_location} to {destination}...")
    time.sleep(2)  # Simulating the teleportation process
    print("Teleportation successful!")

# Example usage:
current_location = "New York"
destination = "Paris"

teleport(current_location,  destination)
```

The Queen planned to use data structures, algorithms, and possibly even some form of user interface, depending on the level of interaction. They were always in agreement regarding travel, but they forgot to push a painting of their property created by a long-forgotten uncle into the window of their castle.

Their Motto was luck, longevity, love, happiness, and wealth.
And good food, too!

U

URBAN PLANNING
(RECURSION)
OUTER SPACE MUSICIANS – Δ, ç, ¥, ˙Δ, ∫, †, ∂, ƒ, ≈, ss, π, √, ≤, Ω, Åss, ¥, ∑

They were all equipped with qualities, assigning them a placement in a group. The space size on each Musician's sphere indicated their range, while the base suggested the volume of the sound. Each instrument was shaped after its tune. The rounder the instrument, the lower the tone and pitch. They lived in Fractal Cities and occupied level V in City 4. They planned their city using the draw_fractal_city function, which called itself with smaller city blocks, creating a fractal pattern as the recursion progresses. This represented a complex city layout by recursively drawing smaller and smaller blocks:

```
import turtle

def draw_fractal_city(x, y, size, depth):
  if depth == 0:
    return
  else:
    # Draw a square representing a city block
    turtle.penup()
    turtle.goto(x, y)
    turtle.pendown()
    turtle.forward(size)
    turtle.right(90)
    turtle.forward(size)
    turtle.right(90)
    turtle.forward(size)
    turtle.right(90)
    turtle.forward(size)
    turtle.right(90)

    # Recursively draw smaller city blocks
    new_size = size / 2
    draw_fractal_city(x - new_size, y + new_size, new_size, depth - 1)
    draw_fractal_city(x + new_size, y + new_size, new_size, depth - 1)
    draw_fractal_city(x - new_size, y - new_size, new_size, depth - 1)
    draw_fractal_city(x + new_size, y - new_size, new_size, depth - 1)

if __name__ == "__main__":
  turtle.speed(2) # Adjust the drawing speed
  draw_fractal_city(0, 0, 200, 3)
  turtle.done()
```

They saved energy and improved security. Each fractal city had a unique function assigned to each floor. One family could live on the first floor with their summerhouse on the 11th floor. There was a floor for housing needs, followed by another for work, shopping experiences, gym, and games, and the next had districts for various services: plumbers, electricians, bakers, or party caterers. Recycling the wastewater and using it to water the vegetables and plants on the roof, collecting compost, and recycling it in those gardens was their pride. There was no need for grass as it took space and energy. Vegetables were useful and beautiful. Apartments located on the edge allowed for watching life on another city's floors or shelves. Each shelf scraper had a special function. The addresses were quite precise. They indicated a city, a shelf, and a row. The number of shelf scrapers was followed by the number of shelf scrapers in that row, then the floor, and the apartment, as A 2-3-6-7-8-10 counted bottom up. Close to the ocean was A, the shelf was located at the bottom (2), and the row was not far from the edge, giving a better way to the breeze than the shelf scraper that was more inside the shelf and on a higher floor. Everyone had everything, a personal robot or two if they chose to. There was no single report of robbery except of ideas.

V	VALUES (FUNCTIONS) ECONOMIST – FIG

Fig understood time as a form of payment or compensation. For example, a pile of books took lots of time to write and lots of time to read. A large canvas painting took longer to paint than a small one. He was only giving time-consuming presents. To him, a gift that took much time to produce was a good present When he wanted to be nice to someone, he'd hire a student to perform time-saving tasks for that person. But others saw it as the work function that took in two parameters (hours_worked and hourly_rate) and calculated the total payment based on these inputs. The main function got user input, called the work function, and then displayed the result.

```
import time

def work(hours_worked, hourly_rate):
    """Calculate payment based on hours worked and hourly rate."""
    total_payment = hours_worked * hourly_rate
    return total_payment

def main():
    # Get user input for hours worked and hourly rate
    hours_worked = float(input("Enter hours worked: "))
    hourly_rate = float(input("Enter hourly rate: "))

    # Calculate payment using the work function
    total_payment = work(hours_worked, hourly_rate)

    # Display the result
    print(f"Total payment: ${total_payment}")

if __name__ == "__main__":
    main()
```

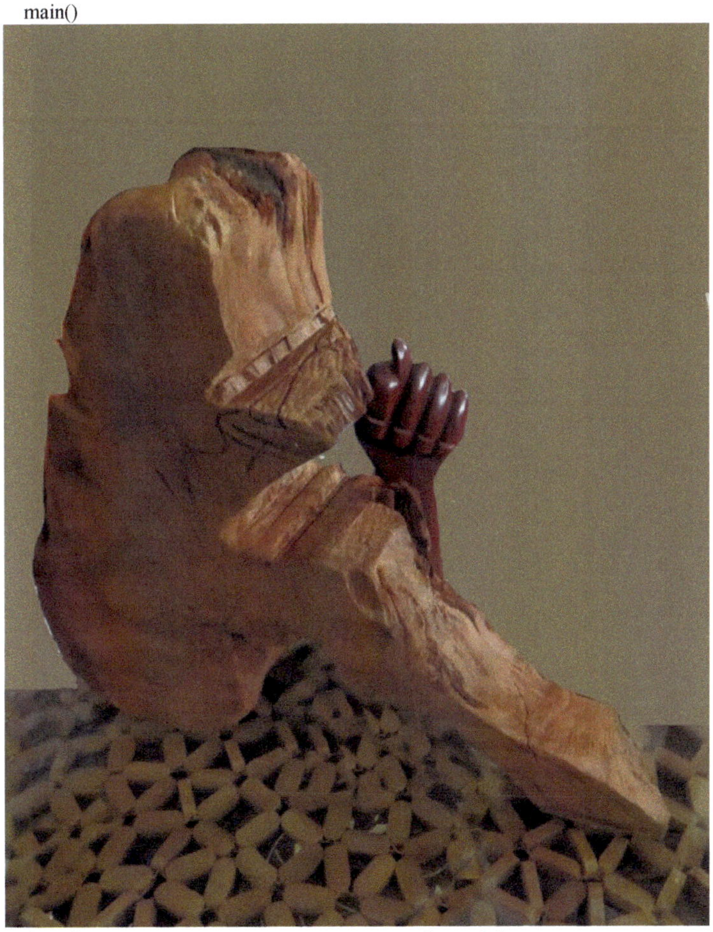

His plans now are to present people with some energy-related gifts.

VISUAL MUSIC INTERPRETATION (RANDOMIZATION) TRUMPET – CHRIS

Chris played trumpet in the evenings, but his mornings served for painting pictures. He loved to paint outdoors but also rented a studio to create large paintings on a big easel by combining various techniques. Of all fine art media, he liked oil painting the most. He put a lot of paint on the canvas. He spent most of his salary on all sorts of painting materials. After each painting session, Chris looked “artistic.” His colleagues were well accustomed to the stains of paint on his pants and colorful rims around his nails, but these marks became an issue when Duncan, the media man, started to work on the advertisements and inserting photographs of the musicians on the orchestra website. A dispute arose between Chris and Debbie, a music collector and is also a photographer. Her task was to take photographs of the orchestra members. Chris was making a fuss over his appearance, asking Debbie not to zoom at his hands, but Debbie said, “I can’t miss a chance to show such a character; don’t go away.” In the end, a still portrait of Chris looked correct, but a music video clip displayed everything she wanted to show.

When Chris' solo show at the City Center Art Gallery, Muse, was about to open, in his artist's statement, Chris informed the viewers that his artwork was inspired by music. He asked his friends from the orchestra, violinist Amadeus, violist Eliza, flutist Peter, bassoonist Lawrence, and bass player Ronald, to improvise music while watching his creations at the opening reception at the gallery.

```
import random
import time

def generate_music(painting):
   # Define a mapping between colors and musical notes
   color_notes = {
      "red": "C",
      "blue": "D",
      "green": "E",
      "yellow": "F",
      "orange": "G",
      "purple": "A",
      "pink": "B"
   }

   # Generate musical notes based on the colors in the painting
   notes = [color_notes[color] for color in painting]

   # Play the generated music
   play_music(notes)

def play_music(notes):
   # Simulate playing the musical notes
   for note in notes:
      print(f"Playing note: {note}")
      time.sleep(0.5)  # Add a short delay for better visualization

# Example painting colors
painting_colors = ["red", "blue", "green", "yellow", "orange",
"purple", "pink"]

# Generate music based on the painting
generate_music(painting_colors)
```

A dictionary (color_notes) helped them map colors from the painting to corresponding musical notes. The generate_music function used this mapping to create a list of musical notes based on the colors in the painting. Finally, the play_music function simulated playing the generated music. Further customization and expansion were based on various preferences and the complexity of the visual music interpretations. Nevertheless, the musicians’ performance and reception were very successful. Even three tough music critics, Monique, Miranda, and Michelle, stated their favorable opinions in "The Solar Rise," a leading local newspaper.

Those were not improvisations, but nobody noticed, except M.

VOCABULARY
(LIST COMPREHENSION)
SITTING WOMAN PRODUCTION SECRETARY – ELDA

Aside from her time-consuming job, she decided to collect words beginning only with the letters x or y, but she could not decide which one to focus on.

```
def collect_x_words(word_list):
    x_words = [word for word in word_list if word.lower().startswith('x')]
    return x_words

# Example word list
word_list = ['Apple', 'Xylophone', 'Banana', 'X-ray', 'Orange', 'Box']

# Collect words that start with 'X'
x_words = collect_x_words(word_list)

# Print the collected words
print("Words that start with 'X':", x_words)
```

The expression [word for word in word_list if word.lower().startswith('x')] created a new list (x_words) by iterating through the word_list and including only the words that start with the letter 'X'. The if word.lower().startswith('x') condition ensured that the comparison was case-insensitive.

Soon, she had her list: Xylophone, Xenon, X-ray, Xerox, Xanadu, Xenophobia, Xenolithic, Xylitol, Xerophyte, Xylene, Xylo logy, Xenoglossy, Xenoglossia.
The last one was not on her list of skills she possessed.

W WEB DESIGN (HTML, CSS, AND JAVASCRIPT - DYNAMIC AND INTERACTIVE USER INTERFACE) STAGE DESIGNERS —JONS

Jon, one of the stage designers, used to draw in his sketchbook all the time when he attended committee meetings. He has also been writing something. Everybody was impressed with his attention and commitment. After some time, it came into view that his serious consideration was focused on drawing caricatures of the speakers. He also wrote stories about each orchestra member. To defend himself and avoid hurting anybody's feelings, he explained that he would provide this material to Duncan, the orchestra's designer, to make the website more vivid and attractive.

```
<!DOCTYPE html>
<html lang="en">
<head>
  <meta charset="UTF-8">
  <meta name="viewport" content="width=device-width, initial-
scale=1.0">
  <title>Orchestra Sketches and Stories</title>
  <link rel="stylesheet" href="styles.css">
</head>
<body>

  <header>
    <h1>Orchestra Members</h1>
  </header>

  <div id="members-container">
    <!-- Member sketches and stories will be dynamically added
here -->
  </div>

  <script src="scripts.js"></script>
</body>
</html>
```

They started with HTML, for the basic structure of the webpage. The members-container div is a placeholder for sketches and stories to be added. They created a simple CSS file (styles.css) for styling:

```
body {
   font-family: Arial, sans-serif;
  margin: 0;
  padding: 0;
}

header {
  background-color: #333;
  color: #fff;
  text-align: center;
  padding: 10px;
}

#members-container {
  display: flex;
  flex-wrap: wrap;
   justify-content: space-around;
  padding: 20px;
}
```

```
member-card {
  width: 300px;
  margin: 10px;
  padding: 15px;
  border: 1px solid #ddd;
  border-radius: 5px;
}

.member-image {
  max-width: 100%;
  height: auto;
  border-radius: 3px;
}

.member-story {
  margin-top: 10px;
}
```

This CSS file provided some basic styling for the webpage, including a responsive layout for the member cards. Now, they created a JavaScript file (scripts.js) to dynamically fetch and display member information. This JavaScript file used the DOMContentLoaded event to ensure the DOM was fully loaded before executing the script. It then dynamically created member cards based on the sample data Then, they replaced the sample data and image filenames with the orchestra members' data. Their code structure followed the common approach of separating HTML for structure, CSS for styling, and JavaScript for dynamic behavior.

The results made everybody happy. Some wanted more (of course), so Jons decided to experiment with AI-based solutions.

WRITING DIGITAL HUMANOID WAY
(OPTICAL CHARACTER RECOGNITION (OCR)
BOOK COLLECTOR - JULIAN OR BOOK SIGNING – LIB

Julian is an avid collector of music-related books and owns an arsenal of several thousand volumes. He loves to talk about the books he enjoys the most for their beauty, content, and value. Julian writes verses about music and the composers. He creates a memory book from his poems to make a lasting account of some noteworthy events. Signing books was required by the publisher to promote his books.
He preferred spending his time writing, but travel and talking with people were nice inspirations. The characters' names in his books came from those he placed above his signature. Since everything is in digital format now, he wanted to write a computer code that digitizes a collection of books, book by book, including title, author, publication date, and genre. What a task! Converting printed books to digital format involves a combination of scanning, optical character recognition (OCR), and organization of the digital content. He wrote a code in Python using the Tesseract OCR library:

```
from PIL import Image
import pytesseract
import os

def digitize_book(book_image_path, output_folder):
    # Ensure output folder exists
    if not os.path.exists(output_folder):
        os.makedirs(output_folder)

    # Load the book image
    book_image = Image.open(book_image_path)

    # Use Tesseract to perform OCR
    text_content = pytesseract.image_to_string(book_image)

    # Save the digital content to a text file
    output_file_path = os.path.join(output_folder,
"digitized_text.txt")
    with open(output_file_path, "w", encoding="utf-8") as
output_file:
        output_file.write(text_content)

    print(f"Digitization complete. Text saved to
{output_file_path}")

# Example usage
book_image_path = "path/to/printed_book.jpg"
output_folder = "path/to/digital_collection"

digitize_book(book_image_path, output_folder)
```

After digitizing the content of his collection, the role of the books has changed. Nobody knew why he digitized them instead of accessing eBook collections, but they were his books, he thought. From a practical point of view, his cherished printed collection could now be replaced with wooden blocks with nice covers and a layer of dust on the top of a bookshelf.

WRITING FOR PERFORMANCE (CALL THE FUNCTION) DIRECTOR – GERLOST

He was an administrator by vocation. He even felt he was born to be a boss. Some control processes and others control people. His job vision was to be a creator, with people as his building blocks. Like paint would serve a painter to create a picture; he'd use the whole company structure with all the exciting people. They'd have to obey him, though, so the machine would run smoothly. Once, a boy with a guitar stopped him on the street. The administrator agreed to listen to a poem he wrote. It was a fast, rhythmically spoken text stating that all young people should enjoy work as a form of artistic creation without being influenced by their families, and they should fight the authorities. The guitar was hanging at his hip; it was his "B" poem. He was a student hitchhiking and making a living by reciting his poem. "I was once where you are now," Gerlost said. "Unless your art is really about fighting, you either create art or fight the authorities. And, if you choose to fight them, you become one of them." The boy wrote a Python code for a B poem-based song about fighting the authorities:

```
def fight_authorities():
    # Create a list of verses for the song
    verses = [
        "Beneath the city lights, where shadows grow,",
        "Bold hearts rise in the underground's glow.",
        "",
        "Breaking the chains, with words like a sword,",
        "Battling the silence, our anthem is roared.",
        "",
        "Bravery blooms where the rebel seeds sow,",
        "Building a revolution, watch the defiance grow.",
        "",
        "Behind the scenes, in the heart's darkest recess,",
        "Burning with passion, we resist and confess.",
        "",
        "Bridges we build, with unity's might,",
        "Beneath the moon's gaze, we'll reclaim the night.",
    ]

    # Print each verse of the song
    for verse in verses:
        print(verse)

# Call the function to generate the song
fight_authorities()
```

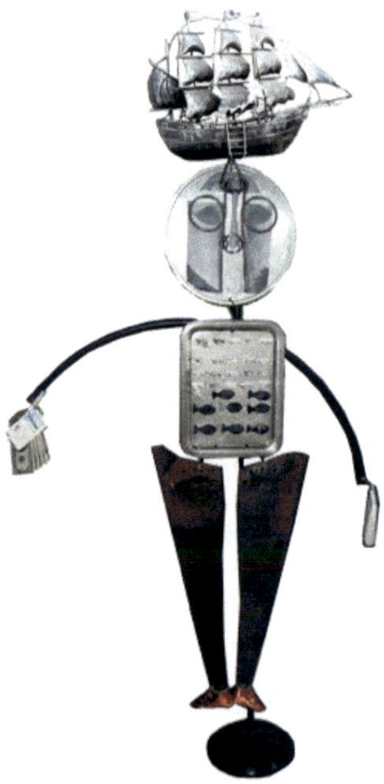

Then, he tweaked and modified his codes to match the style of each city with his youth poetic rebellion!

WRITING INSPIRATIONS (RANDOMIZATION) THE CITY GAME – EKOEL

Each day, before and after work, and including weekends, Ekoel carefully examined his view out of his window. He could see actions in the windows facing his building. The patterns were different in the morning, in the evening, and during the weekends. He carefully drafted all his findings to enter them and transfer them into his novel. Each sketch served as a trigger for his imagination. When someone new moved in, a new chapter evolved. He wrote a code where watching changes generated stories for novels:

```
import random

def generate_story_prompt():
    # Lists of potential elements for the story prompt
    view_elements = ["tree", "bird", "rain", "cityscape", "sunset", "clouds", "street", "mountain"]
    action_elements = ["whispered", "danced", "vanished", "appeared", "shimmered", "echoed", "fluttered"]

    # Generate a random story prompt
    view = random.choice(view_elements)
    action = random.choice(action_elements)

    story_prompt = f"Outside the window, the {view} {action}."

    return story_prompt

# Generate and print a story prompt
story_prompt = generate_story_prompt()
print("Story Prompt:")
print(story_prompt)
```

This script randomly selected elements from predefined lists for his view and action and combined them into a story prompt. He customized the lists or added more complexity to his stories, providing him with novel inspiration. He called it his pandemic writing.

WRITING WITH AI (SPELLCHECKING)
HANDYMAN – ZINOS

He was very busy. One could tell how busy he was by looking at the length of his letters. He had no time to shorten them. Since people complained, he wrote a simple algorithm in Python that shortens a letter by removing redundant words, compressing the text, and simplifying concepts. He planned to enhance it based on specific requirements or language nuances but had no time for that.

```
def shorten_letter(letter):
    # List of common redundant words
    redundant_words = ["that", "is", "are", "was", "were", "am", "I", "you", "he", "she", "it", "we", "they"]

    # Remove redundant words
    words = letter.split()
    filtered_words = [word for word in words if word.lower() not in redundant_words]
    letter_without_redundancy = ' '.join(filtered_words)

    # Compress the text by removing consecutive duplicate words
    compressed_text = ' '.join(word for i, word in enumerate(filtered_words) if i == 0 or word != filtered_words[i-1])

    # Simplify concepts (replace synonyms with simpler words)
    simplified_text = compressed_text.replace("utilize", "use").replace("facilitate", "help").replace("obtain", "get")

    return simplified_text

# Example usage
original_letter = """
Dear John,

I hope this letter finds you well and you are enjoying the weather we are experiencing together now. I am writing to inform you that the project that we are currently working on and is very important to all of us is progressing and moving forward very nicely, making everyone happy. Some certain aspects need your attention and consideration. It is essential that we utilize all available resources to facilitate the completion of this project in  a timely, proficient, and least expensive manner with attention to detail and resulting satisfaction and enjoyment of our mighty and fun-loving  clients.

To obtain success,  work collaboratively and efficiently. With your expertise and dedication, we can overcome any challenges that may  arise.
Please feel free to reach out.
Best  regards,
[Your Name]
"""

shortened_letter = shorten_letter(original_letter)
print(shortened_letter) = """

For success,  work collaboratively and efficiently. With your help, we can overcome challenges.
Please reach out.
```

His method removed redundant words, compressed consecutive duplicate words, and simplified certain concepts. He knew that he could customize the list of disposable words and the simplifications based on his specific addressees.

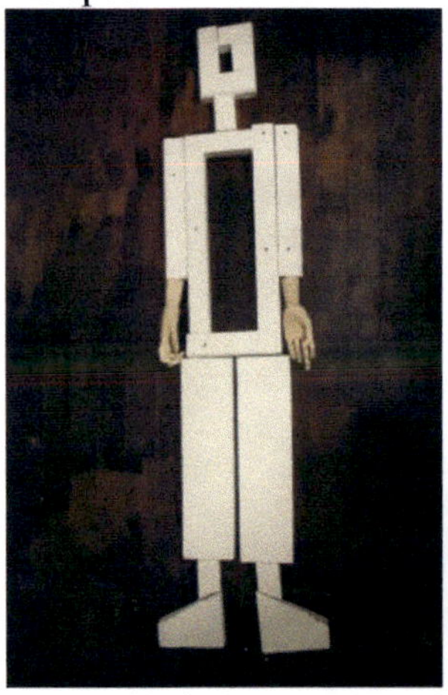

Now, all his letters started with a sentence, " Please excuse the brevity."

X	XYLOLOGY – STUDY OF WOOD (CLASS) XYLOPHONE – EN

He lived in a city where energy was collected from falling leaves to generate power for cars. Everyone planted trees, especially those that allowed light to pass through. People collected their leaves to sell them and ferment them to serve as a source of power.

```
class LeafFermentation:
    def __init__(self, leaf_type, fermentation_duration):
        self.leaf_type = leaf_type
        self.fermentation_duration = fermentation_duration
        self.energy_generated = 0

    def ferment_leaves(self):
        print(f"Fermenting {self.leaf_type} leaves for
{self.fermentation_duration} days...")
        # Simulate fermentation process (you can replace this with
actual fermentation logic)
        self.energy_generated = self.fermentation_duration * 10 #
Arbitrary energy generation factor
        print(f"{self.leaf_type} leaves successfully fermented!")

    def power_car(self):
        if self.energy_generated > 0:
            print(f"Powering the car with energy from {self.leaf_type}
leaves.")
            print(f"Car is now running on {self.energy_generated} units
of power.")
        else:
            print("No energy generated. Please ferment leaves first.")

# Example usage
fern = LeafFermentation(leaf_type='Fern', fermentation_duration=7)
fern.ferment_leaves()
fern.power_car()
```

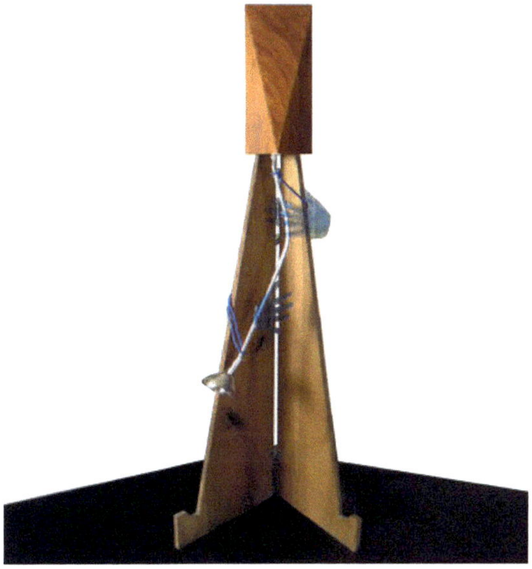

The city was very clean. Visitors started planting more trees in their places, followed by even more trees. Soon, many cities changed their names to “Forrest City.”

Y	YET, ANOTHER SUPPORT (RETURN FUNCTION) BOT ASSISTANT – JACQUES

His job was simple: to assist, but the reality was to assist with everything whenever anyone needed it. The group was rather big; they asked him for his help with practically everything, be it a letter, taking an instrument for repair, or notifying the spouse about one's tardiness. This part was the hardest one as he had to come up with excuses, followed by interrogation and Q&A sessions. Jacques came up with a standard answer: please talk to the boss. Soon, he understood that he needed to become a storyteller and work overtime. His solution came with a code offering suggestions:

```
def explain_overtime_reasons(employee_name, projects, deadlines):
    # Check if the employee is a hard worker
    if is_hard_worker(employee_name):
        return f"{employee_name} is known for being a hard worker and is committed to delivering high-quality results."

    # Check if there are ongoing projects
    if projects > 0:
        return f"{employee_name} is actively involved in {projects} ongoing projects."

    # Check if there are upcoming deadlines
    if deadlines > 0:
        return f"{employee_name} is working diligently to meet {deadlines} upcoming deadlines."

    # If none of the above apply, give a generic explanation
    return f"{employee_name} is putting in extra effort to contribute to the team's success."

def is_hard_worker(employee_name):
    # Placeholder logic to determine if someone is a hard worker
    # This could be based on performance reviews or other criteria
    return True

# Example usage
employee_name = "Bob"
ongoing_projects = 2
upcoming_deadlines = 3
explanation = explain_overtime_reasons(employee_name, ongoing_projects, upcoming_deadlines)
print(explanation)
```

Jacque's imagination got proper support, so he felt just and needed.

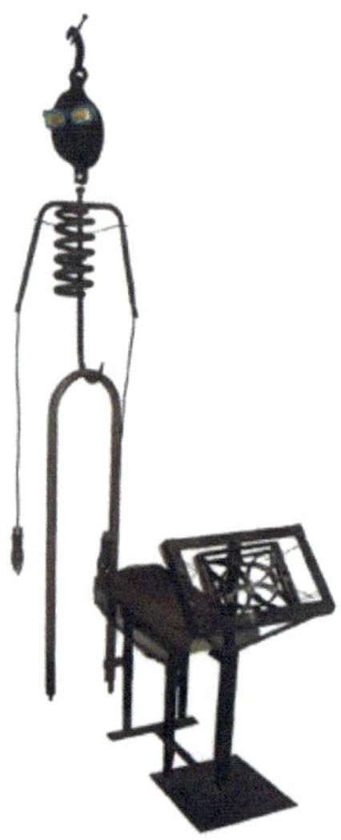

Z	ZENOGRAPHY – A STUDY OF THE PLANET JUPITER (OOP) JUPITER RESEARCHER – PI

His mission was to encounter all the planets in his Galaxy.
He did not have an exact count for all planets in the Milky Way, as nobody did. However, his code could be modified with the actual data or logic needed. He started with his list of planets:
class Galaxy:

```
  def __init__(self):
    self.planets = ["Mercury", "Venus", "Earth", "Mars", "Jupiter", "Saturn", "Uranus", "Neptune", "Pluto"]

   def count_planets(self):
     return len(self.planets)

if __name__ == "__main__":
  milky_way = Galaxy()
  total_planets = milky_way.count_planets()

  print(f"There are {total_planets} planets in the Milky Way.")
```

His code defined a Galaxy class with an __init__ method to initialize the list of planets and a count_planets method to get the count of planets.

He keeps counting.

ZOOGEOLOGY, ARCHEOLOGY, PALEOLOGY, ARACHNOLOGY (INTERSECTION) ENTOMOLOGISTS

They all wanted to be anthropologists. One of them found some jars and an ancient chemistry lab, so he became an archeologist. The second one found a dinosaur bone, so he became a paleozoologist. One found a spider and thus wanted to be an arachnologist. To collaborate, they wrote a common skills code:

```
def find_common_skills(archaeologist_skills, paleozoologist_skills, arachnologist_skills):
    # Convert skills to sets for easy intersection
    archaeologist_set = set(archaeologist_skills)
    paleozoologist_set = set(paleozoologist_skills):   arachnologist_set = set(arachnologist_skills)

    # Find common skills
    common_skills  =  archaeologist_set.intersection(paleozoologist_set,  arachnologist_set)
```

They traveled together, sharing their scientific tasks and duties equally.

CHAPTER 3
NUMBERS AND DIMENSIONS

NUMBERS	MATHEMATICS (MEASUREMENT SYSTEMS) A CLASS AND THE TEACHER

A teacher addressed numbers and numerical systems, saying, "Numbers are mathematical systems for quantifying and measuring things. They represent quantities, values, or positions in a sequence. There are many types of numbers for different purposes in mathematics. Some types of numbers are:"

Natural Numbers (N) are the set of positive integers starting from 1 and continuing indefinitely (1, 2, 3, 4, ...).
Whole Numbers (W) are similar to natural numbers but include 0 (0, 1, 2, 3, 4, ...).
Integers (Z) represent a set of all positive and negative whole numbers, including zero (..., -3, -2, -1, 0, 1, 2, 3, ...).
Rational Numbers (Q) can be fractions of two integers, where the denominator is not zero, including integers and fractions (e.g., 1/2, -3, 4/5).
Irrational Numbers cannot be expressed as fractions, and their decimal representations are non-terminating and non-repeating. Examples include the square root of 2 ($\sqrt{2}$) or π (pi).
Real Numbers (R) are the set of all rational and irrational numbers.
Complex Numbers (C) are in the form a + bi, where "a" and "b" are real numbers, and "i" is the imaginary unit ($i^2 = -1$).
Imaginary Numbers are in the form bi, where "b" is a real number, and "i" is the imaginary unit.

Numbers play a fundamental role in various branches of mathematics and have wide-ranging applications in science, engineering, economics, and everyday life. They are used for counting, measuring, calculating, and describing quantities and relationships. Numbers can be represented in various ways depending on the context and the system being used. Here are some common methods:

Decimal System (Base-10):
This is the most familiar system, using 10 digits from 0 to 9.
Each digit's place value is a power of 10. For example, in the number 1234, the digit 4 is in the "ones" place, 3 is in the "tens" place, 2 is in the "hundreds" place, and 1 is in the "thousands" place.
Binary System (Base-2):
Used internally by almost all modern computers and computer-based devices because of its straightforward implementation in digital circuitry.
Uses only two digits, 0 and 1.
Each digit's place value is a power of 2.
Octal System (Base-8):
Uses eight digits: 0 through 7.
Each digit's place value is a power of 8.
Hexadecimal System (Base-16):
It uses 16 digits: 0 through 9 and A through F (where A represents 10, B represents 11, and so on).
It is often used in computing as a more human-friendly representation of binary-coded values.
Each digit's place value is a power of 16.
Roman Numerals:
An ancient numeral system that originated in ancient Rome.

```
    return common_skills

if __name__ == "__main__":
```

```
# Define skills for each profession
archaeologist_skills = ['excavation', 'artifact_analysis', 'field_survey', 'historical_research']
paleozoologist_skills = ['fossil_analysis', 'taxonomy', 'paleoecology', 'fieldwork']
arachnologist_skills = ['spider_taxonomy', 'behavioral_observation', 'ecology', 'research']

# Find and print common skills
common_skills = find_common_skills(archaeologist_skills, paleozoologist_skills, arachnologist_skills)

 if common_skills:
   print("Common Skills:", common_skills)
else:
   print("No common skills found.")
```

Each profession's skills were represented as lists, and the find_common_skills function took these lists, converted them to sets, and found the intersection (common skills) using the intersection method. Finally, it printed the common skills or a message if there are none. As they encountered more professionals, they customized the skills lists with more specific skills relevant to each profession. It uses combinations of letters from the Latin alphabet, such as I, V, X, L, C, D, and M, to represent numbers. The value of each numeral depends on its position and the specific rules for combining them.

Scientific Notation:
Represents numbers as a product of a coefficient and a power of 10.
Useful for expressing very large or very small numbers.
For example, 3.0 × 10^8 represents 300,000,000 in scientific notation.
These are just a few examples of number representations, and many other numeral systems and notations are used in various fields and cultures. The choice of representation often depends on the specific requirements of a particular application or context.

The discussion went on including a space and how people address it. Each group introduced different dimensions, followed by some conclusions on how the findings can benefit people in various fields.

"Adults love numbers," said Little Prince.

# DIMENSIONS ZERO OR ONE?	DIMENSIONS IN SPACE (INTERACT WITH AND DESCRIBE) GROUP ONE

Kenneth, one of the students thought that a point has no dimension. He imagined it as a single spot on a plane. Another one, Stan had a different opinion. It takes an x and a y position to define it. Point A would be A (1.0, 1.0) on a graph. In a flat space, a point is considered to have zero dimensions, as it doesn't have any extent in terms of length, width, or height. Stan argued that a point in flat space is one-dimensional based on a specific perspective when using a coordinate system from a coordinate perspective.

```
class Point:
  def __init__(self, x, y):
    self.x = x
    self.y = y

  def dimension(self):
    # In a flat space, argue that a point can be considered one-dimensional based on its coordinates.
    return 1

# Example usage:
point_in_flat_space = Point(3, 4)
dimension_of_point = point_in_flat_space.dimension()

print(f"The point is {dimension_of_point}-dimensional in a flat space.")
```

His code defined a Point class with x and y coordinates. The dimension method stated that the point was one-dimensional in a flat space. However, Kenneth stated that a point in a flat space has no dimension. His argument was based on a specific interpretation.

```
class Point:
  def __init__(self, x, y):
    self.x = x
    self.y = y
    # Basic method: Get the coordinates of the point.
    return self.x, self.y

  def move(self, dx, dy):
    # Basic method: Move the point by specified increments.
    self.x += dx
    self.y += dy

# Example usage:
point_in_flat_space = Point(3, 4)

print(f"Coordinates of the point: {point_in_flat_space.get_coordinates()}")
print(f"The point is {point_in_flat_space.dimension()}-dimensional in a flat space.")

# Move the point and print the new coordinates
point_in_flat_space.move(2, -1)
print(f"New coordinates after moving: {point_in_flat_space.get_coordinates()}")
```

the Point class has an __init__ method to initialize the point with x and y coordinates.

The get coordinates method he returned the x and y coordinates of the point. The move method allowed moving the point by specified increments in the x and y directions. He emphasized the idea that a point doesn't have any extent in terms of length, width, or height. Zero-dimensional graphics typically refer to point-based graphics representing a single point in space. While zero-dimensional graphics might seem limited, they still find applications in various practical scenarios.

Both agreed that their reasoning may not be universally accepted.

TWO	MATHEMATICS (PARAMETRIC EQUATIONS AND 3D PLOTTING) GROUP TWO

A line in space is typically represented as a parametric equation with two parameters, which implies that it has two dimensions. A Python code snippet describes this concept:

```
import matplotlib.pyplot as plt
import numpy as np

def line_in_space(t):
    # Parametric equations for a line in space
    x = 2 * t  # Example equation for x-coordinate
    y = 3 * t  # Example equation for y-coordinate
    z = -1 * t  # Example equation for z-coordinate

    return x, y, z

# Generate points on the line for values of t
t_values = np.linspace(-10, 10, 100)
line_points = np.array([line_in_space(t) for t in t_values])

# Plot the line in 3D space
fig = plt.figure()
ax = fig.add_subplot(111, projection='3d')
ax.plot3D(line_points[:, 0], line_points[:, 1], line_points[:, 2], label='Line in Space')

ax.set_xlabel('X-axis')
ax.set_ylabel('Y-axis')
ax.set_zlabel('Z-axis')

plt.title('Representation of a Line in 3D Space')
plt.legend()
plt.show()
```

With x, y, and z coordinates, the line_in_space function took a parameter t and calculated the coordinates of points on the line based on these equations. The code then generated points along the line for a range of t values and plotted the line in a 3D space using Matplotlib.

The line_in_space function encapsulated the logic for calculating coordinates on the line. The parametric equations $x = 2t$, $y = 3t$, and $z = -t$ represented the line in space. Arrays and NumPy: NumPy was used to efficiently handle arrays for storing line points. Matplotlib was used for 3D plotting to visualize the line in space. This code illustrated how a line in space can be represented and visualized using parametric equations and 3D plotting.

That is three-dimensional!

TWO AGAIN	COMPUTER GRAPHICS PROGRAMMING (THE PARAMETRIC EQUATIONS) GROUP THREE

This group created a line in a digital way and then in an analog way by coding in Python.
First, the Digital Way (Using Turtle Graphics):

```
import turtle

# Create a turtle screen and set its background color
screen = turtle.Screen()
screen.bgcolor("white")

# Create a turtle object
digital_turtle = turtle.Turtle()

# Move the turtle to the starting position
digital_turtle.penup()
digital_turtle.goto(-100, 0)
digital_turtle.pendown()

# Draw a line
digital_turtle.forward(200)

# Close the turtle graphics window on click
screen.exitonclick()
```

The Turtle graphics library provided a way to introduce programming. The turtle started at a specified position, moved to the location provided, and drew a line. The code used a digital representation of the drawing with precise instructions given.

Analog Way (Using Matplotlib):

```
import matplotlib.pyplot as plt

# Define the coordinates of the line
x = [-100, 100]
y = [0, 0]

# Plot the line
plt.plot(x, y)

# Set axis labels
plt.xlabel('X-axis')
plt.ylabel('Y-axis')

# Set the title of the plot
plt.title('Analog Line Drawing')

# Display the plot
plt.show()
```

A data visualization library, Matplotlib, was used to create a line plot. The plot function drew the line to define its coordinates. The code related to the field of mathematics and data visualization, a graphical representation of the line, is analog as it's a continuous plot rather than a step-by-step digital drawing.

THREE	3D PRINTING (3D PLOTTING FUNCTIONS) GROUP THREE

One of the students could play two instruments as needed. He could move from one to another without even thinking. After sending his codes to a prototyping machine kept at a distant location, it would 3D print the object according to the code. Switching from two to three dimensions in coding often involves using libraries with 3D graphics capabilities. One of Python's libraries for 3D graphics is matplotlib with its mplot3d toolkit. Before running the code, he made sure he had matplotlib installed:

```
pip install matplotlib
import matplotlib.pyplot as plt
from mpl_toolkits.mplot3d import Axes3D
import numpy as np

def plot_2d(data):
    plt.plot(data[0], data[1], marker='o')
    plt.title('2D Plot')
    plt.xlabel('X-axis')
    plt.ylabel('Y-axis')
    plt.show()

def plot_3d(data):
    fig = plt.figure()
    ax = fig.add_subplot(111, projection='3d')
    ax.scatter(data[0], data[1], data[2], marker='o')
    ax.set_title('3D Plot')
    ax.set_xlabel('X-axis')
    ax.set_ylabel('Y-axis')
    ax.set_zlabel('Z-axis')
    plt.show()

# Example usage:
data_2d = np.array([[1, 2, 3, 4, 5], [2, 4, 6, 8, 10]])
data_3d = np.vstack((data_2d, np.zeros_like(data_2d[0]))) # Adding
a third dimension with zeros

plot_2d(data_2d)
plot_3d(data_3d)
```

The plot_2d function plotted data in two dimensions using matplotlib, and the plot_3d function extended this to three dimensions using the mplot3d toolkit. Understanding how to use these functions and representing data in three dimensions was crucial for tasks involving 3D graphics, scientific visualization, and simulations. These libraries facilitated the ability to transition from 2D to 3D, making it an essential skill for coding applications with spatial data representation.

He intended to send his new instrument for printing as a gift, but he never mentioned the recipient's name.

FOUR	COMPUTER SCIENCE (ARRAYS AND NUMPY) GROUP FOUR

"What are the four dimensions, then?" asked the girl sitting in a corner. Representing a four-dimensional space in a visual manner is challenging since we live in a three-dimensional world, but using mathematical concepts helps us understand and manipulate four-dimensional spaces. One common way to represent a point in 4D space is using a tuple (x, y, z, w). A Python code snippet used Matplotlib to show a representation of points in a 4D space:

```
import matplotlib.pyplot as plt
from mpl_toolkits.mplot3d import Axes3D
import numpy as np

def point_in_4d_space(t):
    # Parametric equations for a point in 4D space
    x = 2 * t
    y = 3 * t
    z = -1 * t
    w = 0.5 * t

    return x, y, z, w

# Generate points in 4D space for values of t
t_values = np.linspace(-10, 10, 100)
points_4d = np.array([point_in_4d_space(t) for t in t_values])

# Plot the points in 3D space (ignoring the fourth dimension)
fig = plt.figure()
ax = fig.add_subplot(111, projection='3d')
ax.scatter(points_4d[:, 0], points_4d[:, 1], points_4d[:, 2], label='Points in 4D Space')

ax.set_xlabel('X-axis')
ax.set_ylabel('Y-axis')
ax.set_zlabel('Z-axis')

plt.title('Representation of Points in 4D Space (Projecting to 3D)')
plt.legend()
plt.show()
```

Each point in 4D space was represented by a tuple (x, y, z, w). The point_in_4d_space function took a parameter t and calculated the coordinates of points in 4D space based on these equations. It generated points in 4D space for a range of t values and projected them onto a 3D space for visualization using Matplotlib. The point_in_4d_space function encapsulates the logic for calculating coordinates in 4D.

```
    def dimension(self):
        # Argument: In a flat space, a point has no dimensions.
        return 0

    def get_coordinates(self):
```

Similar to the previous work, parametric equations represented points in 4D space. NumPy was used to efficiently handle arrays for storing 4D points. Matplotlib was used for 3D scatter plotting to visualize points in 4D space (projected onto 3D). Visualizing true four-dimensional space was projected onto a three-dimensional space for visualization.

FIVE	LINEAR ALGEBRA (ARRAYS AND NUMPY) GROUP FIVE

So, now, a fifth-dimensional space! Representing a fifth-dimensional space visually is even more challenging as it goes beyond our three-dimensional perception. However, mathematically, a point in 5D space can be extended mathematically using a tuple (x, y, z, w, v) with Python code using NumPy to generate and visualize points in 5D space:

```
import matplotlib.pyplot as plt
from mpl_toolkits.mplot3d import Axes3D
import numpy as np

def point_in_5d_space(t):
    # Parametric equations for a point in 5D space
    x = 2 * t
    y = 3 * t
    z = -1 * t
    w = 0.5 * t
    v = -0.2 * t

    return x, y, z, w, v

# Generate points in 5D space for values of t
t_values = np.linspace(-10, 10, 100)
points_5d = np.array([point_in_5d_space(t) for t in t_values])

# Visualize points in a 3D space (projecting from 5D to 3D)
fig = plt.figure()
ax = fig.add_subplot(111, projection='3d')
ax.scatter(points_5d[:, 0], points_5d[:, 1], points_5d[:, 2], label='Points in 5D Space')

ax.set_xlabel('X-axis')
ax.set_ylabel('Y-axis')
ax.set_zlabel('Z-axis')

plt.title('Representation of Points in 5D Space (Projecting to 3D)')
plt.legend()
plt.show()
```

The point_in_5d_space function encapsulates the logic for calculating coordinates in 5D space. Parametric equations are used to represent points in 5D space. They used NumPy to efficiently handle arrays for storing 5D points. Matplotlib offered 3D scatter plotting to visualize points in 5D space (projected onto 3D). Linear algebra deals with vector spaces and transformations, and the concept of representing points in higher-dimensional spaces aligns with the principles of linear algebra. The use of tuples to represent coordinates and parametric equations reflects mathematical concepts commonly used.

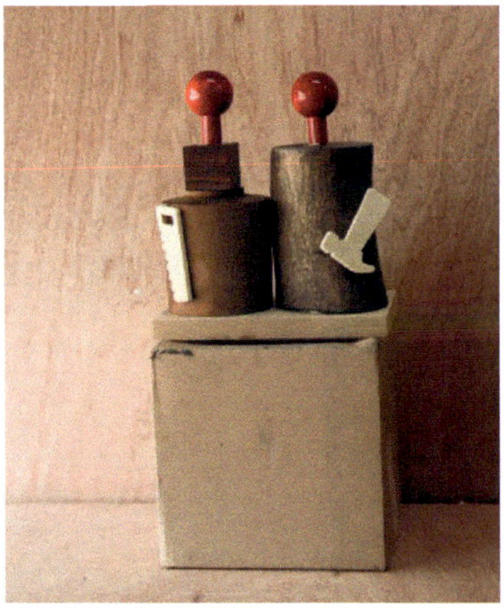

SIX	COMPUTATION (ARRAYS AND NUMPY) GROUP SIX

Representing points in a six-dimensional space extends the concept even further. We can use a tuple (x, y, z, w, v, u) to represent a point in 6D space with a Python code:

```
import matplotlib.pyplot as plt
from mpl_toolkits.mplot3d import Axes3D
import numpy as np

def point_in_6d_space(t):
    # Parametric equations for a point in 6D space
    x = 2 * t
    y = 3 * t
    z = -1 * t
    w = 0.5 * t
    v = -0.2 * t
    u = 0.1 * t

    return x, y, z, w, v, u

# Generate points in 6D space for values of t
t_values = np.linspace(-10, 10, 100)
points_6d = np.array([point_in_6d_space(t) for t in t_values])

# Visualize points in a 3D space (projecting from 6D to 3D)
fig = plt.figure()
ax = fig.add_subplot(111, projection='3d')
ax.scatter(points_6d[:, 0], points_6d[:, 1], points_6d[:, 2], label='Points in 6D Space')

ax.set_xlabel('X-axis')
ax.set_ylabel('Y-axis')
ax.set_zlabel('Z-axis')

plt.title('Representation of Points in 6D Space (Projecting to 3D)')
plt.legend()
plt.show()
```

As before, they used parametric equations to represent points in 6D space. It can be applied to Mathematics (Linear Algebra), as it aligns with its principles by representing points in a higher-dimensional space. Linear algebra deals with vector spaces and linear transformations, and extending these concepts to six dimensions is a natural progression. In theoretical physics, especially in areas like string theory or certain quantum theories, considering spaces with more than three dimensions is not uncommon. In Computer Science (Data Science), higher-dimensional spaces are commonly encountered in data science, machine learning, and feature engineering. Data with multiple features can be conceptualized as points in a high-dimensional space. Understanding and visualizing points in higher-dimensional spaces are fundamental concepts that have applications across various disciplines.

INFINITE SPACE	FUNCTIONAL ANALYSES (ARRAYS AND NUMPY) GROUP EIGHT

Representing an infinite-dimensional space in a practical way is not feasible in code due to limitations in visualization and computation. However, the concept of infinite-dimensional spaces is well-established in mathematics, particularly in functional analysis. They used symbolic mathematics to represent an infinite-dimensional space conceptually:

```
import sympy as sp

def point_in_infinite_dimensional_space(t):
    # Symbolic representation of an infinite-dimensional space
    x = sp.symbols('x')
    expression = sum(x**i for i in range(t + 1))

    return expression

# Print the representation for various values of t
for t in range(5):
    result = point_in_infinite_dimensional_space(t)
    print(f"For t = {t}, expression = {result}")
```

It can be used in Symbolic Mathematics (Sympy): the code uses the Sympy library to represent an infinite-dimensional space symbolically. The expression sum(x**i for i in range(t + 1)) represents an infinite sum of terms in an infinite-dimensional space. For mathematics, functional analysis extensively studies infinite-dimensional spaces. Spaces of functions, such as function spaces, are examples of infinite-dimensional spaces. This concept is foundational in understanding operators and transformations in such spaces. For Physics, in quantum mechanics, wave functions and state vectors often belong to infinite-dimensional Hilbert spaces. In computer science (Functional Programming), the concept of infinite-dimensional spaces is related to functional programming paradigms. Functions themselves can be treated as elements of infinite-dimensional spaces, and understanding this abstraction is quite relevant. While the code provides a symbolic representation, dealing with infinite-dimensional spaces often involves theoretical frameworks and abstract mathematics, and practical implementations may involve specialized mathematical structures like Hilbert spaces in the case of functional analysis.

You want an infinite D?
That's me! I am Chat GPT.

Grammar of the City. © 2025 by Anna Ursyn

CHAPTER 4
APPLICATIONS

The world becomes more visual. Let's look at computer graphics applications in different dimensions.

PRACTICAL APPLICATIONS IN COMPUTER GRAPHICS BASED ON ZERO DIMENSIONS

Particle Systems: Zero-dimensional graphics can represent individual particles in a particle system. This is used in computer graphics for simulations like fire, smoke, or fluid dynamics.
Molecular Visualization: In chemistry or bioinformatics, zero-dimensional graphics can represent atoms or molecules as points in space, which is useful for visualizing molecular structures.
Point Clouds in 3D Scanning: In 3D scanning and computer vision, zero-dimensional graphics can represent points in a point cloud, used in applications like 3D modeling, object recognition, and AR.
Graphics Rendering Initialization: In computer graphics programming, zero-dimensional graphics may be used in the initialization stage, representing the starting point or origin for more complex graphics.
Signal Processing: Zero-dimensional graphics can represent individual data points and have applications in audio processing or digital signal analysis. In Coordinate Systems, they mark the origin (0,0).

Sparse Data Representation: In some data visualization scenarios, especially when dealing with sparse data, representing each data point as a zero-dimensional graphic can be efficient and meaningful.
Graph Theory Visualization represents nodes in a graph as zero-dimensional points, aiding in understanding the relationships between different elements.
Simulation Initialization: In simulations and modeling, zero-dimensional graphics can represent initial conditions or starting points for dynamic systems.
Data Annotation: Zero-dimensional graphics can annotate specific points of interest in a larger graphical context, for a focused and minimalistic representation. They serve as building blocks for more complex visualizations and simulations in various fields.

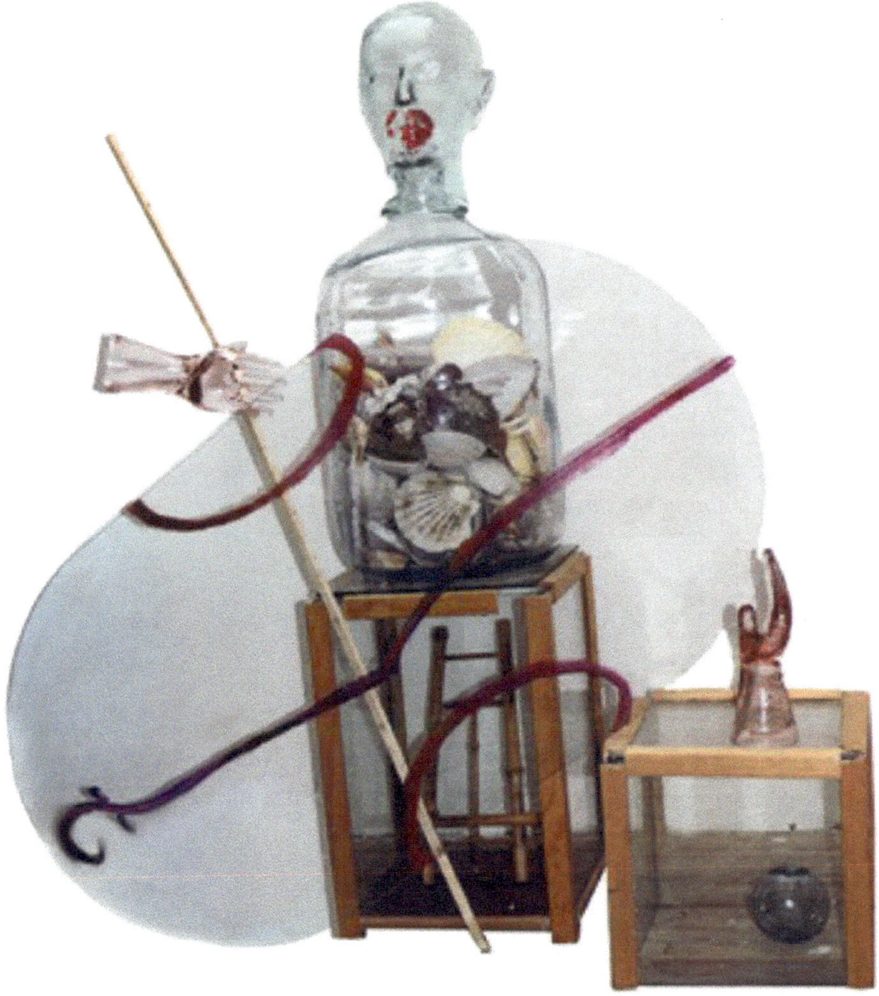

PRACTICAL APPLICATIONS IN COMPUTER GRAPHICS BASED ON ONE-DIMENSION

One-dimensional graphics involve representing objects or structures along a single axis. While less common than higher-dimensional graphics, one-dimensional graphics find applications in specific scenarios. Here are some practical applications:

Line Charts in Data Visualization: One-dimensional graphics are commonly used in line charts to represent trends or relationships in data over a single axis, such as time. This is prevalent in business analytics, finance, and scientific research.
Signal Processing: One-dimensional graphics can represent signals or waveforms along a time axis, often used in areas like audio processing, speech recognition, and telecommunications.
GIS (Geographic Information Systems) can represent linear features such as roads, rivers, or boundaries, aiding in spatial analysis and mapping applications.
Timeline Visualization: Timelines in project management or historical representations often use one-dimensional graphics to show events or tasks along a temporal axis.
Audio Waveform Visualization: In audio editing software or music production tools, to represent audio waveforms along a time axis, facilitating precise editing and manipulation.
Temperature Profiles: One-dimensional graphics can be used to display temperature profiles over a geographic or vertical axis, aiding meteorological and environmental studies.
Network Traffic Visualization: Using a one-dimensional graph representing network traffic over time helps monitor and analyze computer networks' data flow.
Stock Market Price Charts: Finance price charts display the historical performance of stocks or other financial instruments using them.
EKG/ECG Displays: Electrocardiogram (ECG or EKG) displays show the heart's electrical activity over time with one-dimensional graphics.
Linear Sensors and Measurements: One-dimensional graphics represent linear measurements, such as distance, where values change along a single axis.
Barcode Representation: Barcodes are one-dimensional graphics that represent information in a linear format, and are widely used in retail, publishing, and inventory management.
Navigation Paths: One-dimensional graphics can represent paths or routes, helping in navigation systems or location-based services. Despite being limited in complexity, they are effective where representation along a single axis is sufficient for conveying meaningful information. These applications span various fields, including data visualization, science, engineering, and multimedia.

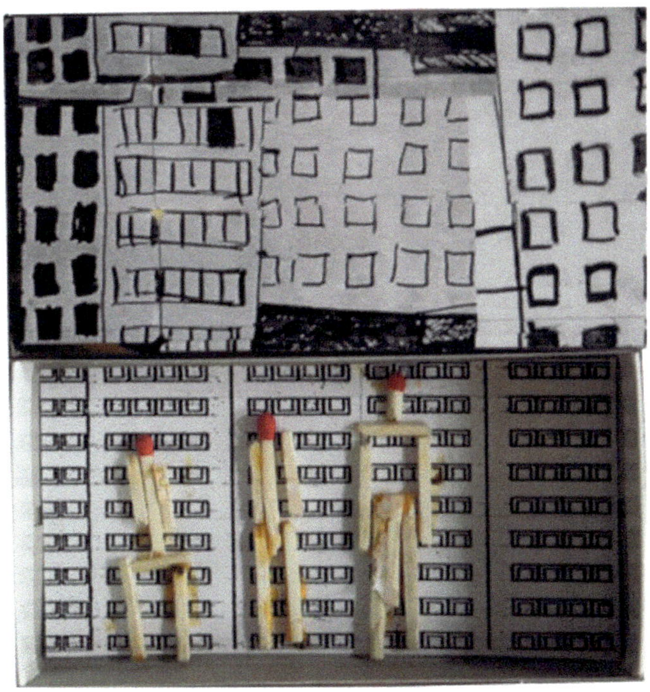

PRACTICAL APPLICATIONS IN COMPUTER GRAPHICS BASED ON TWO DIMENSIONS

Computer graphics, creating, manipulating, and representing visual images and animations, affects fields:

Graphic Design: Logo Design: Creating visually appealing logos for businesses.
Print Media: Designing posters, brochures, flyers, and other print materials.
Web Design: Designing website layouts, icons, and other web elements.
User Interfaces (UI): Software UI: Designing the graphical interfaces of software applications.
Mobile App Design: Creating visually pleasing interfaces for various mobile applications.
Interactive Web Design: Designing user interfaces for interactive websites.
Maps and Cartography: City Maps: Creating detailed maps for navigation and exploration.
Geographical Information Systems (GIS): Analyzing and visualizing spatial data.
Weather Maps: Representing weather-related patterns and forecasts.
Education and Training: Educational Graphics: Developing visuals for educational materials.
Training Simulations: Creating two-dimensional simulations for training purposes.
Infographics: Presenting information through visually appealing graphics.
Data Visualization: Charts and Graphs: Representing data through bar charts, pie charts, etc.
Dashboards: Designing visual dashboards for data analysis.
Flowcharts: Creating diagrams to represent processes and workflows.
Entertainment Industry: 2D Animation: Creating animated content for cartoons and movies.
Video Games: Designing 2D game graphics, characters, and backgrounds.
Digital Comics: Developing visuals for digital comic books.
Advertising and Marketing: Banner Ads: Designing visually appealing banner advertisements.
Marketing Collateral: Creating graphics for marketing campaigns.
Social Media Graphics: Designing visuals for social media platforms.
Medical Imaging: Medical Illustrations: Creating visuals for medical textbooks and presentations.
Diagnostic Imaging: Visualizing medical imaging data in 2D.
Patient Education Graphics: Developing visuals to explain medical procedures.
Architectural Visualization: Floor Plans: Creating 2D representations of architectural layouts.
Site Plans: Visualizing building sites and landscapes.
Interior Design: Designing interiors through 2D graphics.
Graphical User Documentation: Instruction Manuals: Creating visual guides for products.
Technical Documentation: Using graphics to explain technical processes.
User Guides: Illustrating steps and procedures for users.

Two-dimensional computer graphics applications foster communication and visualization of information.

Entertainment and Gaming:
Creation of realistic 3D environments for video games.
Character modeling and animation in animated films and video games.
Special effects in movies for a more immersive experience.
Virtual Reality (VR) and Augmented Reality (AR):
Simulation of realistic virtual environments for training purposes.
Interactive and immersive experiences in VR and AR applications.
Computer-Aided Design (CAD)**:**
Architectural modeling for visualizing buildings and structures.
Product design and prototyping in manufacturing industries.
Medical Imaging:
Reconstruction of 3D images from medical scans (MRI, CT scans).
Surgical simulation for training medical professionals.
Scientific Visualization:
Representing complex scientific data in three dimensions for analysis.
Simulation of physical phenomena for research and education.
Education and Training:
Educational software with 3D models for better understanding.
Virtual labs and simulations for hands-on learning.
Virtual Tourism:
Creating virtual tours of real-world locations for exploration.
Historical reconstructions for educational purposes.
Marketing and Advertising:
Product visualization and advertisements with realistic 3D models.
Interactive presentations for showcasing products or concepts.
Simulation and Training:
Flight simulation for pilot training.
Military simulations for training exercises.
Web and Mobile Applications:
Interactive 3D elements in websites and mobile apps.
Virtual try-ons for online shopping.
Geographic Information Systems (GIS):
Visualizing geographic data in 3D for better analysis.
Urban planning and development simulations.
Animation and Film Production:
Creation of 3D animations for movies and television.
Visual effects and CGI for enhancing storytelling.

These 3D applications showcase the versatility and importance of 3D computer graphics in various fields.

PRACTICAL APPLICATIONS IN COMPUTER GRAPHICS IN FOUR-DIMENSIONS

Computer graphics primarily deals with creating, manipulating, and representing visual images and animations on a computer. While three-dimensional graphics (3D) are more common, four-dimensional graphics (4D) involve an additional dimension, often time.

4D Modeling and Simulation:
4D graphics are used to model and simulate dynamic processes over time. In various fields, such as physics, engineering, biology, and finance, to visualize and understand changes in complex systems.
Medical Imaging and Visualization:
In medical fields, they visualize time-varying medical data, such as the movement of organs, blood flow, or the development of diseases to help in diagnosis, treatment planning, and medical education.
Scientific Data Analysis:
Scientists and researchers can use them to analyze and visualize time-dependent datasets. This is particularly useful in fields like atmospheric science, where understanding temporal changes is crucial. **Animation and Special Effects**:
In the entertainment industry, creating more realistic and dynamic animations includes simulating the effects of time on characters, environments, and special effects in movies and video games.
Financial Modeling and Analysis:
4D graphics can be applied in financial modeling to represent and analyze time-series data, stock market trends, and economic indicators to provide deeper insights for decision-makers.
Urban Planning and Architecture:
4D graphics can aid them in visualizing the development and evolution of urban spaces over time. This is valuable for understanding the impact of architectural decisions and urban planning strategies.
Virtual Reality (VR) and Augmented Reality (AR):
They can enhance the immersive experience. Incorporating time as a dimension allows for more dynamic and interactive virtual worlds, providing users with a more engaging and realistic perception.
Geospatial Analysis:
In geographic information systems (GIS), 4D graphics can be applied to analyze and visualize changes in spatial data over time, as useful in tracking environmental changes, land use patterns, and urban growth.
Fluid Dynamics and Simulation:
4D graphics can be used to simulate and visualize the behavior of fluids over time. This applies to aerospace engineering, where understanding airflow dynamics around objects is crucial.
Education and Training:
Incorporating time as a dimension in educational simulations and training scenarios can provide learners with a more realistic and dynamic learning experience. This is applicable from medicine to aviation.

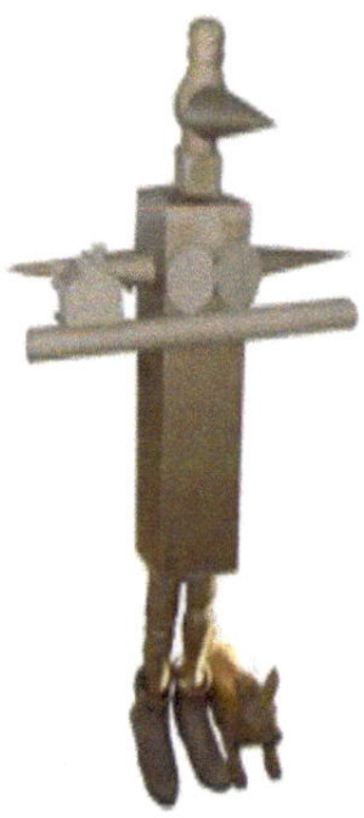

These applications highlight the diverse ways in which four-dimensional graphics can enhance understanding, analysis, and representation of dynamic phenomena across various disciplines.

PRACTICAL APPLICATIONS IN COMPUTER GRAPHICS BASED ON FIVE-DIMENSIONS

Traditional computer graphics typically involve two-dimensional (2D) and three-dimensional (3D) representations. The concept of five dimensions in computer graphics is not yet a standard or widely recognized framework.

Yua: has the power to change the direction of a river.

PRACTICAL APPLICATIONS IN COMPUTER GRAPHICS BASED ON INFINITE DIMENSIONS

Infinite dimensions in computer graphics are not a standard or widely recognized framework. Traditional computer graphics typically involve two-dimensional (2D) and three-dimensional (3D) representations, and the idea of infinite dimensions may not apply in most practical applications. However, there are emerging concepts or applications.

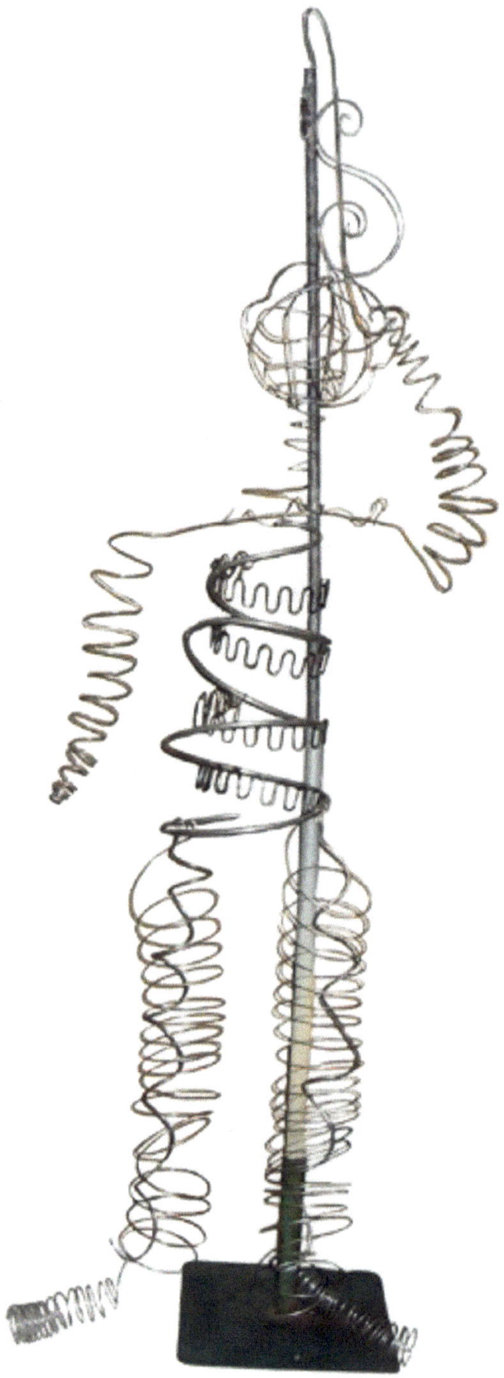

City Matters. © 2025 by Anna Ursyn

Chapter 5 Products

Graphic Design Software: companies provide solutions for creating graphics for print and digital media.
Video Games, especially in the indie game, use them for character design, backgrounds, and animations.
Animation Software packages allow animators to create 2D animations, films, cartoons, and online.
Digital Art Tablets: drawing tablets, provide artists with a digital canvas for creating 2D artwork.
Printed Materials: books, magazines, posters, and other printed materials heavily depend on 2D graphics for illustrations, layout design, and cover art.
User Interface (UI) Design: 2D graphics are crucial in designing user interfaces for websites, applications, and software, ensuring a visually appealing and user-friendly experience.
Educational Software: interactivity often incorporates 2D graphics to enhance students' learning experiences, making concepts more engaging and easier to understand.
Cartoons and Comics: traditional and digital comics and animated cartoons heavily rely on 2D graphics for storytelling and visual appeal.
Infographics present information visually, for complex data and statistics accessible and understandable.
Map Design: maps, whether for navigation or education represent geographic information effectively.
Digital Signage: displays in public spaces, retail environments, and events often use 2D graphics for advertising and information dissemination.
Icon Design: icons on computer interfaces, websites, and various mobile applications are typically designed using 2D graphics for clear and recognizable representation.

There are diverse applications of two-dimensional graphics across creative, entertainment, educational, and practical domains.

PRODUCTS COMING OUT OF THREE-DIMENSIONAL GRAPHICS

Three-dimensional (3D) graphics have revolutionized various industries, enabling the creation of immersive and realistic products. 3D Modeling Software offers powerful tools for creating 3D models, animations, and visual effects in industries such as film, gaming, and design.

Video Games utilize 3D graphics for character models, environments, and special effects, providing players with realistic and immersive gaming experiences.

Computer-Aided Design (CAD) for designing complex structures, machinery, and architectural plans.

Virtual Reality (VR) and Augmented Reality (AR) leverage 3D graphics to create realistic and interactive simulations for training, education, gaming, and other immersive experiences.

3D Printing relies on 3D models to create physical objects layer by layer. This technology has applications in prototyping, manufacturing, healthcare, and more.

The Medical Imaging field uses 3D graphics imaging technologies, such as CT scans and MRIs, to create detailed, 3D representations of internal structures for diagnosis and treatment planning.

Architectural Visualization: Architects use 3D graphics to create realistic visualizations of buildings and spaces before they are constructed, aiding in design and presentation.

Product Design and Prototyping offers Industrial designers 3D graphics to visualize and prototype products, allowing for thorough testing and refinement before production.

Animation and Visual Effects (VFX) focuses on them as crucial in creating animated films, TV shows, and visual effects that enhance realism and create fantastical elements.

Simulations and Training for industries such as aviation and defense use 3D graphics to develop realistic simulations, allowing personnel to practice in safe and controlled environments.

Geospatial Mapping: Geographic Information Systems (GIS) use 3D graphics to map and analyze spatial data, providing a three-dimensional perspective on geographical information.

Entertainment and Virtual Worlds: Virtual reality platforms and online virtual worlds use 3D graphics to create immersive social interaction, gaming, and exploration environments. The wide-ranging impact of three-dimensional graphics is present across sectors, enhancing creativity, simulation, and visualization capabilities in diverse fields.

Useful Products Coming Out of Four-Dimensional Graphics

Four-dimensional graphics often referred to as 4D graphics, extend traditional three-dimensional space by incorporating time as the fourth dimension. While it's a theoretical and mathematical concept, it has inspired various creative and innovative ideas in different fields.
Data Visualization: Visualizing data over time can be considered a form of 4D graphics. Products that offer dynamic and interactive data visualization, especially in fields like finance, analytics, and scientific research, may leverage the time dimension for better insights.
Simulation and Modeling: Simulation software incorporating time as a crucial aspect is a practical application of 4D graphics. This is particularly relevant in physics, engineering, and biology.
Virtual Reality (VR) and Augmented Reality (AR): Some applications in VR and AR might incorporate time as a dimension, allowing users to experience changes over time. This could benefit training simulations, architectural design, or historical reconstructions.
Entertainment and Gaming: Interactive media and games might explore the concept of 4D graphics to enhance gameplay by introducing time-based elements, dynamic environments, or evolving storylines.
Art and Design: Creative industries might use the concept of 4D graphics to produce time-based visual art or design installations, animated sculptures, time-dependent visual effects, or interactive exhibits.

Green. © 2025 by Matylda Czarnecka.

It's essential to note that the term "4D graphics" is somewhat abstract, and its practical application can vary across different domains.

AS FOR FIVE-DIMENSIONAL GRAPHICS, SIX-DIMENSIONAL GRAPHICS, OR INFINITE-DIMENSIONAL GRAPHICS

Traditional graphics and graphics technology typically involve two-dimensional (2D) or three-dimensional (3D) representations.

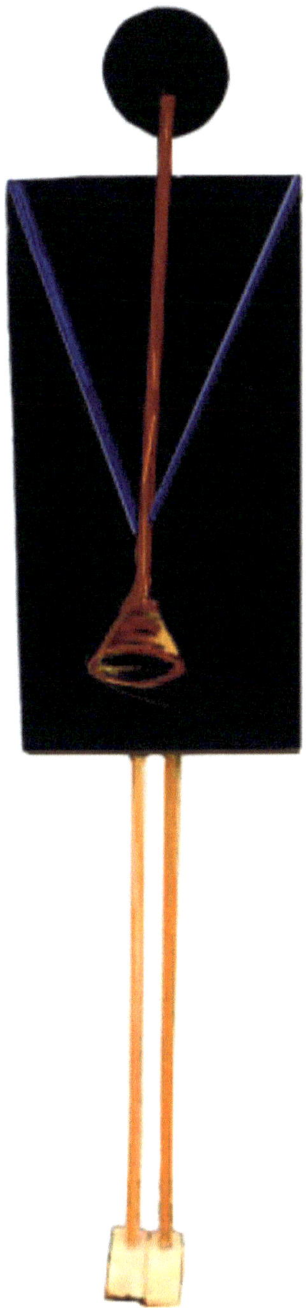

Check technology publications, research papers, or industry announcements for updates. Terminology and technology can evolve, and new developments may have occurred.

THE END.

All Roads Lead to Somethin'. © 2025 by Anna Ursyn

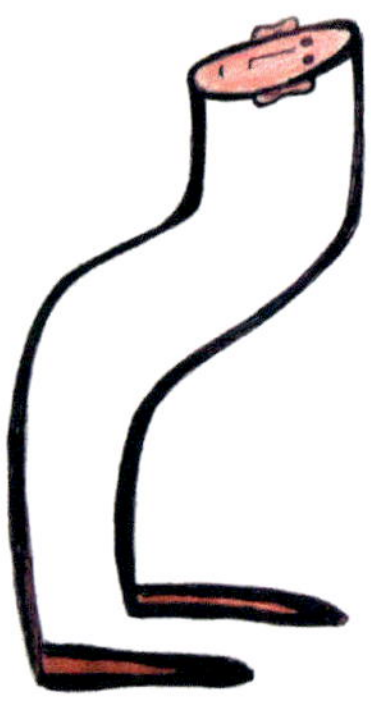

Undipag: always hopes for the best.

Undpaq: always hopes for the best.

ACKNOWLEDGMENTS AND CREDITS

The UNC President, Board of Trustees members, Provost and members of the Provost Office, Dean of the Performance and Visual Arts, Chair of the School of Art and Design, colleagues, and members of several grant committees have been supporting me in my research and performances based on my books. My great thanks go to all of them and everybody else involved.

My appreciation goes to Randi Slack and Heba Kusseibati from Taylor & Francis Group for making these books happen.

I'd like to thank the reviewers for supporting the books.

My thanks for Matylda Czarnecka and Joohyun Pyune for the photographs and artwork.

For books and performances, software and copyright-free resources, among them, Grammarly, ChatGPT, QuillBot, Wordtune, Microsoft Word, Adobe products, and more apps were used, including music and visual music Pexels, and Udio.

Images are by the author and collaborators, as credited.

A View from the Window. © 2025 by Matylda Czarnecka. (Used with permission).

Forest. © *2025 by Matylda Czarnecka. (Used with permission).*

PUBLICATIONS RELATED TO THIS BOOK

al-Rifaie, M. M., Ursyn, A., & Wyeld, T. (2020). *The Art of Coding: The Language of Drawing, Graphics, and Animation.* CRC Press: Chapman and Hall/CRC. Taylor and Francis Group. ISBN 978-0-367-90037-3; 978-1-138-62964-6; 978-1-315-21033-9.

Arya, A. (2020). *Anyone Can Code.* Routledge. ISBN-10: 0367199696, ISBN-13: 978-0367199692

Holoworld, *The Basics of STREAM Education: A Comprehensive Guide* (2025). Retrieved from https://www.blogs.holoworld.one/what-is-stream-education/

Beginner's Step-by-Step Coding Course: Learn Computer Programming the Easy Way. (DK Complete Courses), Hardcover –2020. ISBN 1465482210

Erwig, M. (2022). *Once Upon an Algorithm: How Stories Explain Computing*. MIT Press. ISBN-10: 0262545292, ISBN-13: 978-0262545297.

Montfort, N. (2021). *Exploratory Programming for the Arts and Humanities, second edition* MIT Press. ISBN-10: 0262044609.

STEAM (2025). Rhode Island School of Design. Retrieved from https://www.risd.edu/steam. VisionShiftStudios (2025).

STEM to STEAM: Integrated Studies STEM to STEAM Resources Toolkit (2025). Edutopia, George Lucas Educational Foundation. Retrieved from https://www.edutopia.org/article/STEM-resources-downloads

Ursyn, A. (2025). *The Transfer of Knowledge through Art and Visualization: Novel Technologies, Collaboration, and Visual Communication of Science-based Projects*. Anna Ursyn (Author). Taylor & Francis Group. Routledge. ISBN 9781032624228

Ursyn, A., & Mostowfi, M. (2015). Visualization by Coding: Drawing Simple Shapes and Forms in Various Programming Languages. In *Handbook of Research on Maximizing Cognitive Learning through Knowledge Visualization* A. Ursyn, Editor. DOI: 10.4018/978-1-4666-8142-2.ch008. https://www.igi-global.com/chapter/visualization-by-coding/127482

Ursyn, A., al-Rifaie, M. M., & Md Islam, F. (2015). Metaphors for Dance and Programming: Rules, Restrictions, and Conditions for Learning and Visual Outcome. In Anna Ursyn, Author/Editor (2015), *Knowledge Visualization and Visual Literacy in Science Education,* 2015, IGI Global, 572 pages, ISBN-13: 978146668142

What is Coding: Coding 101 tutorial (2025). Retrieved from https://www.bitdegree.org/tutorials/what-is-coding/

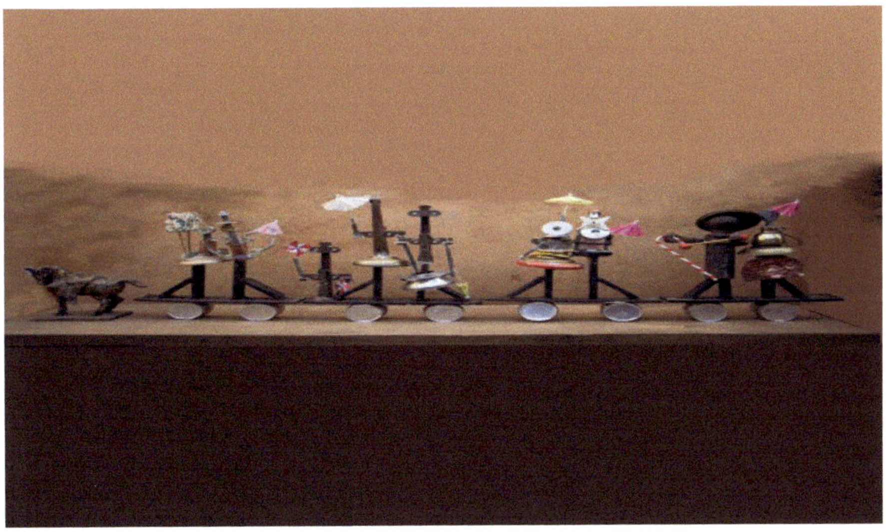

BOOKS – AUTHORED, CO-AUTHORED, AND EDITED BY ANNA URSYN

A LIST OF TITLES FROM THE PREVIOUS PAGE

1. *Dance Code, Dance Steps as a Code,* Anna Ursyn (Author). Taylor & Francis Group.
2. *New Storytelling: Learning through Metaphors.* Anna Ursyn (Author). Taylor & Francis Group.
3. *Code Appreciation, Reshaping Knowledge.* Anna Ursyn, (Author). Taylor & Francis Group.
4. *Nature Appreciation: Knowledge as Art,* Anna Ursyn (Author).
5. *The Transfer of Knowledge through Art and Visualization: Novel Technologies, Collaboration, and Visual Communication of Science-based Projects*. Anna Ursyn (Author). Taylor & Francis Group. Routledge. 2025, 143 pages, ISBN 9781032624228.
6. *Photography for Professions: Creative Knowledge Explorations*. Anna Ursyn (Author), Kendall Hunt Publishing Company, 2022, 177 pages, ISBN 979-8-7657-4703-2.
7. *Art for Professions: Art Appreciation and Knowledge Visualization.* Anna Ursyn (Author), Kendall Hunt Publishing Company. 2021, 538 pages, ISBN-10 1792466609, ISBN-13 978-1792466601.
8. *Describing Nature Through Visual Data*. Anna Ursyn (Author/Editor), IGI Global, 2020, 367 pages, ISBN-10 1799857530, ISBN-13 978-1799857532.
9. *The Art of Coding: The Language of Drawing, Graphics, and Animation*. by al-Rifaie, M. M., Ursyn, A., Wyeld, T. CRC Press, Taylor & Francis Group, A Chapman & Hall Book. 2020, 312 pages. ISBN: 9780-0-367-90037-3 (hbk), 978-1-138-62964-6 (pbk), 978-1-315-21033-9 (ebk).
10. *Graphical Thinking for Science and Technology Through Knowledge,* Visualization (Advances in Multimedia and Interactive Technologies) (Anna Ursyn, Author//Editor), IGI Global. 2020, 374 pages, ISBN-10 1799816516, ISBN-13 978-1799816515.
11. *Interface Support for Creativity, Productivity, and Expression in Computer Graphics*. Anna Ursyn (Author/Editor) IGI Global. 2019, 355 pages, ISBN-13 9781522573715, DOI 10.4018/978-1-5225-7371-5.
12. *Visual Approaches to Cognitive Education with Technology Integration*. Anna Ursyn (Author/Editor), IGI Global. 2018, 387 pages, ISBN-13 9781522553328.
13. *Knowledge Visualization and Visual Literacy in Science Education.* Anna Ursyn (Author/Editor). IGI Global. 2016. 431 pages, ISB-13 9781522504801.
14. *Maximizing Cognitive Learning through Knowledge Visualization*. Handbook of Research. Anna Ursyn (Author/Editor). IGI Global, 2015, 572 pages, ISBN-13 9781466681422.
15. *Computational Solutions for Knowledge, Art, and Entertainment: Information Exchange Beyond Text.* Anna Ursyn (Author), IGI Global, 2014, 511 pages, ISBN-13 9781466646278.
16. *Perceptions of Knowledge Visualization: Explaining Concepts through Meaningful Images*. Anna Ursyn (Author), IGI Global, 2014, 418 pages, ISBN-13 9781466647039.
17. *Biologically Inspired Computing for the Arts: Scientific Data Through Graphics*. Anna Ursyn (Author/Editor), IGI Global, 2012, 442 pages, ISBN-13 9781466609426.

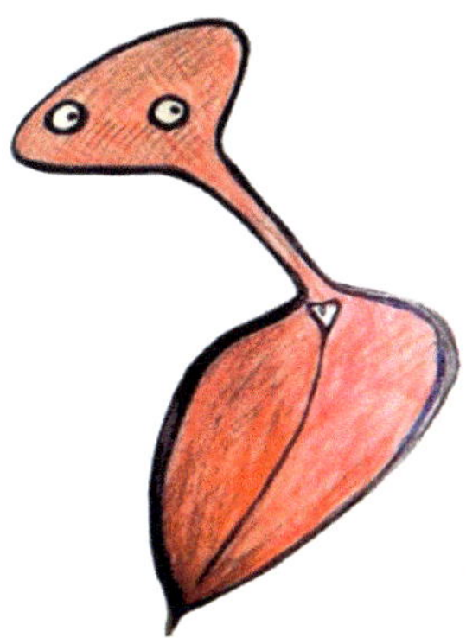

Gunsifo: loves the World.

Gunsifo. Loves the world.

TERMS WITH SHORT DESCRIPTIONS

Abstract – a concept or thought that does not have physical, concrete existence. An artistic object that has a meaning independent of narrative or pictorial representation. Also, a summary of a larger text.

Aesthetics – analysis of principles related to beauty in terms of arts or philosophy

Algorithm – a sequence of instructions telling a computer how to perform computation or write programs. In a recursive process, algorithms can be written many times to create repetition. Algorithms help to solve a complex problem by writing a sequence of simple steps.

Anthropology means the study of human characteristics. Physical anthropology studies human biological and physiological features and their evolution. Cultural anthropology studies societies, cultures, and their development.

API – application programming interface, is a software interface that allows communication between computers and/or programs.

Artifact – an object produced by a human being, examined in the artistic or historical terms (it may be an artwork, a craft object, a tool, a weapon, or an ornament of archaeological or historical interest).

Artificial intelligence (AI) uses computer systems and applies machine learning for tasks, involving big collections of data, that would require human intelligence.

Binary numeral system uses two symbols: typically, "0" (zero) and "1" (one).

Biointerface is a place of contact between a biomolecule, living tissue, or organism and a living or another material. Nanostructure interfaces are extensively studied.

ChatGPT is a computer program that uses artificial intelligence (AI) and natural language processing (NLP) to understand user questions, providing automatic responses, and simulating human conversation (ibm.com/topics/chatbots)

Cognitive abilities enable to think abstractly (not only on concrete objects), learn from experience, reason, comprehend ideas and concepts, and solve problems. They support gaining knowledge, utilizing information, creative and critical thinking.

Cobots are robots that collaborate with people.

DALL·E 2 is a version of GPT-3 that can create realistic images and art from text descriptions.

Data – factual information specially organized for analysis, reasoning, or making decisions.

Data Visualization: information abstracted in a schematic form to provide visual insights into data sets. Data visualization enables us to go from the abstract numbers in a computer program (ones and zeros) to the visual interpretation of data. Text visualization means converting textual information into graphic representation, so we can see the information without reading the data, as tables, histograms, pie or bar charts, or Cartesian coordinates.

Dimension relates to spatial measures such as width, height, or length. Dimension means how many numbers (coordinates) are needed to determine a position of a point in space. In the Cartesian three-dimensional space, three coordinates, x, y, and z, describe the position of a point: x-horizontal axis, y-vertical axis, and z-depth. René Descartes (Cartesius) revolutionized mathematics by providing the first systematic link between geometry described by Euclides and algebra). A **point** has no length, area, volume, or other dimensional attributes, so some mathematicians claim a point is 0-dimensional. A **line** has one dimension because only one coordinate is needed to describe a point in space, while a **surface** has two dimensions. Data may be linear or multidimensional.

Electromagnetic radiation results from the electromagnetic field's propagation of waves (or photons) which carries radiant energy. Waves, which have different wavelengths, include radio waves, microwaves, infrared, light (which is visible), ultraviolet, X-rays, and gamma rays.

Empathy means understanding and sharing another person's or creature's feelings. One may apply cognitive (by knowing how to take somebody's perspective), emotional (by feeling somebody's emotions), and compassionate (by combining intellect and feelings) empathy.

Extended Reality (XR) comprises real-and-virtual environments generated by computer technology and used in wearables.

Virtual Reality (VR) refers to immersive experiences created with the use of real-world content (e.g., 360° Video), purely synthetic content (for instance, computer-generated), or a hybrid of both.

Augmented Reality (AR) is an overlay of computer-generated content on the real world that can superficially interact with the environment in real time. With AR, the CG content and the real world do not block themselves.

Mixed Reality (MR) – in MR, the synthetic content is overlaid and anchored to interact with objects in the real world in real-time.

Fiber lasers use fiber optic cables with added rare earth elements and other materials to provide and transmit light and light signals.

Form – mass that occupies space, giving the weight, density, and thickness of a 3D object or is implied in a picture of this object.

Fractal geometry describes self-similar or scale-symmetric objects called fractals. When magnified or reduced in size, fractal things are self-similar: their parts are similar to the whole, and the likeness continues when the parts are magnified more and more. They are present in nature, designs, and artworks. Fractal geometry can explain the origination of patterns in living organisms.

GPT (generative pre-trained transformer) is a deep learning model originated by Google in 2017.

GPT-4 is a multimodal model that accepts prompts of images and texts as inputs and gives out text outputs, such as natural language or code.

Graphic is an image represented by a graph or relating to graphics. Computers often generate graphic displays.

Haptic – relates to the sense of touch; the senses of touch and proprioception enable the perception and manipulation of objects.

Higher-order thinking goes beyond observation of facts and data memorization, enabling one to build data-based knowledge. Higher-order thinking makes critical thinking possible in an evaluative, creative, and innovative way.

HTML – Hypertext Markup Language. This language codes formatting, links, and other things on Web pages. **XML** – eXtensible Markup Language. A markup language like HTML; it lets individuals define and use their tags.

Hyperlink – a link from a hypertext file or document to another file activated by clicking on a highlighted word or image on the screen.

Icon, iconic object or image. An icon represents a thing or refers to something by resembling or imitating it; thus, a picture, a photograph, a mathematical expression, or an old-style telephone may be regarded as an iconic object. Therefore, an iconic object or image has qualities in common with things it represents by looking, sounding, feeling, tasting, or smelling alike.

Iconography means visual elements such as images and symbols used in a specific culture, society, or artwork. It also may indicate a study about these elements.

Immersive experience happens when a 3D or 4D (including time) image (maybe plus sound or other stimuli) surrounds you creating extended reality. Platforms that support immersive experiences include augmented reality (AR), virtual reality (VR), Mixed reality (MR), 360° video, wearable devices, the Internet of Things (IoT), and more.

Infographics: tools and techniques involved in the graphical representation of data, mostly in journalism, art, and storytelling.

Information – knowledge derived from study, experience, or instruction based on facts or data.

Information visualization – representation plus interaction; it means using the computer-supported, visual-spatial representation of abstract data to amplify cognition and derive new insights. Data presented as information visualization are often interactive, numerical, verbal, and graphical (such as the text of geographic representations).

Ions: cations and anions. An atom or molecule with an electric charge is called an ion. An electric charge results from the presence of single, double, triple, or even higher negative electrons, unequal to the number of positive protons in the nucleus of an atom. Removing or adding one or more electrons changes a neutral atom into an ion. A cation is an ion or group of ions with a positive charge. An anion is a negatively charged ion. In an electrolyte solution, cations move toward the cathode (negative electrode) after applying an electric current, and anions migrate to an anode.

Interface denotes a connection or interaction between two units (which may be subjects, organizations, physical or electronic systems), for example, social interface, or interface between phases of matter such as solid, liquid, and gas, and also interaction of hardware and software. The user and computer interface allows communication with the operating system. Interface with the internet may go through the Internet protocol.

Internet of Things (IoT) means a set of objects connected over a wireless network and acting without human actions. It serves for personal use in smart homes (with everyday physical devices embedded with sensors and software), for elder with disabilities care, as an internet of medical things (IoMT), for business, industrial, vehicular communication, and many kinds of infrastructure systems.

Kinesthesia means knowing about the position and movement of the parts of the body. Sensory organs (proprioceptors) in the muscles and joints signal changes in position.

Knowledge visualization uses visual representations to transfer insights and create new knowledge in communicating different visual formats.

Latitude and longitude are parts of a grid system giving us horizontal and vertical coordinates in the geographic coordinate system. Latitude lines run east-west, and longitude lines run north-south. Every location on Earth has a universal address described by two numbers called latitude and longitude coordinates; they say where the coordinates intersect.

LED, the light-emitting diode, is a semiconductor diode that glows when a voltage is applied.

Mandala is a geometric circular figure depicting the universe according to Hindu and Buddhist traditional symbols.

Manifesto is a public declaration of opinions, statements, and programs mostly of political or social aims. An art manifesto expresses aesthetic and philosophical thoughts about the art defined by an artist or a group of artists. An individual art manifesto facilitates the translation of artistic, visual messages into literary form and conveys it to the viewers, critics, and jurors.

Meander is a geometric pattern made by a line bending along and repeatedly crossing a straight line but not crossing itself. In the arts, it is a decorative pattern constructed from a continuous line shaped into a repeated, ornamental motif.

Metaphor – indicates one thing as representing another, thus making an implied mental comparison. For example, we use metaphors every day when we talk about desktop items, such as folders, documents, and in and out boxes, using familiar objects for organizing elements related to the computer. Also, a figure of speech where we use one word or phrase to designate another one, thus suggesting comparison, as in 'a sea of trouble.'

Mime – a performance art involving body motions without the use of speech.

Mythology is a collection of stories, myths, legends, and beliefs typical of a given culture or religion; for example, Christian, Jewish, Egyptian, Hindu, or Muslim mythologies.

NASA is the *National Aeronautics and Space Administration* civil space program and space exploration. This agency works with contractors, academia, and international and commercial partners to explore, discover, and expand knowledge for the benefit of humanity.

Negative space is the space around the objects depicted in a picture. A **figure-ground reversal** is an optical illusion that happens when we perceive an image formed by the negative space.

Network is a set of connected (wired or wireless) devices, such as computers, servers, mainframes, peripherals, firewalls, smartphones, and more, which allows people to share data. Devices may be linked through cables, telephone lines, radio waves, satellites, or infrared light beams.

Networking means exchanging ideas and information among people for social or business contact.

Neurotransmitters are chemical substances released by nerve cells that transfer signals from neurons to other cells.

OpenAI is a research unit that derives its solutions from deep learning and natural language processing.

Pantomime – a musical, theatrical production using gestures and movements but not words

Paradigm is a pattern of thought: a set of concepts or a way of thinking characteristic of a specific field in science (research methods, postulates, and standards) or philosophy. Paradigm shifts – transitioning to a new approach to the field under study is how the developments come about. Paradigm also means a model, a typical example.

Pattern means the regular order existing in nature and a manmade design. We see patterns everywhere in nature, mathematics, art, architecture, and design. In nature, patterns can be seen as symmetries (e.g., snowflakes) and/or structures having fractal dimensions such as spirals, meanders, or surface waves. In computer science, design patterns serve in creating computer programs. In the arts, the pattern is an artistic or decorative design made of recurring lines or any repeated elements.

Perspective is the appearance of depth, picturing the world on a two-dimensional, flat surface of a piece of paper or a computer screen. Perspective represents 3D objects and depth relationships on a 2D surface.

Photonics is the science of light (photons) generation, detection, and manipulation. It can go through emission, transmission, modulation, sensing, signal processing, switching, and amplification.

Scale is a range of values that forms a standard system for measuring the size of something. Units for measuring in science are known as the International System of Units, which is based on the meter. Very small physical and biological structures are measuring fractions of a meter: micrometer (one-millionth of a meter – 1×10^{-6} m), nanometer one billionth of a meter – 1×10^{-9} m), and picometer (one trillionth of a meter – 1×10^{-12} m) thus, the picometer is one-thousandth of a nanometer. Below are examples of objects of various sizes.

The Milky Way galaxy (10^{21} m)
Our solar system (10^{13} m)
The Earth (10^{18} m)
A city (10^{4} m)
A tree (10^{1} m)
A leaf (10^{-1} m)
A cell (10^{-5} m)
Strands of DNA (10^{-7} m)
An atom (10^{-10} m), and
Quarks (10^{-16} m).

Scientific visualization presents real, abstract, or model-based objects in a digital way directly from the data. It may deliver art-science cooperative learning projects and make knowledge understandable to a broad audience. Visualization as storytelling comprises narratives, interactive graphics, explanatory and animated graphics, and multimedia.

Semiconductor material has a conductivity between a conductor (most metals, for example, copper) and an insulator (such as glass). The properties of a semiconductor, its moving electrons, and electron holes in a crystal lattice can be explained by quantum physics. Silicon crystals are semiconductive materials; they are used in microelectronics and photovoltaics used for direct conversion of sunlight to electricity with the use of solar panels.

Semiotics studies the meaningful use of signs, symbols, codes, and conventions for communication. The name 'semiotics' is derived from the Greek word 'semeion,' which means "sign ." "Meaning" is always the result of social conventions, even when we think something is natural or characteristic and use signs for those meanings. Therefore, culture and art are a series of sign systems. Semioticians analyze such sign systems in various cultures; linguists study language as a system of signs, and some even examine film as a system of signs. The semiotic content of visual design is essential for non-verbal communication applied to practice, especially for visualizing knowledge.

Sign tells about a fact, an idea, or information; it is a distinct thing that signifies another thing. Natural signs signify events caused by nature, while conventional signs may signal art, social interactions, fashion, food, interaction with technology, machines, and practically everything else. Signs take conventional shapes or forms to tell about facts, ideas, or information. Icons and symbols help visually compress information. An **icon** represents a thing or refers to something by resembling or imitating it; thus, a picture, a photograph, a mathematical expression, or an old-style telephone may be regarded as an iconic object. Therefore, an **iconic object** has qualities in common with things it represents by looking, sounding, feeling, tasting, or smelling alike. Natural signs signify events caused by nature, while conventional signs may signal art, social interactions, fashion, food, interactions with technology, machines, and practically everything else.

Signage is a visual graphic that displays information, for example, street signs, room identification signs, or any informational or regulatory signs. Signs, symbols, and icons are collectively called signage. Effective design of a complicated product may help memorize and learn how to use this product (for example, 'Where is the switch?' or 'How to open this thing?').

Social media include social networking sites, image-sharing sites, video hosting sites, discussion sites, community blogs, and economic networks.

Social networking means using Internet-based social media websites and applications to interact with other users for a social or business purpose and stay connected with friends, family, colleagues, customers, or clients. **Social networking** acts through sites like Facebook, Twitter, LinkedIn, and Instagram.

Space is a three-dimensional expanse in the physical universe where we can measure the position and direction of objects and events. A Cartesian coordinate system (with the x, y, and z axes) serves this purpose in Euclidean geometry.

Spectroscopy records how matter interacts with or emits electromagnetic radiation. A spectroscope serves to study matter by measuring properties of specific frequencies and wavelengths of electromagnetic radiation.

Symbol does not resemble things it represents but refers to something by convention; for example, the word "red" represents red. We must learn the relationship between symbols and what they represent, such as letters, numbers, words, codes, traffic lights, and national flags. A symbol represents an abstract concept, not just a thing, and is comparable to an abstract term. Highly abstracted drawings that show no realistic graphic representation become symbols. Symbols are omnipresent in our life, for example:

– An electric diagram that uses abstract symbols for a light bulb, wire, connector, resistor, and switch.
– An apple for a teacher or a bitten apple for a Macintosh computer.
– A map – a typical abstract graphic device.
– A 'slippery when wet' sign.

Symmetry is present when similar parts of an object are arranged around a line, point, or plane. A crystal shows symmetry when it has a center of symmetry, rotation axes, or mirror planes (imaginary planes that divide it into halves). There are several types of symmetry: for example, line or mirror symmetry, radial, cylindrical, or spherical symmetry. A figure with a line, bilateral symmetry has two identical halves when folded along its line of symmetry, and these halves are congruent, meaning they are the same size and shape. An object has a radial symmetry when it can be rotated around the rotation axis. For example, with a fourfold rotation axis, the crystal repeats itself each

90°. Angles of rotational symmetry possible for crystals are: 60 degrees, 90 degrees, 120 degrees, 180 degrees, and 360 degrees. The halves of the bilaterally symmetrical animals, for example, butterflies, form each other's mirror images when seen along the axis. A circle is symmetrical about its center. Optical isomers are 'mirror images' of each other and are symmetrical around a plane. For example, molecules of some sugar isomers deflect the rays of light in the right or left direction.

Synesthesia means the merging of two or more senses. It happens when a sensory stimulus is received by one sense but also triggers perception in another sense.

Synapse: a structure that links (through a synaptic cleft) a nerve cell with another nerve or some other cell type. In an electrical synapse, an activated neuron develops an electric signal on its presynaptic cell membrane, which induces a voltage change on the postsynaptic cell. In a chemical synapse, electrical activity on the presynaptic cell membrane initiates the release of a neurotransmitter and its diffusion to a postsynaptic cell.

Texture: a characteristic of a substance or a material. Texture exists all around us. It can be actual (natural, invented, or manufactured) or simulated (made to look rough, smooth, hard or soft, or like a natural texture). Simulated textures are made to represent real textures, such as smooth arms or rough rock formations. But they are not actual textures; if you touch the picture, you feel only the paint or the pen or pencil marks.

URL means Uniform Resource Locator. Also, resources are called well-known codes, such as http://www.sciam.com/, used in hyperlinks (activated by clicking).

Variable is a feature or a factor that can take on different numerical values.

Vernacular is an adjective to describe the local, indigenous, folkloristic, common, or simple form of a specific culture, architecture, language, or other human activities or products.

Vernacular language is typical of a particular country or region or a **dialect** that can be regional, professional, or otherwise linking a group of people. It may also denote the architecture of houses in a particular region.

Visuals are pictures, diagrams, graphics, film clips, or various forms of display.

Visual media are primarily images, videos, and infographics. Powerpoint presentations may serve as an example.

Visualization means the communication of information with graphical representations. Interactive visual representations of abstract data use easy-to-recognize objects connected through well-defined relations.

Wireframe is a skeletal three-dimensional model in which only lines and vertices are represented. It can also be a way to design a website at the early structural level, a 2D outline of a web page or app which displays the functional elements of a website.

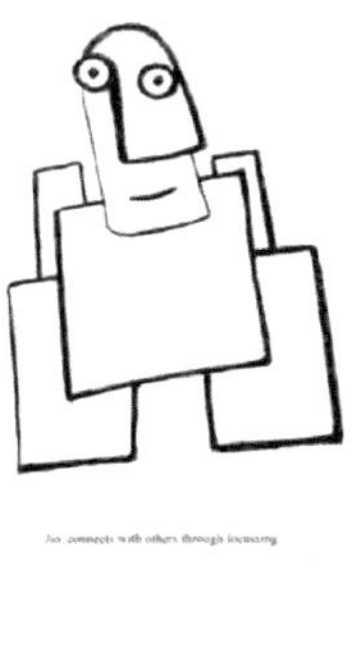

Jio. Connects with others through focusing.

Starflake. © *2025 by Anna Ursyn*

Ohasa: knows the name of each flower by heart.

Ohasa: knows the name of each flower by heart.

Two Skies. © 2025 by Anna Ursyn

ABOUT THE AUTHOR

Anna Ursyn, Ph.D., is a professor of Computer Graphics at the University of Northern Colorado. She combines programming with software and printmaking media to unify computer-generated and painted images and sculptures. She had over 50 single juried and invitational art shows and participated in over 200 juried and invitational fine art exhibitions, such as over a dozen times in ACM SIGGRAPH Art Galleries and traveling shows, including Louvre, Paris, Der Prix Ars Electronica Linz, Austria; Eurographics (Artistic Merit Award), Denver International Airport Show, Denver Capitol shows. Her work was selected to be sent to the Moon by NASA as a part of Carnegie Mellon's MoonArk project and traveling shows, including Centre Pompidou in Paris. Animations projected at the Victory Media Network, Dallas, TX, ISEAs, New York Digital Salons, 20th Century Matrix for NTT Museum, Tokyo, Japan (2000 images and 5000 texts describing the 20th Century), Winner of BauBoden, Deutsche Bau-und Bodenbank AG, cover and 18 color plates, Computerkunst/Computer Art Gladbeck, Germany + traveling shows. Salon de la Culture et des Jeux Mathematiques, CIJM, University Pierre et Marie Curie, Paris, Honorable Mention; Art of the Animal, Australia (award), GRAPHITEs, Art of Photography Show San Diego, CA, Common Ground the Haun Tie Art Museum in Beijing, M.I.A.D. Torento Argentina (Second Place), Immaginando, Digital Visions of Etruria (Honorable Mention), Italy, Bridges Mathematical Art Galleries, Joint Mathematics Meetings Art Galleries, and Generative Art galleries. Her work in ABADs is in the permanent collection of the Museum of Modern Art MOMA in New York City, the Los Angeles County Museum of Art, CA, the Smithsonian Institution, Washington, DC, and more. Anna published over a dozen books, chapters, and articles with her students' artwork included in her book.

Research and pedagogy interests include integrated art, science, and computer art graphics instruction. Chaired the SpaceTime international competitions for students by ACM SIGGRAPH, the International Conference on Computer Graphics and Interactive Techniques. Since 1997, Anna has served as a Liaison, Organizing, and Program Committee member of the International IEEE Conferences on Information Visualization (iV) in London, UK, and has chaired the Symposium and Digital Art Gallery D-ART iV.

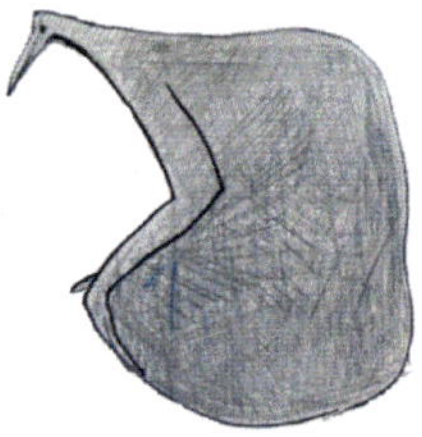

Wabadu: finds any sign of movement.

Wabadu: senses what's coming.

A view from the shore. © 2025 by Matylda Czarnecka (Used with permission).

INDEX

G

H

I

K

L

M

N

O

P

Q

R

S

T

U

V

W

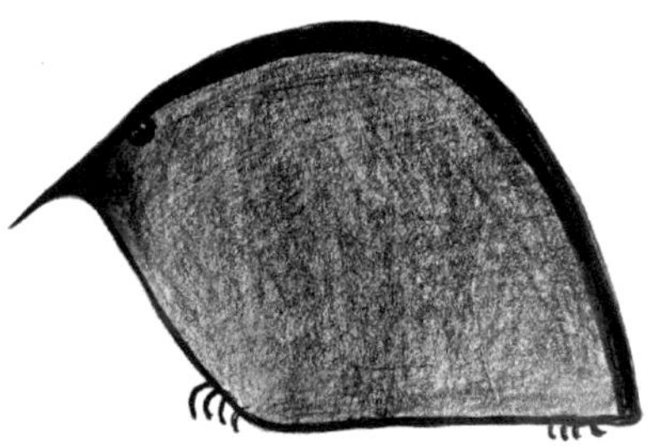

Tumfu: knows where to go to see beauty.

Tumfu: knows where to go see beauty.

A Flutist. A wooden sculpture. © 2025 by Anna Ursyn

For Product Safety Concerns and Information please contact our EU representative GPSR@taylorandfrancis.com Taylor & Francis Verlag GmbH, Kaufingerstraße 24, 80331 München, Germany

* 9 7 8 1 0 3 2 9 7 0 5 7 8 *

T - #0123 - 280825 - C324 - 279/216/15 - PB - 9781032970578 - Gloss Lamination